PUPPETMASTER

THE SECRET LIFE OF J. EDGAR HOOVER

RICHARD HACK

New Millennium Press
Beverly Hills

Copyright © 2004 by New Millennium Entertainment

All rights reserved. No part of this book may be produced or transmitted
in any form or by any means, electronic or mechanical, including
photocopying, recording, or by any information storage and retrieval system
without permission in writing from the publisher.

Library of Congress Cataloging-in-Publication Data Available

ISBN: 1-893224-87-2

Printed in the United States of America

New Millennium Press
301 North Canon Drive
Suite 214
Beverly Hills, CA 90210

www.newmillenniumpress.com
Please visit our website for a complete list of all book
and periodical sources for this title.

Book design by Carolyn Wendt

10 9 8 7 6 5 4 3 2 1

For Troy David Stratos,
finally.

Everything secret degenerates,
even the administration of justice;
nothing is safe that does not show
how it can bear discussion and publicity.

Lord John Emerich Edward Dalberg Acton
(1834–1902)

Also by Richard Hack

Madness in the Morning

When Money Is King

Jackson Family Values

Memories of Madison County

Next to Hughes

Richard Hack's Complete Home Video Companion for Parents

Hughes

Clash of the Titans

CONTENTS

DEATH OF
AN ICON

M*ay 2, 1972. 4936 Thirtieth Place NW, Washington, D.C.* There was an unnatural stillness about the place, sucked dry of breath and emotion, the space thick and unmoving. Only the steady ticking of a mantel clock bore witness as an old man lay dying on the floor. Unconscious, in the master bedroom, he pulled at air in a futile struggle against the inevitable. Stubborn, obdurate, unwilling to accept his own mortality. But then, J. Edgar Hoover had always fought against the odds. This night, however, would be different. This night, he would lose.

By 7 A.M., the low morning sun was streaking through the closed kitchen window as Hoover's longtime housekeeper, a black woman named Annie Fields, adjusted the venetian blind above the sink and began to prepare breakfast. She didn't mind that her employer was fussy and preferred to think of her as a maid. The work was easy even if Mr. Hoover was not.

The breakfast menu never varied—two soft-boiled eggs (positioned just so in porcelain cups that Hoover had inherited from his mother), white toast with softened butter, and black coffee in a flowered teacup—served each morning at exactly 7:30. With clockwork efficiency, as the food reached the dining room table, so too would Hoover. He would have risen an hour earlier, spent a cursory 15

1

minutes riding his Exercycle, showered, dressed, and watched Frank McGee and Barbara Walters on NBC's *Today* to learn of any breaking news.

This morning, however, at the commanded half past seven, Hoover greeted neither the day nor his breakfast. He did not lumber down the steps and across the room, brushing his perfectly pressed suit as he looked for invisible lint. He did not give his usual "humph" as he molded his thick body into the mahogany chair at the far end of the table, nor did he purse his lips as he inspected his eggs for correct consistency.

By 7:45, in fact, the eggs were no longer even on the table. Annie had brought them back into the kitchen and placed fresh ones in rapidly boiling water on the stove top. Hoover's two cairn terriers, G-Boy and Cindy, danced at her feet in anticipation of discarded toast, blissfully unaware that outside, Hoover's chauffeur, Tom Moton, had arrived in his boss's armored Cadillac limousine. As usual, Moton was early, leaving plenty of time for him to take a feather duster and remove pollen clinging to the car's polished chrome grille.

When Moton learned that Mr. Hoover had failed to appear for breakfast, he was confused. "Not like Mr. Hoover, no sir," he said as Annie rambled on. She hadn't heard the shower running. No sound from the television, either. Nothing but the ticking of the mantel clock. Instinctively, the pair began to speak in whispers much like mourners at a funeral or congregants at church.

By the time James Crawford arrived at the back door a half hour later, Moton and Annie were openly fretting. Of the three, Crawford had worked for Hoover the longest, nearly 40 years. He had begun driving the man he called "the Boss" shortly after Hoover had been named head of the newly formed Bureau of Investigation, long before it was called the FBI, and had given up the position only five months earlier. He had reluctantly passed his chauffeur's cap to Moton, his wife's brother, hoping to spend more time with his family.

Yet, somehow, the Boss always found some chore he felt only Crawford could handle. This morning it was planting some fancy rosebushes, Zephirine Drouhin Antique Climbers according to their labels. The flowers had arrived the previous day from Hoover's favorite nursery, Jackson & Perkins. The bare root bushes were laid neatly along the back of the house, arranged in precise order for planting. That was hardly surprising. Everything about Hoover was precise. He would have it no other way.

So when the Boss was nearly an hour late for breakfast, there was legitimate cause for concern. As the three servants huddled in the kitchen discussing the situation, it became obvious one of them would have to investigate, violating Hoover's inflexible dictate that he was never to be disturbed in his room. Since Crawford was the only member of the trio who actually had a key to the bedroom, he was elected to explore the inner sanctum, darkened against prying eyes as if light itself were the enemy.

As Crawford made his way out of the kitchen, he moved through a maze of clutter he knew well. Winding through the living room and into the hall, Crawford's mind raced as his feet fell heavily on the thickly padded stairs leading to the second floor. *Surely,* he thought, *the Boss is merely sleeping.* The rapid beating of his heart denied the truth of his unspoken words. Crawford knew Hoover had not overslept. Hoover *never* overslept.

Arriving at the top of the stairs, Crawford made his way down the corridor. He paused, but only for a second, then knocked, knowing there would be no answer, yet hoping that he was wrong. As he hesitantly tried the door-knob, he found the door unlocked. Strange. The Boss *always* locked himself in for the night, like some enigmatic treasure in danger of being ravaged.

Pushing open the door, Crawford moved into the dark space cautiously, uncertain. The black of the room was blanket thick, the windows blocked by shades and draperies and further covered by Chinese screens. Still, the light from the hallway was enough for Crawford to make out the bulky, unmoving form lying on the floor next to the bed. Reaching it, he found flesh cold to the touch, a body hardened by rigor mortis.

J. Edgar Hoover, the man who personified law and order in modern America, was dead. Wearing silk pajama bottoms and no shirt, he seemed smaller now—no longer the giant who, for nearly half a century, molded the Federal Bureau of Investigation and cast it in his own concept of purity and allegiance. Old and crumpled, Hoover had died as he had lived, alone and isolated.

As an adrenaline surge spiked nerve endings into motion, Crawford raced from the room, calling out to Annie, his fluttering heart threatening to fly from his chest and across the room. "The Boss is dead, on the floor!" he blurted out, knowing that life as he had known it for the past four decades was about to change. America was about to change as well, and for a few brief moments only the three black servants gathered excitedly in a Washington, D.C., kitchen were privy to the fact.

That changed quickly, of course, as calls were made—the first to Hoover's constant companion and second-in-command at the FBI, Clyde Tolson. Tolson had to know first, for he, above anyone, would understand the implications. Since 1931, it was Tolson who had assisted the Boss as his chief cheerleader, administrator, organizer, and best friend. *Too* good of a friend, some said, as rumors of a homosexual relationship between the two men refused to die despite repeated denials.

Tolson himself had been in ill health for several years, with a serious heart condition and advanced high blood pressure. He also had suffered several strokes that left him partially paralyzed. Even as Crawford made the call, he wondered if word of Hoover's death might finish the job and kill Tolson as well. Yet when the associate director of the FBI answered the telephone and heard the news, his reaction was not one of hysteria or grief but rather stoic silence, which Crawford attributed to shock.

The methodical Tolson called upon his FBI training one last time, and immediately reported the director's death to Hoover's titular boss, acting Attorney General Richard Kleindienst, 48 years old and only three months into the job. Placing the telephone receiver back on its hook, Tolson moved more out of habit than grief. As he had for the past 41 years, he crossed the room, exited his apartment, and rode the elevator to the building's lobby to await Hoover's limousine. Each morning the pair normally rode the short distance to the Justice Department together; each evening met again for dinner.

The previous evening, Hoover had cut short a photo session with a retiring agent to return with Tolson to his apartment, worried about the toll his assistant's schedule had been taking on his health. Together they dined on Omaha Steaks, baked potatoes, baby peas—with vanilla ice cream for dessert. All of Hoover's favorites. *A perfect final meal,* Tolson thought as he watched Moton drive up in the familiar armored Cadillac.

Washington, D.C., survives on its ability to spread news through a network as infinite as it is structured. Even as Moton was helping Tolson into the back seat of the black limousine, word began to spread systematically about the death of a man many considered to be indestructible. As each person received the shocking news, the groundswell grew in direct proportion to the importance of the man.

Annie Fields telephoned the Boss's longtime executive assistant, Helen Gandy, catching the elderly woman just as she arrived at her office. It was Gandy's first call of the day, recorded simply enough on the FBI log at 8:40 A.M. The entry listed simply "Annie," with no indication of the tragic news she delivered. Gandy had worked for Hoover for 54 years, having first met the director when she was a file clerk in the Justice Department. Petite, attractive, and exceedingly likable, she became Hoover's secretary at the age of 21, having assured her boss that she had "no immediate plans to marry."[1]

In keeping with Helen's characteristic efficiency, she responded with calculated precision, calling the assistant to the director, John Mohr, to her office to inform him of Hoover's death. She shed no tears; in fact, she was totally devoid of emotion as she related the news. The Boss would have wanted it no other way.

It was left for Mohr to tell his own boss, third in command Mark Felt, the deputy associate director. Despite his many years with the Bureau, Felt had held his current position for only 10 months, and, as such, had yet to prove himself to Clyde Tolson or Helen Gandy. Mohr, by contrast, was a Tolson confidant and had been an FBI agent for 33 years. Tolson knew he could rely on Mohr to handle the funeral arrangements and inform the various Bureau offices that their venerable leader was dead.

By the time Hoover's longtime physician, Dr. Robert V. Choisser, was summoned to 4936 Thirtieth Place NW, President Richard Nixon had learned the news from his chief of staff, H. R. Haldeman, who had been informed by Kleindienst. "Jesus Christ! That old cocksucker!" the president was later quoted as saying of the man who many considered to have made Nixon's run for the White House possible.[2]

Choisser was equally surprised at the news, having only months before given Hoover a complete physical and a clean bill of health. It was 10 A.M. before the doctor arrived at Hoover's colonial home to examine the body, nearly two hours after it was discovered. By then, Crawford had lifted it off the floor and placed it on the bed, draping a blanket over Hoover's bare skin. Annie, who could not bring herself to look at the body, cleaned the bathroom but otherwise left the scene untouched.

Elsewhere on Thirtieth Place NW, it seemed like a typical spring morning. The sky was spotted with enormous clouds, more sharp edged than billowy, like cotton balls washed in alcohol. On the street, neighbors walked their dogs, blissfully unaware that an icon had fallen.

Inside Hoover's home, however, serenity had given way to aberrant activity and constricted emotion. Clyde Tolson sat in the living room, occupying the same pale-green occasional chair he always used when visiting. Alone, introspective, his lips moving in silence, Tolson seemed oblivious to the federal agents who had just arrived to stand guard at the front and back doors under orders from John Mohr. In the kitchen, Annie Fields and Tom Moton sat drinking coffee, talking about their boss's death in disbelief, while upstairs Choisser completed his examination and left Crawford to wait for attendants from Joseph Gawler's Sons Inc. funeral home on Wisconsin Avenue to arrive.

By the time a nondescript station wagon pulled into the alley behind Hoover's home just after noon, most of Washington and indeed much of the world were abuzz with the news of Hoover's passing. They shared a common thread of shock, so permanent a fixture had Hoover become in law enforcement legend, so indelible his contribution. No one knew that more than Richard Nixon, who had been bickering for months with the FBI director over his failure to bend the law for some presidential "black bag" jobs—extracurricular and highly illegal break-ins that for years had been standard practice for FBI agents and were now forbidden by the agency's head.

Though Nixon was as surprised as anyone at Hoover's passing, he greeted the news with a sense of relief. It was the perfect solution. He no longer had to deal with the "Hoover situation" and could now appoint a more adaptable person in position to replace the deceased director. That afternoon, the president wrote in his private diary:

> He died at the right time: fortunately, he died in office. It would have killed him had he been forced out of office or had resigned even voluntarily.
>
> I remember the last conversation I had with him about two weeks ago when I called him and mentioned the fine job the Bureau had done on the hijacking cases. He expressed his appreciation for that call and also expressed his total support for what we are doing in Vietnam.
>
> I am particularly glad that I did not force him out at the end of last year.[3]

Yes, the perfect solution. And the perfect opportunity to sanctify the fallen icon with a state funeral. Nothing better than pageantry to bury any lingering rumors of animosity and showcase the president in an election year.

Nixon's special assistant, Pat Buchanan, wrote the president's official statement, which the president delivered to a subdued nation.

> All Americans today mourn the death of J. Edgar Hoover. He served his nation as Director of the FBI for 48 years under eight American Presidents with total loyalty, unparalleled ability and supreme dedication. It can truly be said of him that he was a legend in his own lifetime.

For millions, he was the symbol and embodiment of the values he cherished most: courage, patriotism, dedication to his country and a granite-like honesty and integrity. In times of controversy, Mr. Hoover was never a man to run from a fight. His magnificent contribution to making this a great and good nation will be remembered by the American people long after the petty carpings and vicious criticisms of his detractors are forgotten.

The FBI he literally created and built is today universally regarded as the finest law-enforcement agency in the world. The FBI is the eternal monument honoring this great American.[4]

Nixon ordered all flags on government buildings to be lowered to half-staff, except the one flying atop FBI headquarters. That one was to continue to fly at full staff as a symbol of Hoover's courage "in resisting the vicious attacks on his organization."[5]

Others echoed Nixon's praise, including Warren E. Burger, chief justice of the Supreme Court, who said that Hoover, "in dedicating his life to building the FBI . . . did so without impinging on the liberties guaranteed by the Constitution and by our traditions." Senator Edward Kennedy added, "Even those who differed with him always had the highest respect for his honesty, integrity, and his desire to do what he thought was best for the country." Senator Edmund Muskie, an outspoken Hoover critic, straddled the political fence by stating, "Some of us may have questioned some of his approaches in recent years, but no one could question his loyalty or dedication to his country."[6]

Not everyone saw Hoover's passing as a loss, but few were willing to speak on the record for fear of retaliation. One who did was Martin Luther King Jr.'s widow, Coretta Scott King, who said, "We are left with a deplorable and dangerous circumstance. The files of the FBI gathered under Mr. Hoover's supervision are replete with lies and are reported to contain sordid material on some of the highest people in government, including presidents of the United States. Such explosive material has to be dealt with in a responsible way. Black people and the black freedom movement have been particular targets of this dishonorable kind of activity."[7]

The secret files to which she referred were said to be filled with salacious goodies of scandal. They were the source of much of Hoover's power, and their very existence had kept him in the director's chair through 16 attorneys general. His was more than just a Washington record. It was the mark of a supreme diplomat who was said to have managed the files' contents, revealing none of their details except perhaps to those individuals in a position to be hurt by their exposure: movie stars, writers, journalists, athletes, judges, congressmen, senators, even presidents. It was a silent form of blackmail: hardly subtle but enormously effective as long as none of the information ever became public knowledge. And for nearly half a century, J. Edgar Hoover saw to it that not a single word did. Ever. The files were so secret, in fact, that almost no one knew for certain if they even existed. But J. Edgar Hoover knew. That was enough.

Even before the president permitted Hoover's death to be publicly announced, he ordered those files to be secured. The word was passed in regimental fashion: Nixon told Haldeman, Haldeman told Kleindienst, Kleindienst told Mohr. Mohr responded by sealing off the late director's office at the FBI. "In accordance with your instructions," Mohr memoed Kleindienst midday on May 2, "Mr. Hoover's private, personal office was secured at 11:40 A.M. today. It was necessary to change the lock on one door in order to accomplish this. To my knowledge, the contents of the office are exactly as they would have been had Mr. Hoover reported to the office this morning. I have in my possession the only key to the office."[8]

Convinced, Nixon moved to capitalize on the publicity opportunity inherent in the director's funeral. Awash with enthusiasm to gain the greatest television exposure possible as part of his reelection campaign strategy, the president informed Kleindienst that he wanted Hoover to be afforded a "proper and dignified state funeral,"[9] complete with live coverage on all three commercial networks plus public television. Little consideration was paid to Hoover's prior request to be buried in a Masonic ceremony, nor was any regard given to Helen Gandy, who had begun to make arrangements with the Supreme Council, 33°, Scottish Rite of Freemasonry, headquartered on Sixteenth Street NW. Rather, the mood at the White House was one of cautious celebration, a time for the president to publicly mourn the nation's loss of a legend while privately planning to regain long-sought control of the Federal Bureau of Investigation.

Officially, it fell to the acting attorney general to appoint Hoover's successor, though in reality Nixon would make the final decision. Anxious to preserve intact

what he saw as the nation's premier crime-fighting organization, Kleindienst placed a call to Cartha D. "Deke"
DeLoach. DeLoach had served in the FBI for 28 years, rising to deputy director, Hoover's lieutenant immediately
under Clyde Tolson, before leaving in 1970 to join PepsiCo
as a vice president. DeLoach knew the FBI as well as Hoover
did, and he had the respect of his fellow agents, as well as
a spotless reputation.

"Deke, I'm going to recommend to President Nixon
that you be appointed interim director," Kleindienst said
to the astonished DeLoach.[10] Though the onetime agent
eventually turned down the offer, Kleindienst nevertheless placed DeLoach's name into consideration for the
position. It was just before noon, and Hoover's body had
yet to be moved from his bed.

The employees of Gawler's funeral home were used to
handling high-profile interments. Gawler's had handled
the funerals of John F. Kennedy, several Supreme Court
justices, more than a dozen senators, and as many diplomats. Yet J. Edgar Hoover was different. The epitome of
secrecy and intrigue, Hoover was as much a mystery as
the bureau he created.

As the two men from Gawler's walked in through the
back of Hoover's home and into his private sanctuary,
they entered a museum that was caught in time and
pressed for space. Against a conflicting background of
dated wallpaper and contemporary furniture sat souvenirs of a privileged life: carved amber statues of the
goddess Kuan Yin, porcelain Foo dogs on elaborate
wooden stands, Ming vases, ivory Buddhas, a trio of
Philip Kraczkowski bronzes, stuffed partridges converted

into bookends, a half-dozen ivory elephants, a sterling sil-
ver oil lamp, a Peruvian drinking cup, and male nudes in
marble, plaster, and porcelain—all showcased on
mahogany tables draped in lace and sitting on Oriental
carpets layered on top of one another and covering every
inch of available floor space.

In the living room, the foyer, and along the staircase,
the walls were the place of history: plaques awarded for
achievement; pictures with presidents Harding, Coolidge,
Roosevelt, Truman; and framed letters of commendation.
At the bedroom door, a bust of Hoover stood guard.

The downstairs clutter and exaltation stood in marked
contrast to the master suite, where traditional maple furniture and a two-hundred-book library gave the room a
heavy, lived-in look that the remainder of the house
lacked. If the four-poster double bed, chest of drawers
with thick glass protecting its top, nightstands stuffed
with pens and reading material, and an aging RCA color
console television weren't exactly *Architectural Digest*,
they did at least speak to the man who escaped from public life here. The sole reminder that Hoover was someone
special was found in a small statue of the FBI director,
carved in wood and kept safe in a glass case on a table.

As the attendants from the funeral home placed
Hoover's body on a wheeled gurney, shielded him against
prying eyes with a blanket, and carried him out through
the back alley, the muted sounds of chaos were building
on what passed for a front lawn. Television news crews
competed with print journalists for position on the artificial grass that Hoover had installed four years earlier. The
too-green Astroturf was an impulse purchase after James

Crawford endured brain surgery in late 1968. As Hoover later explained to his horrified neighbors, he was worried that his chauffeur, who did double time as his gardener, might no longer be able to handle the Kentucky bluegrass that grew thick and manicured in his yard. Rather than find a new lawn man at cost, Hoover had the FBI install Monsanto Corporation Chemgrass. That same artificial surface was now crisscrossed with cables and sound equipment as the world's journalists flattened Hoover's budding flower beds in an effort to command a favorable location.

Their frustration upon learning that the body had been removed undetected was compounded by the announcement from local coroner Dr. James L. Luke that Hoover's demise was caused by hypertensive cardiovascular disease—a common heart attack brought on by high blood pressure. That Hoover was neither being treated for high blood pressure nor taking medication to correct the problem did not seem to alarm Luke, who saw no reason to conduct an autopsy and permitted Gawler's to prepare the corpse for viewing later in the evening.

Throughout the halls of the FBI, there was a palatable uneasiness. Not grief, really. More a sense that the enormous boat that had become the Bureau was suddenly rudderless, cast adrift. The fact that there was no storm did little to quell the apprehensions of those who remained aboard, leery of the future.

Even as both houses of Congress continued throughout the afternoon to deliver eulogies to the late director, voting that his body should lie in state in the Capitol Rotunda, Helen Gandy and John Mohr were dealing with far more pressing matters: the selection of a coffin, a burial suit, flower arrangements, and limousines, plus the preparation of Hoover's family plot at the Congressional Cemetery where the late director's mother, father, and baby sister were laid to rest. To complicate matters, the pair was getting little assistance from Clyde Tolson, who as acting director of the Bureau and the executor of Hoover's estate was professionally and legally responsible for making many of those decisions.

Tolson's structured world had crumbled. So accustomed was he to being in Hoover's shadow that once the camouflage was removed, he felt naked and exposed, ill prepared to function and even less equipped to make a rational decision. The paperwork of the Bureau did not decrease because its director had died. There were memos to be signed, assignments to be made, meetings to be scheduled, and instructions to be delivered. Tolson's secretary, Dorothy Skillman, had inherited many of her boss's duties by default, signing his name to documents and referring decisions to associates, in particular John Mohr. It was therefore entirely possible that Assistant Attorney General L. Patrick Gray III had no idea that he was being shuttled from office to office in a political game of musical chairs when he arrived at FBI headquarters at three o'clock on Tuesday afternoon.

Gray moved easily through the crowd of reporters that had descended on Hoover's office on the fifth floor of the Justice Department building that day. The onetime naval officer had returned to government service to serve under Nixon, and eventually was appointed an assistant attorney general for the civil division. Now working as Kleindienst's unconfirmed assistant, Gray was eager to prove himself. He walked down the familiar halls looking for Tolson. Like everyone else in the Justice Department, Gray had heard about Hoover's secret files, and that even he was mentioned in the contents of several. The president, of course, had his own file, and now Nixon wanted its contents protected by more than a new lock on the office door.

Dorothy Skillman didn't have to do more than shake her head as Gray approached. Tolson's door was open and his office obviously empty. What Gray didn't know, and Skillman wasn't saying was that Tolson wasn't returning that day or any day. She had yet to receive official word, but she knew nonetheless. She was too efficient a secretary not to realize the effect the director's death would have on her boss. Yet not even Skillman knew the toll it had taken.

As Gray moved down the hall toward John Mohr's office, across town Tolson had just pulled himself away from the extraordinary scene that continued to unfold on Hoover's front yard. Though no one had entered or left the house for more than three hours, the news crews kept their vigil as if watching the pot might make it boil. Reaching for his briefcase, the leather worn over years of service, Tolson looped his partially paralyzed left hand through the handle and pulled the case to his side.

It was an effort to move his tired legs, but to remain in the living room was even harder. He resented the stares of pity from the special agents on guard, as if he too had died right along with the director. Without comment, Tolson shuffled passed them toward the stairs and made his way to the guest bedroom on the second floor. He knew it well. When he was released from the hospital after his last stroke, he spent over a month being cared for in that very room.

As comfortable as an old shoe, with just the right amount of wear, the room was more Tolson than Hoover, an accommodation the director made to his old friend. Nowhere else in the house were there Navajo rugs, a souvenir from their trip to Arizona as were the pottery ashtray and Indian figurine. The wing chair had a faded slipcover, which Hoover had not replaced for it was Tolson's favorite.

Sinking slowly to the edge of the bed, Tolson took care as he removed a single sheet of paper from his briefcase. It was written in the wobbling hand of an old man who could no longer control his fingers. He reread the words he had written several hours earlier, as if to remind himself they were still correct.

"I cannot continue to operate effectively in my current position, nor assume the responsibilities incumbent as Acting Director of the FBI," the note began. Tolson's resignation signaled the end of a career that had spanned nearly as many decades as that of J. Edgar Hoover. It was unfair that Hoover had died first, leaving him behind. He had neither the talent nor the desire for a life outside the shadow of his famous friend. Satisfied that the letter would suffice, he clumsily folded it in thirds, and returned it to his briefcase, snapping shut the latch on the leather strap for emphasis.[11]

Back at the Department of Justice, Gray had reached the office of John Mohr, his patience running thin. He was being treated like a messenger boy, not as a representative of the president of the United States. Mohr sensed that the assistant attorney general was irritated even as he waved him to a seat, and found a hint of pleasure in Gray's frustration. Rushing to complete the funeral arrangements for the late director, Mohr had little patience for interference from the White House, despite Nixon's intention to turn the event into a national display of government pomp. He had even less patience when the real reason for Gray's personal visit became clear. Gray wanted immediate access to Hoover's secret files.

"I told him in no uncertain terms that there were no secret files," Mohr later testified before a special House subcommittee.[12]

The unscheduled meeting between the two men was as brusque as it was brief, yet it set the tone for future dealings between the White House and the FBI. The president's reaction to the rebuff was one of contempt toward Mohr and distrust of his denial. This was a battle Nixon intended to win, and win quickly.

That evening Mohr made no mention of Gray's visit as he stood next to Tolson in the chapel of Gawler's funeral home. There, all eyes were on the open casket and the once powerful man inside it. In the rush to prepare the body, the makeup artists at the funeral home had washed Hoover's hair, removing the dark rinse that the director had applied weekly to stave off time. His gray hair and eyebrows gave the corpse a unfamiliar pall, which, when coupled with Hoover's puffy skin and too-pink rouge, made the body look like a poorly rendered wax figure. "He looked like a wispy, gray-haired, tired little man," said one agent who had flown in for the viewing. "There, in the coffin, all the power and the color had been taken away."[13]

For Tolson, who was already suffering emotionally and physically, the sight of Hoover looking vulnerable and weak was unacceptable even in death. Those who arrived near the end of the evening found the coffin closed. And it remained closed throughout the days that followed.

The following morning at eleven o'clock, Hoover's body was moved in the first act of an elaborate state funeral choreographed by the Department of Defense and coordinated by Colonel Vern Coffey, army aide to the president. More than 40 pages of documents detailed the preparations necessitated by the protocol, with all the timed scheduling of a shuttle launch.

It had rained the previous night and into the morning, the sort of quiet, gentle shower created by God for funerals. At the Capitol, an honor guard from all branches of the armed services lined the 35 steps leading to the Rotunda. And there was a quietness about the place, as if all of Washington had taken a deep breath at the same moment.

The hearse bearing the body arrived precisely at 11:25, and soldiers in dress uniform snapped to attention. The air was silvered, shadowless, as eight pallbearers struggled with the $3,300 brass casket. Lined with lead and covered in an American flag, the coffin weighed over half a ton, a fact evident in the pained expressions of those duty bound to make their slow march into the Capitol look effortless. Two suffered minor injuries in the process and were quietly hustled to the sidelines, but not before they slid the casket onto the black catafalque first used at the funeral of Abraham Lincoln. It was an honor previously reserved for presidents, military heroes, and congressmen. And now J. Edgar Hoover.

Inside the Rotunda, the nation's leaders were assembled, tightly packed in their respective sections cordoned off by thick velvet ropes. The entire Supreme Court, swathed in their black robes of service; members of Nixon's cabinet; senators; and congressmen—all poised to pay their final respects to a man most found intimidating even in death. They had come to laud his service, his integrity, and the FBI, which Chief Justice Warren Burger said was "an institution that is, in a very real sense, the lengthened shadow of a man."[14]

There were no notes of discord inside the Capitol, and Hoover's sometimes stormy tenure as head of the FBI seemed forgotten in the rush to praise one whom Burger labeled "a man of great courage who would not sacrifice principle to public clamor."[15]

Even before the brief private tribute had ended, lines were forming outside the Capitol as the public solemnly waited to bid farewell to a national hero. Faces raw and moist with tears, they stood silently in the rain for one hour, two hours, four. Before the day was over, more than 25,000 visitors had entered the Rotunda to pay their final respects in an outpouring of respect that awed even veteran politicians. There was no mention of secret files or hidden sexual agendas. Rather, the motivation behind the vigil was one of loss and admiration. Perhaps as a validation of the skill with which Hoover spun his public image, he was cast as the most unique kind of civil servant: honorable, patriotic, of impeccable integrity.

At the White House, however, President Nixon held no illusion of Hoover's character. His consuming love of gossip, publicity, and power were familiar faults. Only the extent of his knowledge was unknown. Without Hoover, the FBI was a powder keg of information likely to explode onto the headlines without regard for its victims' celebrity status or political stature.

Moving quickly to gain control, Nixon reached into the ranks of malleable fronts and selected Nixon team player L. Patrick Gray III, the assistant attorney general, to head the Bureau on a temporary basis until the presidential election in November. Because Gray's appointment would not be permanent, it required no congressional approval, thus denying the House and Senate an opportunity to scrutinize the selection. At three o'clock in the afternoon on May 3, as the rain fell over the Capitol dome, Gray accepted his appointment. Later at a press conference, White House Press Secretary Ronald L. Ziegler said that Nixon wanted to "name a man in whom he had complete personal confidence." That Gray was a personal friend as well was sidestepped by Ziegler with, "I think you will find that Patrick Gray is not a political man."[16]

If not political, Gray was most certainly dogged as he returned to John Mohr's office to question him once again about the location of the secret files—this time as Mohr's newly appointed boss. Although the answer was the same, the discussion was not. According to testimony before a House subcommittee, Gray screamed that he was "a hardheaded Irishman" whom nobody pushed around. Mohr countered that he was a "hardheaded Dutchman" who could stand his ground against anyone.

As echoes of the argument traveled the length of the corridor, Helen Gandy paused briefly before turning back to her work, sorting through Hoover's "Official and Confidential" files kept in her office. Not secret files, per se; but rather private ones, yet scandalous enough to be separated out from the central filing system because of their sensitive nature.

When Gray passed Gandy's desk after leaving Mohr's office, he paused long enough to question her actions. The efficient executive assistant was upfront, informing him that she was separating Hoover's private files from those that were FBI property, on instructions from Clyde Tolson. Out of innocence, naiveté, or stupidity, Gray never asked to examine the files. The mere mention of Tolson's name made him blanch.

After receiving his appointment as the new FBI director, Gray's first call had been to Tolson. More than just a courtesy, he intended to make it clear that a new order of authority was now in place at the Bureau. Tolson, comfortably ensconced in Hoover's home, refused to take Gray's call and instead made one of his own to Helen Gandy.

In his last official act as associate director of the FBI, an organization to which he had devoted his life for the past 44 years, Tolson instructed Hoover's executive assistant to destroy the director's files, and protect and preserve his image forever. Gandy had, in fact, already begun the task, per protocol established by the director himself in the event of his death. Now satisfied that his work was done, Tolson authorized release of his letter of resignation, hung up the phone, and poured himself a whiskey from Hoover's private reserve.

Helen Gandy smiled sweetly at Gray and turned back to her work, dismissing the new acting director. He was an interloper into her world and that of the FBI. A pretender to the throne. To her, he would never be anything more.

The following morning, several thousand FBI agents, police officers and other members of law enforcement lined the route from the Capitol to the National Presbyterian Church, saluting as the hearse carrying the fallen FBI director rolled past surrounded by 11 motorcycle patrolmen. Television cameras broadcasting the state funeral followed the cortege through the streets of Washington and watched as an honor guard of body bearers unloaded the casket in front of the white stone church built only five years earlier.

President Richard Nixon, leading the eulogies, called the civil servant "a giant [whose] long life brimmed over with magnificent achievement and dedicated service to the country which he loved so well. . . . He became a living legend while still a young man, and he lived up to his legend as the decades passed," Nixon said in eulogy. "He personified integrity; he personified honor; he personified principle; he personified courage; he personified discipline; he personified dedication; he personified loyalty; he personified patriotism."

Clyde Tolson and Helen Gandy watched from their seats at the side of the chapel, hidden from the 1,200 in attendance. Nixon had positioned himself; his wife, Pat; Patrick Gray; and former first lady Mamie Eisenhower in the first row of pews, directly in front of the television cameras.

As the eulogies ended and the chapel filled with the a cappella voices of the army choir, Tolson was helped into a wheelchair and out the side door to a limousine supplied by Gawler's. He wanted neither pity nor attention, yet received both an hour later at Hoover's graveside at the Congressional Cemetery. There J. Edgar Hoover was laid to rest in the family plot not far from the Anacostia River. Looking lost, confused, and deep in grief, Tolson received the flag that had graced Hoover's coffin with a simple "thank you" after the short service. As James Crawford wheeled him to the waiting limousine, none among the mourners spoke. They simply watched in silence as Hoover's most trusted friend and colleague disappeared behind a grove of maple trees. Only then did they retreat to their cars to brave the midday traffic in Washington.

Cemetery workers lowered Hoover's 1,400-pound coffin into his burial vault, the bier mechanism straining under the load. Even as the first shovelfuls of dirt were cast into the grave, black children from the neighborhood began dancing around the tomb, removing yellow mums from the presidential wreath.

A cemetery worker yelled at the youngsters. "You leave those flowers alone now, hear? This here's the grave of a *great* man," he said. "Ya gonna learn 'bout in school," he added under his breath, never realizing how right he would be. In the years to come, the story of J. Edgar Hoover would reveal a legacy unlike any other in this country's history. And secrets—so many secrets. Secrets that were the source of his power and the well of intrigue that ultimately threatened to undermine democracy itself.

ONE

TO BE GOOD IS NOT ENOUGH, WHEN YOU DREAM OF GREATER THINGS

Annie Hoover was not dressed for giving birth. Her flowing black hair, dislodged from its hairpins, clung to the starched lace clasped at her throat by a brooch of pearls and aquamarine. The pin had been her mother's and, as such, gave the woman comfort during the intensity of her labor. Her dark gown was damp with perspiration, its billowing skirt pulled high to her waist. A porcelain tub of hot water lay between her legs, held tight by the pressure from her feet.

For Dr. John P. Mallan, it had been a long night. New Year's Eve always was. Pregnant women throughout Washington seemed to perceive the stroke of midnight as some magical signal to begin childbirth, and Anna Margaret Scheitlin Hoover was among them. Since this child was her fourth, however, she saw no reason to summon Mallan. She knew *perfectly* well how to give birth. But her husband, Dickerson, was naturally nervous even on the most casual day, and so Mallan was requested to aid in the delivery, and "administer a calmative to Mr. Hoover."[1]

It had been an unusually cold Christmas, with just enough snow to make walking difficult. The steps in front of the Hoover home at 413 Seward Square SE seemed especially slick as Mallan climbed them in the dark of predawn January 1, 1895. Annie's oldest son, named Dickerson after his father, heard yells for help and found the elderly doctor gripping the handrail outside the front door of the white stucco house. Inside, the home was warm from the heat of coal stoves, as gas lamps cut velvet shadows across the bedroom.

When John Edgar Hoover arrived an hour and 40 minutes later at 7:30 A.M., Annie brushed tears from her eyes with the back of her hand and accepted a gentle kiss on the forehead from her relieved husband. The baby, looking rather red and annoyed according to his sister Lillian, cried only briefly before nursing at his mother's breast. "He was immediately hungry," Annie later wrote, "while I found the thought of food unbearable."[2]

Annie had always been a rather fussy eater. Even when she had married her husband in a ceremony labeled "the largest Capitol Hill ever had," she refused to partake of the beef roast at the reception. The Metropolitan Presbyterian Church parish hall accommodated the young bride with a plate of "new potatoes and apple sauce."* She had just turned 18; her husband was 22.

The new baby, called Edgar, arrived as the family was still in mourning from the death of daughter Sadie Mar-

---

* The Metropolitan Presbyterian Church was completed in 1872, with the cornerstone laid by President Ulysses S. Grant. Located on Fourth Street SE, not far from the Library of Congress, the church is now known as Capitol Hill Presbyterian.

guerite, who had succumbed to diphtheria at age three while the family was on vacation in Atlantic City a year and a half earlier. "I am free from my binds," Annie wrote, "though not my grief."[3]

Mrs. Hoover devoted herself to the infant, spending any extra household funds on new outfits for the boy and the fanciest high-wheel pram she could afford. "I must have wheeled Edgar a thousand miles around Capitol Hill," his brother later lamented. "It was my daily chore to take [him] out for an airing. I'd tuck his bottle under the pillows of the baby carriage and sometimes we would be gone for hours."[4]

As the boy began to grow, he displayed a rather remarkable memory for his age, learning the alphabet before his second birthday and printing words by the age of three. For his father, who worked as an engraver for the U.S. Coast and Geodetic Survey, the oldest scientific agency in the federal government, his son's talent suggested that he might follow in his footsteps.[†] Yet young Edgar showed little interest in his father's work, preferring to spend his time with his mother in the garden. By the time he entered his first year at Brent Elementary School several blocks from his home, Edgar was a precocious reader with a shy personality that intensified when he developed a stutter as the school year was ending.

While his father chose to comfort his son with promises that the condition would pass with time, young Hoover's mother took him to specialists in search of an immediate

---

†   The Coast and Geodetic Survey was responsible for charting the nation's waterways, generating topographic maps of its coastline, and triangulating its surface as the foundation for land maps.

cure. One physician suggested that Edgar speed up his speech, theorizing that a fast talker lacked the opportunity to stutter. The boy launched into the assignment with an unflappable determination to practice speaking text in record time—in the process earning himself the nickname "Speed." He spread reading material across the floor in his makeshift room—the converted rear parlor—and in the course of accomplishing his goal, achieved an unexpected bonus: He improved his reading skill far beyond that of the average first-grader, expanding his growing library with books on history, geography, and religion.

Studying the Bible was a requirement in the Hoover household, and Edgar found the stories of the Old Testament exciting, with their tales of pestilence and salvation. Each evening the Hoovers read the Bible to their three children around a lamp-lit table and tested them on the lessons learned. While attendance at the Lutheran Church of the Reformation was not mandatory, Edgar was an eager worshiper who loved the regimentation of the service, and sang joyfully in the choir.

Dr. Donald Campbell MacLeod, who had moved into the Capitol Hill neighborhood when Edgar was four, was the minister at the nearby First Presbyterian Church. Introduced to MacLeod at a sandlot baseball game, Edgar found a hero in the man whom he later wrote was his "ideal of manhood."[5] It had less to do with MacLeod's calling from God than it did with his ability to reach youngsters' hearts.

"He was a vigorous, forthright Calvinist, whose rigorous sense of duty and clear-cut view of right and wrong did nothing to suppress his sense of humor or his joy in life," Hoover reflected many years later. "His Saturday appearance at our makeshift ball park was an occasion for rejoicing. When we were shorthanded, he played. When we had enough players, he umpired. And when Donald MacLeod was on the diamond, you played by the rules, you played fair, and you came away with a code of good sportsmanship."[6]

MacLeod was everything that Edgar's father was not. He was charismatic, athletic, spontaneous, and fun-loving—qualities that Dickerson Hoover neither understood nor possessed. The elder Hoover was regimented, studious, and nervous, continuously praying for relief from mysterious demons that pierced his skull and invaded his mind. Unwilling to accept advice from doctors, he warned his family against prescribed medicine. "Stew from the devil's stove," he called it.[7] With his long nose, thick mustache, and dark hair parted down the middle, he carried himself stiffly, like a frozen stalk of celery, neck and body moving together as if his head were unable to rotate on his shoulders.[8]

He was, however, deeply in love with his youngest son, and tried his best to imbue Edgar's personality with a sensitivity he found lacking in his other children. On his frequent business trips for the Coast and Geodetic Survey, Dickerson wrote endearing letters to "my dear Edgar," filled with descriptions of places and people worlds away from his son's sheltered life, which revolved around an eight-square-block area of provincial Washington. Each letter was laced with open affection and a longing for home. "Love to all with a kiss for yourself," he wrote in one. "I have a big favor to ask you. It is give Mama a hug and a long sweet kiss. Good Bye, Papa."[9]

Yet his father's tales of travel to St. Louis, New York, and Chicago failed to excite Edgar. "Everybody is in a rush," Dickerson wrote his son about St. Louis. "The Mississippi is very high and the water is like clay"—hardly words to stimulate a child's imagination, especially when Donald MacLeod was playing Indian scout and taking the neighborhood boys on expeditions to Rock Creek Park in search of Daniel Boone or La Longue Carabine.[10]

As MacLeod became an important male figure in the boy's life, his role sculpted a foundation on which the adult Hoover would remain rooted for his lifetime. It was the stuff of patriotism, valor, piety, and reverence, valued prizes in turn-of-the-century Washington.

The city of J. Edgar Hoover's youth was isolated and parochial in its beliefs; a place of cobblestone streets and horse-drawn carriages, where wide lanes with thick elm trees bordered the refined homes and maintained gardens of the working middle class who took pride in their neighborhood in the shadow of the Capitol. This was a Washington that found Grover Cleveland in the President's Mansion (the preferred term over the White House), and the Washington Monument was alone among memorials in a parklike setting. Blacks were known as "colored folk," and were welcomed as servants but not as equals. Racism was the accepted norm. These were, after all, the sons and daughters of Civil War veterans, only two generations removed from slave owners, with residual emotions and bigotry festering just beneath the surface.

On Sunday afternoons, racism entered the Hoover household as Edgar's grandmother Margaret Scheitlin, who lived conveniently across Seward Square at number 414, would settle herself in the Hoover parlor, extolling tales of her father, John Hitz, who was the appointed consul from Switzerland in 1853, and was succeeded by her brother, John Jr., to the same post in 1864. Whenever he joined his sister in the Hoover home, the heavily bearded Hitz would read from the Bible, casting down sinners with the enthusiasm of a revivalist missionary. The fury of hellfire and brimstone left Edgar wide-eyed and determined to escape the fate of drunkards and heathens—two characteristics Hitz routinely credited to the blacks.[11]

As a youngster, J. Edgar Hoover's only exposure to other races was through the servants who routinely came and went in the household. His mother's treatment of the family's maids and cooks, while not particularly abusive, was hardly tolerant. "And what do you think of Bell this morning?" Annie wrote her son in a letter she left pinned to his headboard. "She came in and as soon as I came into the kitchen, you should have heard her impudence. I waited until she got through and then I told her after she was through with her work, she could quit us. I was not paying her for her insolence which surprised her very much and seemed to knock the wind out of her, so when you come home, we'll have someone else. I think she has been with us a little too long."[12]

No blacks were in his segregated school, and none attended his church. In fact, few lived within the inner city at all, having been pushed out in search of lower-priced housing. Discrimination in the city's restaurants, barbershops and beauty salons, butcher shops, and music halls extended beyond just blacks, however. With the

turn-of-the-century increase in the immigrant population, the very core of America's white Protestant majority
began to feel threatened by unfamiliar customs, foods,
and clothing. The nation's capital reacted by expanding
Jim Crow legislation that legalized segregation and discrimination. When blacks and other minorities were
allowed to mix with whites, they were expected to use
separate entrances, bathrooms, drinking fountains, and
telephones. For a white youngster, this was less discrimination than it was reality, something to be protected, not
questioned. And so it was with J. Edgar Hoover, raised to
think of himself as American and determined to defend
what he saw as his heritage.

In 1906, at the age of 11, Edgar began keeping daily
diaries in which he meticulously recorded his activities
and observations, as well publishing a neighborhood
newspaper that he called the *Weekly Review*. The two-page
mimeographed handout told of life in Seward Square,
especially the more catastrophic elements:

> An accident happened on the Capital Traction Railway,
> about 3:00 o'clock Tuesday, between 4th and 5th
> Streets, S.E. A cartridge was placed on the car tack by
> some boys. It got caught in the slot and broke the plow,
> so that the car could not run. It caused a great deal of
> excitement.

Editor J. E. Hoover reported on the crowds lining the
blocks around Poli's Theater to hear Guido Deiro—the
America Premier of the Piano Accordion. He listed the
Rules of Good Health (as taught at Brent School). He cov-

ered society by reporting on a meeting of the Hot Air Club at Mrs. Griffith's—"They had a very good time." And he alerted his neighbors (who paid a penny a piece for the weekly bulletin) that "Mr. D. N. Hoover of 413 Seward Place, S.E., found a five-dollar gold piece. It was made into a pin."

Though Edgar rarely mentioned his mother in the *Review,* when he did, she made the headlines. "ESCAPED FROM DEATH: On Friday, about 12:15 o'clock, Mrs. Hoover, of 413 Seward Square S.E. came near losing her life. She was frying some eggs for lunch, and the blaze caught to her back, but she managed to put the fire out on her arm, and someone in the kitchen put out the fire on the back."[13]

Eager to make his own money, the youngster shopped his talents among local businesses, looking for part-time work. The results were less than promising according to Edgar's diaries, in which he noted that "Mr. Pollan, Mr. Mors, Mrs. Benedict, Mr. Lunt and Miss Lawrence had no jobs. Mrs. Mors said to come back when Mr. Mors went home."[14]

Finally, out of either desperation or ingenuity, Edgar created a job for himself carrying groceries for customers of the Eastern Market. Built in 1873 by the city from an Italianate design created by local architect Adolf Cluss, the market was the most important single source of fresh food for the nation's capital. As patrons left the brick building, arms overloaded with bags of produce and meat, Edgar offered to carry the bulky packages for a flat fee of 10 cents "regardless of distance," according to a note in his diary.

"I started earning money," Hoover later wrote, "by carrying groceries. In those days, markets did not hire delivery boys, but I discovered that if one stood outside a store, a customer laden with purchases would happily accept a helping hand and gratefully tip anyone who aided with a heavy load. The first such commission I got was to carry two baskets two miles for which I received a tip of ten cents. I realized that the quicker I could complete each chore, the more money I could earn, so I spent most of the time running. Because I ran back to the market and was outside the Eastern Market every day after school and from 7 A.M. to 7 P.M. each Saturday, I could earn as much as two dollars a day. In those days that was a king's ransom."[15]

With his newly demonstrated independence, Edgar's mother felt more comfortable leaving him in the care of his older brother and sister. She even began accompanying her husband on his business trips to New York and Boston, remaining in contact with her children through letters. "Dear little Edgar," began one note from New York, "While Mama is writing you this little letter, the Steam Cars are flying past my window, the elevated road passes right by the window, the street cars in front of the door—New York is a very busy place." Never totally without concern for his health, she wrote, "Take good care of yourself and if you feel badly take some number 10 and if you should have a cold some number 7.‡ Am very glad you are using our room," she added, referring to her

---

‡　Packaged preparations from the Hoovers' local pharmacy were placed in numbered envelopes.

youngest child's lack of his own private space in their house.[16]

The following year, however, Edgar finally received a room of his own when his brother married and moved into the house next door with his new bride. Now 12 years old and thinking of himself as liberated, he cast off the knickers and sailor suits of his youth and committed himself to serious study, continuing to show a fondness for history and math. From his new bedroom window, he could see into the backyard garden where his mother cultivated lily of the valley, forsythia, roses, and a grape arbor. In the summer, Edgar would spend his free time there alone, protected from the afternoon sun, lying in the grass and inhaling the fragrance.

The garden became a place of healing as well when Edgar fell ill in July of 1908 with a staphylococcus infection that presented itself in the form of a large and unsightly red boil on his nose. Refusing to leave the privacy of his home, the boy stoically suffered his embarrassing infirmity in the seclusion of the backyard while his mother applied hot towels to the infection on his face. When the boil finally drained, it left behind scar tissue and indented Edgar's nose with his trademark bulldog profile, which biographers would later incorrectly link to a sports injury. It was a story Hoover encouraged as an adult, the whole truth being somewhat less dramatic.[17]

By now, Edgar had become the focus of his mother's life, his importance in the household amplified with the marriage of his sister Lillian on June 20, 1908, to her boyfriend, Fred Robinette. The ceremony, performed by Dr. MacLeod at the First Presbyterian Church, featured "solemn hymns and traditional music."[18] After the marriage, Lillian moved out of the Hoover house on Seward Square and left Edgar happily at the center of his parents' attention.

Throughout the year, Edgar continued to keep meticulous notes in his small leather-bound diaries, noting with unbridled enthusiasm his accomplishments in school, practical jokes he played on his friends, and what he labeled "noteworthy excursions." On one trip, he ventured to Fort Myer, Virginia, to watch Orville Wright demonstrate the plane he designed for use by the Army Signal Corps. "Went to Fort Myers [sic] & Arlington. Wright flew to Alexandria & back in 14.2 mi. I was the first outsider to shake Orville's hand."[19]

As further proof of Edgar's impending adulthood, one night at dinner he announced to his parents that he intended to enter Central High School that September rather than his neighborhood school Eastern High. It was an astonishing decision, made without discussion and apparently accepted without one as well. While little mention is made in the boy's diaries of the choice to attend a different school than his brother and sister, the announcement reflected Edgar's growing confidence in his ability to compete among the best in the city. Although Central, like Eastern, was a public school, it catered to the academically gifted student by offering a curriculum of foreign language, classic literature, and advanced science in preparation for college. Unlike his brother, Dickerson, who was working for the Steamship Inspection Service, Edgar hoped to continue in school and pursue a law degree. Central High School, three miles away from his neighborhood, represented an opportunity to achieve an education and make contacts not to be found in Seward Square. Edgar, who was now signing his name "J.E.," though still answering to the nickname "Speed," adopted the motto "To be good is not enough, when you dream of greater things," attributed to Albert Einstein.[20] And J.E. was indeed dreaming big.

He entered Central High in the fall of 1909, and approached his new school with the vigor of achievement, joining the library club and the choir. Speed even attempted to join the junior varsity football team, but was turned away before the first practice because of his stature—thin and a few inches shorter than the other players. Undaunted, he then tried out for track, where his slight build proved an advantage in short sprints, in which he excelled.

Slow to make friends, Edgar concentrated instead on a difficult class schedule—physics, chemistry, Latin, and history. Even the most taxing subjects were easy to grasp and praise from his teachers was routinely noted on his report cards. Outside the classroom, and away from track, he spent time with his uncle Halstead, his father's youngest brother, who taught music at the school and lived with Edgar's paternal grandmother until she died. Often, during his lunch hour, Edgar would walk to his uncle's home and read poetry to his grandmother, who had a particular affection for John Keats and Lord Byron.

Despite the heavy demands of his class work, Edgar never failed to attend church services on Sunday. He followed his brother Dickerson, who had left the church the family attended, the Church of the Reformation, to join

Donald MacLeod's First Presbyterian congregation. In his diary dated September 11, 1910, Edgar wrote, "I joined the Presbyterian Church & took my first communion with Dr. D. O. McLeod [sic]."[21] In addition, Edgar taught a Sunday school class at First Presbyterian. He made a special effort to introduce himself to the membership of elders, many of whom held positions in government, presenting them with mimeographed business cards that read "John Edgar Hoover, Student, Central High School, Washington, D.C."[22]

In Edgar's sophomore year, he joined the prestigious Debate Society, long a stronghold of intellect and wit among his peers. For the onetime stutterer, it was a striking achievement as he pressed forth his position in debates on women's suffrage, immigration, and civil rights.

Edgar's was a life without much leisure, at least compared with that of other teenagers. Yet he never tired of the routine. Instead, he thrived on the discipline. Only on the walk to and from school did he allow himself a moment to relax. He marveled at the construction taking place around him. The Union Station and Plaza on Massachusetts Avenue, the House Office Building on Independence, and the District Building on Pennsylvania had all been built within the past year. And the statues. The streets of Washington were becoming a veritable art museum, the Borglum statue of General Philip Sheridan being Edgar's favorite. He commented to his brother that gazing at the statue in the dazzle of the afternoon sun he saw the reflected glory of God.[23]

As Edgar found his own path, he erected rigid boundaries within which he functioned and expected others to do likewise. He found a satisfaction in the regimen and predictability of an ordered existence, and transferred his tendency toward regulation to his own benefit when he joined the Central High School Brigade of Cadets. The brigade was composed of the most popular or gifted male students divided into companies that practiced elaborate drills and marches and competed against one another in citywide contests. Membership came with strict conventions and a demanding practice schedule. The cadets of Central High received uniforms—gray slacks, high-collar navy blue jacket, gold epaulets on the shoulders signifying rank within the organization. Although the uniforms were traditionally worn to school twice a week on practice days, Edgar took to wearing his on Sundays as well, proud to display his new status as a member of the elite school group.[24]

Even as Edgar carefully crafted his future, keeping careful records of his contacts, making lists of his expenses and income from odd jobs, and pushing himself to excel in his studies to maintain the highest grade point average in his class, a pall hung over the Hoover household. Edgar's father was behaving unpredictably, lashing out at imagined slights and spending hours alone in the basement of the house. The basement had always been Dickerson's domain. He had fashioned a distillery of sorts where he made ginger ale that he distributed to the neighborhood children. After converting an old workbench into a reading desk, he spent hours studying the classics. He had a particular fondness for Henry David Thoreau and never seemed to tire reading *The Maine Woods*, which he had been given in 1906 and practically memorized.

The family began to notice a change in Dickerson's behavior, not so much in what he was doing, but rather in what he was not doing. During the fall of 1911, there were periods when the man came home from work and retired to his basement office without dinner or speaking. He would go without sleep, refusing to allow anyone to even enter the basement. Annie was at first mildly amused by his sudden eccentricities, explaining to neighbors that he was "busy discovering," as if ambiguity could explain his constant absence. She eventually came to look upon his change in personality as a slow pull into a bottomless pit of unknown origin or depth.

When, in early 1912, she suggested he see a physician, he recoiled with such hysteria that Annie summoned the doctor to him. And he was not just any doctor. Jesse C. Coggins ran the Laurel Sanitarium, a hospital for the mentally insane and disabled in nearby Laurel, Maryland. For years, Annie had been patient with her husband's stories of real or imagined assaults on his mind. Yet even she was uncertain how Dickerson would react to the arrival of a doctor known for treating the mentally ill.

Dickerson had taken a leave of absence from his job at the Survey at the request of his supervisor, who found his work suffering due to unexplained anxiety. The appearance of Coggins at his doorstep did little to alleviate his symptoms. When introduced to the doctor, Dickerson went to a washbasin and began to splash himself with cold water. The display would have been extraordinary enough had it stopped there; but he did not stop, lowering his head closer and closer to the porcelain bowl, splashing wildly until he finally dissolved in tears. Annie started to rush to his side, only to be held back by Coggins, who moved to help Dickerson himself. Reaching for a towel, the doctor began to dry off the man, who seemed to find some comfort in the physician's touch. That evening Dickerson was admitted to the sanitarium, where he remained for several months.

The official diagnosis was severe depression brought on by a nervous breakdown. Coggins ordered shock treatments, common at the time, which apparently drove Dickerson further into himself and his delusions. During the entire length of Dickerson's stay at Laurel, Annie Hoover and son Dick made regular visits, according to Dick's eldest daughter, Margaret. But never once would they discuss what they saw.

"It was a subject that was invisible. Even though we all knew, we were told not to talk about it. And we didn't," Margaret said. "They said it was a breakdown. And that was all they said. It was a sad time, particularly for J.E."[25]

Edgar's reaction to his father's hospitalization was one of denial. He never mentioned it in his diaries, to friends, or to his pastor. It was as if his lack of acknowledgment might make the reality disappear. "I'm not sure," Margaret said, "but I think he was ashamed."[26]

Edgar redoubled his efforts at school, pushing himself to excel in classes in French, calculus, and biology. Rather than simply memorizing facts, he queried his teachers to discover *why* things were as they were—the origins of words, the formulas for equations, the motivation behind political decisions.

With the family income drained due to his father's illness, Edgar began baby-sitting his niece, Margaret, while his brother worked overtime. It was a lesson in economy and frugality the young Hoover would never forget. Unable to entertain or freely spend on even the smallest extravagance, Annie continued to dote on her younger son, spoiling him with adulation. That the praise she lavished was excessive was lost on Edgar, however. The teenager luxuriated in her compliments and attention, never sensing for a moment that they were the proud ramblings of a mother who had lost her sense of self.

Margaret was aware of changes in her grandfather Dickerson's behavior upon his return to Seward Square. He seemed to have little memory of who she was—in fact, much of his memory had been altered. His eyes were sunk deeply into his face, gaunt and pained from his treatment at Laurel. He was able, however, to return to work in mid-1912, though he never again kept a full-time schedule.

As Edgar entered his senior year at Central High, he was elected captain of Company A, an enormous honor among cadets. It placed him in charge of six different squads that composed the company and put him in competition with the other two companies at Central. Lawrence Biff Jones, who went on to play football at West Point and eventually became the academy's coach, led Company B. David H. Blacklock, in charge of Company C, fought in two world wars, retiring with the rank of brigadier general in 1950 at the age of 55.[27]

For J. Edgar "Speed" Hoover, leading Company A during the inauguration of President Woodrow Wilson was a culmination of structured achievement started years earlier. Marching in the ceremony had long been a tradition for the cadets of Central, and from his first day in the brigade, Edgar plotted his goal and achieved it on the morning of March 4, 1913.

The day dawned cloudy, but cleared up during the early morning, according to the memoirs of Irwin H. Hoover [no relation], who had worked as an usher at the White House for 42 years. Edgar had risen early to assemble his squads, in preparation to march down Pennsylvania Avenue. He had planned to bring the cadets to the street the previous afternoon, but a massive march in favor of women's suffrage disrupted traffic and caused riots near the Treasury Building. Nearly 8,000 suffragists, many on horseback, some on floats, demanded the right to vote for women. It was not a cause that Edgar favored, yet when he heard that some of the marchers had been attacked by a few of the half-million onlookers lining the parade route, he rallied to the defense of the women.

On inauguration day, he advised his cadets to be "alert to lingering scum," and proceeded to direct them in perfect cadence past the newly installed president and first lady. Edgar and his Company A were popular favorites with the crowd and mentioned in newspaper coverage of the inaugural parade. The Central High student paper, *Brecky*, said, "Army and Navy men, critical to the last degree have been unstinting in their praise of the appearance made by [Company A], some officers even going so far as to say that in point of military excellence, the High School Cadet Regiment was second only to the West Pointers among all the marking organization in that immense martial array."[28]

Later in the year, the Cairo Hotel, at 14 stories the tallest building in Washington, hosted the Brigade of

Cadets' annual dance.[§] Wearing a side saber, Edgar led his
company at the regimental ball, and was accompanied by
his parents, who served as chaperones for the event. He
apparently did not dance, however, for his dance card,
which he saved until his death, was totally blank.[29] It
should perhaps come as no surprise, since he had few
friends and certainly no girlfriends.

Serious and determined, Edgar was resolved to leave
his mark as a leader, and as a leader he was without peer
at Central High. Ranked fourth in his class scholastically,
Edgar was selected valedictorian based on his "academic
achievement and moral character."[30] Few in his class
would have denied the 18-year-old the honor; his transformation from shy stutterer to winning debater and cadet
captain had been nothing short of remarkable.

Parting from Company A was harder for Edgar than
anything he had yet accomplished. For three years, the
cadets had provided him with structure, opportunity, education, and glory. When it was time to return his uniform,
Edgar wrote a piece for *Review,* the Cadet newspaper, and
had it delivered to each member of his company. "I want
to take this opportunity of thanking and complimenting
the men of Company A," he wrote. "The Company is
accredited on all sides for being the best six-squad company on the field . . . There is nothing more pleasant than

---

§　The Cairo Hotel was designed and built by local architect Thomas F.
Schneider. After its construction, the public was outraged by its height
and its potential as a fire hazard, since no ladder could reach to the top.
As a result of the outcry, Congress passed the Height of Buildings Act,
which made it illegal for any building in Washington to be higher than
the Capitol dome.

to be associated with a company composed of officers and men who you feel are behind you heart and soul.

"The saddest moment of the year was not when I saw the Adjutant turn toward his right; but was when I realized that I must part with a group of fellows who had become a part of my life. And in conclusion, let me say that I want every man of Company A of 1912–13 to look upon me as their friend and helper wherever we might go after this year."[31]

In his high school yearbook, J. Edgar Hoover was described as "a gentleman of dauntless courage and stainless honor. 'Speed' is one of the best Captains and Captain of one of the best companies that have even been seen at Central . . . He is some debater, too . . . 'Speed' intends to study law at college, and will undoubtedly make as good in that as he has at Central."[32]

Indeed, Edgar had been offered a full scholarship to attend the University of Virginia School of Law. Founded in 1826 by Thomas Jefferson, the law school was famed for the quality of its faculty as well as placement opportunities in the government arena. Had J. Edgar Hoover accepted the offer, and continued to achieve academically, his future as an attorney would have been his to write.

Yet Edgar, like his brother before him, had little choice but to decline the opportunity. The university's gift did not include room or board, and Dickerson Hoover could ill afford to send his youngest son to an out-of-state college. Moreover, his father's health had yet to improve, and Edgar was reluctant to leave his mother because of it. There was no hesitation on Edgar's part; no second-guessing his future. With a maturity that belied his age, the onetime debater and cadet captain applied for and was accepted as a night student at George Washington University in its four-year Masters of Law program. The school did not have the prestige of the University of Virginia, but it was only four blocks from the White House and in the shadow of Seward Square.

Using his acceptance at George Washington as a reference, Hoover obtained an entry-level job as a junior messenger in the Order Division of the Library of Congress, a few blocks from his home. Though his pay was only $30 a month (slightly *less* than he was earning carrying bags of produce from the Eastern Market), he was eager for the structure it provided, as well as the education it afforded. Equally as important, the Library of Congress had a work schedule that allowed him to leave at 4:30 p.m., giving him 20 minutes to make his law classes a half mile away.

When Hoover began working there in 1913, Henry Putnam had been in charge of the library for 14 years. Under Putnam's direction, the library was restructured to include the nation's state and local libraries as an extended part of its organization for the first time. Moreover, Putnam was able to maneuver his way through the politics that had hampered his predecessors. His budgets were approved and his administrative needs met without becoming entangled in the mesh of personalities and political subcommittees.

For Hoover, it was his first direct exposure to the inner workings of Washington and a primer on politics from a superb administrator. Certainly, Hoover's experience at the Library of Congress provided him with equally as much education as anything he was learning at George

Washington University. By the time he graduated with a master's degree in 1917, Hoover had developed several talents that set him apart from others in his class. He had four years of experience as a civil servant on his record, and he had taken more than 4,000 pages of carefully indexed notes on the law.

On July 26, the day after Hoover passed the bar exam in the District of Columbia, he accepted a position with the Department of Justice as a low-level clerk. Although Hoover never publicly confirmed the fact, it was widely assumed that his mother's cousin William Hitz, a federal judge, was responsible for recommending him for the position.

The irony was that after working for years to find out who he was, J. Edgar Hoover was now struggling to reinvent himself. He was no longer satisfied with being the smartest or the most regimented. Woodrow Wilson had changed all that when he declared war on Germany three months earlier, and plunged the country into sacrifice and service in the name of democracy and freedom.

It was then that Hoover discovered he was neither soldier nor politician. His calling was far more pure. He was a patriot, one willing to do whatever was necessary to preserve the America of his youth, and the ideology of his dreams. He knew that now as he carefully dressed in his best work suit, ready for the challenge and eager to be tested.

Outside the window on Seward Square, a wash of yellow caught his eye. A branch of forsythia was preening. Hoover stared, wondering why he had never noticed the beauty of the flower. Now he no longer had the time. There was a war to fight, and to win.

TWO

ALIEN
THREAT

John Lord O'Brian was clearly overwhelmed. As the newly appointed head of the Justice Department's War Emergency Division, O'Brian, a distinguished attorney in his own right, was entrusted with prosecuting German aliens who were involved in what politicians politely called "intrigues." More precisely, the country was awash in paranoia that German spies were active in the United States attempting to sabotage the country's fledgling war effort.

In 1917, slightly more than 400,000 Germans lived legally in America. With the declaration of war, *all* of them suddenly were suspect. Determining whether these suspicions were true or imagined was an enormous task, and one that O'Brian labored to tackle. He divided the responsibility between three offices: two for registration and litigation, and one O'Brian labeled the "Alien Enemy Bureau." The AEB's mandate was the internment and parole of enemy aliens, as well as the issuance of permits that allowed innocent aliens to remain in sensitive areas—be they ports, military bases, or war armament sites. In a memo written to Attorney General Thomas W. Gregory, O'Brian placed Special Assistant District Attorney Charles W. Storey in charge of the AEB. He also made note of a low-ranking clerk named Hoover:

(a) Questions effecting arrest and internment of alleged alien enemies, Mr. Storey.

(b) Questions relating to the parole of men in detention including the important work to be done in connection with the Department of Labor, relating to interned seamen, Mr. Saxon, assistant to Mr. Storey, aided by Mr. Hoover, special agent.[1]

This small mention in the O'Brian memo was the first acknowledgment of J. Edgar Hoover's official responsibility within the Justice Department. He was now known as a special agent—one of many specialty assistants to the attorney general. It was, to be sure, a meteoric rise for the novice lawyer—who had been on the job for less than five months. It was also no accident of fate.

Hoover had attracted attention by working 12-hour days, seven days a week. "I discovered he worked Sundays and nights, as I did myself," O'Brian commented in a CBS interview shortly after Hoover's death. I promoted him several times, simply on merit."[2] Initially, Hoover's work consisted of maintaining the Justice Department's complex filing system. Under O'Brian, however, Hoover's assignment became far more personal as he helped pursue men and women he labeled "low-life vermin"—German saboteurs.

While American soldiers were fighting in the trenches at Le Hemel, the Marne River, and Albert in western Europe, Hoover launched a search for international subversives on domestic soil. With the same obsessive devotion he had previously shown to learning the Psalms, the Song of Songs, and certain passages of the Gospels, he now memorized the faces and facts behind various radicals, mercenaries, and German immigrants. The young attorney took it upon himself to protect Americans at home, even as the first American soldiers were being injured and killed abroad. Later in life Hoover suggested that he never enlisted because his position with the Justice Department made him draft exempt. In reality, the Selective Service Act was passed on May 18—several months before Hoover left the Library of Congress—making Hoover very eligible for service. Regardless, Hoover did perform effectively in his position within the AEB, and was meticulous in his documentation of alien transgressions and subterfuge.

The country had turned itself into a simulacrum of informants and spies, a clothesline patrol with neighbors reporting neighbors, and abundant violations of civil liberties taken in the name of protecting democracy. Volunteers organized themselves into the American Protective League, founded in March 1917 by a Chicago advertising executive named Albert M. Briggs. The group numbered 250,000 at its peak, and stretched across 600 cities. For 75 cents, members received a badge that read, "Auxiliary to the U.S. Department of Justice" and thus armed began their work as amateur spy hunters.

The APL appealed to Attorney General Gregory because it gave the country—particularly older men above the age of conscription—a hand in fighting the war at a time when many felt helpless. It mattered little that most of those who were acting suspicious turned out to be cheating husbands. There was always the chance that they were involved in political espionage.

Meticulously, Hoover and a team of 14 others began the work of sorting through the barrel to find the rotten apples. Over the next two years, Hoover's efficiency in the processing of aliens and the thoroughness with which he evaluated each case proved invaluable to his superiors, who continued to reward his determined dedication through salary increases and heightened responsibilities. Such was Hoover's importance by the end of 1918, he was authorized to hire a confidential secretary. The woman, Helen Gandy, was in charge of typing Hoover's recommendations and maintaining his growing files, allowing the special agent to concentrate on helping to calm the hysteria that had risen across the nation.

From his small office in the seven-story Denrike Building at 1435 K Street, Hoover began to gather a small group of subordinates in whom he trusted and to whom he delegated responsibility. They shared similar characteristics and ethics, including a patriotic attitude, a clean-cut appearance, and an unencumbered family life that allowed them to devote well over 40 hours a week to their jobs. They also appeared to be intensely loyal despite the condescension that had begun to creep into Hoover's demeanor. The fledgling civil servant had developed an unpopular habit of ridiculing those who dared to disagree with his interpretation of the law, dismissing them with a flutter of the hand as if clearing the air of annoying cobwebs. Still, no one faulted his ability to deliver results.

Without benefit of uniforms or heroics, the Alien Enemy Bureau pulled the strings that quietly began to entrap foreign radicals protesting against the U.S. government's involvement in the war. Undercover agents infiltrated small grassroots organizations and attended protest rallies. Within weeks, the number of radicals spreading propaganda began to fall; internment centers were filled with a goulash of foreign immigrants and naturalized citizens, as well as American draft dodgers who openly mocked the newly passed Selective Service Act.

Many of the draft evaders belonged to the No-Conscription League, a group founded by Russian immigrants Emma Goldman and Alexander Berkman. Goldman, a charismatic speaker and advocate of birth control, equal rights, free speech, and union organizations, attracted the attention of Attorney General Gregory with her open protests against forced military service. "We . . . in America, will doubtless meet the full severity of the government and the condemnation of the war-mad jingoes, but we are nevertheless determined to go ahead," she wrote in material circulated at her protests. "We feel confident in arousing thousands of people who are conscientious objectors to the murder of their fellowmen and to whom a principle represents the most vital thing in life."[3]

Goldman was not to be disappointed. In June 1917, she and Berkman were arrested and charged with violation of the Selective Service Act, and a month later found guilty of conspiracy to violate the law and sentenced to two years in prison. The lead prosecutor, Assistant U.S. Attorney Harold A. Conant, took Goldman's own words out of context and used them against her, and even went as far to suggest she was somehow involved in the 1901 assassination of President William McKinley.[*]

---

[*]   Leon Czolgosz, a U.S. citizen born in Detroit, confessed to the assassination of President McKinley. In the course of his interrogation, he admitted having attended a public lecture given by Emma Goldman.

Much of the country followed the drama surrounding the Goldman case already convinced of the outspoken Goldman's guilt, J. Edgar Hoover among them. For Hoover, however, the case was more than a curiosity to be forgotten when the next tattooed lady came to town. This was a signpost for his future direction; a clear indicator that the nation was in no mood to harbor anyone who would dare speak against a president fighting a war or the laws that gave him the power to do it.

Hoover studied the subtleties of the case, taking transcripts of the testimony home and marking Conant's arguments with extensive notes long into the night. It was a propitious course of action, for by 1919, not only was Goldman imprisoned, but nearly all enemy aliens as well. By the time the Allied forces signed an armistice with the Germans at Compiègne in France in November 1918, J. Edgar Hoover was quickly running out of foreign radicals to persecute.

In February 1919, as Attorney General Gregory submitted his resignation, Hoover began actively campaigning to keep his own job, pushing John O'Brian for his continued support. "At the end of the war, at the time of the Armistice, [Edgar] told me he would like to continue in the permanent side of the Department of Justice, and I took that up personally with the new Attorney General A. Mitchell Palmer."[4]

Palmer, a burly Progressive Democrat and outspoken supporter of women's suffrage and trade unions, found himself burying his own opinions in favor of President Woodrow Wilson's more conservative stance. Empowered by victory in the Great War and determined to capitalize on his increased popularity, Wilson moved to rid the country of any radicals who remained vocal in their opposition to his presidency.

The previous year, the Bolsheviks had successfully overthrown the czarist monarchy during the Russian Revolution, and replaced it with the Communist philosophy of Vladimir Lenin. Aware of the United States' large Russian population, Wilson feared that Bolsheviks might attempt to duplicate their triumph in America, and encourage a revolt across the country. No longer was the war on distant shores. Suddenly, the threat was very close and seemingly real.

Palmer was instructed to clamp down on dissidents, under the power granted to the Department of Justice by the Sedition Act of 1918, which said, in part, that it was illegal to "willfully utter, print, write, or publish any disloyal, profane, scurrilous, or abusive language about the form of government of the United States, or the Constitution of the United States."[5] To aid in this dragnet of undesirables, Palmer found an eager accomplice in a young attorney who worked a little longer, organized a little better, and had a burning desire to cleanse America—J. Edgar Hoover.

The 24-year-old Hoover was friendless within the halls of the Department of Justice, rarely associating with his co-workers outside the office setting. Typically, when his fellow employees arrived at work in the Denrike Building just before 9 A.M., Hoover was already at his desk, engrossed in profiling a newly uncovered radical or subversive. He was still there when they left for the night. The presumption was that the special agent in AEB was dedicated to his position and untethered romantically.

Inside the Hoover home on Seward Square, the shades were drawn, shuttering the rooms from the happiness of the outside world. There was little humor here, crushed by depression and the paranoia that mental illness can bring. It was the horror J. Edgar Hoover lived each night as he returned home to witness his father's venting of imagined persecution and his mother's continual sobbing.

Dickerson Hoover had been forced into retirement the day before America entered World War I in 1917. After working for the government for nearly 40 years, he was dismissed without a pension, without severance, and without hope. Deeply depressed, he became lost in a world of remembered dreams and sorrows, thinking and rethinking, yet failing to ever quite come to a conclusion. At first his melancholy had been sporadic, hardly interfering with his performance at work. Yet by 1917, there were fewer good days amidst a series of unexplained absences that left Dickerson's superiors little choice but to terminate the troubled man. With no work, little money, and the pressure of an unpredictable mind, he traveled to a kinder place inside his mind, safe from his wife's criticism.

Annie Hoover felt the loss more than her husband did, of course. At the garden club, at the butcher shop, even during afternoons in the park, it was hard to avoid the stares, and she watched in silence as the gossip spread. There was talk, usually accompanied by a shake of the head or pursed lips. Talk she could have handled, but the loss of Dickerson's $2,000-a-year salary was harder to admit and explain.

Now his family's sole source of income, J. Edgar Hoover pushed himself through the ranks of special agents, watching for opportunities and creating them when they failed to appear. He was, after all, his mother's child, trained to be persistent and meticulously precise. And he had learned his lessons well. Annie had instilled a sense of responsibility in her son, albeit one woven around guilt. For the youngest Hoover, there was no thought of marriage or dating or even a continuing education beyond his law degree. His duty was to his family, in particular to his mother, and he was careful not to disappoint.

Hoover's mother was his best friend, his confidante, his disciplinarian, and his rock. She alone knew how he liked his food prepared. She alone knew how to select his clothes, approve his friends, budget his money, and keep him well. And when he worked those long hours, often alone and certainly far beyond expectations, it was fine if it pleased Attorney General Palmer, but it was *necessary* to please Anna Margaret Scheitlin Hoover.

Late in his life, Hoover commented that his earliest memory was a trip to Virginia Beach in which he nearly drowned in the Atlantic Ocean. His memory was not of the cold salt water or the riptide, but rather the smell of his mother's woolen bathing suit as he sought comfort at her side.[6] Though she stood just over five feet tall, Annie Hoover was a formidable woman, a dowager empress of unrequited expectations and shattered dreams. Throughout his life, Hoover heard her endless tales of her sacrifices and suffering, sentenced to live out her days as the wife of a government printer while aspiring to be a Washington hostess whose invitations were coveted and her parties the stuff of envy. Failing to gain such notoriety, even among her neighbors along Seward Square, Annie committed herself to raising her youngest son to achieve the level of fame she could not. If God had afflicted her husband with a weak mind filled with doubt and shadows, at least He had given her a willing student in Edgar, who venerated her every word and genuflected at her altar of adulation.

When his mentor, John Lord O'Brian, left the Department of Justice, and Mitchell Palmer arrived to replace the departing Thomas W. Gregory, Hoover saw an opportunity to make himself indispensable. His files of dissidents were unique, organized according to Library of Congress guidelines and refined to fit the profiling that matched the political climate of the day.

Following the dictates of President Wilson, Gregory had created a bureau called the Radical Division to identify and deport alien Anarchists and Communists. Swept along on the wash of patriotism after the victory of World War I, the country was eager to rid itself of any semblance of an antidemocracy movement regardless of whose civil liberties were violated. And the very foundation of the Radical Division was Hoover's files.

At the time, the Justice Department had begun to flex its muscles in the area of national security. After many years of attempting to create an investigation unit, first under Attorney General Charles Bonaparte during the administration of President Theodore Roosevelt, and with continued pressure from Bonaparte's successor, George W. Wickersham, the Bureau of Investigation was officially formed in 1909 with 64 agents. By 1919, the Bureau had grown to 301 agents and had a budget of more than $2 million. Its mandate was clear: Rid the country of undesirables, particularly immigrants with radical ideas.

The shakeout period that followed the war found countries around the world attempting to reestablish their political footing. Outspoken advocates of Socialism, Communism, Fascism, and Anarchy were being closely watched for the first time following the success of the Bolsheviks in Russia. In Hungary, France, Scandinavia, Germany, and Austria, the message of a people's republic was growing. Fear that a revolt was heading into the United States was fanned by the American press, which suggested that a Red insurgency was imminent. And a citywide labor strike in Seattle seemed to reinforce the fact that workers were indeed preparing to revolt.

In the early months of 1919, homemade bombs began exploding across the country—left on doorsteps, placed in crowded terminals, and shipped in packages. Public outcry peaked when the tranquillity of a June evening was shattered by a massive explosion in front of the home of Attorney General Palmer. The Palmers had just retired for the night, and across Dupont Circle the assistant secretary of the navy, Franklin D. Roosevelt, and his wife, Eleanor, were returning home from dinner and exiting their limousine. The blast was powerful enough to send shards of glass and broken bricks into their car, though both the Palmers and the Roosevelts escaped personal injury.

The attack was apparently the work of a suicide bomber who was killed in the explosion. The blast scattered leaflets promising death to the capitalist class.[7] Palmer was so shaken by the incident that he immediately recruited William J. Flynn to head the Bureau of Investigation and stop the growing Communist threat. The former head of the U.S. Secret Service, Flynn had been instrumental in organizing the New York police force and was anxious to prove himself on a national level.

The infiltration of Communists into America following World War I seemed to be a natural platform from which to test the Bureau's jurisdiction and effectiveness. Flynn's partner in the effort was the newly appointed head of the Radical Division, J. Edgar Hoover. With his new title, Hoover received an increase in salary to $3,000 a year. After four years on the job, he was making $1,000 more than his father had earned at the end of his entire career.

For Hoover, the opportunity was more than a chance to clean up the radical fringe. This was his moment to enter the national stage, propelled into the spotlight by the nation's most famous Anarchists, Emma Goldman and Alexander Berkman. As soon as the pair were released from prison, having completed their sentences, Hoover served them with deportation papers, arguing the government's case. In a memo to Palmer's special assistant, John Creighton, Hoover had labeled the pair "two of the most dangerous anarchists in this country." He recommended their immediate deportation, stating that if they were permitted to return to the community, it would "result in undue harm."[8] What he did not say was that his personal handling of their individual cases was intended to thrust him into the national spotlight and further his career.

The attorney general, quick to realize the positive public relations coup at hand, authorized Hoover to proceed, placing "all necessary manpower" of the Justice Department at his disposal.[9] Moving to place Berkman under arrest even as he was leaving prison, Hoover traveled by train to the Atlanta penitentiary and personally questioned the Anarchist about his role in public demonstrations and distribution of antigovernment material. Throughout the proceeding, Berkman remained defiant, attacking the Wilson administration in particular, and democracy as a whole.

The decision to deport Berkman came easily, so obvious was his hatred for the U.S. government, and his insistence that he planned to continue campaigning against the administration's policies. Emma Goldman, in contrast, was not as cooperative a target. She was, by way of marriage, a naturalized citizen, and an extremely popular and charismatic speaker.

In developing his case again Goldman, Hoover did not restrict himself to proving that she participated in antigovernment rallies and Anarchist activities. She made no effort to camouflage her positive views of anarchy or even her involvement in legal protests. Such behavior not only was part of her history, but it also was an intricate aspect of her personality.

For Hoover to convince the Immigration Department that Goldman qualified for immediate deportation, he needed to build a case that linked her with a direct violation of the law. To accomplish that goal, the leader of the Radical Division attempted to prove that Goldman was the leader of a group of Anarchists that claimed direct responsibility for the 1910 bombing of the offices of the *Los Angeles Times*. Additionally, as Assistant U.S. Attorney Conant had done before him, he suggested she was also behind the assassination of President McKinley, evoking all the emotions and outrage of that tragic event.

It was a turning point for the young attorney, desperate to make a name for himself. There can be little doubt that Hoover was well aware his charges were false. They had been thoroughly disproven in previous investigations, which even the smallest amount of research would have unearthed. In Hoover's mind, however, his assertions were justified if they helped to push a dangerous woman from the safety of her haven in America. And he was supported in his prejudice by a country only too willing to trounce the civil rights of a few to save the civil rights of many.

Through relentless effort, unsupported allegations, political game playing, and the appearance of intense research, Hoover successfully presented the government's case. On November 25, 1919, Alexander Berkman was ordered deported by the immigration bureau, followed four days later by his onetime consort, Emma Goldman.

The victory capped a month of activity against Russian nationals that began with a surprise raid by the government on the Federation of the Union of Russian Workers. The FURW was a trade union made up of aliens who, after five years in the country, had made no effort to become citizens. They were seen as a breeding ground for dissidents, and were thought to be advocating the overthrow of the U.S. government. On November 7, 1919, the Bureau of Investigation and the Bureau of Immigration launched a series of raids in 12 cities including New York, Chicago, and Los Angeles, netting 18 FURW officers and 232 members—all of whose names were on lists provided by Hoover. Severely beaten in the course of the roundup, the aliens were forced to sign confessions that most could neither read nor understand.

Hoover viewed the operation's success as a statement of support for his anticommunist efforts, and immediately looked for an opportunity to publicize his pro-democracy victory. He found the perfect stage with the USS *Buford,* an Irish-made army transport that the Labor Department had borrowed from the War Department to carry Goldman, Berkman, and 247 other deportees back to Russia. Nick-named the "Red Ark," the ship was rushed into service to prevent any of the deportees from having time to appeal their convictions.

At 4 A.M. on December 21, the Anarchists boarded the *Buford,* having been hastily collected from various prisons, bused to Battery Park, and then ferried to Ellis Island. The night wind arced through the canyons of the city as a few onlookers huddled against the bitter cold. William Newell Vaile, the freshman congressman from Colorado, stood with Hoover throughout the night and later reported on the deportation from the floor of the Capitol, labeling Hoover "a slender bundle of high-charged electric wire."

Emma Goldman held a distinctly different opinion of the man whose personal vendetta had predicated her downfall. When asked by Hoover if he had given her a "square deal," Goldman replied, "Oh, I suppose you've given me as square a deal as you could. We shouldn't expect from any person something beyond his capacity."[10]

In the days prior to the deportation, Hoover had requested maps of the Siberian frontier so that he might acquaint himself with the "vacation that a few of our anarchist friends will take shortly."[11] He joked with head of Immigration Anthony Caminetti that he was "throwing a goodbye party" to which the commissioner might invite a "few close friends."[12] And he made himself available to the press as the transport ship left port, answering questions about the case and otherwise basking in the media attention.

"Goldman had several trunks and a half dozen suit cases filled with her belongings and she took with her a lot of money she has collected from her followers in America," Hoover told a reporter from the *New York Tribune*. "Berkman and most of the others had plenty of money. Just before we left [Ellis Island], one of the men wanted me to cash a check for $3,000. I refused and suggested he send it to some of his friends remaining in this country and have them get the money. He said he wouldn't trust the check into our hands for transmission. 'All right,' I said, 'take it to Russia and trust the Bolsheviki.'"[13]

Palmer was so pleased with the favorable publicity that he offered Hoover the remainder of the year off and "an additional three or four days in the New Year to properly celebrate" his birthday.[14] Hoover declined the offer, informing the attorney general that he would not rest until the nation was free "of all radical low-life that threaten God fearing Americans."[15]

The search for subversives notwithstanding, Hoover did find time to enjoy a small celebration in honor of his twenty-fifth birthday. On New Year's Day, 1920, the family, less Hoover's father, who was once again hospitalized, shared a pot roast dinner in their Seward Square home. It was rare that Hoover had agreed to attend the party, rarer still that he had brought along a guest.

Thomas Franklin Baughman was notoriously handsome, incredibly ardent, outrageously fickle, and J. Edgar

Hoover's only friend. The men had met as students at George Washington University, where both studied law and were brothers in the same fraternity, the Alpha Nu chapter of Kappa Alpha. The order, inspired by Robert E. Lee, stood for character, honor, duty, and reverence to God, and seemed an odd choice for a womanizer of Baughman's reputation. Yet the muscular sportsman's public persona was everything Hoover knew he could never be, and as such was idolized by the shy student.

Baughman lived with his widowed mother and often brought her to the Hoover home to sit in front of the Victrola with Annie and listen to Caruso recordings. "La donna é mobile" regularly reduced the women to tears. They cried together as well when Baughman joined the army to fight against the Germans, and were both present to greet the soldier when he returned a highly decorated captain in the artillery.

On October 27, 1919, Hoover hired his dear friend as a researcher in the Radical Division, placing him in charge of the extensive correspondence generated in Hoover's tracking of the Communist Party and its members in the United States. Through a series of undercover informants, Hoover was able to identify some 2,700 alleged members of the party. In the course of four months, he generated nearly 3,500 letters, memos, and personal files in an exhaustive sweep of the country. The sheer output of paperwork was staggering, considering each was dictated and hand-typed by Helen Gandy, with many overseen by Baughman.

As the two friends celebrated Hoover's birthday, they reviewed what was about to be the most daring wholesale roundup of dissidents ever attempted in America. Based solely on names supplied by Hoover, Acting Secretary of Labor John Abercrombie placed his signature on nearly 3,000 arrest warrants. In doing so, Abercrombie ignored the advice of Secretary of Labor William B. Wilson, who had taken a leave to care for his dying wife.

To Wilson, himself an immigrant who had started working in the coal mines at age nine and later rose to the position of secretary-treasurer of the United Mine Workers union, Hoover's list of suspicious aliens was itself suspect. The only common offense among them was membership in the Communist Party or the competitive Communist Labor Party. Yet for Hoover, and apparently for Abercrombie, that was enough to warrant deportation.

In coordinating the simultaneous raids across the country, Hoover worked with Bureau of Investigation chief Flynn and Flynn's assistant, Frank Burke, who was placed in charge of the operation. The complicated roundup involved 33 separate cities, with undercover operatives in each advised by Burke's memo to "have meetings of the Communist Party and Communist Labor Party held on the night set. I have been informed by some of the bureau officers that such arrangements will be made. This, of course, would facilitate the making of the arrests."[16] He left it to his agents' "discretion as to the methods by which you should gain access to such places."[17]

On the evening of January 2, 1920, Hoover and Baughman operated telephones in the office of the Justice Department, receiving reports from various agents across the country systematically raiding meetings of the two Communist parties. Like fish caught in a dragnet, the immigrants squirmed helplessly, struggling to avoid the inevitable. And at first it seemed as if Hoover's wholesale roundup had made escape impossible. Yet as any drag fisherman knows, there are often surprises to be found in the net.

In total, more than 5,000 arrests were made in 24 hours. Unfortunately, the same speed that made the raids so successful also made the arrests and detention a nightmare. Since local jails were ill-equipped to deal with the massive influx of prisoners, the immigrants were kept in holding rooms that were often little more than storage tanks, typically without heat or toilet facilities.

Matching detainees to arrest warrants became a nearly insurmountable task as well. Alternative spellings of names and identification cards printed in languages other than English confused local police, who received no help from the detainees. American citizens caught in the dragnet had to be released immediately because the Immigration Act of 1918—the basis for the wholesale arrests—applied only to foreigners.

Attorney General Palmer, who advocated expelling the Communists, quickly took credit for the successful roundup, only to be caught in the backlash that developed as details of the raids became known. As Americans were released from custody, they began to speak out against the inhumane conditions that existed within the holding tanks, as well as the lack of warrants for many of those arrested. In many cases, blank warrants had been used during the arrests, with names filled in after the fact.

As the public began to question the validity of the Palmer raids, Hoover redoubled his publicity machine, churning out propaganda to validate his contention that members of the Communist and Communist Labor parties were dangerous and a threat to liberty. Those newspapers that favorably covered the raids received Hoover's promise of access to Palmer's files on the cases, a direct violation of federal law. Although there is no record that such access was actually granted, the promise was the first example of an association with the press that continued throughout Hoover's lifetime.

When the cases came up for public hearing, Hoover initially volunteered to present the government's case for deportation. He was quoted in the *New York Times* suggesting that the detainees arrested with Communist Party cards in their possession were prejudged cases for deportation. "Deportation hearings and the shipment of 'Reds' from this country will be pushed forward rapidly," Mr. Hoover declared. Second, third and as many other 'Soviet Arks' as may be necessary will be made ready as the convictions proceed, he said, and actual deportations will not wait for the conclusion of all the cases,"[18] according to the *Times*.

Frightened and unable to understand the charges against them, the majority of aliens who remained in custody had little hope of a proper defense. Counsel hired by the Communist Labor Party pointed to the illegality of searches done without warrants, and the innocence of immigrants who just happened to be at a meeting of their fellow countrymen. They suggested that many of those arrested with cards identifying them as members of the Communist Party thought the small certificates granted them library privileges or served as a passport to leave the country. Palmer was intent on seeing that they did.

Acting Secretary of Labor Louis F. Post, taking over for John Abercrombie, who was running for the Senate, complicated the government's case when he refused to approve the paperwork that would have forced those convicted to leave the country. During subsequent hearings before the House Rules Committee, Post publicly lashed out at Palmer and the country's conservative newspapers, claiming they had created "a great terroristic scare in the country." Post's attorney went so far as to claim that Palmer had "an absolute ignorance of American principles."[19]

Palmer responded by alleging that after the bombings of 1919, including the one that nearly took his life, he was given a public mandate to make the country safe.

> I say that I was shouted at from every editorial sanctum in America from sea to sea. I was preached upon from every pulpit; I was urged—I could feel it dinned into my ears—throughout the country to do something and do it now, and do it quick, and do it in a way that would bring results to stop this sort of thing in the United States. . . . I accept responsibility for everything [my agents] did. If one or two of them, overzealous or perhaps outraged as patriotic American citizens—and all of them were—by the conduct of these aliens, stepped over the bounds and treated them a little roughly, or too roughly, I forgive them. I do not defend it, but I am not going to raise any row about it.[20]

Palmer delivered his statement with the conviction of a wronged patriot. He not only believed he was right, but also misjudged public opinion of his position, assuming it would carry him to the Democratic presidential nomination. Though Hoover continued to support his superior, few within the Departments of Justice, Labor, or Immigration followed suit.

After Post succeeded in overturning nearly 3,000 requests for deportation of the Communists, Palmer declared that a revolution was brewing across America, predicting that May 1—May Day—would see riots and bombing "in this fine country and overseas as well." Though extensive precautions were taken in large cities across the United States, including the cancellations of leaves and vacations for police officers and firefighters, there was not a single incident of uprising or Communist-inspired violence on that day.

The backlash against Palmer was harsh and nationwide. Branded a fanatic, the attorney general pushed for a national platform of support and continued to raise money for his presidential candidacy. Yet his lot had been cast among the zealots, and not even the support of the old Democratic machine was enough to ensure the nomination, which ultimately went to James M. Cox, the governor of Ohio. Despite his defeat, Palmer never altered his opinion of aliens, who he saw as the source of democratic decay. In an article written for the magazine *Forum*, he wrote, "The whole purpose of communism appears to be the mass formation of the criminals of the world to overthrow the decencies of private life, to usurp property, to disrupt the present order of life regardless of health, sex or religious rights."[21]

It was a sentiment Hoover shared, a conviction that there was a conspiracy underfoot that the government could not see. With Palmer's defeat, Hoover knew his only hope of convincing Washington that the threat was real was to redouble his efforts at locating and profiling offenders.

With the support of the outgoing attorney general, Hoover restructured the Radical Division to enlarge its scope. He changed its name to the General Intelligence Division and redefined its mission. "While the work of the General Intelligence Division was at first confined solely to the investigations of the radical movement," Hoover wrote in a memo on October 5, 1920, "it has now expanded to cover more general intelligence work, including not only the radical activities of the United States and abroad, but also the studying of matters of an international nature, as well as economic and industrial disturbances incident thereto."[22]

It was a move designed to make his contribution unique among government agencies, to cross divisional lines and politics, to link Republicans and Democrats, to appeal to the common need of all mankind to feel secure. And at its very foundation were Hoover's files. Originally limited to dissidents, he began to expand his record keeping to include those who opposed his thesis on the threat of Communism. He quietly investigated department heads, university and religious leaders, judges, senators, and congressmen.

Confiding only in Helen Gandy, Hoover began to cross-reference his files on index cards, eliminating strict alphabetical entries and breaking down subjects into categories based on methods developed at the Library of Congress. The simplicity of the system was plain enough if you understood it; if you didn't, finding information was impossible. He made certain of that.

On November 2, 1920, Americans elected a new president, leaving most government employees to worry about their future job security. Hoover was not one of them. Each night as he made his way back to Seward Square, back to the home where he was born, back to the watchful eyes of his mother, Hoover was secure in the knowledge that familiarity brings. He was creating a place for himself, a niche he alone could fill. It was a solitary world, built of resolve and bound by a determined work ethic. He made no secret of his power base. In fact, he loved to discuss his ever-growing files. Not their contents, of course. Those were his to know alone; files full of secrets and hidden agendas, to be revealed only when the time was right.

Hoover knew all about secrets and about keeping them. He had several himself. His father's illness, for instance. Few outside Laurel Sanitarium really knew the extent of the disease. Few would ever know.

And then there was his only friend. No one knew how often Hoover watched him work, watched him with women, watched him flash his easy smile, framed by his mustache and accentuated by perfect teeth. No one knew how much he treasured the gift he had given him months before—a photo of the handsome man, with the dark piercing eyes and the meaningful gaze. And no one knew that alone at night, Hoover found solace in the picture and its inscription: *To "Speed" Hoover: With Much Affection. Thomas Franklin Baughman.*[23]

THREE

SEX, LIES, AND THE FBI

The spring of 1921 arrived hot and sunny, forcing open the cherry blossoms along the Potomac's Tidal Basin, and returning straw hats to fashion down Pennsylvania Avenue. J. Edgar Hoover, now dressing to draw attention, had his hat steamed and blocked at the Hecht Company on Seventh Street, and began wearing it to work as if to prove he was not in mourning over the death of his father, for he, in fact, was not.

Dickerson Naylor Hoover had spent the last few months of his life being shuttled between Seward Square and Laurel Sanitarium as doctors attempted to break his chronic depression. Seemingly too tired to live another day, the elder Hoover refused to eat much in the way of solid food, existing for several months on little more than tepid fish soup and bread dipped in orange juice. Already slight in weight, Dickerson grew bony and fragile as autumn leaves, spoke to no one—least of all his doctors—and simply prepared for death.

His son, busier than ever with his career, chose not to visit, claiming his father's silence "caused him discomfort." Apparently the feeling was mutual, for on the few occasions when Hoover's father returned to their home on Seward Square, he would wail in pain at the sight of his son. Other than these unexplained outbursts, he remained stoic and unspeaking, his head hunched down low to his shoulders, his eyes pressed into the black holes of their sockets, his face so thin his cheekbones appeared ready to launch themselves through his parchment skin.[1]

Dickerson's death certificate attested that he died of "melancholia" exacerbated by "inanition," which Webster defines as the "loss of vitality that results from lack of food and water." To those around him, Dickerson Hoover simply appeared to fade away, lost in a world of oppression and paranoia. For Hoover and his mother, the death of father and husband was less a loss than a relief from the constant pall he cast over their home. The lack of funeral services either in the house or at the grave site in the Congressional Cemetery reflected their sudden freedom after years of being pulled into an abyss of despair.

In the days following Dickerson's death, Annie Hoover forsook the customary black of mourning by ordering several new outfits in "neutral fabric" for $22, plus assorted "summer accessories" in anticipation of a renewed social life.[2] She had the bill sent to her youngest son, who was now in a better position to afford luxuries, thanks to yet another promotion within the Department of Justice.

Soon after President Warren G. Harding took his oath of office in March 1921, he attempted to make good on a campaign promise to cool the sensationalism of war-baiters and hatemongers. "America's present need is not heroics, but healing; not nostrums, but normalcy; not revolution, but restoration; not agitation, but adjustment; not surgery, but serenity; not the dramatic, but the dispassionate; not experiment, but equipoise; not submergence in internationality, but sustainment in triumphant nationality. . . ," Harding said.[3]

To help restore the country to normalcy, Harding selected his poker-playing buddy and campaign manager Harry Daugherty to be his attorney general. It was a risky move. Daugherty, who more than earned his nickname, "Foxy," had orchestrated Harding's push to the White House through a labyrinth of deals, promises, and trade-offs, and as attorney general it was payback time.

The first to benefit was Daugherty's close friend William J. Burns, head of the William J. Burns International Detective Agency and at the time the most famous private eye in America. Daugherty and Burns had grown up together in Ohio in the sleepy town of Washington Court House, on Paint Creek. Daugherty appointed Burns to replace William J. Flynn as director of the Bureau of Investigation over the objections of almost everyone who knew the detective and his propensity for shady associations.

After aiding Daugherty during the Harding campaign with various clandestine investigations, Burns had been guaranteed the post. As the new head of the Bureau, he was expected to be absolutely loyal to the administration but not to exactly work full-time, since part of his deal allowed him to continue operating his private business. Burns, therefore, needed a crackerjack assistant to run the Bureau in his not-too-unusual absence. Daugherty's suggestion: J. Edgar Hoover.

Hoover had been lobbying heavily for the job ever since Daugherty's arrival the first week of March. He initially impressed the new attorney general with his knowl-edge of the Communist infiltration in America, of which

Daugherty was completely ignorant. Hoover took it upon himself to educate the attorney general about radicals as well as introduce him to his extensive files—files that just happened to include the names of many of Harding's political enemies.

Although it took a few months for Hoover to ingratiate himself with Daugherty, who initially found Hoover to be "quite the dandy with his white linen suits and pocket squares,"[4] the attorney general eventually saw the wisdom of maintaining a continuing voice within the Department of Justice. And so it was that on August 22, 1921, J. Edgar Hoover joined the Bureau, an organization he would ultimately head for a lifetime.

By the time Hoover assumed his new position at a salary of $4,000 a year, Daugherty had made certain that his full cadre of chums was in place throughout the White House. Chief among them was Jess Smith, a onetime haberdasher and department store owner from Ohio who was Daugherty's factotum and rumored lover, and with whom he lived at 1509 H Street, a 10-minute walk from the White House. The house quickly became known as the "Love Nest," not for the alleged romance between Daugherty and Smith, but for the number of women President Harding is suspected of having bedded there.

Owned by the publisher of the *Washington Post,* Edward B. "Ned" McLean, and his wife, Evalyn, the house had once been the office of McLean's father, who himself was said to have had trysts there. With Daugherty and Smith in residence, the "Love Nest" became the unofficial office of the attorney general, who recruited McLean as an agent for the Bureau at a salary of $1 per year. The publisher liked to think of himself as an adventurer, albeit a repeatedly drunken one, and his status as a special agent only added to his reputation. The house itself was rather grand, even though Evalyn, accustomed to her estate, "Friendship," in Georgetown and the 1,200-acre Belmont Farm in Virginia, thought it small. The bedrooms, of course, received the most use. Jess Smith's was a spectacle of pink taffeta; the attorney general's was flowered chintz. And President Harding ended up using them both. In return, Daugherty and Smith had free run of the White House and the rest of the District as well.[5]

Hoover was aware of the arrangement, just as he was of Smith's role within the Justice Department. Though never an official employee, Smith had an office in the same building as Hoover and routinely sent correspondence typed by department stenographers on official stationery. Hoover regularly found Smith rifling through the files, amused at Smith's confusion over their seeming disorder. While Smith had difficulty locating files, he did not have a problem accepting payoffs to make them disappear. Much to Hoover's dismay, even when files were moved for safe-keeping, the investigations into their subjects had a dis-arming way of being closed without prejudice.

Since Burns and Daugherty were not only aware of Smith's behavior but orchestrating it, Hoover wisely chose to remain outside of the intrigue, concentrating on the administration of the department and its agents, now numbering 400. Ironically, Hoover's impeccable perform-ance camouflaged the extent of the illegal practices taking place under Daugherty's watch—practices that were gen-erating millions of dollars in cash flow.

While Jess Smith handled payoffs involving ongoing Bureau investigations in rather straightforward fashion, the real money pouring into Daugherty's slush fund came through Prohibition graft. The Eighteenth Amendment to the Constitution, which made it illegal to manufacture, sell, or transport intoxicating liquor, became effective on January 16, 1920. As distilleries across the country shut down their taps, bootleggers and booze traffickers began producing illegal liquor and delivering it to major cities throughout the country. When local police departments attempted to locate the stills and confiscate the contraband, organized crime quickly countered with bribes and payoffs. Nowhere was the door easier to open than in the Justice Department of the United States where Harry Daugherty made it possible for America's underground to deal direct through his own private connection, Gaston B. Means.

Means was originally hired by Burns as a special agent at a rate of $7 a day. A onetime double spy for Germany and Britain during the war, Means had first found his way into Burns's employ in 1910 when he joined the Burns Detective Agency. With his deceptively sweet face and muscular physique, Means manipulated his way through life, not only scoffing at laws but bragging about his success at ignoring them.

At the top of his list of accomplishments was the alleged murder of a wealthy widow from Chicago, Maude A. King. Mrs. King made the mistake of going hunting one day with Means in North Carolina, and ended up being carried out of the woods with a bullet hole in her head. Means claimed the woman had accidentally shot herself, and was acquitted of any wrongdoing, if only for lack of evidence. Some weeks later, when he presented a forged will leaving him $150,000, the rightful heirs of Mrs. King countered with their own authentic document, leaving Means with bloodied hands but no payoff.

At Daugherty's suggestion, Means became the liaison between the attorney general and the booze traffickers, operating out of a Bureau-provided house at 903 Sixteenth Street NW where he lived with his family, employed three servants, and kept his chauffeur-driven Cadillac. Each week Means arranged for payoffs from bootleggers anxious to purchase protection from federal arrest and prosecution. Using a drop at the Vanderbilt Hotel in New York, Means routinely collected payments ranging from $10,000 to $50,000 for the guarantee of no interference in the bootleggers' business as well as access to government-bonded liquor warehouses. In 1930, Means revealed his part in the payoffs, bragging that they generated more than $7 million—money split among Means, Burns, and Daugherty.[6]

Hoover first met Means in October 1921, when he "lumbered into the Department of Justice where I then was a subordinate and immediately began to investigate everything within reach. A bulky man, with a heavy body and long, gorilla-like arms, there was about him the air of a person eternally reaching a climax. It was all simulation. Underneath his excited exterior, Gaston Means was cool and cunning and crafty."[7]

He despised Means's deceiving looks, his crude behavior, his surreptitious activities, and his arrogant style. Though he was unable to convince Burns that Means was a detriment to the Bureau, he did manage to keep him out of his office, refusing to even glance in Means's direction for fear of being sullied through association. "Those of us who were honest kept quiet about where we worked," Hoover later said. "We didn't want people to think we were crooks."[8]

With illegal activity swirling around his department, Hoover remained focused on responsibilities he thought were the proper domain of the Bureau of Investigation. While Burns busied himself with using Bureau agents to assist in breaking a strike of 400,000 railroad shop workers, Hoover was drawn into the mysterious world of the Ku Klux Klan at the request of Paul Wooton, the Washington correspondent for the *New Orleans Times-Picayune*. Wooton arrived unannounced at Hoover's office in late 1922, carrying a personal letter from the governor of Louisiana, John M. Parker. Hoover felt the sweat on Wooton's palm as he shook the journalist's hand and watched with apprehension as the clearly nervous reporter shifted uneasily from right foot to left, refusing to sit, as if he were being watched and needed to end his visit quickly.

Wooton had every reason to be concerned. At the time, the Klan was running rampant in Louisiana, preaching its message of white supremacy, and regularly kidnapping blacks and burning the initials "KKK" into their foreheads with acid. Worse still, murders were taking place sporadically throughout New Orleans and nearby parishes. Local police were reluctant to get involved either out of intimidation or because of their own participation in the murders.

Certain his mail was being searched and censored and his telephone tapped by the Klan, Governor Parker sent Wooton with a written request for federal help. The newspaperman suspected he was being followed and knew his presence in Hoover's office was itself dangerous, his darting eyes suggesting the degree of his anxiety.

While Hoover accepted the letter, he did not acknowledge that the Ku Klux Klan had violated any federal statutes, preferring to believe the group's efforts were limited to harmless intimidation. Nevertheless, he agreed to discuss the situation with Daugherty and promised to protect Wooton's identity. Daugherty, preoccupied with his Prohibition graft, had little time for the non-money-making lunacy of an angered South and dismissed Parker's hysteria out of hand. To keep Hoover busy, however, he instructed him to investigate the legitimacy of Parker's assertions and to present a written analysis of the situation.

Even though he believed blacks were basically lazy and unreliable, "low Red Cap sorts" according to a memo he sent to Daugherty, Hoover thought it best to placate Parker by suggesting that the governor appeal directly to the president of the United States to voice his concern, referencing Article IV, Section 4 of the Constitution, which authorized the federal government to protect states "against domestic violence."

Hoover was surprised to learn that Parker did as he suggested, sending President Harding a letter dated October 2, 1922, in which he requested federal troop intervention. In his letter, Parker alerted Harding that "due to the activities of an organized body reputed to be the Ku Klux

Klan . . . not only have the laws been violated, but men taken out, beaten and whipped. Two men [Watt Daniels and Thomas Richards] have been brutally murdered without trial or charges . . . my information tonight is that six more citizens have been ordered to leave their homes (in Morehouse Parish) under penalty of death. These conditions are beyond [my] control." There was panic in his plea when he added that his own police forces in the state were "publicly recognized as members of this Ku Klux Klan."[9]

The Mer Rouge Murders, as the killing of Daniels and Richards became known, made headlines for the gruesome condition of the victims' bodies when they were pulled from Lake LaFourche. The men had last been seen leaving a local barbecue and baseball game when hooded attackers armed with rifles forcibly removed them from their car and marched them into the woods. Initially knocked unconscious, the men were lashed to large wagon wheels and their bodies repeatedly clubbed, breaking their legs, arms, shoulders, and hips.

Ignoring calls from the Mer Rouge residents, local police were slow to take action, even as witnesses reported a gasoline-fed fire burning on the banks of the lake. There, in the shadows of hoods and flames, the heads of Daniels and Richards were surgically removed and their bodies dumped into the water of the remote rural area. The gruesome discovery of the bodies by divers guarded by state militia should have caused a public outcry. Rather, local sentiment was mixed, as Klansmen intimidated those who dared speak out against what they saw as racial cleansing "for the good of race pride."[10]

Though Harding ordered Bureau agents to investigate the case, he did it more for his own protection than in response to Parker's request. Based on the prevailing elitist politics, the Klan was considered an order dedicated to the preservation of the propertied class, and the fight against gambling, liquor, drugs, and prostitution. Harding himself had been sworn into the Klan earlier in the year in an effort to maintain his political base. The Klan's Imperial Wizard, William Joseph Simmons, conducted the secret initiation in the Green Room of the White House, with Harding rewarding those on the induction team "War Department license tags that allowed them to run red lights all across the nation."[11]

Hoover apparently was ignorant of Harding's involvement in the organization. He was, however, anxious to advance legitimate investigations within the Bureau. While he fundamentally agreed with white supremacy, he was outraged by vigilante violence regardless of its motivation. It was the challenge that the Klan posed to legitimate authority that upset him, coupled with its propensity to violate the law. "The Ku Klux Klan contaminates the courts—the very basis of our civic protection," Hoover wrote Burns in December 1922. "It is bad enough when the pulpits and the legislative halls of the land are scourged with the course of Kluxism, but when the courts and processes of justice are directly attacked, it is time for positive and drastic action."[12]

Despite the aggressive posture, the Bureau did not launch a wholesale investigation into Klan activities at the time, but instead limited itself to the investigation into the murders in Mer Rouge, Louisiana. With information furnished by Hoover's special agents, the police arrested local doctor and former Mer Rouge mayor Bunnie McEwin McKoin and a deputy sheriff, charging them with the murders. McKoin, an outspoken member of the Klan, had reported shots fired at his car several months earlier in an assassination attempt. The prosecutor proposed that Daniels and Richards were killed in retaliation. McKoin also had the skill necessary to decapitate the victims. Ultimately, however, the accused were not indicted for what was labeled "lack of evidence" and subsequently released, while the *Times-Picayune* suggested a more plausible reason: "a majority of the grand jurors were Klansmen."[13]

Struck by the obvious bias in the region, Hoover fought back with a familiar tactic: opening a file and launching an investigation into the personal life of an individual—in this case Imperial Kleagle Edward Young Clarke. Clarke, known as Atlanta's P. T. Barnum, appealed to Hoover's curiosity not simply because he was credited with turning the Klan into a major success story but because he had a private side that included carnal passion with his widowed partner, Mrs. Elizabeth "Bessie" Tyler, and assorted teenage girls as well.

Bessie was a self-educated woman who utilized her ample breasts and flattering curves to seduce businessmen initially into having sex, and later for self-promotion. An early version of a public relations guru, the buxom woman was said to have married and had a daughter at the age of 14, and was widowed the following year. With a child to support, she turned her talents to exploitation and met Clarke during her promotion of the annual Harvest Festival, an Atlanta tradition that mixed food, crafts, and fiddling contests. Together she and Clarke formed the Southern Publicity Association, and its initial clients, including the Salvation Army and the American Red Cross, gave it a well-deserved reputation for helping wholesome charities. It was not until Clarke and the voluptuous Tyler met William Joseph Simmons that public relations history was made.

As Bessie remembered it, she and Clarke were introduced to the Imperial Wizard after her son-in-law joined the Klan. "We found Colonel Simmons was having a hard time [getting] along. He couldn't pay his rent. The receipts were not sufficient to take care of his personal needs. He was a minister and a clean living and thinking man, and he was heart and soul for the success of his Ku Klux Klan. After we had investigated it from every angle, we decided to go into it with Colonel Simmons and give it the impetus that it could best get from publicity."[14]

With the help of Clarke and Tyler, membership in the Klan expanded from a little more than 3,000 in the summer of 1921 to 100,000 by the end of the following year. In addition to becoming quite wealthy—he received money for each recruit—Clarke became nationally known as the Klan's spokesman and defender, drawing on its Christian roots and belief in the purity of women.

Assigning special agents to tail Clarke's every move, Hoover patiently waited for the pious publicist to break the law, keeping notes on his associations, habits, and activities. In less than three weeks, the determined assistant director of the Bureau received word that Clarke had traveled from Houston to New Orleans in the company of a young woman with whom he was having a sexual relationship. Alerted by Hoover, local police in New Orleans broke into the couple's hotel room and arrested Clarke, charging him with violating the White Slave Traffic Act. Passed in 1910, the act (officially known as the Mann Act) made it illegal for a man and a woman to cross state lines to commit an immoral act. Although originally intended to curtail prostitution, the law worked just as well when applied to unmarried yet consenting adults. Clarke was indicted in Texas and pleaded guilty to the charge in federal court, paying a fine of $5,000.[15]

While the arrest was small consolation to a nation still at the mercy of the Klan's vigilantes, it nevertheless reminded Hoover of the power of clandestine information. It was something the man virtually running the Bureau of Investigation would not forget. Indeed, he was about to build his reputation on that very principle.

In May 1923, Hoover was able to look upon his career with both pride and confusion. While he had found his niche and seemed to be making an impact on what he saw as growing lawlessness in America, those around him seemed to be intent on breaking as many rules as he was determined to enforce.

Alone in his office late at night, Hoover was repeatedly tempted to resign, feeling certain that it was only a matter of time before the corruption around him resulted in the collapse of the entire Bureau. No longer could he feel justified in looking the other way; no longer was it safe to pretend it wasn't happening.

Inside the Bureau, whispers spread the news that the Harding administration was about to be hit by a major scandal, which also intensified Hoover's gloom. At the center of the rumors was a reported scam in which Secretary of the Interior Albert B. Fall had colluded with several oil barons from the West, leasing oil rights to government-held reserves for personal gain. Fall immediately denied the allegation, and at first Hoover was convinced of his innocence.

Hoover's mother, however, was less trusting, relying not on insider gossip but the astrological readings of Madame Marcia. Marcia Champney held her mystical court in her small house at 1509 R Street, midway between Dupont and Logan Circles, having been thrust into Washington high society on the palms of Edith Galt, whom in 1909 Madame Marcia accurately predicted would marry the president of the United States. It mattered little that the president at the time, William Howard Taft, was already married. Edith Galt was both widowed and patient, and when she found herself on the receiving end of a proposal from Woodrow Wilson, the next president to enter the White House, Madame Marcia's career was written in the stars.

By the time Florence Kling Harding became First Lady and routinely summoned the astrologer for personal sessions, scheduling an appointment with Madame Marcia required both money and connections. Annie Hoover had both, thanks to her son, who regularly gifted his mother with astrological readings. That Madame Marcia should alert Annie to political intrigue within the Harding administration was as likely to have originated from Marcia's gossiping clients as it was from her clairvoyant skills. Regardless of its origin, when Annie Hoover relayed the information that scandal was afoot, Hoover wasted little time in checking out her facts.

Interestingly enough, Madame Marcia's flash of perception did not center on Secretary Fall, despite the gossip swirling around Washington. Rather, the clairvoyant advised Annie to be wary of Jess Smith, who, she warned, was not only corrupt, but likely to be murdered. Knowing that her son maintained an office close to Smith's, Annie raced back to Seward Square full of caution and warning of doom.

Hoover reacted to the prediction with characteristic disbelief yet mentioned it to Frank Baughman as he did most things. The two men continued to be inseparable, sharing lunches, dinners and late-night drinks and dances with the women Baughman always seemed to attract. Hoover was fascinated by the ease with which Baughman handled himself, the way he leaned into a conversation no matter how unimportant.

Baughman had encountered Smith only the day before at the new apartment Smith shared with Daugherty. The pair had moved out of the "Love Nest" to a large two-bedroom residential unit in the posh Wardman Park Hotel not far from Dupont Circle. While dropping off paperwork to Daugherty, Baughman overheard a heated argument between the roommates. Perhaps argument was the wrong word, he later informed Hoover. More a stern warning. The talk was of Smith's impending arrest on charges of influence peddling. As Herbert Hoover, then Harding's secretary of commerce, would later write in his memoirs, the president himself had called Smith to the White House to admonish him for playing fast and loose with his privileged position in the Justice Department. Harding was direct and frank about his desire to avoid scandal, and told Smith he intended to have him arrested.[16]

The next day, Smith and Daugherty fled Washington to spend the weekend in their cabin in Columbus, Ohio, which they lovingly called the "Shack." Smith was understandably tense, suspecting that any moment he would be taken into custody. Come Sunday, however, no federal agents had appeared. On the train back to Washington, Smith bolted the door to his cabin and paced back and forth within the confines of the small room.

On Monday, he attempted to play golf at the McLean estate, Friendship, only to return to his apartment and hastily write a new will on a brown-paper bag. By 7 A.M., May 30, 1923, Smith was dead, a .32-caliber revolver found on the floor next to his right hand.[17]

The mystery surrounding Smith's death sent the Washington press into a feeding frenzy, circling the Department of Justice as vultures would the dying wounded. It helped neither Daugherty nor the Harding administration that a special agent who had been assigned to keep watch over Smith discovered the body after hearing a shot at 6:40 in the morning. According to press reports at the time, after discovering the body the agent telephoned Bureau director Burns, who lived in the apartment directly below the pair at the Wardman Park. Burns notified the police, but not before alerting the president *and* the hotel manager, Elmer Dwyer. By the time Sergeant J. D. Marks arrived at the apartment, so many people had entered Smith's bedroom to view the body that preserving the crime scene, if indeed there had been a crime, became next to impossible.

Marks noted that Smith's head was partially inside a wire-mesh wastebasket containing burned papers, and there it remained until coroner, J. Ramsey Nesbitt arrived. "He apparently had shot himself while sitting on the edge of the bed. His body slumped off on the floor, the head striking a metal wastebasket at the head of the bed and overturning it so that the head was partly in the basket," Nesbitt told the *Daily News*.[18]

Hoover and the Bureau were drawn into the investigation as a precautionary measure when rumors began to surface that the perceived suicide might actually have been murder—an apparent effort to silence an increasingly fragile Smith and keep the multiple indiscretions of the Harding administration under wraps. Burns ordered that Hoover's file on Smith be delivered to Daugherty, after which it mysteriously disappeared forever.

As the heat began to build within the administration to defuse the suspicions of the press, Hoover endeavored to stay under the radar. He meticulously detailed every procedure he authorized by associating it with a federal statute or law. He remained personally aloof to the intrigue gripping the Department of Justice by being clinical in his analysis of the situation. People were reduced to file numbers and their offenses categorized by subject. Since no one was above suspicion in Hoover's mind, even the president had a file into which Hoover placed observations and comments by members of Harding's Secret Service staff. The silent observer, he quietly bided his time in the background, seeing all, saying nothing, waiting to see which way the political climate would turn.

Meanwhile, hoping to divert attention from the potential scandal within his administration, Harding announced plans to take an extended tour across the country to Alaska, with the First Lady, and assorted members of his staff, including Harry Daugherty. After Smith's death, however, Daugherty was quietly dropped from the guest list and replaced by Frederick Gillett, the Republican Speaker of the House from Massachusetts.

The absence of the president from Washington did little to cool the rumor mill, of course. If anything, talk of corruption at the very core of the administration increased as Burton Kendall Wheeler and Thomas J. Walsh, the Democratic senators from Montana, announced their probe into Albert Fall and his handling of leases in the federal oil fields. Daugherty's response was one of vengeance, ordering Hoover to uncover negative material on Wheeler, newly elected and perceived more vulnerable than the widely respected Walsh.

"Agents of the Department . . . surrounded my house," Wheeler said. "Watched persons who went in and came out, constantly shadowed me, shadowed my house, and shadowed my wife."[19] What agents weren't doing was uncovering information on Fall. Two months earlier, in March 1923, Fall had resigned as secretary of the interior hoping to assuage those who questioned his integrity. Unfortunately for Fall, in the months prior to his resignation, he had made rather substantial renovations on his Three Rivers Ranch in New Mexico, renovations that could not be easily financed by his salary.

Fall was protected from a Bureau investigation because of his friendship with Daugherty, who instead placed those called as witnesses under scrutiny. Hoover eagerly complied, but only after he received instructions in writing, once more protecting his own reputation. "He was a little like the soldier who follows his commander's order to kill. If the wrong man gets shot, the guy who pulled the trigger only has to point his finger toward his captain to escape responsibility,"[20] a retired FBI agent said, recalling Hoover's alibi for his conduct.

Despite the Bureau's best efforts at intimidation, Wheeler and Walsh uncovered damaging evidence against both Fall and Daugherty. Implications of a Senate investigation played heavily on Harding's mind, as Herbert Hoover remembered. The then secretary of commerce and his wife had joined the president and his party aboard ship sailing to Alaska.

> One day after lunch when we were a few days out, Harding asked me to come to his cabin. He pumped at me the question: "If you knew of a great scandal in our administration, would you for the good of the country and the party expose it publicly or would you bury it?" My natural reply was, "Publish it, and at least get credit for integrity on your side." [Harding] remarked that this method might be politically dangerous.[21]

Harding never revealed the full extent of his knowledge to Herbert Hoover or the nation. The twenty-ninth president of the United States died on August 2, 1923, before returning to Washington. He had fallen ill from what his doctors initially labeled "poisoning from bad sea food [sic]," contracted while in Seattle on July 27 during

a stop on the trip home. Harry Daugherty had unexpectedly shown up and sat alone with the president for several
hours. That evening Harding collapsed and was taken by
train to San Francisco. Canceling his speeches and personal appearances, Harding remained secluded in the
Palace Hotel. For the next few days, he appeared to be
responding to treatment. However, on the evening of
August 2, he began to perspire heavily and ultimately died.

Several years later, Gaston Means wrote a book in
which he suggested that the president's wife had poisoned
him in retaliation for his dalliances in Daugherty's "Love
Nest." Others believed Daugherty poisoned him when he
came to Seattle. The official cause of death was a heart
attack. Yet, as Herbert Hoover later said, "People do not
die from a broken heart, but people with bad hearts may
reach the end much sooner from great worries."[22]

When Herbert Hoover was called upon to dedicate
Harding's tomb in Marion, Ohio, he declared, "Warren
Harding had a dim realization that he had been betrayed
by a few of the men whom he had trusted, by men who he
had believed were his devoted friends. It was later proved
in the courts of the land that these men had betrayed not
only the friendship and trust of their staunch and loyal
friend, but they had betrayed their country."

Despite the best efforts of the Department of Justice to
intimidate witnesses and obscure facts, in October 1923
Senator Thomas Walsh convened a special committee to
investigate Fall and his handling of the leases on three oil-
rich parcels of land under his jurisdiction: one in Elk Hill
and one in Buena Vista Hills, California, and the third in
Teapot Dome, Wyoming. As the case moved forward, the

Senate learned Fall had leased rights to the Elk Hill
reserve to Edward L. Doheny of California's Pan American
Petroleum Company, while at the same time receiving a
"loan" of $100,000 in cash, wrapped in brown paper and
delivered in a black satchel. Subsequently the Senate discovered that Fall had leased the Teapot reserve to his
friend Harry F. Sinclair, who headed the Mammoth Oil
Company, after he received "six heifers, a yearling bull,
two six-month-old boars, four sows and for his foreman,
an English thoroughbred horse."[23] In addition, Fall also
received $390,000 in cash and bonds.

In early 1924, the Teapot Dome scandal exploded
across the headlines of America and into the very heart of
Washington, D.C. Former vice president Calvin Coolidge,
who became president after Harding's passing, had so little confidence in Daugherty's integrity that he went outside the attorney general's office to name independent
counsel to prosecute the government's case. Though he
had lost the new president's confidence, Daugherty
showed little willingness to resign. Rather, he continued
to pursue Wheeler even as the bombastic senator was
attacking him. J. Edgar Hoover sat next to Daugherty and
his defense counsel during Wheeler's hearings which
charged Daugherty with interfering with the inquiry into
the former interior secretary.

The star witness was none other than Gaston B.
Means, alleged murderer, extortionist, and special agent
of the Bureau of Investigation. Given Means's reputation,
Daugherty assumed few would believe anything Means
had to say. It was a calculated risk Daugherty was about
to lose. The testimony delivered by the rogue investigator

was so damaging and explicit that it changed the flavor of the entire hearing, which thereafter became known in the press as the "Means Trials."

As Don Whitehead wrote in his book *The FBI Story*:

> Means said he had arranged to have agents sneak into senator's offices, open their mail, search their files and spy on them in an effort to find something damaging which could be used to stop their attacks on Daugherty. Means said he delivered his reports to Jess Smith. He indicated that he never dealt with anyone below the Daugherty-Smith-Burns level of authority.[24]

While it would take years before the scandal was totally settled, it took only until March 28 for Daugherty to be forced out of office by Coolidge. He was replaced by Harlan F. Stone, the dean of Columbia University's School of Law. Though Daugherty managed to avoid a prison sentence after two hung juries could not decide his fate on charges of conspiring to defraud the federal government, Fall was not so lucky. He was sentenced to a year in prison and a fine of $100,000.*

Bureau of Investigation director William Burns was immediately at the top of Stone's list for dismissal, given his close association with Daugherty as a member of the

---

* A complete account of the Teapot Dome scandal can be found in *Teapot Dome* by M. R. Werner and John Starr. For a thorough rendering of the corruption of the Harding administration, see *Incredible Era: The Life and Times of Warren Gamaliel Harding* by Samuel Hopkins Adams, as well as the excellent *Florence Harding: The First Lady, the Jazz Age, and the Death of America's Most Scandalous President* by Carl Sferrazza Anthony.

so-called Ohio Gang. It did not help America's most famous detective that he admitted to a Senate committee in early April that he said nothing when Daugherty had perjured himself about sending agents to Montana to find damaging information on Wheeler. Burns, of course, not only knew about the operation, but was intricately involved in it.

After several weeks passed and Burns still had his job, he began to fall into old habits and believed that he was untouchable. The reality of the moment became more apparent when Stone, who had been busy shoring up the crumbling halls of the Justice Department, finally got around to the corrupt head of the Bureau of Investigation.

When William J. Burns swaggered into the office of the attorney general on May 9, 1924, he anticipated receiving an endorsement of his performance. Stone, huge and grim behind a large, polished mahogany desk, a perpetual scowl carved into his brow, was silent for a moment, staring at the arrogant detective before him. When Stone finally spoke, he bluntly demanded that Burns resign or be fired. The blood drained from the Irishman's face, and the freckles that covered his nose and cheeks seemed to lose all color. Incapable or unwilling to respond, Burns refused to answer, and was promptly escorted from the Denrike Building and onto the street. Only later that evening on the radio did Burns hear about his resignation.

The following morning, Stone made a decision that would have a far-reaching impact. At 11:30 A.M. on May 10, 1924, Stone asked J. Edgar Hoover to report to his office. What unfolded over the next few moments has been recounted thousands of times, its retelling a mandatory tradition for new agents entering the Bureau. The simple version has Hoover, the man who effectively ran the Bureau's day-to-day operations, being offered the job as its acting director. Later in life, however, the version Hoover would tell made a point of filling the story with drama and pathos, suggesting he had to pause and think about his options before answering.

"I'll take the job, Mr. Stone, on certain conditions," Hoover claimed to have stated.

"What are they?" Stone asked, presumably impressed that Hoover hadn't jumped at the opportunity.

"The Bureau must be divorced from politics and not be a catch-all for political hacks. Appointments must be based on merit. Second, promotions will be made on proven ability and the Bureau will be responsible only to the Attorney General."

"I wouldn't give it to you under any other conditions," Stone replied. "That's all. Good day."[25] Hoover turned without smiling, and walked into the pages of history.

FOUR

THE
ELECTRIC WIRE

Mrs. Mabel Walker Willebrant worked her broad lips into a slow smile as she placed the telephone receiver back in its cradle. She had just received news that pleased her, and since Mrs. Mabel Walker Willebrant found very little lately that she could honestly say made her happy, she took this occasion to stop and relish the moment.

Her boss, Attorney General Harlan Stone, had taken her advice about J. Edgar Hoover. When he asked her opinion, she had not hesitated to label young Hoover a "firebrand," for to Mabel Walker Willebrant that was exactly what he was. She knew the word well, having been called it herself on several occasions. For the portly and stern assistant attorney general, "firebrand" was a compliment: someone who liked to stir things up, a rouser who intended to get things done.

"He's honest and informed and one who operates like an electric wire, with almost trigger response," she had told Stone, and it seemed to seal his decision.[1]

Hoover himself would never credit Mrs. Mabel Walker Willebrant with his appointment, of course. It didn't matter that she was the highest-ranking woman in the Coolidge administration, or that she was the assistant attorney general in charge of prosecuting bootleggers.

She was, after all, a woman, and a controversial one at that. "The Prohibition Portia," they called her. Brilliant, unattractive, dedicated, and divorced. Like J. Edgar Hoover, she lived her job, and it certainly did not hurt that she thought him to be talented, consistent, and yes, a firebrand.

Still, at this stage of his career, it did not serve the new acting director of the Bureau of Investigation to have a woman holding the spotlight on his glory. That honor he chose to give to Secretary of Commerce Herbert Hoover, or more precisely, Hoover's executive secretary, Lawrence Richey. Richey was a former special agent with the Secret Service who had guarded Theodore Roosevelt, later became a private eye handling cases for the government, and then reentered civil service at the request of Herbert Hoover, who needed a factotum. When Stone asked the commerce secretary about a potential replacement for William J. Burns, Hoover mentioned it to Richey, and Richey is said to have commented: "Why should they look around when they have the man they need right over there now—a young, well-educated lawyer named Hoover."[2]

It seems doubtful that J. Edgar Hoover would have been an unknown at this point having already served as Burns's second-in-command for several years. More likely, Stone asked for references on the assistant director from those around him, and Richey gave feedback along with others. It was, however, Mrs. Mabel Walker Willebrant's unique position within the Justice Department that made *her* recommendation the decisive one.

Harlan Stone was an imposing man, nearly six feet five inches in height, with thick bones and a scowl perpetually etched in his brow as if the next decision he had to make would change the course of history. Oftentimes, of course, it was true, as it was on May 10, 1924, when he shook the hand of J. Edgar Hoover and confirmed his appointment.

After the new acting director of the Bureau of Investigation left the office of Harlan Stone, he placed a telephone call to his mother. It was little more than a validation of what Annie Hoover had long anticipated. She was well aware of the hours her son toiled late into the night, never failing to bring home boxes of paperwork. She saw the sacrifices he had made. And she swelled with pride at being the mother of the director of the Bureau of Investigation. Not *acting* director. Director. Which is exactly what she said to her friends when she put on her best spring bonnet and set about spreading the word around Seward Square.

As he sat down to dinner that evening, Hoover found a sapphire ring on his plate, a token of Annie's unbridled pride. On the platinum band, six diamonds flanked a star sapphire. It was the perfect appetizer to the special pot roast meal prepared by the cook and supervised by Hoover's mollycoddling mother. Several months earlier, she had traveled to Bailey Banks and Biddle, a jewelry store known for the quality of its clientele as well as its gems, to purchase the ring, in preparation for this evening.

If it hadn't been for Annie's clothesline telegraph spreading the news around the neighborhood, her son's promotion might have gone unnoticed throughout much of Washington. There was no formal announcement of

Hoover's ascension to the top drawer in the Bureau, no posting on the government employee's bulletin board. Stone saw no need for it, for he truly believed this appointment was temporary, as reflected in a memo widely circulated throughout his department. That memo—the first in a new file Hoover created as the head of the Bureau—commanded little attention from its one-sentence length.

May 10, 1924.

Mr. J. Edgar Hoover
Bureau of Investigation
Washington, D.C.

Dear Sir:
You are hereby authorized to assume the duties of Director, Bureau of Investigation, with the title of Acting Director.

Very truly yours,
Harlan Stone
Attorney General.

If it meant little to most within the Department of Justice, it was vindication for the image-conscious acting director, who promptly ordered a wooden nameplate for his new desk in his new office adjacent to Helen Gandy whom he nominated to replace Mrs. Jesse Duckstein, Burns's former secretary.

It was the first order of business that Hoover undertook without direct supervision from Stone, who anticipated keeping an extraordinarily tight rein on the troubled department.

The new attorney general certainly did not want a repeat of past indiscretions and thoroughly expressed his expectations in a memo sent on May 13, 1924. It covered six points that Hoover was expected to follow precisely and immediately.

1. The activities of the Bureau are to be limited strictly to investigations of violation of law, under my direction or under the direction of an Assistant Attorney General regularly conducting the work of the Department of Justice.

2. I desire that the personnel of the Bureau be reduced so far as is consistent with the proper performance of duties.

3. I request that you go over the entire personnel of the Bureau, as conveniently as may be done, and discontinue the services of those who are incompetent or unreliable.

4. I, some time ago, gave instructions that the so-called "dollar-a-year" men should be discontinued, except in those cases where the appointees are in the regular employment of this Department. Please see that these instructions are carried out with all convenient speed.

5. Until further instructed, I desire that no new appointments be made without my approval. In making appointments, please nominate men of known good character and ability, giving preference to men who have had some legal training.

6. I am especially anxious that the morale of the
Bureau be strengthened and I believe a first step in
that direction is the observation of the foregoing
suggestions.[3]

The acting director had been given direction, and he
saw in it an opportunity to prove his efficiency. Not in
months, not in weeks, but within days he reported back
to Stone that he had, in fact, acted on the attorney general's mandate. Gone were the "dollar-a-day" men, including Ned McLean. Gone were many of the incompetents,
including Gaston B. Means (then serving time in a federal
penitentiary while on temporary suspension from the
department)[4] and Alaska P. Davidson, the Bureau's first and
only female agent at the time.* In their place was a new
policy requiring future applicants to have a degree in law
or accounting.

Within months the number of agents dropped from
441 to 402, and the clerical support staff plummeted from
216 employees to 99. No longer was favoritism shown by
hiring friends or associates of congressmen, senators,
judges, and cabinet members. And field offices no longer
were run as independent organizations, but as satellite
operations of the Bureau of Investigation.

---

* Alaska P. Davidson was hired as a special agent under William J. Burns.
She was 54 years old at the time and had only three years of public school-
ing. Emma Jentzer, occasionally credited as the first female agent, was
hired as a clerk in 1910 by the Bureau's first director, Stanley Finch.
Jentzer performed a variety of duties in the Bureau, and was placed undercover in 1917 during investigations into the activities of Emma Goldman.
At the time of her hiring, women were not considered to be qualified to
perform the duties of special agents.

Pinning a map of the United States on the wall in his office, Hoover sectioned the country into 53 areas, each with a field office headed by a special agent in charge (SAC). In several cases, that agent was the office's only employee and responsible for representing federal law in that area. "I look to you as the Special Agent in Charge as my representative and I consider it your duty and function to see that the Special Agents and other employees assigned to your office are engaged at all times upon government business," Hoover memoed the field on July 1, 1924. "You are to exercise even closer supervision over the work of the Agents under you," he commanded.[5]

To cut down on the confusing and often counterproductive stream of paperwork, Hoover refused to accept reports from individual agents, instructing them instead to report only to their SAC. The SACs in turn would report to Hoover or those running the Bureau's six divisions he created. Division One was Hoover's own, the director's office. And, of course, it held the director's files, including the drawer labeled "Official and Confidential."

Division Two would be headed by the assistant director, who was as yet unnamed. Division Three and Division Four covered the various investigations undertaken by the Bureau. Division Five monitored the Bureau's chief clerks, and Division Six handled identification, Hoover's concept of a central clearinghouse for criminals and their statistics. It did not matter that the divisions were at best illusionary. He knew there was no assistant director as yet, nor any Department of Identification for that matter. But Hoover was nothing if not devoted to structure, and with his six divisions, his department's structure was now in place.

Amid the swirl of reorganization, Hoover's own General Intelligence Division, the one he had captained to glory and then scandal during the postwar years, was dissolved by order of the attorney general. While Stone was dean of the law school at Columbia University, he had been a severe critic of the Palmer raids, criticizing Palmer and stating that it appeared "he has proceeded on the theory that such aliens are not entitled to the constitutional guaranty of due process of law." Now that Stone was attorney general, he intended to see that the civil liberties of immigrants were no longer eclipsed, and instructed the director of the Bureau to stop investigating radicals immediately.

It was not a decision that made Hoover exceptionally happy, particularly when he suddenly found himself on the receiving end of a visit from Roger Baldwin, director of the American Civil Liberties Union. Baldwin had written to Stone demanding proof that the Bureau's efforts to generate incriminating evidence against radicals had ceased.

In one of the most remarkable transformations in American history, Hoover, the anticommunist, welcomed Baldwin, the pro-radical, like a long-lost friend. The Harvard-educated Baldwin had arrived poised for confrontation, yet was so dazzled by Hoover's apologies for past injustices and his pledge of the Bureau's commitment to individual freedom that he left the Department of Justice in a state of near euphoria. The following day, he wrote to Stone and shared his enthusiasm about a man he felt he had totally misjudged.

"I spent an hour with Mr. Hoover of the Bureau of Investigation after seeing you," Baldwin wrote. "I think I owe it to him and to you to say that I think we were wrong in our estimate of his attitude. That estimate was based upon some of the unfortunate performances of the Bureau in a previous administration in which Mr. Hoover doubtless played an unwilling part. What he told me of the details and changes made in the administration of the Bureau all indicate that the reorganization meets every suggestion any of us could possibly make, and that it has already been carried out faithfully in accordance with your stated general policy."[6]

When he received the letter, Stone allowed his stern demeanor to soften, his hardened scowl melting into a wry smile as he dashed off a note to Hoover, enclosing the letter from Baldwin. "Memorandum for Mr. Hoover, Acting Director, Bureau of Investigation. Will Mr. Hoover please note. This may be embarrassing praise, but I suppose we will have to endure it like the hot weather."[7]

Baldwin was pleased and Stone was pleased. Each thought that he had reworked the Bureau in his own image, and both were being led down an illusionary path of compliance by the acting director. Though it would not become known until several years after his death, Hoover not only did not stop his profiling of radicals with the dissolution of the General Information Division (GID), but he also continued to infiltrate meetings of the ACLU with undercover agents. Even more telling, he began a file on the attorney general of the United States, his boss, Harlan Fiske Stone, and redoubled his efforts to uncover damaging information on Roger Nash Baldwin.

As Hoover streamlined the operation of the Bureau, standardization became the key to cost efficiency as well as employee productivity. Taking the cookie-cutter approach, he viewed agents in the field as interchangeable—all college graduates, all dressed alike: immaculate white shirt, plain tie (red was forbidden for its Communist association), and gray suit. Filing systems were standardized based on Hoover's own catalog maintained in Washington. Even office layouts were duplicated from one city to the next, allowing agents to move between locations, prefamiliarized with policy, procedure, and organization.

When he was being observed, Hoover based his behavior strictly on Stone's dictates, instinctively aiming to exceed expectations. Working well into the evenings, seven days a week, he was always available, always cooperative, and ever precise. Every memo, instruction, and disciplinary action was triple-checked for accuracy and appropriateness. The smallest typo mandated the severest reprimand. And every letter received by Hoover's office generated one in response, which by December amounted to more than 50 letters and memos per day.

Exactly seven months after naming Hoover the acting director of the Bureau of Investigation, the attorney general requested an appointment with his temporary employee. It was unusual for Stone to make appointments with Hoover in advance. Stone seemed to prefer to interrupt Hoover's workday at will, keeping track of Hoover's response time to his requests. Yet during the first week of December 1924, the attorney general telephoned Hoover personally and requested that he present himself in his office at 2 P.M. on the tenth of the month.

In the days that followed the phone call, Hoover's mind raced with various scenarios ranging from apocalypse to promotion. At lunchtime on December 10, he left his office to pace down K Street, stumbled unto a pair of black cats, and convinced himself that he was about to be fired. By the time 2 P.M. arrived, Hoover was a cable of nervous energy from which his entire future hung. As it happened, Stone's own lunch appointment ran late, and he did not return to his office until nearly 20 minutes after two. By that point, Hoover had lost any pretense of composition, and in his eagerness to greet Harlan Stone bumped into the attorney general, scattering his papers across the polished parquet floors.

The amusement Stone took in retelling the story was amplified by Hoover's efforts to always appear in control, an efficient administrator with no room for failure.[8] This day, of course, Hoover would not fail; rather, Stone took pride in announcing his decision to appoint the 29-year-old civil servant as the director of the Bureau of Investigation. It would be one of Stone's last official acts as attorney general. The following month, President Calvin Coolidge nominated Stone to replace the retiring Joseph McKenna on the Supreme Court of the United States.

Even though Hoover already had been effectively doing the job he was now officially entitled to call his own, he was given a generous salary boost from $5,000 a year to $7,500. In celebration, Hoover and Frank Baughman escorted their mothers to New York City to see Fred Astaire and his sister, Adele, in the Gershwin brothers' *Lady, Be Good!* at the Liberty Theater on Forty-second Street.

It was an evening that Hoover would not easily forget, from the grand theater with its sculpted "Liberty Bell" and eagles to the toe-tapping Astaires' performance of "Fascinating Rhythm" and an aftershow invitation to meet the stars. While Adele looked suspiciously at the man she thought was rather frightening ("something about his eyes"), Fred would later remember Hoover for his handshake ("a vise grip") and his nervous energy ("a bit like a terrier").[9] Hoover himself would remember the evening as his introduction to his first celebrity outside of politics. It was an association he would learn to cultivate. For now, however, he was content with nurturing his Bureau and its investigations.

The Washington press was seemingly less than eager to learn about the new head of the Bureau, and Hoover received barely a mention in most newspapers. The exception was the *Washington Evening Star*, which ran a lengthy article by Robert T. Small about the appointment.

> The days of the "Old Sleuth" are over. The oldtime detective, the man of "shadows" and "frame-ups" and "get the goods in any way you can" is a thing of the past. . . . As an assistant to Burns, young Hoover got some education in the arts of the old school. But most of these he is casting aside. He is striking out along new and clean lines. He is not going to have men snooping around the offices of Senators and Representatives. He is going to try and do his work in a big and legitimate way. Young Mr. Hoover, of the new school of crime detection, has no entangling alliances. Among his friends he is known to be as clean as a hound's tooth.[10]

Hoover's incorruptibility was advanced even further in an article that Small wrote for the news journal *Literary Digest* the following month. In it, Small described Hoover as a "scholar, a gentleman, and a scientist."

> Attorney-General Stone cast aside all of the ancient notions of how a bureau of investigations, which is the Department of Justice name for secret service, should be conducted.
>
> Detectives of the old school the whole world over, from Scotland Yard to Tokyo, will be watching this new idea in Washington. Naturally they are skeptical. They look askance at the appointment of a young lawyer, thirty years of age, to head one of the most important branches of the Government's system for the control and apprehension of criminals . . .
>
> He looks at detective work from a new angle. He sees the evidence side. Instead of merely "getting the goods," he is concerned with making the "goods" stick in court . . .
>
> Perhaps that sort of thing is too idealistic. Perhaps the old third-degree style will come back. But anyway, we will see.
>
> Hoover is a homebred here in Washington. He was a high school cadet and used to march to the tunes of Sousa's famous march dedicated to these boys. He is also in the Military Intelligence Division of the Officers Reserve Corps. Furthermore, he plays golf. Whoever could picture an "Old Sleuth" doing that?[11]

The answer, apparently, was many, for with the dawn of 1925, the mood of America began to change. It was a time of financial abundance. Industrial production was reaching an all-time high, employment was up, and America's wallets were open in a free-spending frenzy with afternoons spent golfing on the local greens. It was the Roaring Twenties and on the surface, at least, a new freedom dominated the landscape. Flappers and speakeasies flaunted themselves in the face of a temperance movement determined to clamp down on frivolity. Though legally prohibited, liquor seemed to flow more freely than ever. The rumrunners and bootleggers operated right under the gaze of state law enforcement officials and outside the jurisdiction of Hoover's Bureau of Investigation.[†]

"I want to bring to your personal attention certain conditions existing in the Bureau in the past and which I do not intend shall continue in the future," Hoover wrote to his agents in the field. He continued:

> I do know that some years past, the forces of the Bureau of Investigation did not enjoy the best reputation . . . I am strongly of the opinion that the only way whereby we can again gain public respect and support is through proper conduct upon our part.
>
> I am determined to summarily dismiss from this Bureau any employee whom I find indulging in the use of intoxicants to any degree or extent upon any occasion. This, I can appreciate, is a very drastic attitude and I shall probably be looked upon by some elements

---

† The enforcement of the Eighteenth Amendment authorizing Prohibition was the responsibility of the Prohibition Bureau of the U.S. Treasury Department.

as a fanatic. I am not, however, one of those who may be classed as a "white ribbon" advocate,[‡] but I do believe that when a man becomes a part of this Bureau, he must so conduct himself, both officially and unofficially, as to eliminate the slightest possibility of criticism as to his conduct or actions. . . . I, myself, am refraining from the use of intoxicants . . . and I am not, therefore, expecting any more of the field employees than I am of myself.

The Bureau cannot afford to have a public scandal visited upon it in view of the all too numerous attacks made . . . during the past few years. I do not want this Bureau to be referred to in terms I have frequently heard used against other governmental agencies. . . .

What I am trying to do is to protect the force of the Bureau of Investigation from outside criticism and from bringing the Bureau of Investigation into disrepute because of the isolated circumstances of misconduct upon the part of employees who are too strongly addicted to their own personal desires and tastes to properly keep in mind at all times and upon all occasions the honor and integrity of the service of which they are a part.[12]

The integrity that concerned Hoover drove his performance both at work and at home. When he said he had stopped drinking liquor, he meant it, removing even his mother's treasured sherry from her house. His was a life

---

‡   White ribbons were worn by members of the Woman's Christian Temperance Union and came to signify those in favor of Prohibition.

dominated by control—of his emotions, his finances, and his leisure—and as he spun the illusion of propriety for himself, the web touched all those around him.

Most certainly, it impacted his niece Margaret, who at 17 moved in with her uncle and grandmother after her father, Hoover's brother Dick, bought a house in Maryland. While the accommodation allowed Margaret to finish attending Eastern High on East Capitol Street just a few blocks from Congress, it also turned her uncle into the gatekeeper for her developing love life. "J.E. used to scare my dates half to death with his stare—as if he knew something about them," Margaret remembered. "These poor boys would literally break into a cold sweat just waiting for him to come down the stairs. He had this strange effect on people."[13]

During this time, Hoover began to smoke Lucky Strike cigarettes, his one documented vice, which according to Margaret had been prescribed by his doctor to help alleviate stress caused by work. "His doctor had recommended that he smoke a cigarette after dinner to relax. The problem was that he didn't like to smoke alone . . . so he suggested that I smoke too. Well, I'm still smoking and he stopped years ago," she said in 1972 a few months before his death.[14]

Hoover's choice of Luckies was interesting given his concern for his appearance and presentation. Lucky Strike advertised itself as a woman's cigarette, coaxing American females to "reach for a Lucky instead of a sweet."

As Hoover worked to present his case for a unified Bureau of Investigation to Congress, the day-to-day details of running the Bureau and its investigations fell to Harold

"Pop" Nathan, a well-read special agent from the Bureau's office in Pittsburgh. One of a few Jewish agents who survived the downsizing during Hoover's initial year as director, Nathan held an arts degree from the City College of New York, was an opera buff, liked classical literature, and spent his vacations touring museums around the country. Yet it was his skill at organization and administration that prompted Hoover to offer him the job of assistant director of investigations in 1925. Nathan became Hoover's second-in-command, having won the post over Frank Baughman, who was named the supervisor of the headquarters' staff.

Although much has been made of Hoover's attachment to the 28-year-old Baughman, his selection of the 45-year-old Nathan over his college friend speaks to Hoover's determination to succeed in refocusing the Bureau. The challenge was difficult, especially given the Bureau's limited mandate in investigations. Strictly speaking, the Bureau was legally allowed to enforce few laws: the Mann Act (aimed at controlling intrastate prostitution) and the Dyer Act (which made it illegal to transport stolen motor vehicles across state lines) generated most of its cases. The Bureau also investigated charges of bank fraud, mail fraud, theft of government property, and bribing or impersonating government officials.

These were hardly the types of cases likely to generate the kind of nationwide exposure Hoover craved. For that he needed a grandstand, a showcase, a platform on which to build his reputation and that of his unknown Bureau. His agents were not permitted to make arrests or even carry firearms (then solely the province of state and local police), which made it nearly impossible to generate even a shred of publicity no matter how diligent his efforts were.

Returning to his files as the key to his strength, Hoover envisioned a Bureau that maintained records not only on radicals and politicians but on die-hard criminals as well. Criminal records at the time were principally the responsibility of prison wardens and police chiefs scattered across the country. Initially, Hoover conceived a plan to centralize criminal records within the Bureau of Investigation, files that would be under his sole control and administration. It was only a small leap for America's newest head cop to add fingerprints into the mix.

A relatively new science at the time, fingerprint identification and cataloging was a hodgepodge affair, with records kept primarily at Leavenworth Penitentiary in Kansas and the National Bureau of Criminal Identification in Chicago, a branch of the International Association of Chiefs of Police. Founded in 1893, the IACP had spearheaded the collection of fingerprints from crime scenes. Yet it was only after Congress authorized the Bureau of Investigation to coordinate the "exchange of identification records with officers of the cities, counties, and states" that Hoover realized the level of authority equal to his grand illusion.

Having placed himself at the nucleus of the nation's law enforcement officials, Hoover and his Bureau suddenly became essential to crime analysis throughout the country. On July 15, 1925, the newly anointed prime minister of prints spoke before the IACP to secure his position, stressing the need for "universal cooperation" in the "uniting of the forces of the guardians of civilization in the face of the common danger"—the rise in criminal activity across the nation. Hoover, indeed, had arrived. Until that moment, little effort had been given to organizing information from state and local police in a single central location outside of the preliminary work done by the IACP. Hoover was nearly alone in speaking out on issues of nationwide crime while aggressively mentoring his team of special agents to prepare for their eventual place in crime fighting.

As if cued by necessity, several months later tragedy struck at the very core of the Bureau in the form of a notorious car thief named Martin James Durkin. On October 11, 1925, Durkin shot to death special agent Edwin C. Shanahan—the first agent killed in the line of duty.[§] Upon hearing of the shooting, Hoover was reported to have roiled in anger, saying "We've got to get Durkin. If one of our agents is killed and the killer is permitted to get away, it will be open season on all our agents. Get him!"[15]

Get him they did, although it took months as more than 200 agents pursued the elusive Durkin across Illinois, Missouri, Kansas, Oklahoma, Texas, New Mexico, Arizona, and California, all without benefit of any authority, since no federal law had been broken. Durkin was subsequently tried in state court for murder, receiving a

---

§   In Don Whitehead's book, *The FBI Story*, the author incorrectly names the agent Edward B. Shanahan, an error duplicated in numerous other books. Edwin C. Shanahan was born in 1898 and became an agent in February 1920. Shanahan's son, Dennis, followed his father's lead, becoming an agent in 1948, serving 28 years before retiring in 1976.

sentence of 35 years, which were added to the 15 years he got from federal court for illegally transporting a car over state lines.**

The manhunt helped draw attention to Hoover, who accepted the nation's praise for having "removed a filthy killer from the street." It was a triumph he highlighted in his subsequent report to Congress for his first full year as director. In the report, Hoover pointed to arrests that yielded a total of 4,494 years in prison and fines equal to $1,038,856.42. The figures were a sobering reminder that crime was on the rise, right along with apprehensions.

Dressed in a white linen suit with coordinated pocket square and tie, Hoover was ever eloquent, selling his snake-oil statistics with the energy of an evangelist. And it was with great pleasure that Hoover listened to the astonished praise of congressmen at the news that the Bureau had recovered goods and money worth more than $6.5 million. The way Hoover phrased it, with a budget of slightly more than $2 million the Bureau seemed to be actually making a profit for the government. That Hoover's "recoveries" weren't really federal property but mostly returned autos, recouped bank funds, and miscellaneous stolen goods was a detail that mattered only if it was brought up. As it happened, no one did.

With each passing year, the numbers grew larger, Hoover more dramatic, and the press ever more enthused with this man they found to be a hero in public service.

** Martin James Durkin served his sentences in the Statesville Penitentiary in Joliet, Illinois, and Leavenworth Federal Prison in Leavenworth, Kansas, finally gaining release on July 28, 1954.

With each newspaper and magazine mention, Annie Hoover removed her sewing shears from the top left-hand drawer of the dining room buffet, and clipped the story for a scrapbook she had begun on her youngest son. Dutifully, she pasted the clippings onto its pages to be reviewed later by Hoover himself. No matter that her older son was far more famous as the inspector general of the U.S. Steamboat Inspection Service. Her younger son was saving America.

Hoover had a private telephone with an unlisted number installed for use by his night supervisor, a Bureau hotline to keep him abreast of breaking news at home. "Lincoln 3004" rang directly in his bedroom. Few outside the Bureau had this number. One who did was Clyde Anderson Tolson.

A native of Laredo, Missouri, Tolson was serving as the confidential secretary to Coolidge's secretary of war, Dwight F. Davis,†† when he was invited to dinner by Herbert Hoover's confidential secretary, Lawrence Richey. It was a Tuesday night in 1927, unseasonably warm for October, and Richey and Tolson walked the few blocks from their offices to the Mayflower Hotel, remarking about the unusual weather and the stillness in the air.

Tolson was celebrating his graduation from George Washington University. He had gotten his law degree at night, just like J. Edgar Hoover had, Richey pointed out. Richey had barely uttered the name when he spotted his

---

†† Though he served in various government and military positions, Dwight F. Davis is best known for having started the Davis Cup International Tennis Tournament while he was a student at Harvard University in 1899.

friend and fellow Mason across the hotel's dining room, having dinner with Frank Baughman and special agent Charles Appel. Introductions were exchanged, as were business cards, with Hoover prodding Tolson to telephone if he was interested in discussing a career in the Bureau.

The tall, slender, and quiet Tolson took advantage of the offer, meeting privately on several occasions with Hoover in his office and finding the director far different than he expected. His sense of humor and easy laugh were so spontaneous that Tolson felt relaxed around the Bureau chief, drawn into his yarns of bank robberies and car thefts.[16]

For Tolson, the idea of becoming a special agent was little more than fantasy, the public perception at the time being one of shoot-outs and cross-country chases in pursuit of car thieves on the lam. The son of a Missouri farmer, Tolson strived for refinement, not crime busting, preferring to perfect his penmanship over engaging in physical activity. His long-term goal was to return to Iowa, where his parents now lived, and practice law privately.

J. Edgar Hoover had other plans for the 27-year-old, whom he found to be articulate, attractive, and most important, meticulous in his attention to detail. Tolson's mind was capable of retaining volumes of unrelated facts. His experience in the War Department had honed that talent, and Hoover saw unlimited potential for the new attorney in an administrative role in the Bureau of Investigation.

Tolson applied for a position in the Bureau in January 1928. He made little secret of his intention to remain in its employ only long enough to gain the experience that would later benefit his law practice. Acting special agent in charge T. H. Tracy interviewed Tolson at Hoover's request and submitted a report, long buried in the Bureau's files.

Agent states that applicant told him that he does not desire a position as a matter of remuneration as he can hold his present position as long as he cared to; that he desires a position as Special Agent for the reason that he wants to obtain practice of law in his home town, Cedar Rapids, Iowa [where his parents had moved]. After being questioned as to how long he would remain with the Bureau, assuming he obtained the position, he answered about a year and a half or two years, but after that he could not say. Applicant impresses Agent as being a substantial sort of man, very courteous, his manner is pleasing, and his personal appearance excellent, his bearing upright. Agent states that the fact applicant has considerable tact can safely be inferred from the position he has occupied for the past 5 years; that there is no question in his mind but that applicant possesses many qualifications far above the average applicant; that in dictation he has confidence, poise, and his diction is excellent; that applicant seems to be of a social type and although physically fitted for it, might be displeased with rugged work, this was brought out by the manner of his questions concerning the apprehension of fugitives and undercover duties; that he is convinced that applicant would make an excellent Agent and be a credit to the Bureau, but his frankness in stating that he only intends to remain with the Bureau for a period of 2 years would seem to militate against him and render employment speculative.[17]

Tolson's application included references from Secretary of War Davis, who wrote that he would "personally appreciate anything that may be done to assist applicant in getting located"; former secretary of war, Newton D. Baker, who found Tolson "to be a boy of fine presence, serious attention to his duties, and excellent intelligence"; the judge advocate general of the U.S. Army, Major General John Hull, who said that Tolson was "very courteous, absolutely trustworthy and . . . an exceptionally bright, clean cut young man"; and Thomas Pernis, a letter carrier from Cedar Rapids, who stated that he had "known applicant about seven or eight years, that he was a very bright and ambitious young man, and that he knows the applicant is not at all *dissipated* [italics added for emphasis]."[18]

The most curious comments came from John W. Martyn, executive assistant to the secretary of war, who mentioned that Tolson "showed no particular interest in women; that his habits and associates have always been of the best."

> Agent questioned Mr. Martyn as to whether or not applicant would accept a bribe in any form or nature. Agent was informed that if applicant were so inclined and was of a mercenary temperament he could have derived a great number of benefits through the position he holds; that applicant has been tried in that respect in a discreet manner and applicant was found to be above reproach.[19]

In April 1928, Tolson accepted the Bureau's offer and received his training as a special agent in the district field office in Washington, D.C., before being transferred to Massachusetts as a special agent in the Boston office. By September, however, Hoover sent word that he needed Tolson back in Washington promoting him to supervisor of the clerical staff at the Bureau's headquarters. Nine months later, Hoover moved Tolson yet again, this time appointing him special agent in charge of the Buffalo, New York, office.

Tolson had yet to unpack when, five days after arriving in Buffalo, Hoover ordered him to return immediately to Washington. An emergency at headquarters required his attention. Although the exact nature of the emergency is lost in history, Tolson's transfer coincided with the marriage of Frank Baughman, who, as a new family man, suddenly stopped being available for dinners and late nights at the office. Baughman pointed out with considerable pride that Hoover served as best man at the ceremony, a wedding to which Tolson was not invited. Whatever the reason, Tolson suddenly found himself sharing the title of assistant director with "Pop" Nathan, having been appointed to the number two spot after less than 24 months as an agent.

It was a heady time for J. Edgar Hoover, who now had a private chauffeur, a private secretary, an executive assistant, and two assistant directors who managed to maintain his growing appointment schedule. With the election of Herbert Clark Hoover to the presidency, the head of the Bureau of Investigation had instant entree into the White House. For both Hoovers, it was a comfortable arrangement, as each attempted to control a growing crime problem sweeping across the country.

Only a month before Herbert Hoover took office in
March 1929, seven men were gunned down in a garage on
Chicago's Clark Street in a gangland execution that rattled
an already skittish nation. The St. Valentine's Day Massacre drew attention to gangsters such as Al Capone, who
was rumored to be behind the murders, and unfortunately glamorized criminals in the process. Capone was
just one among a multitude of bootleggers competing for
territories with machine guns singing a song of violent
death while sitting atop stockpiles of illegal booze and
millions of dollars in tax-free cash.

The Treasury Department's Prohibition squads were
hardly making a dent in the freewheeling empires of the
mobsters who flaunted their disregard of federal laws and
regulations. For J. Edgar Hoover, these gangs headed by
amoral outcasts were the living embodiment of the statistics he drummed religiously into the minds of senators
and congressmen. Though they played out like a Hollywood melodrama, the crimes were real, and as the death
toll mounted, the country demanded protection from its
government.

Given the lack of federal laws that addressed interstate
crimes, Hoover was basically without ammunition to correct the problem, even as many in the nation were looking to the Bureau to be the anticrime headquarters that
Hoover claimed it to be. Strapped by the inactivity of the
lawmakers, Hoover was forced into confronting the paradox of his situation. Politicians were both the problem
and the answer. Corruption in government did not mirac-
ulously disappear despite the best efforts of Herbert
Hoover and Calvin Coolidge before him. As America suf-

fered through the collapse of the stock market in October 1929 and the beginning of the Great Depression, crime became the *only* way that many felt they could make a living. It was all made easy through the political bosses of cities across the country who controlled the police, the judges, and often the press.

It was discouraging news to J. Edgar Hoover, who saw the continuing swirl of crime move from state to state like some self-perpetuating weather pattern. He was pessimistic by nature, and as the economy continued to falter and crime statistics continued to rise, he added insecurity to his already complicated list of personality traits.

Hoover had seen how the political future of President Hoover was being undermined by public sentiment, and as he faced the New Year in 1932, what he saw was uncertainty. In any other year, he would have turned to his mother for support and consolation, for she above all others knew how to restore the confidence he desperately needed to inspire others. But Annie Hoover was herself not well. Stricken with sudden abdominal pains in February, she was bedridden and heavily medicated.

Distracted by the onset of her condition, Hoover brought in nurses by day and sped home each evening to sit at her bedside. Stubbornly refusing to be treated by doctors, Annie instead read the writings of Mary Baker Eddy, the founder of Christian Science. Not that Annie particularly believed in Eddy's teachings. She was more interested in the strength of the woman who had overcome illness through prayer. "Faith, faith," she whispered to her son, as she pulled his face close and kissed his forehead in dramatic resignation.

With his insecurity threatening to derail his career and his mother's condition worsening, Hoover fell to his knees by the side of her bed and began to pray a rapid-fire litany of confessions and fears. Only then did his mother see the extent of her son's uncertainty, his staccato wants and needs tripping over one another to get attention.

Whether by divine intervention or sheer will, two days later Annie Hoover rose from bed and dressed herself, dismissing her nurses and resuming control of her life. Her granddaughter Margaret later characterized the recovery as a "truly miraculous return from near death."[20] But then, her son's transformation was no less astonishing.

During the first week of March 1932, the insecurity that had gripped Hoover was transformed into a renewed determination to keep his job and reform America's crime-fighting machine. His catharsis was empowered by a single crime—one so tragic it would hold the country in its grip and change J. Edgar Hoover's life forever.

FIVE

CRIMES OF
THE CENTURY

M arch 1, 1932. *Amwell Road, Hopewell, New Jersey.* Anne Morrow Lindbergh wrapped the fur collar of her wool coat tightly around her neck as protection from the cool air blowing through the forest of seasoned oak trees and across the flat ground that surrounded her new home. She and her husband, the famed aviator Charles Lindbergh, had named the place Highfields, for it sat atop a great hill that was part of the Sourland Mountains just north of Princeton, New Jersey.

The whitewashed fieldstone house loomed large on the cleared ridge, the ground frozen and unlandscaped. A pile of discarded lumber was stacked next to the three-car garage, the remains of construction that was nearly finished. Anne felt the gravel on the driveway mold to the rubber soles of her shoes as she walked toward the back of the house, away from the stone wall that circled the property. When she reached the far corner of the building, she stopped just outside the library window with its newly painted shutters and freshly glazed glass. She quickly removed some pebbles from her pocket—she had picked them up from the driveway at the beginning of her walk—and tossed them one at a time toward the second-story French window.

A tiny woman, Anne stood just over five feet tall, but her pitching arm was as accurate as it was strong. The pebbles hit their mark clattering against the pane. Within seconds, Betty Gow appeared at the window, and seeing Mrs. Lindbergh, the Scottish nanny lifted up 20-month-old Charles Augustus Lindbergh Jr. onto her hip to see his mother standing below. Charlie, as the baby was called, smiled at his mother and released a quick laugh that sounded strangely tinny, like pennies dropping into a metal can.[1]

The baby had been ill with a cold, and Anne had decided to stay the night in New Jersey rather than return with the baby to her parents' home in New York as was her custom. It was a decision she would regret for the rest of her life, for later that evening, perhaps just after nine o'clock, the littlest Lindbergh was snatched from his crib in what was soon labeled the crime of the century.

J. Edgar Hoover had just fallen asleep when his private telephone rang shortly after 11 P.M. As he reached through the darkness for the handset, Hoover knew that it was his night supervisor calling with a message from the Bureau. It gratified him to be needed, even at this inconvenient hour. What he did not know was that the news he was about to receive would set in motion a chain of events destined to propel him out of Washington notoriety and into the national spotlight.

Upon hearing of the apparent kidnapping of the Lindbergh baby, Hoover was immediately outraged. The crime was heinous and certain to take a huge emotional toll on the parents. He asked to be kept informed as the situation developed, and hung up the phone. Though he tried, he failed to fall back to sleep. The air was alive with anticipation and its presence precluded anything as ordinary as slumber.

When the next call arrived, at 1:22 A.M., Hoover not only was still awake but had dressed in anticipation of going to the office. After learning that Corporal Frank A. Kelly, an eight-year veteran of the New Jersey state police, had found a ransom note demanding $50,000 and the warning not to "making anyding [sic] public or for notify [sic] the Police,"[2] Hoover immediately summoned his driver and left for the Department of Justice.

Minutes later, Hoover walked into the Denrike Building and found it a mini-epicenter of activity as agents and associates gathered after hearing the news. It mattered little that kidnapping was not a federal offense or under the direct auspices of the Bureau. This was a major crime, and Hoover immediately telephoned the New Jersey state police to offer his department's help.

Colonel H. Norman Schwarzkopf, head of New Jersey's police department, was quite confident in his own ability, and refused all offers of assistance, including those from J. Edgar Hoover.* A graduate of West Point, Schwarzkopf was the first head of the 10-year-old state police force and had minimal case-solving experience. "One of Schwarzkopf's detractors would later note that the only police experience he had was 'as a floor-walker at Bamberger's Department Store.'"[3] Even so, it was more than Hoover could claim at that moment.

What J. Edgar Hoover did possess was the ability to trace fingerprints and act as a central clearinghouse of

---

* Colonel H. Norman Schwarzkopf is the father of General H. Norman Schwarzkopf, commander of Operation Desert Shield and Desert Storm during the Persian Gulf War.

information. Rebuffed but not deflated, Hoover appealed directly to President Herbert Hoover early on the morning of March 2, asking for official access to "all documents and material evidence regarding the Lindbergh baby kidnapping."[4] At the same time, New Jersey governor A. Harry Moore took the extraordinary step of sending a telegram to the president as well as to governors of every state east of the Mississippi, requesting that representatives of appropriate police departments meet the following day in Trenton to discuss the Lindbergh case and coordinate their efforts to find the kidnappers. President Hoover designated J. Edgar Hoover as his representative at the meeting, which took place on March 5.

The *New York Times*, in reporting Hoover's selection as the president's delegate, labeled the head of the Bureau of Investigation as "keen-eyed and reticent" and suggested that he was a "firm believer in the Sherlockian methods of matching wits with the underworld. His record of achievements in the eight years he has directed the nation's principal investigative agency is a testimonial to the soundness of his theories."[5]

With several hundred police chiefs and investigators in attendance and Schwarzkopf in command, Hoover took an uncomfortable subordinate role, though he did manage to position himself in widely circulated publicity photographs after the event. He also took the opportunity to visit the Lindbergh estate where he was refused an audience with the Lindberghs themselves, who referred to him as a "fussy little man."[6] Instead, he was permitted to visit the nursery, the library, and the garage, which had been turned into a communications center with a 20-line switchboard.

After Hoover's visit, the story began to circulate among law enforcement officers that the Bureau director had noticed a bird landing on the roof of the house and suggested it was a homing pigeon with an important message about the kidnapping. Apparently, Hoover was oblivious to the fact that the pigeon would have had to have been housed at Highfields if it were indeed returning home. Hoover would later deny the story when asked about it by the press, growing more annoyed each time by the suggestion that he could be so easily distracted.

Unknown to Hoover at the time, his old nemesis Gaston B. Means found the Lindbergh kidnapping as inviting a target as the director did, but for very different reasons. Recently released from the penitentiary, Means contacted Evalyn Walsh McLean, the estranged and very rich wife of Ned McLean, with an incredible story of intrigue and righteousness. Means claimed that he had been asked to participate in the kidnapping of the Lindbergh baby. While he said that he had turned down the offer, he nevertheless was now in a position to rescue the child from the culprits.

Means played up the moment, as he sat in the living room of the Friendship estate, claiming, "I've come to realize that honesty is the best policy." Emory S. Land, Mrs. McLean's friend and a cousin of Lindbergh's mother Evangeline, listened at Evalyn's side. He knew she had long worried that her own son might be kidnapped, and he was hardly surprised when she jumped at the opportunity to aid the Lindberghs.

Means told the impressionable Evalyn that the kidnappers wanted $100,000 in exchange for the baby, while

Means said he would require $4,000 in personal expense money for his trouble. After receiving the Lindbergh's authorization to place Means on the case, Mrs. McLean withdrew the money from her bank, and set the porcine ex-Bureau of Investigation agent on his way.

While Means was presumably dealing with his criminal connections, another go-between had entered the picture in the person of one Dr. John Francis Condon of the Bronx, New York. When Condon, a retired schoolteacher, learned of the kidnapping, he claimed to be so personally affected that he took out an ad in his local newspaper, the *Home News,* to offer his help. "I offer all I can scrape together," Condon wrote in his ad, "so a loving mother may again have her child and Colonel Lindbergh may know that the American people are grateful for the honor bestowed upon them by his pluck and daring."[7]

Condon further advertised that he was willing to meet with the kidnappers, give them money in exchange for the child, and "never utter their names to anyone."[8] The offer riled Hoover for its amateur naiveté, and was made all the more annoying when Condon actually received a response from the kidnappers. Two days after the ad appeared, Condon received a letter from the kidnappers that read in part, "If you are willing to act as go-between in Lindbergh cace [sic] pleace [sic] follow strictly [sic] instruction."[9] Inside the letter was another addressed to Lindbergh that was meant for the aviator's eyes only.

When Condon advised Charles Lindbergh of the communication, the father decided to pay the ransom through Condon and keep the police—and the Bureau—out of the process. While Schwarzkopf attempted to maintain an image of organized efficiency, Hoover, still eager to demonstrate the value of his Bureau, assigned a special 26-man team to solve the crime. Special agent Thomas Sisk was placed in charge.

Drawing upon his proven files, Hoover sent Sisk and his men into New Jersey, New York, and Philadelphia to profile and then interrogate possible suspects. According to special agent Leon G. Turrou, who was a member of the Lindbergh team, despite their diligent efforts the closest the Bureau came to finding the missing baby was when they raided the home of an Italian couple who were horrified to have their own baby mistakenly identified as the kidnapped child. Just before reporting the discovery to Hoover, Turrou claimed to have inspected the baby's diaper and found the child was a girl. "The Lindbergh squad took special pains to keep these blunderings out of the reach of reporters and their carnivorous epithets. The [Bureau] was struggling for recognition and respect, and it couldn't afford the public's horselaughs."[10]

As Hoover's team stumbled its way along the East Coast, Condon placed more advertisements in the *Home News* and arranged a drop-off for the ransom money. On the evening of April 2, 1932, Condon and Lindbergh drove to St. Raymond's Cemetery, close to Condon's home, and in a clandestine meeting worthy of Hollywood, complete with whispered orders and dark shadows, the kidnappers received $50,000 in cash. Fearing for the safety of the baby, Hoover had instructed his agents to stay away from the location and not to interfere.

Unfortunately, after the ransom was paid and Lindbergh received a scrap of paper that claimed the baby could be found aboard a ship docked off Martha's Vineyard near Cape Cod, the body of the child was found on May 12 in a shallow grave less than a mile from the Lindbergh home. Outraged by the discovery, America's heartland responded with an outpouring of sorrow for the Lindbergh family and demands for its government to take control of the situation. Herbert Hoover responded by placing all federal agencies on alert, and appointing J. Edgar Hoover to coordinate the government's effort to catch the criminals. The announcement was void of authority, however. The kidnapping and subsequent murder were still under the jurisdiction of the New Jersey police. It took another six weeks before Congress passed the Lindbergh Law, making it a federal crime to kidnap a person within the boundaries of the United States.

Despite the government's best intentions, the new law still did not cover previous crimes, including the Lindbergh kidnapping itself. The weeks that had followed the crime of the century had denied the director and the Bureau of Investigation their anticipated glory. Hoover was forced to be content with what victories the Bureau *had* scored— including the capture and arrest of Gaston Means.

A little over a week before the baby's body was found, Evalyn McLean had alerted authorities to the former agent's tale of collaboration with the kidnappers—this after Means had demanded an additional $35,000 in payment from the heiress. Hoover ordered agent Charles Appel to set up a surveillance of Evalyn's home. After overhearing the demand for more money, Appel arrested Means, charging the con artist with embezzling $104,000 of Mrs. McLean's money, none of which was returned.

During his trial, Means took the stand in his own defense. He told of meeting with the kidnappers, whom he identified as "No. 19." Gaston himself was "No. 27." Mrs. McLean was "No. 11" and the baby was called "the Book." It was a preposterous tale that few, if any, believed. Listening to the story from his seat in the courtroom, Hoover shook his head in disbelief.

"As he finished his testimony, he stepped down and in lumbering fashion sought a seat beside me," Hoover later wrote.

"'Well, Hoover,' [Means] asked. 'What do you think of that?'

"'Gaston,' [Hoover] answered, 'every bit of it was a pack of lies.'

"He considered this for a long moment, his eyes blinking, his bullet head shoved forward over his bulking chest.

"'Well,' he said seriously, 'you've got to admit that it made a whale of a good story!'"[11]

Ultimately, Means was found guilty of larceny, embezzlement, and conspiracy to defraud, and was sentenced to serve 17 years in federal prison, his colorful stories having failed to convince.

Americans had tired of the crime wave and the stories told about them. Mired in the Great Depression, people wanted relief from lawlessness that showed no sign of disappearing, and a return to the economic prosperity of the past. Moreover, they wanted Herbert Hoover out of office and a new president in his place.

Franklin D. Roosevelt's election in November 1932 sent most of Washington into defense mode, as many prepared for the inevitable firings that come with a major transfer of power. J. Edgar Hoover, who had managed to survive through the Wilson, Harding, Coolidge, and Hoover administrations, feared he would loose his job when Roosevelt appointed a new attorney general.

For once, Hoover's insecurity was justified. Roosevelt had little personal experience with the Bureau of Investigation, and his nominee for attorney general, Senator Thomas J. Walsh of Montana, had little time for J. Edgar Hoover. After all, Hoover had launched an investigation into the private life of Burton Kendall Wheeler, the *other* senator from Montana, and his part in the demise of former interior secretary Albert Fall. An outraged Walsh had served as his colleague's defense counsel in court, and since that time, Walsh had made it clear that he intended to remove J. Edgar Hoover from his position if, and when, he was in a position to do so.

In late February 1933, one week before Roosevelt's inauguration, Walsh accepted his appointment as attorney general and announced his goal to "reorganize the Department of Justice . . . probably with an almost completely new personnel."[12] Hoover received word of the statement before its publication while dining at Harvey's Restaurant with Clyde Tolson. Lawrence Richey delivered the news with the kind of excited glee that exists solely in Washington, a place where gossip is only as hot as the damage it does to another's career.

Hoover pursed his lips in a circle tight with anxiety as he sucked in the words. For a moment the air hung still with silence, unnatural around the fast-talking director. When he finally spoke, Hoover said quietly, "Yes, I believe

the senator has something like that in mind. However . . . ,"
and with that he leaned over and whispered a few words
into Tolson's ear, as the waiters pretended not to notice.
Then, pulling away, Hoover broke a smile—half pain, half
vengeance—and then broke into a laugh.[13]

The 73-year-old Walsh had many in Washington
smiling wryly, for he had just married a very attractive
Cuban woman named Maria Nieves Perez Chaumont de
Truffini, several years his junior despite the length of her
name. Shortly after their honeymoon, aboard a train
heading for the presidential inauguration, Walsh suffered
a heart attack and was found by his bride on the floor of
their compartment. Mina, as she was called, rushed to
find a doctor, who pronounced Walsh dead of coronary
thrombosis.

Hoover, who had planned to meet Walsh as he
stepped off the train in Union Station, instead greeted his
widow. He had taken the precaution of instructing special
agent Edward E. Conray, of the Bureau's office in North
Carolina, to board the train in Rocky Mount and keep
watch "outside her drawing room."[14]

With Walsh yet to be buried, President Roosevelt
offered the post of attorney general to Homer Cummings,
onetime chairman of the Democratic National Committee, who accepted the job without any preconceived
notions of mass firings. Having been given a stay, if only
a temporary one, Hoover launched a campaign to prove
his worth. Fortunately for him, the administration was
preoccupied with the state of the economy and moved to
push more cash into the national pipeline by suspending
the gold standard and replacing it with Federal Reserve

notes. As the nation commenced exchanging the recalled gold notes, several hundred that had been included in the Lindbergh ransom began to surface in various New York banks, providing the first new clues in the cold case and reenergizing the push to catch the kidnappers.

The following month, in a sweeping reorganization of the various federal investigative units, Roosevelt combined the Prohibition Bureau, the Bureau of Investigation, and the Bureau of Identification into the new Division of Investigation, naming J. Edgar Hoover as its head. With Prohibition being phased out by the gradual passing of the Twenty-first Amendment, Hoover essentially was left in charge of his former Bureau. Yet, the new Division of Investigation was under the usual pressure to perform.

Soon after the reorganization, Hoover received word of an early morning machine-gun massacre at the Kansas City Union Station train depot that resulted in the deaths of 30-year-old special agent Raymond J. Caffrey; McAlester, Oklahoma, police chief Otto Reed; two Kansas City policemen, Bill Grooms and Frank Hermanson; and escaped convict Frank Nash, whom the officers were escorting back to Leavenworth penitentiary in Kansas. The killers, who apparently were attempting to free Nash, escaped presumably unharmed, placing Hoover once again at the center of public outrage and renewed determination.

Responding with the rage of Tisiphone, Hoover promised to hunt down the assassins to the very last. "The problems of organized gang warfare and the defiance by desperate armed criminals of the forces of society and civilization can no longer be ignored," he thundered. "Sooner or later, the penalty which is their due will be paid."[15] He ordered the full resources of the Bureau to be focused toward apprehending those responsible, and gave notice to "America's gangsters" that their days were numbered.

Building on the theme that "hoodlums" from the Midwest had to be responsible for such a grievous and public violation of human decency, Hoover used the murders as further proof that his agents needed to be allowed to carry firearms for protection. What he conveniently did not publicize was that special agent Caffrey had been armed with a .38-caliber pistol. Caffrey gad arrived at Union Station with his boss, special agent in charge Reed Vetterli, head of the Bureau's Kansas City office.

They were joined by Hermanson and Grooms to meet the Missouri Pacific, a passenger train carrying Nash. An out-of-shape, hook-nosed bank robber, Nash had escaped in October 1930 from Leavenworth, where he had been serving a 25-year sentence for robbing a mail train in Oklahoma. For several weeks before his recapture, Nash hid in Hot Springs, Arkansas, in the shadow of the Ouachita Mountains in a house he had rented with his wife, Frances, and their young daughter.

On the morning of Friday, June 16, Nash put on his ill-fitting red toupee and left his wife and child to venture into downtown Hot Springs to visit Richard "Tallman" Galatas, who ran the White Front cigar store and pool hall. It was the local hangout for the town prostitutes and vacationing bank robbers and murderers that enjoyed the protection of the corrupt Hot Springs police. The two-story building that housed the White Front sat conveniently on Central Avenue, down the street from the large brick Arlington Hotel, a favorite of Al Capone.

Nash had just left the White Front when he was approached by Oklahoma police chief Reed, and two Bureau agents, Joe Lackey and Frank Smith, who had driven from Oklahoma on a tip revealing Nash's whereabouts. Lackey and Smith, who were illegally armed, and Reed, who had no jurisdiction in Arkansas, took Nash into custody without benefit of a federal marshal and proceeded to drive him to Fort Smith, where they boarded the cross-country Missouri Pacific bound for Kansas City.

When the train pulled into Union Station 15 minutes behind schedule on the morning of June 17, Mrs. Lottie West had just opened the Travelers Aid station she routinely operated in the lobby of the vast terminal. She saw the wedge of officers escorting a manacled man across the lobby and out the south entrance, headed toward special agent Caffrey's parked 1932 Chevrolet. Nash was placed in the front passenger seat, guarded by Lackey, Smith, and Reed in the rear. Hermanson, Grooms, and Vetterli were standing by the passenger door as Caffrey moved across the front of the car to the driver's side. Suddenly, gunmen appeared near the right front of the car, screaming "Hands up! Up!" before letting loose with a spray of machine-gun fire that killed Nash, Caffrey, Hermanson, Grooms, and Reed, and left Vetterli and Lackey wounded. Only Frank Smith escaped injury, having fallen forward and played dead during the carnage.

Later, from his hospital bed, Lackey, who had been shot three times in the back, said he was unable to identify the shooters. "Agent got such a hurried glance at these two men and this glance was through a none-too-clean window," he dictated for the official files.[16]

Smith was too busy playing dead to serve as an eye-witness. "At the first volley . . . the writer dropped his head down below the front end as if shot and remained in that position until the firing ceased. While the writer observed by a glance a man behind the machine gun pointed and shooting in his direction, he was unable to obtain any kind of a description of him and was unable to see anyone else who did the shooting."[17]

Vetterli, who dropped to the ground and ran for cover through the south entrance of the terminal, had been grazed in the arm by a stray bullet. He later said with certainty that one of the attackers was Robert "Big Bob" Brady, a convicted robber who had escaped from the Kansas City prison earlier in the month. Soon after he said he wasn't so certain.[18]

In an effort to stoke the flames of indignation growing across America, Hoover welcomed press coverage of the slaughter and promised that "every effort and every resource of this Bureau [will] be utilized" to capture the gunmen, a sentiment he conveyed to Vetterli as well.[19] Moreover, he wrote a letter to the widow of Frank Hermanson in which he stated, "I trust that his death will not have been in vain and that it will result in the awakening of the public conscience to its responsibility to demand more effective laws and more effective enforcement of the laws in dealing with the criminal element in the country."[20]

Hoover pushed his agents to make an arrest even though they were groping for a reliable suspect. Names were mentioned: Verne Miller, a former lawman turned robber; Wilber Underhill and Harvey Bailey, who had led the prison escape that included "Big Bob"; and Charles

"Pretty Boy" Floyd, who had been identified by Travelers Aid manager Lottie West. West was certain that when she arrived to begin her day at 7 A.M., Pretty Boy was sitting not only at her counter, but in *her* chair, of all things.

Hoover placed special agent Gus T. Jones in charge of the investigation. A onetime Texas Ranger, Jones knew his way around firearms. Yet even as Jones began to track suspects and Hoover assured the public that it was only a matter of time before the murderers were caught, the gangster population showed no signs of intimidation. If anything, they began to flagrantly taunt the Bureau with what seemed like daily bank robberies.

The Bureau was no closer to making an arrest when, on July 23, 1933, Hoover's phone again rang in the middle of the night. This time his office put through a call from Mrs. Charles F. Urschel of Oklahoma City, who reported that her husband, a wealthy oil tycoon and businessman, had been kidnapped from their home during a bridge game and was being held for $200,000 ransom. Armed with the new Lindbergh Law, Hoover personally took charge of the case, which would have undoubtedly made more headlines had Mrs. Urschel not paid the ransom and the kidnappers released their victim unharmed by the end of the week. Sadly for the criminals, Urschel was able to give enough information to the Bureau to enable them to track down the farmhouse where the victim was held—a farmhouse that belonged to the stepparents of Kathryn Kelly, the wife of George "Machine Gun" Kelly. According to a Hoover-authorized version of the story, "In the early hours of September 26, 1933, FBI special agents and Memphis police raided the Kelly hideaway. Caught without a machine gun in his hands, Kelly cringed before the officers and pleaded, 'Don't shoot G-Men! Don't shoot!'"[21]

Though Hoover began to repeat the story so often it earned his agents the moniker of "G-men" for years, Kelly denied he had ever uttered the words. Convicted with his wife of kidnapping Urschel and sentenced to life imprisonment, Kelly insisted he had never even heard the term before and actually said, "I've been waiting for you," as he raised his hands over his head.

The swift conclusion of the Urschel case, coupled with the G-men tag brought Hoover a bonanza of publicity at a time in the country's history when true heroes were rare. If Hoover was less than a knight on a white horse, at least he represented what many saw as an unwavering force against increasing crime. Had they inspected their icon closer, however, they would have found tiny cracks in a resolute character. Each small, and each almost unnoticeable, but when combined together, they suggested a man far more complicated than the imperious crusader for justice he appeared to be.

Most apparent was Hoover's insistence on speedy conclusions to high-profile cases. Despite daily pressure from Hoover's office, a year after the Kansas City Massacre not a single arrest had been made in the case. In truth, the investigation seemed to be heading in unanticipated directions. An autopsy done on agent Raymond Caffrey indicated that he died from a head wound caused by a ball bearing—a type found in the shell of a shotgun. Likewise, Frank Hermanson: head wound, shotgun blast. Ditto Frank Nash. Unfortunately for Hoover, the only shotguns on the scene were the ones inside Caffrey's Chevrolet, in the possession of police chief Otto Reed and Bureau agent Joe Lackey.[22] Of those two, the only shotgun fired was Lackey's; Reed's remained wedged against his hip.

That his own agent might have been responsible for three deaths at the scene, including that of agent Caffrey, was simply not an option Hoover was willing to accept. How much more advantageous it was to believe that a bank robber like "Pretty Boy" Floyd was responsible, even though Floyd had never met Nash and wasn't a killer.

The cherub-cheeked Floyd, who happened to be heading to Missouri at the time, was linked to the murders, as was his traveling companion and friend Adam Richetti, whose fingerprint was suddenly and quite mysteriously discovered on a dusty beer bottle in the basement of a house rented by Verne Miller, one of the names on the suspect list. Though the house had been searched early on in the investigation and Richetti's fingerprint somehow missed, its eventual discovery placed Floyd, Richetti, and Miller together, giving Hoover all he apparently needed to build a case for their arrest as the villains behind the Kansas City Massacre.

Hoover had been alerted to Miller's role when a trace of phone records from Nash's wife indicated calls to Miller's house in Kansas City. Trailing the onetime lawman-turned-gangster proved difficult, however. He did not seem to be hiding, and was reportedly sighted in New York, Boston, and Miami. In truth, Miller had gone underground, with his friend Al Silvers (né Silverman), a member of a New York gang whom Miller had met in the army. Silvers's brother Irwin, an optometrist, innocently hired Miller, who had given his name as Stephen J. Gross Jr., as an optical salesman on his brother's recommendation. Which is how a gangster named Miller resurfaced in Chicago at the Sherone Apartments as a salesman named Gross, wearing glasses and a mustache, and carrying samples of eyewear.

The disguise didn't fool Miller's wife when she opened the door of her apartment at the Sherone and excitedly greeted her long-absent husband on Halloween night. Hoover, who had the place under surveillance, immediately positioned agents inside and outside the building, joined by members of Chicago's finest to supply necessary gun power and make an arrest. For the entire evening of October 31 and well into the next day, agents watched the apartment door. When the door finally opened in late afternoon and a couple stepped into the hallway, agents weren't immediately able to identify the man wearing a fedora pulled down over his face. And by the time agents made their move to capture the elusive Miller, he had bolted down the fire stairs, out the side entrance, and leaped into a waiting getaway car pummeled by a hail of bullets.

As stories of the getaway reached Hoover in Washington, comparing his Bureau to the slapstick antics of movieland's Keystone Kops, his rage reopened an old wound as his agents were revealed to be ill-prepared and uninformed. Far greater a problem than a blundered surveillance was the battering Hoover's image was taking, however. Try as he might to demand respect and create the illusion of a seasoned criminal mind, Hoover was being privately mocked as a bit too manicured to be taken seriously as a detective, and far too affected to be believed as an enforcer of the law. In August 1933, Ray Tucker, writing in *Collier's* magazine, turned the entire Bureau into a burlesque of tailing operatives and clandestine stakeouts, and its director into a publicity-seeking mooncalf.

> The director's appetite for publicity is the talk of the Capital, although admittedly a peculiar enterprise for a bureau which, by the nature of its works, is supposed to operate in secrecy. Although Mr. Hoover issued strict orders against publicity on the part of his agents, he was never bound by them. In every newspaper and magazine article and radio broadcast recounting his field agents' activities, there appears invariably the name of "J. Edgar Hoover, Director of the United States Bureau of Investigation."
>
> For three months last winter, his agents' exploits were the headline attractions on the radio hour of a popular cigarette.[†] Once a week, there came over the air the hoarse, melodramatic overture announcing that "This is Operative J-3, clear all wires." It was a thrilling show, even though 'D of J men' are not known by numbers, and even though they have no authority to order that "all wires" be cleared.[23]

Tucker's biting commentary did not stop at lampooning the sacrosanct Bureau. He saved his most biting comments for the director himself:

---

† *The Lucky Strike Hour,* sponsored by Hoover's favorite cigarette, began in 1932 and became, for a short time, the most popular show on radio.

In appearance, Mr. Hoover looks utterly unlike the story-book sleuth. He is short, fat, businesslike, and walks with mincing step. His black hair, swarthy skin and collegiate haircut make him look younger than thirty-eight, but heavy, horn-rimmed spectacles give him an air of age and authority. He dresses fastidiously, with Eleanor blue as the favorite color for the matched shades of tie, handkerchief and socks. A little pompous, he rides in an expensive limousine even if only to a near-by self-service cafeteria.[24]

Publicly, Hoover dismissed the article as the "rantings of a liquor soaked rat." Privately, he seethed in anger at the way Tucker drew the Bureau in broad, inept lines and Hoover in delicate, "mincing" steps. Nothing, however, was more infuriating than being called fat. While it was true he had gained several pounds as he had matured, it was "solid weight," as Annie Hoover called it. "Nothing wrong with solid weight on a man," she said.[25]

Determined to repair any damage done by the *Collier's* piece by proving the efficiency of his Bureau, Hoover ordered a swift conclusion to the Kansas City Massacre case. Agents Lackey, Smith, and Vetterli were summoned to Washington for "interrogation and training." Hoover left no doubt that he expected his three agents/eyewitnesses to be able to identify their attackers.

While the Bureau continued to pursue Floyd and Richetti as the Kansas City killers well into the winter, Verne Miller's life on the run took a decidedly different route. On November 29, 1933, Miller's naked body was discovered in a remote section of Detroit in a ditch at the intersection of Cambridge and Harlow Streets, not far from Gilchrist's liquor store, a popular gang hangout. His head had been crushed and beaten by something resembling a claw hammer, his body wrapped in a blanket and tied with rope. Only the week before, Al Silvers had been murdered in a similar fashion, his body dumped in Somers, Connecticut, north of Hartford.

With his main murder suspect now himself murdered, Hoover redoubled his efforts to hunt down "Pretty Boy" Floyd and Adam Richetti in an effort to close a case that had become a major cause of embarrassment. He attempted to place the blame on Congress for the Bureau's failure to capture Floyd, Richetti, and other gangsters with nicknames like "Creepy," "Slim," "Bla Bla," and "Baby Face." And then, of course, there was Dillinger.

John Dillinger was not the most famous gangster at the time or the most dangerous. But he was arguably the most *liked* of the crop of machine gun–happy bank robbers who were shooting themselves across the Midwest leaving grieving widows and headlines in their dust. People tended to romanticize "Pretty Johnny" because he stole only from banks and never killed unless provoked. And they were fascinated by his postcards to J. Edgar Hoover—love notes he sent from different states taunting Hoover to tighten the net. How the Bureau's director hated those weekly reminders that Dillinger had escaped from jail yet again. He bragged no jail could hold him and proved it three times in a row. Yet even Hoover had to admit that Dillinger made headlines, and therefore *capturing* Dillinger seemed the perfect answer to Hoover's hunger for publicity and the cleansing of America.

As it turned out, Dillinger was not an easy man to track, despite his continual appearances in public, usually leaping over a bank counter in search of fresh cash. And no one in the Bureau knew that better than Melvin Horace Purvis Jr., a Hoover protégé and, at the age of 29, the special agent in charge of the Bureau's office in Chicago.

For five years, Hoover had taken a special interest in the diminutive agent who was just over five feet tall, buying him presents and sending him an average of one letter a week. It was a curious relationship that existed between the men, with the normally dour Hoover bordering on giddy in his communications that usually began "Dear Mel" and ended "Affectionately, Jayee."

April 3, 1934

Dear Melvin,

I received the True-Vue[‡] and films, bombs, magic trick and your sassy note. What did the True-Vue and films cost? I asked you to get them for me and I intend to pay for them. The films were both educational and uplifting, but I thought they would include a series on "A Night in a Moorish Harem" or was it a "Turkish Harem"? Nevertheless, it was some night and I am still looking forward to you producing a set. Of course my interest is solely as a censor or as Chairman of the Moral Uplift Squad. The bombs are the best yet. I have already caused Miss Gandy to jump two feet and that is something

---

‡ Tru-Vue Films Strips were attached to cards that fit into handheld viewers, and normally featured cartoons or travelogues.

considering the fact that she is now in the heavyweight class. The damned Magic Trick has me almost "nuts" trying to figure out how it is done. . . . Well, son, keep a stiff upper lip and get Dillinger for me, and the world is yours.

Sincerely and affectionately,

Jayee[26]

Taking Hoover at his word, Purvis plunged into tracking every lead into Dillinger's whereabouts, occasionally with disastrous results. Purvis was armed with machine guns and a highly competent investigator, Samuel P. Cowley, senior administrative assistant to "Pop" Nathan based in Washington. Hoover appointed Cowley supervisor of the Bureau's Flying Squad, a traveling team of investigators whose sole purpose was the apprehension of gangsters, and sent him to the Chicago office to join Purvis's push for Dillinger.

On April 22, 1934, Purvis received a tip that Dillinger and his girlfriend, Billie Frechette, plus "Baby Face" Nelson and his wife, Helen Gillis, were vacationing at the Little Bohemia Lodge in Manitowish Waters, Wisconsin. The lakefront hotel, whose backwater sign advertised "Dine, Dance & Swim," was so remote that the closest Bureau offices were in Chicago and St. Paul. After immediately ordering in agents from both locations, Hoover placed calls to the local Washington press, gushing with excitement as he alerted them to stand by for news about the capture of John Dillinger. As it happened, Hoover's excitement was a bit premature. When the agents arrived in the North Woods of Wisconsin late that night and proceeded to walk up the long drive leading to the Little Bohemia Lodge—lest the sounds of their car engines alert the outlaws—they were greeted with the loud barking of dogs who were not pleased that strangers were sneaking through the trees.

Fearing that the dogs might alert Dillinger, Purvis instructed his agents to prepare to fire their weapons. Sadly, three men who had been drinking in the lodge's bar picked that precise moment to leave the hotel and enter their own vehicle parked outside. Believing the threesome were fleeing, Purvis ordered his men to shoot out the tires on the car, but in their enthusiasm his agents instantly killed one of the men and injured the others.

At the sound of gunfire, Dillinger grabbed his gun and slid out an upstairs rear window, fleeing with his partners into the woods. "Baby Face" Nelson, resting in a cabin on adjacent Little Star Lake, escaped in the opposite direction. With the help of the local sheriff, Carl C. Christensen, special agents J. C. Newman and W. Carter Baum tracked Nelson to the nearby home of Alvin Koerner, who operated the town's telephone exchange. Nelson, already trigger-happy and extremely nervous, fired into the agents' car, killing Baum and seriously wounding Newman and the sheriff.

As Melvin Purvis canvassed the normally quiet scene that night in the North Woods, he had only one thing on his mind: how to explain the dead bodies, damaged cars, and lack of arrests to the man waiting for his telephone call in Washington. When J. Edgar Hoover received the news that things had not gone as planned in Manitowish Waters, his reaction was controlled hysteria. Angry at Purvis and humiliated in front of the press, Hoover returned to his home on Seward Square and pondered his fate as cries for his resignation were heard throughout the country. Purvis did offer his resignation, but it was refused.

Time magazine turned the debacle into a rather inventive board game in its May 7, 1934, issue tracking Dillinger's moves in a place called "Dillinger Land."[27] Comedian Will Rogers suggested that since the Bureau was now in the habit of shooting bystanders, "Dillinger is going to accidentally get with some [of them] some time, [and] then he will get shot."[28]

Refusing for once to comment to the press, Hoover instead deferred to Attorney General Homer Cummings, who suggested yet again that Congress was to blame for not passing his crime legislation and adequately funding the Bureau. While few in the House and Senate bought the argument, with Cummings's help Hoover's special agents were finally granted the right to carry firearms on June 18, 1934, and the power to make arrests as well. Hoover finally had received the authority he coveted, and he began to carry a revolver with a mother-of-pearl grip as if to prove the point. Four days later, the Bureau's agents would make the first use of their new authority.

Melvin Purvis, still licking his wounds in Chicago, had been tethered to his desk by Hoover. No longer receiving cute notes from the director, now Purvis was now on the receiving end of damning memos and disciplinary warnings. Then a telephone call came during the third week of July that held the prospect of turning Purvis back into a star. A Chicago madam named Anna Sage proposed a trade—John Dillinger's whereabouts in exchange for half the reward posted on his head and the feds' guarantee of help to halt her anticipated deportation back to her homeland, Romania.

The exact promises Purvis made to Sage were not recorded for posterity. What is known is that on the evening of July 22, Anna put on an orange skirt[§] and accompanied Dillinger and his girlfriend, Polly Hamilton, to Chicago's Biograph Theater to see Clark Gable, William Powell, and Myrna Loy in the film *Manhattan Melodrama*. As the trio exited the theater 90 minutes later, Purvis was waiting, leaning against a doorway, his straw hat cocked just so on his head. Seeing Dillinger, Purvis lit a cigar—the signal for his men to arrest the fugitive. "I was very nervous," Purvis later wrote in his memoir. "It must have been a squeaky voice that called out, 'Stick 'em up, Johnny! We have you surrounded.'"[29]

As Dillinger bolted and attempted to escape down the alley alongside the theater, he was shot multiple times, one bullet entering his neck and exiting through his eye. He was dead at the scene amid a mob of spectators, some of whom dipped handkerchiefs in his blood as a souvenir from the man called Public Enemy Number One.

By midnight, Hoover was in his office, holding a press conference to announce Dillinger's death and praise the agents who had tracked down and killed the criminal. Though Hoover did not credit Melvin Purvis with the Bureau's victory—in fact, Purvis did not fire his gun—the nation's media latched onto the pesky agent, labeling him "The Man Who Got Dillinger," an epithet that would follow him the rest of his life.

The conceit of shared glory was not one that came naturally to Hoover, nor was it one that he intended to learn in his thirty-ninth year. Waking up the following day to headlines

---

§   Under the marquee lights, the skirt appeared red, earning Anna Sage the nickname the "Lady in Red."

that hailed Purvis as a dragon slayer was not part of Hoover's grand plan, and one that Purvis would live to regret.

At the moment, however, there was enough glory to be shared, with Hoover welcoming Purvis and Cowley to Washington and declaring to all who would listen that they were being given raises based on exemplary performance. "The world" that Hoover had promised Purvis for eliminating Dillinger did seem to be a wonderful one—one that would only get more extraordinary several months later, when Purvis tracked down and eventually cornered "Pretty Boy" Floyd in a clover field in Ohio with several other agents and four patrolmen from East Liverpool. There, on the top of a rise, he was shot and killed as he tried to escape. Floyd went to his death denying he had anything to do with the Kansas City Massacre.

His partner, Adam Richetti, had been captured the previous day by police in the nearby town of Wellsville—Richetti having fallen asleep on a blanket near Lon Israel's pig farm waiting for Floyd's return. The town of 2,000 was suddenly overwhelmed with reporters and photographers, all anxious to get the story of "Pretty Boy's" final days. Richetti wasn't talking except to say that he too had no knowledge of anything that happened in Kansas City.

Hoover, taking credit for ridding America of several notorious criminals, preened in the glory of long-awaited triumph. He even joined the flood of media attention that headlined the news with the arrest in September of Bruno Richard Hauptmann for the kidnapping of the Lindbergh baby.

Hauptmann had been identified when he used one of the gold certificates contained in the ransom money to pay for gas at a service station in the Bronx. Agent Thomas Sisk was present when Hauptmann was tailed and arrested for questioning, and later reported the facts to his eager boss. Though the Bureau of Investigation had been only marginally involved in the Lindbergh case and had been consistently denied access to much of the evidence, there was Hoover pictured with Colonel H. Norman Schwarzkopf when the arrest was made. Although Hoover was often photographed sticking pins in a wall map that traced the ransom money as it began to appear in circulation, the Bureau's participation in the case was negligible compared with that of the Treasury Department and the New Jersey and New York state police forces.

When Adam Richetti went on trial for the Kansas City murders, however, Hoover saw a national stage for himself and his Bureau. He had, after all, three agents as eyewitnesses to the carnage—three agents who were conveniently obliged to change their stories of what took place that day.

As he took the stand in Richetti's trial, 20-year Bureau veteran Frank Smith somehow forgot that he was previously unable to identify any of the triggermen in Kansas City. Shown a photo of Verne Miller, Smith said that "this was the man that shot at my head."[30] Hoover was pleased.

Agent Reed Vetterli, who had fallen out of favor with Hoover and been transferred out of the Kansas City office, suddenly remembered that it wasn't "Big Bob" Brady firing a machine gun as Vetterli sprinted toward the south entrance of Union Station. It was "Pretty Boy" Floyd. Yes, it was all clear now. Floyd had fired the shots.[31] Hoover was pleased yet again.

And then there was agent Joe Lackey. Having taken
those three shots to his back, Lackey was now the picture
of confidence and health as he took the stand to answer
the prosecution's questions. Upon concentrating on the
events of that fateful day, he was certain without the slightest doubt that Adam Richetti was the triggerman who
killed policeman Frank Hermanson. When asked, he
pointed with all the authority of a Bureau man at the killer.

"You are pointing to the defendant, Adam Richetti, is
that right?" the prosecutor asked.

"Yes, sir," Lackey responded without flinching.

There was no mention of Lackey's written statement
to Hoover at the time of the shooting. Or Smith's or Vetterli's for that matter. No one brought up the "none too
clean windshield" or the fact that Lackey was uncertain,
just hours after the incident, whether he could "identify
either of these men." And no one spoke of the shotgun
blast from inside the car that hit Hermanson in the head
and splattered parts of his brain across the car fender. No,
no one spoke of that at all.[32]

On October 7, 1938, Adam Richetti was executed for
the murder of Frank Hermanson, pleading his innocence
to his dying breath. Commenting on the verdict, J. Edgar
Hoover said, "Justice has been done." And with that he
turned to the news photographers' exploding flashbulbs,
a contented smile on his face.

SIX

HOORAY FOR HOLLYWOOD

T he strident sound of a baby's cry echoed throughout the director's office of the FBI—nails-against-chalkboard shrill, dominating in intensity. As a rule, babies were not permitted in the hallowed halls of the Justice Department, and certainly not in J. Edgar Hoover's wing, but this particular baby—a cousin of First Lady Eleanor Roosevelt's—had gotten past the guards, cradled in the arms of a senator's wife. One look at the death mask of John Dillinger in the outer reception room of Hoover's inner sanctum had set the baby into a panic attack that no amount of rocking could sooth. Still, the wail of an infant somehow fit into the series of unexpected events in a perfectly horrid day.

When Hoover finally left his office on the evening of March 4, 1935, and entered his waiting limousine, he flicked his wrist with the skill of a fly fisherman and did not speak. Actually, he *dared* not speak, for if he did, he knew that something vulgar would escape his lips, and he did not want to offend James Crawford, his new chauffeur. Crawford knew what the wrist movement meant: Take me home.

Earlier, Hoover had argued with Clyde Tolson over their canceled dinner plans and snapped at Helen Gandy about an overwatered ivy plant sitting in a clay pot that had left an ugly ring on the inside window ledge in their new offices. He dictated a particularly pointed memo addressing the "defacing of government property" and hoped he was mistaken when he saw her eyes begin to pool with tears in response. He disliked any display of emotion in the office, particularly from Miss Gandy.

He was cold, he was tired, and the telephone call that had ended his day refused to stop repeating itself in his mind. "Mrs. Hoover," Gandy had said. He deliberately didn't raise his eyes, or respond in any manner she could see. His silence bespoke his annoyance at the interruption. She knew better than to call him at the office.

Looking out the window of the limousine, Hoover sighed at the brown piles of snow pushed up against the gutter like so much dirty linen. "Come home," his mother had commanded, as if he were a child being reprimanded for playing stickball too long in the street. When he attempted to question her further, she only repeated herself. Then the line went dead.

As he walked up the front steps to the home they still shared, he saw that the shades in the front parlor were still pulled down against the afternoon sun. Annie Hoover always pulled down the shades, plunging the rooms into hues of cinereous gray. "Mother," Hoover called out as he entered the house, moving to pull up the shades as he entered the living room. Getting no answer, he sighed at the thought of a confrontation as he climbed the stairs, pulling himself along by gripping the banister. His small feet struggled to balance his thick legs, log-heavy after an exhausting day. As he reached the top of the stairs and looked down the hall, he saw that the door to his mother's bedroom was closed. Knocking once, he opened it, as if to question her right to shut herself off from the remainder of the house.

Inside the dark room, Annie Hoover was propped up in bed, the covers pulled to her neck. "Not again, Mother," Hoover said, walking to her bedside. "What is it this time?"

"The same," she replied.

For half a year, since shortly after her seventy-fourth birthday in September, Annie Hoover had been complaining of abdominal pain, particularly in the evenings. Obstinate and afraid, she refused to consult a doctor, preferring instead to rely on her youngest child to bring her a sherry and stay at her side until she fell asleep. The scene had played itself out so many times over the past few months that Hoover knew better than to argue. He was, of course, as stubborn as she, but it was easier to walk back downstairs and return with her tonic than suggest that a legitimate medical opinion was what his mother actually needed.

"They talked about you again on the radio, Edgar," she said, after taking a sip, looking at the glass, and then taking another. "Mrs. Monasian heard it too. She came right over and said that Winchell said you were trying to ruin the movie business. I told her you hated criminals, not movies," she said, setting the empty sherry glass on the narrow mahogany nightstand next to her bed.

"You're quite right, Mother. Now get some rest," Hoover said before leaving the room and hurrying down the hallway, making a mental note to write Walter Winchell a special thank-you note.

He had become increasingly friendly with the popular columnist since he began lobbying hard for stricter censorship of Hollywood product—in particular for the passage of a motion picture code that would halt the abundance of feature films that romanticized gangsters. What had started out lowbrow with Edward G. Robinson in *Outside the Law* and *Little Caesar* and continued with James Cagney in *The Public Enemy,* turned classic cinema in *Scarface* from Howard Hughes. With increasing frequency, cold-blooded killers were depicted on celluloid as beyond the law, reaping the benefits of a life of crime and always attracting the most glamorous women.

To Hoover, it was an unconscionable trend that needed to be exterminated right along with the "vermin" he knew his public enemies to be. Though the motion picture industry wrote its own morality code in 1934 as a means of self-censorship, that fixed only part of the dilemma, according to the director of the Bureau of Investigation. G-men needed to be heroes, romantic leads who were incorruptible and unstoppable.

As Hoover saw it, the problem was simple: gangsters got the headlines, and with headlines came fame. To compete, the Bureau needed its own stars—or at least one: J. Edgar Hoover. By September 1934, Mr. Hoover was ready for his close-up, scrubbed, polished, and as artificial as any movie star. It was then that his mother had fallen ill. He wondered silently if there possibly could be a connection, and then quickly dismissed the thought.

In what can be seen only as the lessons of Hollywood coming to Washington, both Attorney General Homer Cummings and Hoover decided in a series of private meetings to launch a publicity campaign designed to mold public perception and enthusiasm. To accomplish that goal, they turned to popular syndicated columnists Drew Pearson and Robert S. Allen, who wrote the column Washington Merry-Go-Round. Both journalists suggested that what the Justice Department *really* needed was not only good press, but its own publicist. And both men recommended their mutual friend, Henry Suydam, the Washington correspondent for New York's *Brooklyn Eagle* newspaper, for the job.

Suydam saw the opportunity to become established within the ranks of government and build contacts from the inside out. By generating press releases for Cummings and letters for Hoover that stressed the competence, efficiency, and indomitable strength of the special agents of the Bureau of Investigation, he did more than that. He created the illusion of the G-man—tall, slender, bright, quick, a man who always got his prey.

It mattered little that no single G-man embodied all the qualities that Suydam painted, especially J. Edgar Hoover. Suydam was spinning illusion, not flesh and blood, at a time when America needed to be saved from a corrupt element of humanity. And in Hoover he had the perfect foil—a leader as serious in his determination to remove crime from the nation as he was to become the spokesman for his own success.

No release was complete without a quote from the director of the Bureau of Investigation. Though never on the scene of an arrest or shootout, Hoover was "in constant touch" with his special agents in the field and only too happy to share the details of their various triumphs.

While the criminals got name play, the special agents, for the most part, did not. Hoover learned his lesson with former protégé Melvin Purvis, when he took the nation by storm and became an overnight hero with the shooting of John Dillinger and then "Pretty Boy" Floyd.

As long as Sam Cowley, who had been given half the credit in finding Dillinger, remained in Chicago, Purvis was forced to share much of the local glory. That changed on November 27, 1934, when Cowley and fellow agent Herman Hollis were mortally wounded by "Baby Face" Nelson in a gun battle near North Side Park in Barrington, Illinois. Purvis was widely reported to have taken an oath in Cowley's blood to avenge the agent's death, unaware that Nelson had also been mortally wounded before he escaped. Nelson's body was found in a nearby cemetery the next day.

Purvis's deathside pledge, however well-meaning, attracted exactly the type of attention that Hoover was determined to prevent, blood oaths not being part of recognized Bureau protocol. Though Purvis got attention from the media, he lost any hope of receiving it from his boss. Overnight, Purvis was unable to reach Hoover for any reason. His calls were unreturned, and the silence became a fog on a mind otherwise darkened by paranoia. It pleased Hoover to watch the slow disintegration of his once proud protégé, so much so that he repeatedly took home Purvis's file, updated weekly with reports from Tolson.[1]

To those inside the Bureau, it came as little surprise that on August 5, 1935, Melvin Purvis submitted his formal resignation as a G-man and ended what was an equally brilliant and disastrous career. That was not the end of his story as far as Hoover was concerned. The director ordered any mention of Purvis's involvement in the Dillinger killing to be removed, with Cowley's name listed as special agent in charge.

When Purvis subsequently lent his name to the Post Cereal Junior G-Man Club, Hoover demanded that the cereal maker list Purvis as a former G-man on all boxes that contained the metal Melvin Purvis Junior G-Man badge. The Bureau placed its own order for Purvis's "Manual of Instructions to All Operatives," at the cost of four Post Toasties box tops, and then had the manual read for any "compromised material." None was found.

The demise of Purvis as America's favorite G-man was a necessary rite of passage to allow Hoover to be declared America's true custodian of crime detection and the keeper of the nation's secrets. "J. Edgar Hoover is the personification of every decent minded citizen who wants to live in a world free from criminals," Suydam wrote in his pitch letters to journalists, most of whom were all too familiar with Hoover's push for attention.[2]

Hoover made himself available for interviews and his Bureau files available for exploitation, particularly to Hollywood filmmakers eager to replace the money being lost from the self-censorship of gangster films. The answer, as Hoover saw it, was not to stop making the popular films, but rather to switch the theme from crime wave to crime busting.

Jack L. Warner of Warner Bros. studios was the first to leap onto the stage that Hoover was constructing, brandishing a story he had optioned from former Warner head of production Darryl F. Zanuck. *G-Men* told the saga of a young lawyer, played by James Cagney, who was raised by gangsters only to join the Bureau to fight the lawlessness around him.* Hoover personally approved the script by Seton I. Miller, who had previously written *Scarface*. In addition, Hoover and Tolson visited the set during production of the film and assigned a trio of agents from the Los Angeles office to provide uncredited technical assistance.

Virtually unknown in Hollywood, Hoover was instantly enamored by the glamour and celebrity of the stars he met—among them Bette Davis, who was filming *The Girl from Tenth Avenue* on the Warner Bros. lot at the time. It was a world far removed from the politics of Washington, and gave Hoover his first indication that he might be welcomed into this place where dreams were made.

When *G-men* premiered in Manhattan on April 18, 1935, Hoover traveled to New York with Clyde Tolson and Henry Suydam, as well as Annie Hoover, who complained, but nevertheless rose unaided from her sickbed for the occasion. The group spent the evening at the Waldorf-Astoria on Park Avenue as the hotel's guests, Hoover in a two-bedroom suite with his mother and the others in nearby rooms. Previously, when Hoover and Tolson traveled to Manhattan on Bureau business, they stayed at the downscale Hotel New Yorker, across from Pennsylvania Station. After the premiere of *G-Men*, however, Hoover developed a decided taste for the opulence of the East

---

* Zanuck left Warner Bros. in 1933 to start 20th Century Pictures. *G-Men* is based on his book, *Public Enemy No. 1*, which he wrote under the pseudonym Gregory Rogers.

Side, as well as nights spent with the rich and famous at the Stork Club on East Fifty-third Street.

Walter Winchell had introduced Hoover to the club in 1934, not long after Prohibition became history. The club, which had been an elegant speakeasy for the society crowd, emerged from Prohibition's shadow as a rejuvenated and very exclusive nightclub and restaurant which routinely turned away more guests than it admitted.

After the premiere of *G-Men* and the sudden popularity of the newly renamed *Federal* Bureau of Investigation, Hoover felt right at home with the stars that joined Winchell at his own table 50, including Ethel Merman who was having a romance with Stork Club owner Sherman Billingsley. It pleased Hoover to be instantly recognized and swept inside when he approached the doorman with Clyde Tolson trailing just steps behind.

He did not realize that Billingsley, behind his back, referred to the FBI director and assistant director as "Mr. and Mrs. Hoover." It was a growing problem for Hoover and Tolson, seen so often in each other's company that outsiders projected a romantic relationship between the two. Had it been true, the two men would likely have been more interesting personalities. Yet nothing in their public behavior suggested anything more than a working relationship that had grown into best-friends status. Both men were quite aware of the gossip, but refused to allow it to impact their friendship, offering further proof that they had little to hide. If anything, Hoover was harder on Tolson because of their association, routinely sending him scathing memos that left little doubt that Hoover was Tolson's boss.

In 1928, after six months of service in the Bureau, Hoover wrote on Tolson's Field Efficiency Rating Sheet the number "86%" over the remarks, "Agent has developed rapidly and is better than average. He is keen, aggressive and deeply interested. Has initiative and tact and is absolutely loyal. Requires very little supervision and investigates thoroughly. Should develop exceptional efficiency as he gains experience."[3]

By mid-1930, when Tolson was being perceived as Hoover's virtual alter ego, the compliments had given way to a series of memos that began, "My patience is about reaching the limit,"[4] "I am particularly disturbed over the supervision and handling of investigative work,"[5] "I am particularly disturbed over what I consider to be a general let-down in discipline,"[6] and "I desire that immediate steps be taken to improve supervision."[7] Hoover described Tolson's work as "careless"[8] and "inefficient,"[9] at exactly the time the Bureau was being touted as the most flawless crime-fighting organization in the world—a bit of a paradox considering Tolson was then rising to assume the number two position under Hoover at the organization.

Nowhere was the Hoover-Tolson show on larger stages than in the Senate and House, where Mr. Hoover and Mr. Tolson walked from their new offices on the fifth floor of the Department of Justice building[†] to appear before the Appropriations Subcommittee in April 1936. Hoover was anxious to increase the budget of the FBI to

---

† The Department of Justice building at Ninth Street and Constitution Avenue NW was designed by Clarence Clark Zantzinger, Charles Borie Jr., and Milton Bennett Medary, and finished in 1934.

$5 million—nearly double his budget of $2,589,500 in 1934. He approached his first meeting in the Senate with confidence, armed with the Bureau's success in eliminating the Dillinger gang, as well as "Pretty Boy" Floyd, "Baby Face" Nelson, "Machine Gun" Kelly, and "Ma" Barker and her sons.‡ What he did not expect was to be attacked on the success of his public relations campaign.

The senior senator from Tennessee, Kenneth Douglas McKellar, had made little secret of the fact that he disliked Hoover's addiction to publicity, and demanded to know if the Bureau was spending any money, "directly or indirectly," on advertising.

"There is not," Hoover responded, a vein expanding in his neck and across his forehead. "We are not permitted in any way to engage in advertising," which was technically true. Henry Suydam was not a Bureau employee, but rather worked for the Department of Justice.

Then what of these movies, McKellar wanted to know. "Do you take part, for instance, in the making of any moving pictures?"

"That is one thing that the Bureau has very strongly objected to," Hoover lied. "You have seen several of the G-men pictures, I believe."

McKellar had, and he found them to be blatant advertisements for the methods and accomplishments of the Bureau—and for Hoover. "Your picture was shown in conjunction with them frequently."

---

‡ Hoover had labeled Kate "Ma" Barker, a "she-wolf . . . a veritable beast of prey." She was killed with her youngest son, Fred, on January 16, 1935, after firing on FBI agents surrounding her hideout in Ocklawaha, on Florida's Lake Weir.

Hoover, of course, knew he had asked that his picture be used in those films. It was a matter of authenticity. Now, he stammered slightly as he made every effort to appear nonplussed, to project innocence. "We declined emphatically to lend any form of endorsement and had nothing to do with their production; furnished no advice, technical advice, or other advice as to the production of those pictures."[10]

Clyde Tolson leaned back in his chair and attempted not to look surprised. There were truths and there were lies. This he recognized as a lie. How could he not? He had been on the set. At least two dozen people had seen him. *Perhaps,* he thought, *that's not really an endorsement.* Suddenly the line between hyperbole and truth was lost.

Tolson knew what was coming next. He wondered how Hoover would respond when questioned about *The G-Men,* the radio show that Chevrolet had sponsored on NBC. He had seen the press release himself and knew Hoover had approved it:

"A new weekly dramatic serial, *The G-Men,* based on actual cases from the files of Federal Bureau of Investigation, opens coast-to-coast Saturday night at 8 o'clock, EST. The continuity will be prepared by Phillips H. Lord, known on the air as Seth Parker. "If there are some who are still dazzled by the false glamour of the gangster," said a representative of the sponsor, "we hope these radio programs will show little glamour is left to the criminal when he comes to the end of the road." The purpose of the broadcast, it is pointed out, is to "hold up a clear mirror to the G man and his activities, and let the true reflection, as contained in the official records, speak for itself.'"[11]

The radio show had run for 13 episodes, beginning on June 20, 1935. Yet, curiously, McKellar never made reference to them, if he even knew they existed. Rather, he moved to make his attack personal, demanding that Hoover explain his exact qualifications for his position with the Bureau.

"Nineteen years with the Department of Justice; twelve of them as director of the Bureau of Investigation," Hoover answered.

"Did you ever make an arrest?" McKellar asked.

"No, sir; I have made investigations," came Hoover's reply.

Not satisfied with that response, McKellar probed, prodded, and otherwise pressed Hoover to admit that he, in fact, had never personally gone into the field to personally arrest anyone. Hoover danced around the issue, and pointed out that he was in charge of all cases. But as to an arrest, he finally had to concede his lack of a personal arrest record.

The unexpected grilling by Senator McKellar left Hoover in such an agitated state that he refused to walk back to his office, or even have Tolson accompany him in his car. While Tolson returned to the Justice Department, Hoover fled to the sanctuary of Seward Square. His mother, still not well but always ready to support her son, listened in silence as Hoover lamented his treatment in front of the Senate, and soothed his hurt pride with copious amounts of Johnny Walker Black Label Scotch.

In a memo that went out to all Bureau offices the following day, Hoover informed all special agents that he
wanted to be apprised of "all developments in on-going
investigations, particularly those involving suspected
murderers and bank robbers. Timing of all arrests is to be
made through the Seat of Government,"[12] "Seat of Government" being Hoover's term for FBI Headquarters in
Washington.

For the next week, Hoover maneuvered himself
through his office with bombastic dominance, as if to
prove he was still very much in control of operations at
the Bureau. Tolson found himself being courted by his
boss in a different manner, according to the waitstaff at
Harvey's Restaurant on Connecticut Avenue. He was
openly complimented by the director, a novelty from a
man who centered conversation on either himself or
criminals. "It was clear to me that [Tolson] was uncomfortable, you know, the way Mr. Hoover was acting,"
waiter Eddie Mount said. "Like he was being buttered up
for something."[13]

Tolson was indeed being handled carefully, for he was
well aware of Hoover's public transgressions during the
Senate subcommittee meeting and in a position to reveal
what he knew. If Tolson was uncomfortable, it was not
because of the compliments, but rather because his boss
thought they were necessary—Tolson being Hoover's
most loyal employee and friend.

That same friendship would be a factor several weeks
later when Hoover was again taken to task, this time on
the floor of the House of Representatives, where the junior
congressman from Washington State, Marion Zioncheck,

leaped to his feet to denounce Hoover's attempts for more money, labeling him a "master of fiction."

> Apparently, Mr. Speaker, one of the most popular illusions that the American people are suffering from today is the illusion that has been deliberately created and built up by the master of fiction, J. Edgar Hoover— the great "G-Man." . . . The dictator, J. Edgar Hoover.

The dictator would have none of Zioncheck's diatribe, standing in irate insult to label the congressman "a public enemy" who should be added to his list of criminals. Tolson, sitting at the director's right, took out his handkerchief from his suit jacket and nonchalantly handed it to Hoover, who patted his brow and upper lip as he sank back down into his seat.

The challenge for Hoover had been made clear. His ability to command his team of special agents was based on their respect—respect built on more than a decade of leadership. He knew now that he must realize his myths to convince himself, and them, that they were true.

Fortunately, on April 30, 1936, Hoover had a ready-made opportunity when he received word that Alvin "Creepy" Karpis had been tracked to an apartment building in New Orleans. "Public Enemy Number One" was wanted for murder, kidnapping, bank robbery, and bootlegging, and his capture became Hoover's personal obsession.

With the echo of McKellar's words still fresh in his mind, the next day Hoover chartered a plane and flew with Tolson and 12 other agents to New Orleans, where they were met by Flying Squad leader Earl "E.J." Connelley, who had replaced Sam Cowley. By all accounts, Hoover was openly enthusiastic about nabbing the elusive Karpis, and announced to all agents that the arrest was his to make.

The exact details of what happened that sunny afternoon in New Orleans will probably never be known, despite the number of eyewitnesses. Special agents were poised on rooftops, on stairways, and in cars. Karpis, his partner Fred Hunter, and a woman posing as Karpis's wife accidentally cooperated by exiting their apartment just as the FBI was closing in. J. Edgar Hoover maintained a confident smile as he gave the following account to the *New York Times*.

KARPIS CAPTURED IN NEW ORLEANS BY HOOVER HIMSELF, the headline read. "We've captured Alvin Karpis, generally known as Public Enemy No. 1—but not to us,"§ Hoover was quoted as saying."

> They were taken without the firing of a shot. Karpis never had a chance. There were too many guns on him. They were in an apartment on the first floor of the building and were leaving the house to enter an automobile when the agents surrounded them.
>
> Witnesses said that when the three left the house, agents armed with sawed-off shotguns and other weapons stepped to the sidewalk, and crisply commanded them to surrender. When the desperadoes made no move, they were seized and rushed from the scene.[14]

---

§ Hoover actually disliked the term, believing it glamorized criminals.

Hoover had added to his story. "We nabbed the three when they came out and entered their car. There was a rifle in the back seat, but neither Karpis nor Hunter had a chance to reach for it. Karpis said he'd never be taken alive, but we took him without firing a shot. That marked him as a dirty, yellow rat. He was scared to death when we closed in on him. He shook all over—his voice, his hands and his knees."[15]

In February 1938, nearly two years later, Hoover lent his name to a book titled *Persons in Hiding,* ghostwritten by journalist Courtney Ryler Cooper. By this point, the Karpis arrest legend had grown further still.

> With necessary reinforcements for the raiding party, we swooped down out of the sky, after an all-night airplane ride from Washington. The apartment house, a good-looking building in one of the better residence districts, was surrounded. Everyone awaited the word to proceed to what we believed must be a desperate battle. . . . [The raid] was to take place on a boulevard crowded with swift moving traffic, leaving only a narrow lane at one side. And just at the moment when we had planned to start toward the house in our automobiles, thus beginning the raid, a man on an old white horse had sauntered into that lane beside the through traffic.
>
> We could not dislodge him without creating attention. We could not pass him—all other space was jammed with fast-moving cars. So we must wait until the jogging man on the old white horse went slowly down the street—*clop-clop—clop-clop—clop-clop.* . . .

At last he was gone. The raiding party moved forward, just in time to see two men leave the apartment house and enter a car. It was Karpis and a pal. We closed in swiftly. The wrists of Alvin Karpis were handcuffed before he could even whirl for his gun.[16]

In 1956, when Don Whitehead wrote *The FBI Story* with Hoover's endorsement, the tale of the Karpis capture had changed once again. While the white horse remained, the handcuffs did not.

As Hoover and his men approached the apartment building by automobile, Karpis and a companion unexpectedly walked out the door. For a few tense seconds, the FBI cars were blocked by a man riding a white horse up the street, then the horse moved out of the way. Karpis climbed into his automobile. Hoover ran to the left side of the car and Assistant Director Earl Connelley** to the right side. Hoover reached into the car and grabbed Karpis before he could reach for a rifle on the back seat.

"Put the handcuffs on him," Hoover ordered. But no one had remembered to bring handcuffs. An agent pulled off his necktie and tied Karpis' hands behind him. 'Old Creepy,' all the bravado gone and ashen with fear, was put aboard a plane to be flown to St. Paul, Minnesota, to stand trial.

** Earl "E.J." Connelley was not an assistant director at the time. In the weeks following the arrest, he would be named an inspector. In 1940, he was promoted to assistant director of major investigation in the field.

Though the special agents at the arrest weren't talking, Alvin Karpis was—at least he did some 35 years later, soon after being paroled for kidnapping. In his 1971 book, *The Alvin Karpis Story,* Karpis said that it was special agent Clarence Hurt, onetime chief of detectives for the Oklahoma City police department, who had approached the car with Connelley and put a .351-caliber automatic rifle against Karpis's left temple. Karpis went on to deny that he had a rifle. "What rifle? What back seat? We were in a 1936 Plymouth coupe that had no back seat," Karpis wrote.[17]

For Hoover, however, the ultimate put-down was Karpis's insistence that the director did not participate in his arrest, and did not even witness it. "He hid until I was safely covered by many guns. He waited until he was told the coast was clear. Then he came out to reap the glory. . . . I *made* that son-of-a-bitch."[18]

Whichever is the authentic story of the apprehension of Alvin Karpis, there is no denying that Hoover altered his version with each retelling, seemingly determined to sacrifice veracity for drama. His lies, or at least exaggerations, were more of proportion than substance.

What is known for certain is that immediately after the Karpis arrest, Tolson received a note from Hoover commending him on his performance during the apprehension. "I want to take this occasion to extend to you both my official and personal commendation, not only of the excellent, but intelligent and courageous manner in which you handled the apprehension of Alvin Karpis and Fred Hunter at New Orleans on last Friday, May 1st. It was another indication of unselfish devotion to duty, and I was indeed proud to be associated with you upon the

occasion when these arrests were made." Hoover signed
the letter, "With expressions of my very best regards and
good wishes, I am sincerely yours, J. Edgar Hoover."[19]

Tolson continued his daily routine of lunching with
the director at the Mayflower Hotel and dining with him
at Harvey's, having negotiated an "arrangement" with the
establishments. As a courtesy, both restaurants allowed
the men to eat and drink for a "token fee of $2.50."
According to waiters who worked for more than a dozen
years serving the pair, even the $2.50 charge was appar-
ently too high, for neither Hoover nor Tolson paid the
tabs, which were eventually picked up by friends, this at
a time when Hoover's salary had been increased to
$10,000 a year.[20]

Now finding a home on the front page of the nation's
newspapers with regularity, Hoover personified law
enforcement with highly publicized consecutive arrests.
After Alvin Karpis in New Orleans, Hoover personally
captured Karpis's friend, limping Harry Campbell, in
Toledo, Ohio, returning him to St. Paul, Minnesota, to
stand trial with Karpis on kidnapping charges. Back in
Washington, when asked if he had led the raid as he had
done in the Karpis case, Hoover answered, "I did—both
of them, but it was a 'we' job, not an 'I' job."[21]

While living in Toledo, Harry Campbell had taken the
name "Bob Miller," and introduced himself to Toledo society as a successful contractor. He made a point of meeting
Sheriff James M. O'Reilly, who had a six-month friendship
with the gangster. "The Sheriff has already admitted associating with this man for weeks," Hoover said, demanding
an investigation. "It seems to me that any one could have

recognized Harry Campbell from his pictures, which were plastered on nearly every wall in the country."[22]

The same day Campbell was apprehended, special agents captured gangster William Mahan in San Francisco, followed four days later with the arrest of kidnapper Thomas H. Robinson in Glendale, California. On the surface, it was a stunning show of investigative prowess, though some believed the speed of the arrests involved far more than mere skill and luck. "The timing has been so dramatic," an editor in the *New York Times* suggested, "that one might almost suspect a touch of stage direction as if J. Edgar Hoover had all three of his quarry in hand and chose to release them one by one. The effect has been not unlike the knitting women at the guillotine in 'A Tale of Two Cities.' The American people has [sic] been counting gangster heads as they dropped into the basket."[23] The FBI director, of course, denied any such choreographed effort.

Hoover was America's hero. There were speeches, dedications, awards. And without any apologies to Senator McKellar, there was Hollywood. Hoover renewed his efforts to court film producers, and welcomed newscaster Lowell Thomas and his cameramen into his offices in the Department of Justice to shoot the 30-minute short *You Can't Get Away with It.*

Hoover introduced the documentary, narrated by Thomas, which illustrated FBI techniques and agent training as well as dramatizing several apprehensions, including that of John Dillinger. Across the country, theater posters proclaimed, "Scoop! The First Authentic (Factual Not Fiction) Pictures of Hoover, Himself, and His G-men." Hoover posed for photographers, looking through a camera lens at Clyde Tolson standing pertly in the picture.

He made it all look so easy, so right, calling the FBI "America's anti-crime academy."[24] If the Bureau was, as Hoover insisted, a well-oiled machine, it did not extend as far as his armored Cadillac limousine. On November 12, 1936, Hoover sent Tolson a detailed memo airing his disappointment:

> I would like to have someone designated in the Bureau to look after the car which I have assigned to my office. I have repeatedly in the past called attention to the fact that apparently little or no attention is given to the checking over and supervision of this car.
>
> Last Saturday, I called attention to the fact that the windshield wiper did not work when the car went up a steep hill. Today, I had occasion to go to Baltimore and during the trip . . . encountered a very heavy rain. The wiper did not work going up the hills and consequently, the speed had to be cut down in order to be able to have proper visibility. I would like to know what action, if any, was taken in order to have the windshield wiper repaired.
>
> I have noted for a week that the electric clock in the rear of the car is between eight and ten minutes slow. Apparently, no one checks the correct time of this clock each day, because if they did, it would be corrected.
>
> I do not know how to obtain satisfactory service on this car. Obviously, the person in the Chief Clerk's office assigned to take care of this matter gives it but indifferent attention. It would seem to me that it should be possible to secure the services of some employee who

would make it his duty each day to check over the various parts of the car and find out whether all parts of the car are functioning properly. This is not a very intricate or complicated arrangement to effect, but of course, it does require some interest upon the part of the employee assigned, not merely casual attention.[25]

The auto was reportedly so heavy that it lumbered through traffic, challenged to carry its load plus passengers to their destination. Tires and brakes had to be replaced on a monthly basis due to excessive wear. A week after Tolson received Hoover's memo, he succeeded in negotiating a unique service contract with General Motors that allowed a trained mechanic to service the car six times a year in the Department of Justice building.

During the first such service, the car was rushed off its lift to race Tolson to a hospital in Baltimore, the victim of an appendicitis attack. Panicked when his assistant became ill over lunch, Hoover demanded that Tolson be taken to the hospital in his vehicle despite the availability of a nearby ambulance service.

After spending a week in the hospital on Hoover-authorized sick leave, Tolson returned immediately to service accompanying Hoover to New York for a four-day tour of the Manhattan Bureau office. The manager of the St. Moritz hotel at 50 Central Park South welcomed the pair with a complimentary two-bedroom suite, while Stork Club owner Sherman Billingsley agreed to pay for all food, liquor, and telephone charges.

Swept up in the media excitement that followed the apprehensions of Campbell, Mahan, and Robinson, Hoover

made "appearances" around New York, signing autographs
and shaking hands as a gaggle of the curious followed him
through the streets. On the evening of December 13, during a late-night dinner at the Stork Club with Tolson,
Hoover was joined by actress Anita Colby, at that moment
well on her way to becoming America's first supermodel.
Twenty-two-years old and a dynamic beauty, Colby openly
flirted with the flattered Hoover, who began to talk in his
staccato prose about unsolved cases in the FBI files. Soon
others were drawn to the fast-paced monologue, including
Ginger Rogers and her mother, Lela, who thrilled to the
tales of kidnapping and treachery. Clyde Tolson, not so
much left out of the conversation as literally pushed away
from the table by the flurry of activity, seemed sullenly
transfixed by the chorus of female giggles and shared looks
of horror.

"He was quite a good story teller," Ginger Rogers
remembered in 1977. "And I think he might have gone on
all night, if my mother hadn't heard the band playing 'Red
Sails in the Sunset' and asked Mr. Hoover to dance."[26]

An embarrassed Hoover, befuddled by the invitation,
quickly excused himself and left the Stork Club with Tolson. "He said something about his inability to dance,
turned the color of an eggplant, and left," Ginger said.
"Mother and I just laughed like crazy—this big G-Man
running away from all these women."[27]

The following night, on December 14, the New York
City police department successfully tracked down librarian–
turned–bank robber Harry Brunette in an apartment on
the Upper West Side. As a courtesy, New York police commissioner Lewis J. Valentine informed the Bureau director

of the pending arrest, planned for the next afternoon. Much to Valentine's amazement, several hours later, without any warning, Hoover appeared at the stakeout with two dozen FBI agents, Tolson among them.

Rushing the apartment on the first floor of the building and demanding Brunette's surrender, Hoover was met with abject silence. Nodding his head in the direction of the door, Hoover authorized Tolson, armed with a Thompson machine gun, to shoot his way into the apartment. As Brunette returned fire, Hoover and Tolson sought what available cover the hallway provided while backup agents tossed tear gas into the apartment, sending neighbors into the street.

For his part, Harry Brunette escaped into a nearby janitor's closet where he continued to fire through the door until he exhausted his bullets and surrendered. While the action of the FBI was concentrated in the hallway, the tear gas had ignited the building, attracting a mob of rubberneckers into the street along with the arriving fire department.[28]

Newspaper headlines touted Hoover's successful capture of Brunette, along with police grumblings that the FBI's director was attempting to "steal the glory." At a hastily called news conference in the ballroom of the St. Moritz, Hoover thanked the police and fire departments for their cooperation, while posturing amazement at the suggestion that he was attempting to generate headlines with machine-gun grandstanding. According to Hoover, his Bureau "never double-crossed anyone," adding "that hindsight was better than foresight," and assuring the press that "all precautions were taken to prevent innocent persons from being hurt."[29]

For Tolson, the arrest was a watershed event in what was to be his first and only use of firearms in the line of duty. He returned to Washington, a triumphant hero with a new nickname: "Killer." Hoover responded with paternal pride at his protégé's performance in the line of duty, calling it "efficient and courageous." Hoover wrote Tolson that he was "subjected, during the course of this raid, to great physical danger, and you measured up to the high standard expected of all men of the Federal Bureau of Investigation. Your courage and fearlessness upon this occasion are to be highly commended."[30]

With the appearance of a smooth commandant, Hoover had reached a plateau both in his life and in his career. He was famous, he was courted, he was financially stable, and he had a growing power unrelated to the current political power in current power. He was, however, far from satisfied. Despite years of speech making, Hoover was troubled by his occasional stutter, practicing long into the night to overcome the affliction.

Then there were the persistent rumors that he was a flit—a homosexual, a queer. He shook involuntarily at the thought, a chill grabbing his body and spiking unsolicited energy through his spine. He hated queers and what they represented. Abnormal sex. Emotional imbalance. And the way they talked, like gossiping women. He hated it all.

Yet alone at night, in the privacy of darkness, he neither pondered ways to stifle the hearsay nor erase the stigma. He felt no need to scream his innocence, or declare his normalcy. He *knew* he was normal. He *knew* it was so. And with that, he rolled over and went to sleep.

SEVEN

ASCENT OF POWER

Whenever J. Edgar Hoover thought of homosexuals, he thought of Barton J. Pincus. "Birdie," as he was known to his classmates, was the son of a Washington, D.C., watchmaker with a storefront not far from Seward Square. When Hoover was a teenager, Birdie, 10 years his junior, discovered his mother's jewelry box and began wearing rope pearls beneath his undershirt, wisely realizing that any outward show of accessories was bound to attract the wrong kind of attention.

After Birdie himself became a teenager, he was discovered after class by a custodian in the wardrobe closet of Eastern High's drama club trying on a hoop skirt and flower bonnet, and was made to stand outside the school in the costume as a token penance for trespassing. Six weeks after the punishment was imposed, Birdie was dead from a self-inflicted gunshot wound.

Annie Hoover called Barton J. Pincus "Daffy." While most who heard it presumed she was referring to Pincus's flamboyant (by Washington standards) behavior, it, actually, was short for daffodil, a reference to her penchant to equate homosexuals with a flower she found particularly unattractive. "Oh, the boy's poor mother," she said when news of Birdie's suicide spread throughout the neighborhood. "I would sooner die myself than endure something like that." At this point in the conversation, she would usually cast her eyes toward heaven, as if to thank God that her own sons had no such predilection.

The only thing that Hoover hated more than homosexuals was Communists. Although he had been compelled to withdraw from his earlier highly visible campaigns to rout the country of Communists at the insistence of Harlan Stone, Hoover was still diligent in their pursuit—albeit quietly. With the arrival of Franklin D. Roosevelt in the White House, Communists were joined by another threat—Nazis. Under Adolf Hitler, the Nazis of the National Socialist German Workers Party had seized control of Germany in 1933. And by 1936, rumors were rampant that Nazis had infiltrated the United States and were nestled within embassies and consulates of the German government.

As the threat of war grew in Europe, the president called on Hoover to begin organized surveillance of Communists and Fascists—"a broad picture of the general movement and its activities as may affect the economic and political life of the country as a whole." The authority was granted to Hoover under a clause in the original Bureau mandate that allowed the secretary of state to request FBI investigations on matters of national interest.* Which is why, on August 25, 1936, Hoover was called to the White House and given the authority verbally by Roosevelt's secretary of state, Cordell Hull. "Go ahead and investigate the cocksuckers," Hull said, or at least that is what Hoover claimed to hear.[1]

---

* See Title II and Title V, United States Code, FBI.

Under the auspices of the General Intelligence Division Hoover began what was to be an open-ended surveillance of anyone he had reason to suspect. No need to be officially a Communist or Fascist to qualify, or for that matter even to have done something illegal; the mere illusion of impropriety was enough to warrant FBI interest.

In a memo to FBI field offices written on September 5, 1936, Hoover instructed his special agents to begin reporting suspected subversive activities of not only Communists and Fascists but also "representatives or advocates of other organizations or groups advocating the overthrow or replacement of the Government of the United States by illegal methods."[2]

Edward A. Tamm, an assistant director and the third-in-command in the Seat of Government, was assigned the task of targeting areas of suspected subversive activity. Tamm's response was startling if only for the scope of its proposed investigations. Under a general classification category, he listed "maritime, steel, coal, clothing, garment and fur industries; the newspaper field; government affairs; the armed forces; educational institutions; Communist and affiliated organizations; Fascist and anti-Fascist movements; and activities in organized labor organizations."[3] Hoover found this to be "a good beginning," according to his notes in the memo's margins.[4]

It was to be an entirely new landscape for FBI surveillance, one supported by the president of the United States, albeit surreptitiously. Nothing would be written from Roosevelt to Hoover. Rather, it was a clandestine operation monitored through face-to-face meetings and mouthed reports. The extent to which Hoover's reach had expanded certainly was not hidden from Roosevelt, who encouraged the nation's top G-man to dig and uncover.

The assignment was unregulated and far-reaching—not unlike an unrelated "flying trip" that was considered "both for business and to an extent for pleasure." It was an eight-day excursion to Havana, Cuba; Nassau, Bahamas; and San Juan, Puerto Rico, by way of Miami. Hoover invited Clyde Tolson to join him as well as Tolson's roommate at the Westchester Apartments, Guy Hottel. A muscular athlete, Hottel had played football while attending George Washington University with Tolson. After graduation, Hottel became an insurance salesman with Aetna, then joined the FBI as a special agent—one who just happened to live with the assistant director.

The planning that preceded Hoover's working vacation indicated just how much his power had grown. Regardless of guise, the trip was an obvious holiday—the first time Hoover had ever left U.S. soil, and the first of many breaks he would take without ever claiming a day of vacation.

Hoover assigned special agent Robert Page Burrus to handle the arrangements, paid in full by the government. Burrus reported back to the director several days before his departure, in a five-page memo that was as telling in its submissive tone as it was for its efficiency.

Dear Sir:

In connection with your anticipated visit to Miami, Florida, and thence to Habana, Cuba; Nassau and Puerto Rico; returning to Miami, Florida, I conferred with Commander V.M. Thompson, Special Assistant to the Secretary of the Treasury, and with Mr. E. T. Ackan, Assistant Secretary of the Treasury, and through Mr. Gibbons have arranged that the freedom of the port at Miami, Florida and Customs courtesy be extended to you and those who will accompany you when you return from your trip, by aeroplane, to Miami, Florida. In order that no possible misunderstanding may arise when you return to Miami, Florida, there is annexed hereto copy of a letter dated February 11, 1936, from the Honorable Stephen B. Gibbons to Mr. John Klein, Deputy Collector of Customs, Miami, Florida, authorizing the extension of the usual Customs courtesies and free entry privileges to you, Mr. Tolson and Mr. Hottel. Complying with the request made in connection with this matter, as embodied in my letter to Mr. Gibbons, your arrival at Miami will not be made known to the press or others not officially interested. The extending to you of the usual Customs courtesies and free entry privileges will eliminate any examination of luggage or other procedures which may cause you any delay or unnecessary loss of time when you return to the United States via Miami, Florida. A copy of the letter from Mr. Gibbons to Mr. John Klein, Deputy Collector of Customs, Miami, Florida is enclosed in an envelope so indicated and marked no. 1.

PROOF OF CITIZENSHIP UPON RETURN TO UNITED STATES VIA MIAMI, FLORIDA
Upon your return to the United States, via Miami, Florida, it would customarily be necessary to exhibit

proof of citizenship. I have, however, arranged through the cooperation of Miss Ruth Shipley [Chief, Passport Division, Department of State] to have instructions issued by Colonel Daniel W. MacCormack, Commissioner of Immigration and Naturalization, Department of Labor, to his representatives at Miami, Florida, to waive the customary procedure in connection with proof of citizenship. Colonel MacCormack is presently out of the city, but upon his return on Monday, February 17, 1936, Miss Shipley will confer with him and see that the arrangements in this respect are perfected.

There is annexed hereto a letter dated February 11, 1936, addressed to you by the Honorable Wilbur Carr, Assistant Secretary of State, in which he makes reference to the general letter of introduction for you to any American Diplomatic and Consular officer within whose territory you may visit. He further states that he has also written to the Honorable Jefferson Caffery, American Ambassador at Habana and to Mr. Henry, American Consul at Nassau concerning your trip. When Mr. Carr was informed of your anticipated trip, he indicated very keen interest and desire to extend every possible courtesy to you, through his office and the offices of the State Department representatives wherever you may visit. This most cordial feeling, I am quite sure, is the result of his recent visit to your office.

There is also attached hereto a letter dated February 11, 1936, signed by the Honorable Cordell Hull, Secretary of State, to the American Diplomatic and Consular officers which refers to your anticipated trip and bespeaks for you and your party such courtesies and assistance which the Diplomatic officers may be able to render, consistent with their official duties.

HABANA, CUBA

Hotel: The Sevilla-Biltmore on the Prado is now the leading hotel and is being occupied by guests who enjoy international prominence.

Amusements and Exclusive Dining Places: I have been informed that the Patio on the Prado caters to the more exclusive class at Habana for dinner and supper and the guests to a large extent are members of the Diplomatic Corps and high government officials. Another place which Mr. Sumner Wells [sic], the former Ambassador to Cuba, recommends as being very exclusive, is the Sans Sousi, which, I understand, is an open air cabaret which caters to the more elite class of Cuban society.

NASSAU, BAHAMAS

I am forwarding herewith copy of a letter dated February 11, 1936, from Miss Ruth Shipley, Chief, Passport Division, Department of State, to the Honorable F. Lammot Belin who resides on an estate known as "On the Edge of the Blue" at Nassau, Bahamas. Miss Shipley has been personally acquainted with Mr. Belin for many years and she referred to him as a career man of the State Department; former Ambassador to Poland, related to the DuPonts of Delaware and a man who has a splendid personality and is enjoying life on his very beautiful estate.

It will be noted in [the] letter that Miss Shipley stated that she had been asked whether she knew anyone in Nassau to whom a letter of introduction could be given for you. I assure you that this is entirely incorrect and that I made no such suggestion really; on the other hand, that you preferred to have time at your disposal to do what you desired to do. Miss Shipley evidently used this phraseology not knowing just what else to say.

Hotel: Fort Montague. I am informed that this hotel is the most exclusive one there.

PUERTO RICO
Hotel: Condado-Vanderbilt is the only hotel which I understand has facilities which are acceptable.

May I respectfully suggest that consideration be given to the use of Travelers' Checks by you while on this trip, and further that you may desire to take out Travelers' Insurance. Might I further take the privilege of suggesting that travel both by plane and by railroad to the South is extremely heavy at this season of the year and that reservations should be made as far in advance as possible.

I am also sending to you an original letter dated February 11, 1936, addressed to me by Miss Ruth Shipley, Chief, Passport Division, Department of State, which indicates the action taken by her and other officials in connection with your trip South. She has exhibited keen interest and cooperation and a desire to be helpful and the thought has occurred to me that you may care to drop her a note of thanks.

Very truly yours,
R. P. Burrus
Special Agent[5]

That the secretary of state should accommodate Hoover by personally writing a letter of introduction to diplomatic and consular officers speaks volumes of the director's increased influence within Washington. After returning from the trip, which by all reports was indeed relaxing, Hoover wrote thank-you notes, paying generous compliments to those in the Passport Division, the Customs Division, and the State Department who made his "working" vacation so productive. He then ordered Burrus's memo destroyed. Only through an error in filing does a copy still exist in FBI records.

Hoover not only took lengthy and multiple vacations at the government's expense, but also built on his reputation as a celebrity with long weekends in New York drinking and eating to excess, having refined his talent for accepting what he termed "accommodations" from hotels, restaurants, and nightclubs. It was typical for such establishments to build their reputations on the backs of Hollywood and Broadway stars. While Hoover remained the only law enforcement official to benefit from such generosity, he hardly found it surprising, since he was, after all, no ordinary policeman.

The Great Depression, having shown signs of being alleviated by President Roosevelt's New Deal in the first three years of his presidency, came roaring back to life near the end of 1936. With Roosevelt's reelection in November, however, the president received what he felt was a resounding mandate to continue his policies of government control and influence. To that end, he found nothing improper in Hoover's clandestine surveillance of private citizens, and was rather proud of the Bureau director's continuing flirtation with celebrity.

On New Year's Eve 1936, as banks continued to fold up like concertinas, Hoover and Tolson traveled yet again to New York to celebrate at the Stork Club at the invitation of columnist Walter Winchell. After resting in their complimentary two-bedroom suite at the St. Moritz, the pair took a ride through Central Park in their chauffeured FBI limousine. They were then dropped off at the long marquee awning at 3 East Fifty-third Street and welcomed by the Stork's uniformed doorman. The atmosphere inside the club was even more festive than usual, with noisemakers, party hats, and confetti streamers competing for attention with the hoots and screams of happy celebrants. It was not, to be sure, a typical Hoover scene, but Winchell had been insistent and assured the director that the positive publicity would be ample reward for his effort.

Winchell seated Hoover and Tolson next to the journalist's close friend, fledgling screenwriter Art Arthur, who had just finished the story for his first film, *Charlie Chan on Broadway,* and boxer Jim Braddock, the newly crowned heavyweight champion of the world. Yet it was Arthur's date, model Luisa Stuart, who would prove to be the historian of the evening. Stuart was seen in a widely circulated photograph taken that evening at the club in which she was pointing a toy gun at a "surrendering" Hoover and Tolson.

"I remember there were jokes about race," Stuart recalled in 1989, "and Hoover didn't want to go on to the Cotton Club because Gene Krupa, the white jazz drummer, played with blacks there. All the same, we did end up going to the Cotton Club, in an FBI limousine. I sat with

Art in the backseat. Hoover and Tolson sat opposite us in those two little seats on hinges they have in limousines. And that was when I noticed they were holding hands—all the way to the club, I think. Just sitting there talking and holding hands with each other."[6]

Unfortunately, Stuart's memory of the evening is more dramatic than accurate. Hoover's FBI limousine in New York was a 1935 Cadillac outfitted with thick windows and a special air cleaner installed in the trunk. The rear seat had been moved forward to hold the equipment and was covered in custom-made mohair. At the time, jump seats in limousines were positioned to allow all passengers to face forward, but Hoover's FBI limousines did not have them installed at all—the carrying of passengers not encouraged. For Stuart and Arthur to have ridden with Hoover and Tolson, they would have had to sit in the front seat with the driver, unable to see Hoover and Tolson in the rear.

Upon arriving at the Cotton Club, Stuart remembered that Hoover became extremely upset when he witnessed interracial dancing. "Hoover got furious after we did get to the Cotton Club, because not only were there black and white musicians, there was a black and white couple dancing—a black man and a white woman."[7]

The original Cotton Club, located in Harlem on 125th Street, had been started by mobster Owney Madden and had an all-white clientele. Blacks were permitted inside the club only as entertainers or waiters. As Jimmy Durante put it at the club's opening, "It isn't necessary to mix with colored people if you don't feel like it. You have your own party and keep to yourself. But it's worth seeing.

How they step."[8] In February 1936, the Cotton Club was closed. Later that year, in September, a downtown version of the original opened on the top floor of a building at Broadway and Seventh Avenue in Manhattan. Again, however, blacks were not welcomed as customers or on the dance floor—even on New Year's Eve.

Moreover, Gene Krupa did not perform that evening or any evening in the new location. The show that night was headlined by tap dancer Bill "Bojangles" Robinson and bandleader Cab Calloway and the stars of the Cotton Club Parade in its twenty-third edition. A photo from the evening shows no blacks in the audience, nor J. Edgar Hoover for that matter.

Though Hoover would be long dead before Stuart claimed witness to his homosexual dalliances with Tolson, he was nevertheless prone to wonder about both Stuart and Art Arthur. In 1937, Hoover opened a file on both of them as well as other friends of Walter Winchell with whom he came in contact. Winchell had the largest file of all, one that eventually grew to 3,908 pages. From Winchell's mentions of Hoover in this column and on his radio program to his associations with known gangsters, the journalist's file suggests that the Bureau was watching Winchell constantly for decades while benefiting from his propaganda.

When Hoover captured Harry Brunette, Winchell's broadcast of the news was more a defense of Hoover than an announcement of the capture. "G-Men led by J. Edgar Hoover last Monday night captured a tough guy," Winchell said. "Not taking any chances, they used machine guns and other weapons and got a very dangerous criminal. Hoover is now being heckled and belittled by several newspapers and writers for making the United States a safer place to live in. The widows and children of agents Baum, Cowley, Hollis and others who have lost their lives, who died for your family and mine, must be appalled by such criticism. Take it from one who knows that they are man-hunters and not glory-hunters."[9]

Yet glory was never far from Hoover's mind, so essential a factor was it in his pursuit of power—albeit power designed to cleanse America of its criminal element. With the capture of the country's most notorious gangsters, Hoover had wiped clean the once-popular list of public enemies, leaving the FBI available for the president's call to arms against what he saw as the growing threat of Fascism.

Unwilling to combat a Congress already fighting many of Roosevelt's New Deal proposals, the president allowed Hoover to operate under the radar of supervision from anyone, including the attorney general to whom he theoretically reported. Roosevelt did this to expedite feedback in order to control his growing paranoia over enemy infiltration on domestic soil. For Hoover, the carte blanche approach delivered by the nation's chief executive was vindication that the organization he created in his own image had become the caretaker of America's trust.

As the world's attention turned toward the increasingly aggressive posture of Germany, the paranoia of Fascist infiltration into the heartland of America became real and certain. The mood was given credence when, in March 1937, columnist Haywood Hale Broun, a member of the legendary Algonquin Hotel Round Table, wrote that an active German American Bund was seeking new members for the Nazi Party. "Actual recruiting is going on, and there is already a considerable body of storm troops here in America," Broun wrote. He said that these were ethnic Germans living and training in the United States and "their loyalty is palpably directed toward Hitler and the homeland."[10]

The FBI launched an investigation into the Bund, an organization that Hoover said "holds the promise to be even more dangerous than the Communist Party in America."[11] Yet even as the Bureau was secretly infiltrating the Bund's activities, Hoover found himself sidetracked not by the Bureau, but by his "other" family. Hoover's mother, who for months had been totally bedridden and was being cared for by a rail-thin live-in nurse named Minerva, began to slip in and out of a coma.

During the last week of January 1938, when Hoover had resigned himself to the fact that his mother was dying, Annie made what was labeled a "miraculous recovery" by her nurse, who was the only source of medical opinion she was accepting. Annie was thrilled when, on Valentine's Day, Clyde Tolson sent an enormous arrangement of long-stem roses—pink, not red, for Annie thought red to be the color of prostitutes. Hoover responded with a thank-you note, distinctive in that it opened with "Dear Clyde": "Mother was quite pleased with the beautiful Valentine flowers which you sent her and asked me to tell you how much she appreciates your remembrance of her on this occasion, Sincerely, J. Edgar Hoover."[12]

Annie Hoover passed away peacefully on the evening of February 22, 1938 at the age of 77 with her youngest child at her bedside. After instructing Minerva to call

Lee's Funeral Home to pick up the body, Hoover kissed his mother's forehead and left the room. As he walked down the hallway toward the bathroom, Hoover hated that his life had changed forever without his consent. His mother was more than his best friend; she was his link to his own mortality.

Undressing, Hoover stepped into the shower and felt the massage of tepid water on his bowed head. For a full 10 minutes he did not move. When he did, it was only to stand naked at the bathroom window, his fleshy body chubby as that of a bar mitzvah boy. The backyard was suddenly alive with memories of his childhood and a life of innocence long gone.

Annie's funeral took place two days later, and she was laid to rest in the Congressional Cemetery next to her husband and young daughter Sadie. Immediately following the interment, Hoover and Tolson left Washington for Miami Beach, where they stayed in a villa at the Nautilus Hotel.† The Nautilus was a genteel oasis of moneyed society where Hoover was the guest of his friend, Harry Viner, the wealthy owner of the Arcade Sunshine Laundry and Dry Cleaners in Washington. Though in mourning, Hoover nevertheless found time to tan his skin to a leathery glow while Tolson, worried about skin cancer, lay protected under a large multistriped canvas umbrella. Upon their return, the pair resembled nothing less than a British settler and an Indian chief.

---

† The Nautilus Hotel was turned into Miami's Mount Sinai Hospital in 1949. It remained a functioning hospital until it was demolished to make way for the Fred J. Ascher Allied Health Careers Building in 1968.

Within months, Tolson and roommate Guy Hottel had moved from his apartment in the Westchester to the fifth floor of the Marlyn Apartments on Thirty-ninth and Cathedral Avenue NW.[13] At the same time, Hoover moved as well, out of the Seward Square home of his birth and into a new $25,000 home located at 4936 Thirtieth Place NW not far from the edge of Rock Creek Park, in an upscale suburb of Washington popular with senators and judges. Gone was the furniture of his youth, replaced by a collection of Chinese antiques that would continue to grow for the remainder of his life.

The colonial brick house sat well back from the street, with an expansive front lawn and a concrete walkway leading to the entrance. A side garden led toward the rear, where it joined an impressive back lawn shaded by old maples. Inside the home, photographs of Hoover's late mother were a feature of every room, including the kitchen. Only the downstairs den escaped Annie's penetrating stare, for here, among Hoover's many honors and awards, he constructed a bar and placed his first television set—a black and white RCA Victor TRK-9 with a five-by-seven-inch screen—a gift from RCA president David Sarnoff. Television was so new at the time, there were no stations yet established in Washington, D.C., and Hoover could use the set only to receive radio broadcasts.

While Sarnoff was eager to place sets in the homes of important Washington politicians and judges for the publicity value, his gift to Hoover was unusual, for Hoover fit neither of those categories. In return for his kindness, however, Sarnoff was rewarded with his very own FBI file. Hoover suspected the Russian immigrant of trying to mold America's political landscape by controlling its broadcasting.

Now 43 and alone, Hoover dissolved into an isolation of his own design. Although he still traveled with Clyde Tolson to New York on weekends and indulged a passion for horse racing in season, Hoover became increasingly less social after the death of his mother, concentrating instead on the legacy of his career. Eager to expand his image as a fearless G-man, Hoover continued his drive to be included in high-profile arrests that might garner positive press coverage. Unfortunately for Hoover, by 1939 gangsters cut from the cloth of John Dillinger and "Pretty Boy" Floyd were in short supply, the result of a successful FBI purge. Yet Hoover did manage to make one last highly praised capture, courtesy of Walter Winchell.

Louis "Lepke" Buchalter, a member of the Lucky Luciano organized crime family, was a professional killer who ran a business called Murder Incorporated. It was said that Buchalter would kill anyone, anywhere, for a price. Yet, despite the name of his organization, murder was hardly his only game. He was also a successful narcotics dealer and an extortion heavyweight, and was skilled in the protection racket and arson for hire.

Wanted in New York for the murder of the owner of a Brooklyn candy store, Buchalter also faced federal narcotics charges, which brought him to Hoover's attention. Walter Winchell became involved when he received an anonymous telephone call at the Stork Club. The caller said Buchalter was ready to turn himself in—but only to J. Edgar Hoover personally, and only in the presence of Walter Winchell.

Initially excited by the prospect of making his first single-handed arrest, Hoover quickly became disillusioned as Buchalter failed to fulfill his promise, repeatedly delaying the date of the rendezvous and causing Hoover to doubt Winchell's ability to produce the warlord. Hoover watched helplessly as Winchell gave weekly updates on his radio show of his progress with the notorious killer's surrender. For the first time in their friendship, Hoover lashed out at Winchell, suggesting that the columnist was playing with their relationship for ratings.

After Winchell conveyed his own frustration to the mystery caller, Buchalter acquiesced. Apparently convinced by Winchell that he had an "understanding" with the federal government to limit his sentence on narcotics charges, the Jewish mobster agreed to surrender to Hoover on the evening of August 24, 1939.

The moon was a mere sliver of light in the night sky as Hoover approached the corner of Twenty-eighth Street and Fifth Avenue in his black limousine, alone in the backseat, his driver in the front. Winchell, who had made arrangements to pick up Buchalter several blocks away, pulled up behind Hoover's car. Buchalter, looking heavier than in his photographs and sporting a mustache, joined Winchell inside Hoover's limousine, where the journalist introduced the murderer to the director of the FBI.

Though Hoover would claim in later years that he walked up to Buchalter who was standing on the street corner—the official version repeated in Don Whitehead's *The FBI Story*—and took him into custody, in truth neither man was ever alone on the street. Special agents were monitoring Hoover's every move from a distance, and Winchell was there to protect Buchalter from "itchy trigger-fingers."[14]

Later that same evening, Hoover called a press conference at FBI headquarters in Manhattan to reveal the arrest of the mass murderer. For his part, Winchell never received any credit, though he found comfort in his increased ratings. "Mr. Hoover said the FBI had managed the surrender through its own sources and that no monetary reward either had been paid or promised," reported the New York Times. "Mr. Hoover said [Buchalter] appeared 'very healthy and contented.'"[15] It might have been said that Hoover was as well, as he continued to manipulate the press.

Hoover was careful never to be photographed holding a drink or gaming at the races, his only remaining vices since he had long ago given up smoking. And while he didn't mind making fun of himself at his own expense, it was his domain alone. The slightest suggestion from anyone else that he was inefficient, ineffective, incapacitated, or effeminate was met with dramatic and swift retribution.

Such was the case when, in January 1940, Hoover made his annual appearance before the House Appropriations Subcommittee, with Tolson by his side. In addressing the FBI's role in watching over internal security, Hoover explained that his General Intelligence Division had responsibility for uncovering "espionage, sabotage, and other subversive activities, and violations of the neutrality relations." Hoover proudly outlined the division's procedure. "We have a general index, arranged alphabetically and geographically, available at the Bureau, so that in the event of any greater emergency coming to our country, we will be able to locate immediately these various persons who may need to be the subject of further investigation."[16]

The members of the subcommittee, unaware of the extent of Hoover's surveillance of citizens, reacted with cries of "Gestapo tactics" and "stampeding of civil rights." New York congressman Vito Marcantonio was particularly offended by Hoover's remarks. "By this type of testimony . . . two facts become obvious: First, we are preparing a general raid against civil rights, a blackout against the civil liberties of the American people, a system of terror by index cards such as you have in the Gestapo countries of the world; second, we are engendering a war hysteria which is a menace to the peace of the United States."[17]

Senator George Norris of Nebraska expressed his concern that the Bureau was "overstepping and overreaching the legitimate object for which it was created," adding that Hoover himself was the "greatest hound for publicity on the North American continent."[18]

That both criticisms were essentially correct only added to the intensity of Hoover's reaction. "Mr. Hoover is in agreement with me that the principles which Attorney General [Harlan] Stone laid down in 1924, when the Federal Bureau of Investigation was reorganized . . . , are sound," countered Robert Jackson, who had replaced Homer Cummings as attorney general. "And that the usefulness of the Bureau depends upon a faithful adherence to those limitations." Despite Hoover's efforts to conduct surveillance across America, Jackson added, "The Federal Bureau of Investigation will confine its activities to the investigation of violation of Federal Statutes, the collecting of evidence in cases in which the United States is or may be a party in interest, and the service of process issued by the courts."[‡19]

While Jackson was attempting to comfort with words, the FBI was taking action of its own. On February 6, 1940, several simultaneous raids netted the Bureau a dozen suspects—all alleged members of the Abraham Lincoln Brigade, a group of Americans who had fought against the Fascists during the recently ended Spanish Civil War. The 12 soldiers of fortune were photographed chained together and handcuffed as they were being taken to jail. Though the raids were authorized by way of indictments handed down by a federal grand jury, newspapers across the country voiced what they saw as unbridled persecution by the government. One editorial screamed that the country had turned into a "Gestapo that can haul citizens off to prison and court in ignominy, imposing any kind of conditions the captors wish without accountability."[20]

The *New Republic* magazine, in an editorial headlined AMERICAN OGPU,** suggested that while in other countries citizens are forced to bend to Gestapos, "in this country, Hoover has the voluntary support of all who would delight in gangster movies and ten-cent detective magazines."

---

‡ Hoover failed to mention that he already was keeping a file on Congressman Vito Marcantonio, opened August 4, 1930, and signed by C. C. Spears, the acting agent in charge of the New York City office of the Bureau. The initial report was generated when Marcantonio was a candidate for assistant U.S. attorney general in New York. By the time of his death in 1954, Marcantonio's file was nearly 1,000 pages in length.

** The Soviet OGPU was a secret police force that arrested, tortured, and murdered thousands of citizens thought to be enemies of the Communist state.

Unrepentant, Hoover flew back to Miami and his villa at the Nautilus late in February, Tolson and Hottel in tow. In a radio exclusive, Walter Winchell reported that "the Federal Bureau of Investigation G-Men swung into action at daybreak and arrested over 30 people in the Federal drive against Miami vice and white slavery. The higher-ups who will be named eventually will shock the state of Florida."[21] Winchell did not report that Hoover's agents also arrested 48 others on charges that varied from bank embezzling to impersonating a federal agent.

One who was not impressed was columnist Westbrook Pegler, who wrote for the *Chicago Daily News* and the *Washington Post,* and received the Pulitzer Prize for journalism in 1940. Pegler had a penchant for continuing to repeat the rumor that the FBI was collecting secret files on Washington politicians. Pegler wrote, "The FBI cooperates with police departments which tap wires of family telephones and even, in one incredible case . . . took photograph records and moving pictures, on suspicion, of conversations and scenes within the bedroom of husband and wife."[22] Hoover, in turn, said that Pegler was guilty of "mental halitosis."[23]

Not everyone was against Hoover's performance. Quite the opposite. Much as Democrats and Republicans seem to look at the same scenario with a different perception, so too did they respond to Hoover, normally along party lines. Hugh S. Johnson, former administrator of Roosevelt's National Recovery Administration and the Works Progress Administration, wrote in the Scripps-Howard newspapers: "This attack on such a man and his work is nothing less than obscene. Sucker commentators and sucker politicians who support this sabotage are unwittingly doing great harm. . . . If the reward for such victories over crime and corruption—such improvements in police methods everywhere—is a political smearing out from public life, then why should any cop be capable, be brave, efficient or honest?"[24] These improvements included the FBI crime laboratories Hoover had started, where fingerprint and blood evidence was analyzed along with firearms and handwriting. The labs' services were free of charge to all federal, state, and local police during the investigation of crimes.

J. Edgar Hoover had turned a small, corrupt agency within the Justice Department into a national police force that redefined the image of law enforcement around the world. The question was less about the job the FBI was doing and more a debate over whether the power being generated by its head was beneficial to the country, let alone Mr. Hoover.

It was a time in the nation's history when uncertainty flourished. The threat of war had too quickly become the reality of war, as America watched Germany attack Czechoslovakia, Poland, Britain, and France, then Denmark, Norway, Belgium, and Holland. Peace pacts were made and broken while the United States declared its neutrality and attempted to focus inward on its own economic depression.

The president was struggling with a disenchanted population that was only too eager to accept increasing handouts from the federal government, including work, Social Security, and medical treatment. For all its proclamations of "land of the free, home of the brave," America

was less a melting pot of immigrants than it was a segregated and suspicious country uncertain whom to trust—
least of all President Franklin Roosevelt.

The one man Roosevelt *did* trust, and trust implicitly,
was J. Edgar Hoover. It was not because Hoover was a personal friend of the president, although Hoover often
claimed that was the case. It was because Roosevelt
respected Hoover's ability to uncover the truth behind an
individual's behavior and maintain a cloak of absolute
secrecy in the process. There was not a single information
leak from the FBI files during the Roosevelt administration. With that assurance of confidentiality, the president
threw wide the net of authority that allowed Hoover to
grow in both influence and power, hoping in the process
to catch as many saboteurs rumored to be entering the
country as possible.

Meanwhile, Senator Norris pushed for an investigation into the practices of the FBI that had led to the arrests
of the Abraham Lincoln Brigade members in Detroit. The
attorney general ordered an internal probe headed by
Henry Schweinhaut, chief of the Civil Liberties Unit of
the Department of Justice. Though hardly an unbiased
figure, Schweinhaut conducted what was considered a
moderately thorough investigation into the apprehensions and concluded, "I am satisfied that the conduct of
the Agents is not subject to the justifiable criticism."[25]

Independently, a consortium of left-wing organizations took advantage of the growing pulse against
Hoover's publicity-laced investigations and called for his
suspension pending an extensive examination of his practices and the widely reported secret files of the FBI. An

unsigned 76-page memo titled "The Investigative Work of the FBI with Reference to Activities Based upon Economic or Political Views or Opinions" was fed to the press, and its contents were splashed liberally across newspapers nationwide.

At the same time, Rhode Island senator Theodore F. Green initiated an independent inquiry into the wiretapping practices of government agencies and various police organizations. While the FBI was not specifically targeted, Green's basis for the inquiry was Hoover's own admission that his Bureau continued to use wiretapping as a means of surveillance despite passage of a federal law in 1934 that made its use a felony.[§]

Although Attorney General Jackson immediately defended the government's need to use wiretaps "in limited cases," pointing to "kidnapping, extortion, and sabotage," he nevertheless made a surprise announcement that the practice would be discontinued, crediting the suggestion for the change of policy to Hoover himself. This did not, however, prevent Hoover from continuing to use wiretaps. He simply had to find ways to legitimately duplicate the information that the taps provided. While publicly maintaining his absolute dislike for such methods of investigation, he lobbied through the press for its return— usually through a Walter Winchell or Drew Pearson mention of how the Bureau was being hampered by the restrictions placed on it by federal law.

---

§ The Federal Communications Act of 1934, U.S.C. 605, states it is illegal for anyone who is not the intended receiver to "intercept any communication and divulge or publish the existence, contents, substance, purpose, effect, or meaning of such intercepted communication to any person."

Even when the objections of his critics were at their loudest, Hoover did not waiver from what he believed was his duty as the nation's police chief. Every day he delivered two dozen or more reports to the president on investigations into various individuals, organizations, and unions. Roosevelt, well aware that the reports represented only a small portion of the cases Hoover was investigating, made every effort to keep the FBI director in his confidence and favor.

On June 14, 1940, Roosevelt sent Hoover a letter that the director later kept displayed in his home. In it the president praised Hoover for his service to the country, adding his thanks for the "many interesting and valuable reports that you have made to me regarding the fast moving situations of the last few months. You have done and are doing a wonderful job, and I want you to know of my gratification and appreciation."[26]

For Roosevelt, it was standard praise in what was little more than a form letter. For Hoover, it was a backslap that proved his value and reinforced his resolve. In writing a response, Hoover gushed that "when the President of our country, bearing the weight of untold burdens, takes the time to so express himself to one of his Bureau heads, there is implanted in the hearts of the recipients a renewed strength and vigor to carry on their tasks."[27]

As controversy continued to mount on the FBI's famed director, he kept a muted stance, insisting that his reputation needed no defense. The only obvious change was the addition of a sign atop the console radio in Hoover's office. It was a copy of an essay titled "The Penalty of Leadership" that read in part: "In every field of human endeavor, he that

is first must perpetually live in the white light of publicity
. . . when a man's work becomes a standard for the whole
world, it also becomes a target for the shafts of the envious
few." Many thought the director had written the words
himself, so closely did he associate with the message. He
made no effort to reveal, if indeed he even knew, that the
piece was from an advertisement for Cadillac that appeared
in the January 2, 1915, issue of the *Saturday Evening Post*.
The advertisement was written by Theodore MacManus
who worked for the luxury division of General Motors.
Hoover had been sent the prose with his latest armored
limousine.[28]

As America nervously watched the world at war, its
president, increasingly concerned about spies within the
borders of the United States, put all acts of sabotage, espionage, and treason, along with violations of the Neutrality Act, under the auspices of the FBI. He also raised an
extra $3,488,000 for the Bureau's use in uncovering
"spies, sabotage and subversive agents."[29]

It was an authority that came into direct conflict with
Congressman Martin Dies of Texas, chairman of the
House Un-American Activities Committee. On the surface, it would appear that Hoover and Dies would be com-
plementary hunters after the same prey, but the Bureau's
director saw the congressman as an interloper into his
jurisdiction and set about organizing an FBI plot to discredit him.

Heading the arsenal of Hoover's top guns was special
agent Louis Burrous Nichols. The George Washington
University graduate had come to the Bureau from his position as a publicity director for the YMCA, and rose quickly

to become assistant to Clyde Tolson, and the FBI's official liaison between the press and the Bureau. He was in a perfect position to feed the media discrediting information on Dies, and advance the image of the FBI at the same time. By infiltrating Dies's committee, the Bureau was able to report on its findings well in advance of the committee's own press releases. Although Hoover's efforts amounted to little more than petty one-upmanship, that the director of the FBI had the time and tenacity to persevere in such trivial game playing outraged Dies, who began generating his own releases battering Hoover and his Bureau.

Taking his case to Roosevelt, Dies complained adamantly about Hoover's counterproductive behavior while keeping quiet about his own. To the president it was all harmless politics, but in the spirit of compromise he requested that the attorney general intervene and approve all releases from the Dies committee before publication, and allowed Dies the courtesy of receiving information from the Bureau's files.

Hoover was, in fact, enlarging his power base within the Roosevelt administration at a meteoric pace. In addition to investigating those suspected of violating federal law, as well as domestic surveillance of suspected saboteurs, Hoover became the contact for British spy William Stephenson. Stephenson was a wealthy Canadian who was named head of British Security Coordination, and headquartered in New York. Operating under the code name "Intrepid," Stephenson contacted Hoover through their mutual friend, boxer Gene Tunney, and requested Hoover's help in intercepting communications from the Germans.

It was to be a rather one-sided relationship. While Stephenson was successful in deciphering coded German messages and passed along reports to Hoover, the Americans, hoping to remain neutral during the war, were hesitant at first to reciprocate. Even so, Stephenson continued to operate successfully in America throughout the war and is generally believed to be the agent on whose life author Ian Fleming based his James Bond "007" character.

The isolationism of the United States at a time when much of Europe was being invaded and captured was not only accepted by Hoover but encouraged by him. He thought little of the British and the French, and was openly antagonistic toward Scandinavians, whom he saw as haughty and pompous. That would all change on the morning of December 7, 1941.

J. Edgar Hoover had just finished lunch—a rather heavy meal of lobster bisque and sirloin steak—in his complimentary suite at the Waldorf-Astoria, when the telephone rang. Clyde Tolson reached over, picked up the receiver, and handed the instrument to his satiated boss. Hoover received the news minutes after the president did.

As a tropical breeze blew from the south across the paradise of Hawaii, 360 Japanese warplanes attacked the U.S. Navy fleet anchored in Pearl Harbor on the island of Oahu, and the adjacent airfield at Hickam Air Force Base. Though the bombing lasted under two hours, 2,400 American lives were lost.

Speaking to the nation, President Roosevelt said gravely, "Yesterday, December 7, 1941—a date which will live in infamy—the United States of America was suddenly and deliberately attacked by naval and air forces of

the Empire of Japan." He admitted that America had been
caught off guard and unprepared. What he did not say
was that some in government placed the blame squarely
on J. Edgar Hoover.

EIGHT

A FOUNDATION
BUILT ON SAND

J. Edgar Hoover's nonstop tirade rumbled through the passenger compartment of the chartered airliner like a cannon pulled over cobblestones. Clyde Tolson, the only other occupant in the cabin, struggled to stay awake as the staccato speech droned on, the occasional high note of inflection rousing him back to the present. Hoover kept repeating himself, stressing that the president *should* have listened. That, of course, was hindsight, 2,400 deaths later.

For several years, Tolson had been hearing Hoover's complaints about the Federal Communications Commission head James Lawrence Fly. Hoover and Fly were embroiled in a running dispute over the legality of tapping coded messages sent between the United States and Japan, Italy, and Germany. Hoover was in favor, Fly was opposed. After months of wrangling, the two men were no closer to a compromise, each certain that his position was legally sound. Citing his inability to provide adequate national security coverage, Hoover asked Attorney General Robert Jackson for a proclamation written and authorized by the president overruling the FCC's authority in the decision. The proclamation was entering its final rewrite stage when the Japanese attacked Pearl Harbor and made the issue rather moot. Those complaining the loudest that Hoover had been denied proper ammunition in his fight were the same ones days earlier who had condemned his efforts.

One message that *was* passed along to the president, however, was an intercepted communication between a Japanese man named Mori in Hawaii and his uncle in Tokyo. The conversation talked of the Pacific Fleet at Pearl Harbor and the uncle questioned which flowers were currently blooming in the islands. The nephew responded: "hibiscus" and "poinsettia." From those two words Hoover deduced that this might indeed be some manner of code, since hibiscus bloomed all year long on the islands.

"It is entirely possible that the information sought in this conversation with Japan might have been a prelude to the proposed bombing of the Hawaiian Islands today," Hoover wrote General Edwin "Pa" Watson, Roosevelt's military aide and confidant, after arriving back in Washington that evening.[1] The letter, held in the collection of the Franklin Delano Roosevelt Presidential Library in Hyde Park, New York, notes that the Bureau relayed the intercepted message to the White House the evening before the attack.

"Hibiscus, hibiscus," Hoover muttered as he poured himself a double shot of 114 proof Old Grand Dad, turned on his console record player, and listened to "Red Sails in the Sunset" by Guy Lombardo. His mind drifted back to Ginger Rogers and her mother, Lela, listening intently to his stories at the Stork Club. Happier moments if not simpler days.

Though work remained his focus, liquor became his friend as he found himself unable to shake the guilt that pulled at his conscience, wondering if he could have done something to prevent the bombing. America was mobilizing for war. More soldiers and fliers and sailors would die. J. Edgar Hoover felt personally responsible for failing his country.[2]

While America was flooded with reports about potential Japanese saboteurs, Hoover silently worried about an elusive double agent named Dusko Popov, who was neither Japanese nor anti-American. Born in Yugoslavia to wealthy industrialist parents, Popov made a lifestyle of gambling, women, and adventure as he traveled around the world in pursuit of pleasure. His playboy image worked well as a cover when, during World War II, he was approached to work for the Abwehr, Germany's intelligence unit. Popov's assignment: retrieve classified information from the British.

Liking Nazis even less than he did war, Popov reported the contact to British intelligence, who in turn recruited the playboy as a spy against Germany. Despite the life-and-death nature of his double-agent persona, Popov remained seemingly aloof to any potential peril, even after the Germans sent him to the United States armed with a questionnaire about various aspects of the American military buildup.

The questionnaire, which Popov had previously shown to the British, was hidden on a microdot via new German technology, and curiously included a list of inquiries about Pearl Harbor. Soon after Popov arrived in New York in mid-August 1941, he reported to the FBI where he met with "E.J." Connelley of Alvin Karpis fame and revealed what he felt were vital clues to a future attack on America. More impressed by the microdot technology than the actual details of the questionnaire, Connelley and SAC Sam Foxworth referred the entire matter to Hoover's personal attention. That Hoover was unavailable was hardly surprising. It was, after all, mid-August and, as he had done the previous three years, Hoover was on a "working" vacation in Del Mar, California, home of the Del Mar Turf Club.

By the time Hoover returned to Washington and then to New York, Popov had settled into a penthouse apartment on Park Avenue and was entertaining French actress Simone Simon, who had just completed the film *The Devil and Daniel Webster*. Upon hearing of Popov's playboy antics, Hoover dismissed the man as something of a joke, agreeing to see him only after receiving word from British intelligence concerning the microdot.

Popov, writing about the incident in his memoir, said Hoover was rude and aggressive during their first encounter. "There was no introduction, no preliminaries, no politesse," Popov wrote. "I walked into Foxworth's office, and there was Hoover sitting behind the desk looking like a sledgehammer in search of an anvil. Foxworth, dispossessed, was sitting silently in an armchair alongside.

"'Sit down, Popov,' Hoover yelped at me, and the expression of disgust on his face indicated that I was the equivalent of a fresh dog turd which had had the audacity of placing itself beneath his polished brogans."[3]

Hoover's voice was loud, his words clipped and as strained as the vein bulging down the side of his neck. "'I'm running the cleanest police organization in the world,' Hoover ranted. 'You come here from nowhere and within six weeks install yourself in a Park Avenue penthouse, chase film stars . . . and try to corrupt my officers. I'm telling you right now, I won't stand for it.' He pounded the desk with his fist as though to nail the words into my brain," Popov wrote some 30 years later, the moment still fresh, the humiliation just as stinging.[4]

There was more pounding and raging, as he labeled Popov a "bogus spy" and a playboy with unrepentant sexual fervor. This from the mouth of the man who "was the person responsible for the disaster of Pearl Harbor."[5] At least if one can believe Dusko Popov.

Yet, according to Bureau files, although Hoover did not trust Popov, he did follow through on the information supplied by the spy, passing it along not only to Naval Intelligence but to President Roosevelt as well. Again, however, the interest was in the microdot technology. Hoover sent a memo to "Pa" Watson on September 4, 1941, enthused by the potential of the microdot, and later wrote that the spyware had been discovered by a Bureau technician working in the crime laboratory.[6]

Now, in light of Pearl Harbor, Hoover thought back to the microdot and the obnoxious playboy who delivered it, not knowing who Popov told of his treatment at the hands of the FBI and its chief. Moving to deflect blame and reinforce his position, Hoover reminded White House Press Secretary Stephen Early of the Mori message and its hibiscus clue, noting in a memo that "the Office of Naval Intelligence scoffed at the significance of the message." Hoover reiterated that the message was considered of such importance by the SAC at the FBI's Honolulu office that he "called an officer from his home, seven miles away, to come to his office for a copy of the Dr. Mori conversation."[7]

The president, who was under increasing pressure to do something about the "Japanese threat," placed Hoover in charge of censorship of the press, giving him the authority to forbid publication or broadcast of information considered "damaging to the war effort of the United States." Even this endorsement did not free Hoover from his sense of culpability or reduce his late-night drinking, which continued through Christmas. Hoover's worry was that Supreme Court Justice Owen Roberts, whom Roosevelt had placed in charge of assigning responsibility for Pearl Harbor, was taking direct aim at him and the Bureau he held so dear.

On December 29, John O'Donnell, writing his Capitol Stuff column in the McCormick chain of newspapers, spun fragments of truth into a public attack on the director. Upon reading it, Hoover instantly became nauseous and hurriedly left his office, buffering himself against the world in his Thirtieth Place NW home and refusing all calls, even from Tolson.

"The nation's super Dick Tracy, FBI Director J. Edgar Hoover, is directly under the gun," O'Donnell wrote, suggesting that direct blame for Pearl Harbor was "in Hoover's lap." Drawing readers further into the plot, O'Donnell added that "long-time Capitol Hill foes of FBI Chief Hoover have been whetting up their snickersnees [large knives], itching to take a crack at the detective hero as far back as the days of kidnappers and gangsters. Leaders are holding them back with the promise that the report of the Roberts Board of Inquiry will provide the ammunition for an all-out drive to oust Hoover from his seat of tremendous power."[8]

As word reached the White House concerning Hoover's erratic behavior, the president asked Press Secretary Stephen Early to call the Bureau's director and relay Roosevelt's continued faith in his competence. It was an unusual break from protocol given that no government official or study had placed Hoover publicly in the crosshairs of responsibility. Even more amazing is that, sources suggest, when the call from the White House came, Hoover believed it was to request his resignation.[9]

The psychological lift that Hoover received from Early's call cannot be overstated, so fragile were his emotions and stability at the time. His relief at the reaffirmation of his importance to the administration can be tangibly felt in the note Hoover sent in response.

> You do not know how much I appreciate your call today and the message you gave me. Please thank the President for me. To think that with all his cares and responsibilities he could think of such a matter is just another evidence of his great heart and understanding. I am deeply touched.[10]

Hoover immediately plunged himself into defending America's war effort while increasing the pressure on FCC head James Fly to release fingerprints of radio operators in the United States. Hoover was joined in this demand by Attorney General Francis Biddle, who had replaced Robert Jackson after Jackson was appointed by Roosevelt to the U.S. Supreme Court. Though Fly was still adamantly opposed to releasing any fingerprints to Hoover, Biddle was persistent. "The situation has materially changed," he wrote Fly on January 2, 1942. "The evidence is strong that messages have been surreptitiously transmitted to our enemies by radio, and that military attacks upon the territory of this country may have been furthered and facilitated thereby. . . . Please think this over; I should hate to have something serious happen which might have been so easily avoided."[11]

Fly eventually acquiesced and sent Hoover all the fingerprints from FCC records. They became a permanent part of the Bureau's files and were continuously checked against known subversives. Yet as unwavering as Hoover was in his determination to gain access to the FCC files, he refused to give his blessing to the president's wholesale roundup of Japanese Americans. On February 19, 1942, Roosevelt signed Executive Order No. 9066, which allowed people of Japanese ancestry—the majority of whom were U.S. citizens—to be forced to move into so-called relocation centers hastily constructed in remote areas in western and southern states.

Names such as Gila River, Heart Mountain, Manzanar, and Tule Lake were colorful camouflage for the reality of life inside tar-paper barracks behind barbed-wire fences. U.S citizens were pulled from their homes at gunpoint and crowded into huts with several other families, where they remained through the war years. Concentration camps for Asians, Hoover called them, and he was outraged not because Roosevelt had issued the order or that Japanese Americans were the targets, but because he felt the camps were unnecessary. Hoover was certain that the FBI had already captured any spies within U.S. borders. He indicated so in a memo to the attorney general, also addressing the pressure on the governor and attorney general of California—the state nearest to Hawaii.

> The necessity for mass evacuation is based primarily upon public and political pressure rather than on factual data. Public hysteria and, in some instances, the comments of the press, and radio announcers, have resulted in a tremendous amount of pressure being brought to bear on Governor [Culburt] Olson and Earl Warren, Attorney General of the State [of California], and on the military authorities. It is interesting to observe that little mention has been made of the mass evacuation of enemy aliens.[12]

Even as much of America was caught up in a surge of animosity toward the Japanese and Japanese Americans, Hoover was typically self-absorbed, nervously waiting for the report from Justice Owen Roberts on who would receive official blame for the military defeat at Pearl Harbor. After extensive hearings, ones at which Hoover never testified, Roberts determined that responsibility lay with the military—specifically Admiral Husband E. Kimmel and General Walter C. Short, the commanders in charge at Pearl Harbor. The FBI was absolved of any wrongdoing.

The relief of the decision manifested itself in a rather peculiar way within the halls of the Bureau. Hoover took umbrage to the fact that neither Roberts nor Roosevelt paid homage to the Bureau's apprehension of hundreds of Japanese aliens who were considered spies and saboteurs. Instead of sharing the pride of accomplishment with his agents, Hoover pressured them to perform even better, galvanizing those in the field to increase wiretapping and enlarge undercover operations inside the relocation camps.

As the first American soldiers were deployed into the European theater of operations, Hoover returned to the familiar halls of the Roosevelt White House, where the president was under fire from a different foe far removed from anything German or Japanese. The aggressor came in the person of William Christian Bullitt, former ambassador to France, who had come upon some information about Undersecretary of State Sumner Welles and was threatening to release it to the press.

Having been a child of privilege, Welles was a longtime friend of Roosevelt and his wife, Eleanor, and was a page at their wedding, carrying the bride's train as she walked down the aisle. A brilliant strategist and accomplished politician, Welles apparently had a secret sexual fantasy that involved oral sex with black males—a desire he managed to keep hidden under the guise of a happy marriage until 1940.

In September of that year, Welles accompanied the vice president, cabinet heads, senators, and congressmen to the Alabama funeral of William Bankhead, Speaker of the House and father of actress Tallulah Bankhead. On the train ride home, Welles joined the other politicians in consuming copious amounts of liquor. Thus lubricated, Welles escaped to his stateroom, where he proceeded to ring for a procession of black porters, proposing that each expose himself to some serious lovemaking.

The porters, after rebuffing Welles's overtures, relayed the story to the train's engineer, who in turn passed the word to Ernest E. Norris, president of Southern Railway-

Company. Norris instructed his porters to forget the incident, but several spread the story that eventually made it to the desk of William Bullitt. Bullitt, who coveted Welles's position, passed the rumor along to the president, demanding that the undersecretary be asked to resign.

Roosevelt, who had long held the theory that anything a man did while drinking was forgivable, scoffed at Bullitt's efforts to discredit Welles, all the while taking the discreet precaution to place Hoover on the scent to uncover what he could about the incident, which under Virginia law was a felony if proven true. Hoover assigned the case to Edward A. Tamm, who delivered his report three weeks later after interviewing many of those involved—Welles excluded.

Hoover wrote a memo to the president on January 26, 1941, in which he confirmed that Welles indeed had "propositioned a number of train crew to have immoral relations with them" but that only one porter, a man named Stone, had been "directly" propositioned and had died two weeks before the investigation was started.[13] Hoover added several provocative asides, including the knowledge that Welles had a similar "problem" while serving as the ambassador to Cuba years earlier. Hoover also mentioned a train trip to Cleveland that had taken place two weeks before the incident being investigated, in which a comparable "situation" had developed between Welles and several "colored" porters.

Hoover deemed the problem more mental than physical, which apparently made it worthy of dismissal. In light of the presumed likelihood of a similar situation occurring, however, Hoover suggested that the president assign a "bodyguard" to watch over Welles on his trips—someone "older and with a history of discretion."

This was, in fact, what Roosevelt did, forgetting about the incident for over a year. Caught up in the war effort, the president was actually amazed when, in mid-1942, Bullitt raised the issue again, this time to Welles's boss, Secretary of State Cordell Hull. Even without scandal, Hull had many issues with his undersecretary. In his seventies and with a propensity to ponder, Hull did not understand the quick-thinking-and-acting Welles, with his 48-year-old energy and seeming limitless power to regenerate. Moreover, Hull was jealous of Welles's close relationship with the president, who often bypassed the secretary of state when Welles was available.

Upon hearing the charges lodged against his ultraconservative and cultured assistant, Hull placed his own call to Hoover, requesting his help. The director, seeing no particular advantage in cooperating with Hull, refused to share what information he had on the incident, claiming he had passed the entire file on to the president's secretary, Marvin McIntyre. That Hoover had his own copy on his nightstand in his private bedroom was hardly information he cared to share.

By sidestepping Hull, Hoover managed to posture and deflect scandal—a balancing act he performed well and often during the Roosevelt administration. The president, of course, was quite aware of much of Hoover's game-playing, as well as his need to lay claim to other's triumphs and capitalize on their weaknesses. Certainly such was the case when, in June 1942, a German U-boat came within 200 feet of a beach off Amagansett, on Long Island, New York, and off-loaded four saboteurs on American soil in what was to be the most unusual invasion in World War II.

Deep fog poured across the sound, thick as porridge and just as bland. Twenty-one-year-old John Cullen, Coast Guard seaman second class,was used to the fog. He saw it nearly every night and heard the familiar moan of horns signaling to lost ships to keep away. He liked the predictability of his watch. He looked forward to it: the cold, moist air blowing off the coast, the taste of salt, the lap of waves against an invisible shore.

This night, however, would be different for John Cullen, seaman second class. As the muted beam of his flashlight sliced ineffectively through the dense night air, he caught sight of a man struggling onto the shore. Then another. And then two more.

Unarmed and uncertain, he approached the men, yelling for them to identify themselves. The oldest of the group—not yet 40, Cullen judged—came up to him, flashed big teeth stained with tobacco or too much booze, and claimed to be a fisherman.

"Our boat ran aground and we're going to wait here until daylight," the man told Cullen, who looked down at the man's hands.

Not the hands of a fisherman, Cullen thought. Nervous now, he felt a burn plumb his chest and settle inside his stomach. Playing for time, he suggested that the men accompany him to the Coast Guard station to wait until daybreak, his mind flushed with scenarios, none having a happy ending.[14]

The four men were reluctant to move away from the shore, not knowing what to say. Cullen, caught between panic and heroism, held his ground, waiting, counting his heartbeats, watching the fingers on the fisherman's hands. Suddenly, one of the men broke the silence, speaking in German. The older man slapped his hand over the other's mouth, shouting for his partner to be quiet. He quickly turned back to Cullen, suddenly desperate and agitated.

"Now listen," the man said in English "I don't want to kill you. You don't know what this is all about. Why don't you forget it? Here is some money. Go out and have yourself a good time." Astonished, Cullen pushed away the fist gripping a wad of cash and stepped backward, prepared to defend himself. "Look in my eyes! Look in my eyes!" the man continued, shoving the bills into the seaman's hand. "Would you know me if you ever saw me again?"

For a few seconds Cullen said nothing, then calmly answered. "I have never seen you before." He took the money and started running back toward the Coast Guard station.[15]

He turned to look again at the shore, but the men were lost in the thick mystery of fog. Later, as he searched with his crewmen for evidence of the foreigners, there was no sign of anything even slightly suspicious. It took until daybreak for the Coast Guard to find the buried German uniforms and ammunition that the men had left behind.

By the time the incident was reported to the FBI the following day around lunchtime, 12 hours had passed since the saboteurs had touched U.S. soil. Hoover met the news with stifled histrionics, quickly laying the blame on inaction by the Coast Guard and promising to hunt down the four men. Other than the contents of the boxes found buried on the beach, however, Hoover had no clues.

The four Germans had used the intervening time to split up into pairs. Their leader, 39-year-old George Dasch, and his partner, 35-year-old Ernest Burger, found their way to a room at Manhattan's Hotel Martinique on Broadway at Thirty-second Street. The Beaux Arts landmark, designed by Henry J. Hardenbergh of Plaza Hotel fame, was opulent and expensive. The luxurious surroundings did little to comfort Dasch, who was having reservations about performing feats of derring-do for the Germans when his loyalties were really with the United States, a country he had called home for the previous 20 years. As Dasch nervously announced his intention to turn himself in to the FBI, Burger joined him in professing allegiance to America.

Unfortunately, while Dasch's motives may have been pure when he took a train to Washington and walked into the offices of the Department of Justice armed with a suitcase full of cash, his story of submarines and late-night landings did not impress FBI Assistant Director D. Milton "Mickey" Ladd, head of the Bureau's Domestic Intelligence Division. Even though Hoover had placed his entire organization on high alert and Ladd was in charge of tracking saboteurs, he dismissed Dasch's story as the invention of a mentally unbalanced publicity hound, and promptly ordered the foreigner to leave.

Impulsively, Dasch opened the suitcase and spilled forth $84,000 in hundreds and fifties across the special agent's mahogany desk. That one move was all that prevented him from being escorted out of FBI headquarters and thrown back into the frontiers of Washington. As it was, when Hoover learned of the story and saw the cash, Dasch was immediately taken into custody and interrogated for the next seven days.

According to Dasch, his group of saboteurs was the first of many to be sent to America by Hitler to destroy "key railroad installations, aluminum factories, power plants, bridges and canal locks, plus targets of opportunity, such as Jewish-owned department stores, that could create public panic."[16] While Dasch was busy revealing classified information about German U-boats, spies, codes, and operations, as well as another submarine drop that already had taken place in Florida, Hoover assembled a team to connect the dots that Dasch had drawn and reap the glory.

On June 20, a week after the Germans had breached the shores of the United States, special agents of the FBI arrested Burger and the two other members of Dasch's group. In another seven days, they had arrested the four saboteurs from the Florida drop in New York and Chicago, having tracked them from their point of entry just south of Jacksonville.

Hoover wasted no time in taking credit for the apprehensions, eliminating Dasch's surrender and information completely from the official record. According to memos Hoover sent to Roosevelt, he assumed control of the investigation into the German submarine landing on June 14, coordinated the arrest of Burger and his two cohorts in New York on June 20, arrested Dasch in New York two days later, and had the remaining men in custody by June 27. Though more than a dozen FBI special agents knew that Dasch was in custody in Washington four days before his "arrest" in New York, no one stepped forward to correct Hoover's version of the truth.[17]

Lewis Wood, writing in the *New York Times,* suggested that "the rapid and effective action of the G-men in seizing the Germans almost as they landed on the sandy beaches gave a feeling of comfort and security. Men and women felt satisfaction and confidence that the government was infinitely better prepared to cope with spies and saboteurs than during the last war."[18]

Hoover was lionized for his efficiency and dedication in preventing what might have been the initial steps of an elaborate scheme to sabotage American businesses and ports by German agents. A public campaign was launched to award the director of the FBI the Congressional Medal of Honor. Not everyone was in agreement, however, that Hoover had shown wisdom in announcing the captures. In a declassified memo to Secretary of War Henry Stimson from Major General George V. Strong, the militarist made the point that "the premature breaking of the story had wreaked our plans for seizing two additional groups of four men each who are apparently scheduled to land on our shores in August."[19]

Major General Strong not withstanding, the campaign to canonize Hoover actually made it to the Senate Judiciary Committee, which recommended that an "appropriate medal" be awarded. Even his enemies had to admit that Hoover had been effective in squashing the infiltration of enemy agents, having sent a direct message to the Germans that the American shores were impenetrable. That he was helped by a secret confession and surrender was counted by Hoover as the luck that plays into events in wartime.

Dasch and company did not share in that luck. The eight men were secretly placed on trial after Roosevelt issued a military order on July 2, 1942, that called for a commission to try the Germans for "offenses against the Law of War and the Articles of War." Further he stated that the "commission shall have power to . . . make such rules for the conduct of the proceedings."[20]

The trial, held in the seclusion of the Department of Justice building, made up its rules as it went, without the benefit of press coverage or independent overseers. It ended with a guilty verdict and a death sentence for all eight men. By the time the outcome of the trial was announced on August 8, 1942, six of the men already had been executed in the electric chair. Only Dasch and Burger were given presidential pardons, and their sentences reduced to confinement at hard labor.*

In 1959, Dasch wrote a book titled *Eight Spies Against America,* in which he told of Hoover's promise that if he stood trial with his co-conspirators to bluff the Germans, he would be subsequently released in secret and provided with a new identity. Once the trial was over and it became evident to Dasch that he was going to spend at least thirty years at hard labor, he looked at the Bureau's director and said, "Mr. Hoover, aren't you really ashamed of yourself?"

---

* Dasch and Burger eventually were deported in 1948 after President Harry S. Truman granted them executive clemency. Dasch returned to Germany, where he was labeled a traitor by the Germans. Despite repeated unsuccessful attempts to reenter the United States, he died alone in Germany in 1991.

ing Dickerson Hoover and his new bride, Annie.

Cadet captain Hoover at the age of sixteen.

John Edgar Hoover at four years of age.

Poised for greatness, new Bureau director J. Edgar Hoover at his desk, December 22, 1924.

Dickerson Hoover suffered from mental illness during the later years of his life.

Annie Hoover lived with her youngest son she died.

ney general A. Mitchell Palmer gave Hoover his first taste of power.

en of the Reds" Emma Goldman in 1917.

MR. HOOVER
DIRECTOR

MR. MOHR
ASSISTANT TO THE DIRECTOR

MR. TOLSON
ASSOCIATE DIRECTOR

MR. DE LOACH
ASSISTANT TO THE DIRECTOR

MR. ROSEN
ASSISTANT DIRECTOR

MR. TROTTER
ASSISTANT DIRECTOR

MR. CALLAHAN
ASSISTANT DIRECTOR

MR. CONRAD
ASSISTANT DIRECTOR

MR. TAVE
ASSISTANT DIR

MR. SULLIVAN
ASSISTANT DIRECTOR

MR. CASPER
ASSISTANT DIRECTOR

MR. GALE
ASSISTANT DIRECTOR

MR. FELT
ASSISTANT DIRECTOR

MR. WICH
ASSISTANT DIR

The FBI hierarchy in 1965.

Actors Dave Vine, Ella Logan, and Jerry Goff in a publicity photograph with John Edgar Hoover, at York's Fox Theater, December 12, 1935.

March 25, 1958, J. Edgar Hoover presented to Helen Gandy, Executive Assistant to the Director, a
h and a plaque bearing her four Service Award Keys in honor of her 40 years of faithful and
ted service to the FBI. With Miss Gandy and the Director at the presentation were the intermediate
of the Director's office. Left to right: W. Samuel Noisette, Johnnie L. Knight, Jr.; Worthington
h; Inspector Frank C. Hollowman; James E. Crawford; Miss Gandy; Maurice G. Anthony; Director
ver; John W. Dalseg; Teresa L. Cuddy; Edna M. Holmes; and Hessie B. Bannon

thy Lamour and J. Edgar Hoover at The Preakness, 1946.

Though insisting that his special agents remain trim, FBI Director Hoover was overweight most of his life (pictured here circa 1950).

e Tolson and Hoover at the Laurel, Maryland horse races, October 8, 1937.

e A. Tolson, J. Edgar Hoover, Guy Hottel and friends in a rare photo of Hoover at play.

Hoover was assigned to head the investigation into the assassination of John F. Kennedy by Preside
Lyndon B. Johnson.

Martin Luther King Jr. arrives at the Federal Bureau of Investigation to meet Hoover. The FBI directo
had labeled King the "most notorious liar" in America.

An FBI agent walking nearby struck me on the face, sending me sprawling to the floor. One of the army guards helped me to my feet, and through the tears brought on by the hot sting of the agent's hand, I saw the Chief disappear down the hall, seemingly surrounded by an impregnable wall of justice and strength.[21]

If Hoover had any second thoughts, they were lost in his rush to take a two-week holiday: his annual trip west to Del Mar where he spent his days at the horse races and his evenings in the company of such stars as Lucille Ball and Desi Arnaz, Bing Crosby, and Jimmy Durante, all of whom were unaware that Hoover had FBI files on each of them. Midway through the vacation, on August 16, the hotel management was notified of a ruckus in Hoover's suite. The sound of dishes breaking mixed with shouts as the director vented his anger at Clyde Tolson over some apparent slight. At one point in the melodrama, Tolson left the suite, slamming the door in evident high dudgeon, according to the hotel staff.

Returning to Washington, Tolson telephoned that he had taken ill on the trip and was absent from work for an additional nine days. According to FBI sources, Tolson was nursing a black eye and bruised lip, compliments of a well-flung ashtray. Hoover remained in Del Mar, limiting his official business to a single half-day trip to the Bureau's office in San Diego. The purpose of the visit was to discuss a radical named Joseph Lash and his relationship with the country's First Lady, Eleanor Roosevelt.

Hoover's relationship with Eleanor Roosevelt was best described as arm's-length distrust. He was at odds with her friendship with blacks, Communists, homosexuals, and others he grouped under the label "bohemian filth." Among them was Joseph Lash.

Lash was an outspoken, charismatic radical who, at age 30, met the First Lady when he testified before the House Un-American Activities Committee investigating the Communist infiltration of the American Youth Congress (AYC). It was the start of a lifelong friendship that attracted the raised eyebrow of Hoover. He saw in their continuing correspondence and liaisons the foundation of intrigue.

To investigate Mrs. Roosevelt required new procedures to be installed at the Bureau—procedures that were anything but legal and certainly unprecedented. In January 1942, Hoover authorized what later became known as "black bag" jobs, assignments that included surreptitious break-ins, burglaries, and surveillance.

The first such job was a break-in at AYC offices by FBI agents, who subsequently photographed letters written by the First Lady to AYC officials. Although no copies remain of the letters themselves, the assignment was referenced in a memo sent to the director from Assistant Director D. Milton Ladd, who listed the correspondence under the heading "Do Not File"—a new category in Hoover's filing system identifying high-security items not to be placed in the central file.

Reference is made to your request that the attached correspondence [of Eleanor Roosevelt],[†] made available by

---

† Blacked out by the FBI in accordance with the parameters allowed by the Freedom of Information Act.

[FBI assistant director] P. E. Foxworth and obtained from the offices of the American Youth Congress in New York City, be reviewed and analyzed. . . . Correspondence contained therein was reviewed and the pertinent information set forth in a blue ["Do Not File"] memorandum transmitted to your office with the developed photographs and the roll of negatives for whatever disposition deemed advisable.[22]

As it happened, Hoover's Bureau was not the only government division conducting illegal break-ins. The U.S. War Department had had its own clandestine organization in operation since 1917—the Military Intelligence Division (MID). Hoover routinely made use of information gathered by the MID, particularly where it concerned Mrs. Roosevelt, who was being watched overtly by the Secret Service and covertly by the MID—a group that also was keeping track of the activities of Joseph Lash.

Their task was simplified in March 1943, when Eleanor Roosevelt traveled to Chicago, and checked into the Blackstone Hotel on South Michigan Avenue. According to a report submitted by FBI liaison agent George Burton to Assistant Director Ladd some nine months later, microphone bugs placed inside the First Lady's suite recorded her having intercourse with the young and rebellious Lash. Burton claimed that the White House "by some means" heard about the clandestine recording and called MID head General George Strong and Colonel Leslie Forney, head of the Army Counterintelligence Corps., for an immediate meeting with the president.

When they reached the White House, they were received by the President, General ["Pa"] Watson and Harry Hopkins [federal administrator and presidential adviser] and were ordered to produce the entire records in this case. Colonel Forney stated . . . that this was extremely embarrassing as the material contained a recording of the entire proceedings between Lash and Mrs. Roosevelt which had been planted in the [Blackstone] hotel room. This recording indicated quite clearly that Mrs. Roosevelt and Lash engaged in sexual intercourse during their stay in the hotel room. . . . After this record was played, Mrs. Roosevelt was called into the conference and was confronted with the information and this resulted in a terrific fight between the President and Mrs. Roosevelt. At approximately 5 A.M. the next morning, the President called for General [Hap] Arnold, Chief of the Army Air Corps, and upon his arrival at the conference, ordered him to have Lash outside the United States and on his way to a combat post within ten hours.[23]

The memo is astonishing on two fronts. First, J. Edgar Hoover believed its contents, including the existence of the salacious recording, and marked the correspondence for placement in his "Do Not File" folders. Second, none of the events ever took place.

Although Mrs. Roosevelt did meet Lash in Chicago, they had dinner together and nothing more. The First Lady's secretary, Tommy Thompson, was present the entire time. Moreover, the president made a point during his administration to remain undemonstrative in front of his staff about personal affairs, and would not have confronted his wife with an audience. Lash, then an Army Air Force recruit stationed in Urbana, Illinois, was reassigned a month after his rendezvous with the First Lady, but it was to a weather station in New Caledonia in the South Pacific, not to a combat post, based primarily on doubts of his ability to perform in a military capacity due to his radical beliefs.

When Mrs. Roosevelt heard about the surveillance from the hotel staff, she complained to her husband, who agreed that the MID might have better ways to utilize its time than monitoring the wife of the president of the United States. Mrs. Rossevelt, however, did not stop arranging rendezvous with the student radical. Not only did the First Lady find Lash extremely bright and intellectually stimulating, but she also used him as a sounding board for her speeches and efforts to involve the youth of America in politics. Mrs. Roosevelt also took a turn at playing Cupid, arranging for Lash to meet secretly with Trude Pratt, a married teacher with whom Lash actually *was* having an affair. For the First Lady, it was apparently an enjoyable diversion from the seriousness of the war effort. Letters in her FBI file convey a sense of affection for the two lovers, who eventually married after Pratt's divorce.[‡]

Such was Hoover's love of gossip that he frequently took portions of the First Lady's "Official and Confidential"

---

‡ Ultimately, Lash was approached to write a biography of FDR and Eleanor Roosevelt after their deaths by their son Elliott. The resulting book, *Eleanor and Franklin,* was awarded the Pulitzer Prize for biography in 1972.

FBI file home to reread speculative reports on her rumored lesbian relationship with Lorena Hickok, the Associated Press reporter assigned to the White House. The First Lady had met Lorena shortly before entering the White House and continued a correspondence with her long after she left the Executive Mansion. "Hick," as Eleanor dubbed her, was under surveillance for much of the time Roosevelt was in office, and letters Hickok wrote the First Lady left little doubt that theirs was more than a passing professional relationship.

"Only eight more days," Lorena wrote in one letter. "Funny how even the dearest face will fade away in time. Most clearly I remember your eyes, with a kind of teasing smile in them, and the feeling of that soft spot just northeast of the corner of your mouth against my lips." It was an image that made Hoover convulse with laughter: "Horse Face" and "Bat Breath"—his nicknames for Eleanor and Lorena—embracing in the Rose Garden, Lorena having moved into the White House as a resident in 1940 to be closer to the president's wife.

It was a compassionate friendship that gave Eleanor comfort when many conservatives in the United States took umbrage at her flagrant associations with an assortment of people Hoover deemed "society's muck." Unlike the strong, independent, assertive spokeswoman who championed youth, radicals, and the poor, the Eleanor revealed in her letters had an almost fragile, childlike vulnerability that reached out for affection. Her run-on sentences did not reflect the precision she demonstrated in other parts of her life; her security was undiminished by her words of love. "Hick darling," the First Lady wrote,

"Oh! How good it was to hear your voice, it was so inadequate to try & tell you what it meant, Jimmy[§] was near & I couldn't say *je t'aime et je t'adore*[**] as I longed to do but always remember I am saying it & that I go to sleep thinking of you & repeating our little saying."[24]

The First Lady's relationships aside, Hoover continued to inundate the White House with memos about an anticipated influx of saboteurs, nonexistent Communist infiltrators, and unexplained press leaks from within the Executive Mansion. Having spent nearly 20 years building the Bureau, fighting corruption and delivering justice, Hoover still found that he needed to prove his worth—now more than ever. The president seemed intent on expanding the scope of intelligence analysis, particularly overseas, and talked about appointing a bureaucrat to administrate the various units. Hoover's name was not on the short list of candidates; in fact, he was yet again rumored to be targeted for replacement. Feeding Hoover's fears of forced retirement was the president's open discussions with William Joseph "Wild Bill" Donovan, the onetime assistant attorney general under Harlan Stone and Hoover's first administrator when he took control of the Bureau of Investigation in 1924. Roosevelt thought Donovan an ideal candidate to form an international counterintelligence division to complement the FBI's homeland security. FDR saw it as a coordinated effort; Hoover labeled it competition.

---

§ Oldest son James Roosevelt was 26 at the time.

** I love and adore you.

In many ways, Donovan was the perfect choice, if only because he was everything Hoover was not. Donovan traveled extensively around the world; Hoover's trip to Cuba and Puerto Rico was his only time off American soil. Donovan was a decorated war hero, ultimately rising to the rank of major general in the army; Hoover had chosen not to enlist. Donovan followed his military training, delegating assignments throughout the ranks of his organization; Hoover centralized control in his own hands, assigning tasks based on personal relationships. And while Donovan believed in fact-based investigations, Hoover relied on rumor and speculation. Yes, Hoover was worried about being replaced; and he, alone, knew all the valid reasons.

Internationally, the concept of intelligence traditionally had been the responsibility of ambassadors who had no training in the spy game. Information that came back to the United States was funneled to various committees from which it might or might not be forwarded to the White House. Information from foreign embassies generally was not shared with the FBI, who in turn did not make its files available to anyone but the attorney general.

Roosevelt named Donovan coordinator of information, reporting directly to the White House, with responsibility to "collect and analyze all information and data, which may bear upon national security, to correlate such information and date, and to make such information and date available to the President."

Traveling extensively, Donovan spoke to ambassadors in dozens of foreign countries, utilizing information their embassies uncovered to fill a pipeline with methodically prepared studies filtered directly to the president. By comparison, Hoover's own memos, far more numerous in number, were replete with often unproven allegations, a hodgepodge of fictionalized truths laced with often uncorroborated facts.

Impressed by Donovan's tenacity and organizational skills, Roosevelt expanded his responsibilities through the creation of the Office of Strategic Services (OSS) in July 1942, appointing Donovan as its first director. Within months, the new director had organized a team of more than 15,000 operatives, who spoke French, Italian, German, and Japanese.

The OSS had been successful in a series of break-ins at foreign embassies, an illegal operation to photograph vital paperwork and confidential codes. In particular, the Spanish embassy in Washington was targeted by Donovan, for it contained a mother lode of poorly guarded information. In successive months—July, August, and September 1942—Donovan's agents broke into the embassy three times, rifling through its safe for the maritime codes held within. Roosevelt was generous with his praise and appreciation for Donovan's performance and made little effort to hide his adulation from the director of the FBI. For days Hoover pouted, sharpening his frayed nerves on Tolson's back and threatening retaliation. He had only days to wait.

When Donovan ordered his agents to climb the walls of the Spanish embassy for a fourth time in early October, Hoover obviously had his ear to the ground. Even as the operatives were quietly cracking the safe inside the office of the Spanish ambassador, the FBI was moving into place. Not quietly or with finesse. No, this operation was meant to be seen, and Hoover had the sirens blaring, lights flashing, and press on the scene—all the better to create a circus atmosphere geared toward one purpose: the humiliation of William Joseph Donovan.

The Bureau director claimed total innocence when Donovan later labeled the act "near treason." The FBI, having arrested the OSS operatives and confiscated the Spanish code ciphers, refused to release the men until Donovan himself appeared before Hoover and took personal responsibility for the operation. Hoover refused to turn over the cipher data except to the MID, and only then at the request of the president.

The move was classic Hoover: obvious in its manipulation but always with the good of the country at the core. It was a triumph of major magnitude that quickened Hoover's step and broadened his smile. For the remainder of his life, Donovan never forgave the director of the FBI. The OSS would die with the end of World War II, eventually mutating into the Central Intelligence Agency. By then Roosevelt would be dead as well, the victim of a cerebral hemorrhage.

With less emotion than that with which one replaces a burned-out bulb, Hoover cleared his desk of Roosevelt material, his "great heart and understanding" no longer relevant. Gone were the files on the president's romances—reports of trysts with his cousin Margaret Suckley; his wife's social secretary, Lucy Mercer (later Rutherfurd); and Marguerite "Missy" LeHand, who was willed half of Roosevelt's $3 million estate—all now secured under the heading "Official and Confidential."

Gone too were the files on Sumner Welles, whom Hoover made certain Roosevelt forced into retirement in 1943. "A strange one," Hoover maintained.

Yet the Welles file was not placed with the stored material on Roosevelt. No "Official and Confidential" here. For Welles, Hoover had a special spot buried deep within the "Personal and Confidential" files, maintained by Helen Gandy. There he placed his most secret documents, the ones he found such fascinating reading, during solitary evenings in his bedroom, sealed against light and prying eyes.

Deviant behavior provided endless fodder for the insatiably curious Bureau director. What he could not or would not do in his own life, he read about in others. The secret files began with Welles, handsome, brilliant, and misunderstood. There were notes about Gustave, Welles's bisexual valet, who, when drunk, had a penchant for chasing scullery maids about the kitchen brandishing a butcher knife and screaming obscenities. There were stories of Welles's own escapades, including the Christmas he nearly froze to death, having stumbled into an icy stream where he was rumored to have followed a black workman on his property.[25] And there was Hoover's personal favorite, the report on Welles appearing drunk in an exclusive hotel just off the Champs-Elysées, in the company of a pair of male prostitutes.

Writer Truman Capote, himself a fan of the transgressed, wrote about the incident in his final book, *Answered Prayers*:

> It was after midnight in Paris in the bar of the Boeuf-sur-le-Toit, when he was sitting at a pink-clothed table

with three men, two of them expensive tarts, Corsican pirates in British flannel, and the third none other than Sumner Welles—fans of *Confidential* will remember the patrician Mr. Welles, former Undersecretary of State, great and good friend of the Brotherhood of Sleeping Car Porters. It made rather a tableau, one especially vivant, when His Excellency, pickled as brandied peaches, began nibbling those Corsican ears.

By the time the file found its place at the front of Hoover's "Personal and Confidential" cabinet, it was already worn and tattered from repeated scrutiny. Other folders would follow in quick succession—files that contained the most sordid of Hoover's discoveries. Words so damaging that just a hint of what they revealed was enough to paralyze entire governments and turn the FBI's director into the most potentially dangerous man in the world.

NINE

ROSES ARE ALSO RED

There was a certain understanding between them—
Hoover and Roosevelt, that is. The president was
crippled, after all. Not by the polio that had attacked him
in 1921 and paralyzed his legs, but by a strict interpretation of the law that kept wiretaps and surveillance from
being used imperiously. Hoover was well aware of the
specifics of federal regulations that tied his hands and
shielded his eyes from free exploration of the truth. Then
came that certain understanding—one that freed both
Bureau director and American president from being
accountable to anyone but each other.

Nothing in writing. Words passed in private meetings, if
at all; more a sense of permission that passed from leader to
administrator and back to leader with information its own
reward. It was an unspoken agreement that served each
man well and delivered nearly unlimited information on
government officials and politicians, movie stars, journalists, and high-profile citizens. Until, of course, the evening
of April 12, 1945, when Franklin Delano Roosevelt passed
away unexpectedly at his home at Warm Springs, Georgia.

The president had been sitting for a portrait by Elizabeth Shoumatoff, an artist friend of Lucy Mercer Rutherfurd's, who had been staying at the Little White House in
Warm Springs at Roosevelt's invitation. Lucy, now a widow

245

and no longer the social secretary to Eleanor Roosevelt, had been the president's mistress while he was assistant secretary of the navy. Incredibly busy and romantically naive, Eleanor did not learn the details of the relationship until 1918, when she accidentally found love letters from her secretary to her husband as she unpacked his suitcase.

Hoover knew of Roosevelt's trysts and maintained a file thick with observations of the pair, as well as reports on the president's dalliances with his cousin Margaret Suckley, who by no small coincidence was also visiting Warm Springs on the afternoon of April 12. After a pleasant lunch, Roosevelt went outside to the small porch, and resumed posing for the oil portrait started earlier in the day. The pain that struck ice pick sharp at the back of his skull left him only seconds to cry out before lapsing into unconsciousness. By the time the First Lady heard about her husband's collapse, the thirty-second president of the United States was dead.

J. Edgar Hoover was not on the original guest list for the Roosevelt funeral, choreographed by Eleanor in the East Room of the White House the following Saturday. He did, however, attend the ceremony anyway, offering condolences to a rather surprised former First Lady, and was photographed standing next to President and Mrs. Harry S. Truman. It was not out of a sense of grief that Hoover had intruded upon the proceedings, but rather as part of a required transition, from old loyalties to new.

The incoming president was not as easy to approach, even for a seasoned veteran like Hoover. Since his early days as a senator, Truman found Hoover far too unregulated and pompous, and was outspoken about his concerns over the extent of the FBI's authority.

On May 12, 1945, the new president wrote himself an internal memo crystallizing his thoughts: "We want no Gestapo or Secret Police. FBI is tending in that direction. They are dabbling in sex life scandals and plain blackmail when they should be catching criminals. They also have a habit of sneering at local law enforcement officers. *This must stop.* Cooperation is what we must have."[1]

Hoover's idea of cooperation was simple: agree with him and there will be no problem. Unfortunately for the director of the FBI, Truman agreed with almost nothing that Hoover had to say, including how he ran his organization and courted the press.

To Hoover, Truman was a "pig farmer from Missouri"[2] who had first been elected to the Senate after Hoover had been FBI director for a full decade. Eleven years later, and Hoover was still looking upon Truman as a newcomer who needed to learn the ropes. It was from this position of superiority that Hoover arranged for a little-known agent named Marion Chiles III to pay a visit to the new president and convey his message of welcome. Chiles, as it happened, had grown up in Missouri—his father, Marion Chiles Jr., was a longtime friend of Truman's. As a surprised Truman welcomed Chiles into the Oval Office, he was highly curious as to why the agent had come.

"With a message from Mr. Hoover," Chiles replied. "Mr. Hoover wants you to know that he and the FBI are at your personal disposal and will help you in any way you ask."

Truman was not playing the game, and sent Chiles packing with a message for the director. "Any time I need the services of the FBI, I will ask for it through my attorney general," Truman announced, dismissing Chiles and Hoover in the same sentence.³

Though Truman was only days into his job as chief executive of the United States, he already had set the stage for a showdown with the Bureau head, and it was one for which Truman was ill prepared. Hoover, after all, had the home-court advantage. He knew Washington, he knew politics, and he knew where all the skeletons were hidden. With the flick of a wrist, he could open a file cabinet and ruin a life, or keep it shut and save a career.

According to that plan, Harry S. Truman was a mere passenger along for a brief ride in a pumpkin chariot that was his to appreciate for as long as it lasted. Hoover, meanwhile, was busy paving the road on which the carriage traveled. He had been doing so for years. Stop the road, stop the chariot. Hoover knew the routine well.

When Chiles returned to Hoover's office conveying the presidential sentiment, Hoover declared a private war on the White House that would last until the end of the Truman administration. As months passed and Truman was absorbed in the final stages of World War II and the peace agreements that followed, Hoover rededicated himself to the cause of eradicating Communists within the borders of the United States. That Russia was playing such an important role in the final treaties at Yalta and later at the Potsdam Conference provoked Hoover, driving an ideological spike between the director and the president. Not that Truman was unaware of the potential of a Cold War and the rising popularity of Communism in Europe. He just did not see it as a major problem: "People are very much wrought up about the Communist 'bugaboo' but I am of the opinion that the country is perfectly safe so far as Communism is concerned—we have far too many sane people."[4] For Hoover, it was *the* problem, a poison that had to be eradicated at all costs.

The mainstay of the FBI's fight against Communism centered on infiltration of the Communist Party and wiretaps of its membership—two practices the White House found disturbing and attempted to discourage, citing violation of civil liberties.

"What the hell is this crap?" Truman was said to have asked when he learned about numerous FBI wiretaps. "Cut them off. Tell the FBI we haven't got any time for that kind of shit."[5]

But Hoover didn't stop. Even without presidential authorization, the surveillance and wiretaps continued. Not because Hoover didn't care about civil liberties. Rather, to the director's way of thinking, in order to protect the civil liberties of many, he had to violate the civil liberties of the few, particularly Communists and those with perceived perversions. Alger Hiss seemed to fit in both categories.

Tall, thin, and debonair, Alger Hiss was something of a legend in Washington. Financially stable and a graduate of Harvard Law School, Hiss was secretary to Supreme Court Justice Oliver Wendell Holmes before joining the Justice, Agriculture, and State departments, accompanying Roosevelt to the Yalta Conference in 1945, and serving as secretary-general of the United Nations. It was a meteoric rise, especially by Washington standards, where careers grow with the speed of oaks.

That the distinguished and erudite Hiss should have had occasion to meet and associate with Communist Party member and college dropout Whittaker Chambers was as unlikely as it was real, for in 1941, Chambers admitted as much. Moreover, he gave a sworn statement to the FBI that not only was he a friend of the dignified Mr. Hiss, but he also had direct knowledge that the diplomat was a spy for the Communist Party.

It was a time in America when lists of suspected Communists were as popular as radio soap operas and equally as discussed over afternoon cocktails. At first the information about Hiss was dismissed as the rantings of a publicity seeker, Chambers being a little-known book reviewer for *Time* magazine. Not the type that would be carrying Russian secrets and certainly not a Russian spy himself.

It actually would take several more *years* of confessions, sworn statements, and attacks on known Communist informants for Chambers's revelations to be taken seriously. By that point, he had risen within the ranks of *Time* to become publisher Henry Luce's favorite writer.[6] In all that time, Chambers was unshakable in his determination to expose Hiss and his Communist leanings.

On May 29, 1946, more than a year after Roosevelt's death, Hoover alerted the president that there was a ring of spies in Washington "noted for their pro-Soviet leanings" and all eager to learn America's atomic secrets.[7] He included Alger Hiss on the list.* Though still not convinced that the

---

* Also on Hoover's list were Under Secretary of State Dean Acheson, Acheson's assistant Herbert Marks, former assistant secretary of war John J. McCloy, Assistant Secretary of War Howard C. Peterson, Secretary of Commerce Henry A. Wallace, Paul Appleby and George Schwartzwalder from the Bureau of the Budget, Edward U. Condon from the Bureau of Standards, and Abe Feller and James R. Newman of the United Nations.

individuals named by his informants were guilty, Hoover was far more concerned about revalidating his own career than about protecting others. As usual, the Bureau's director saw as his mission the gathering of information, not the investigation of guilt, particularly where America's atomic secrets were concerned.

Unfortunately, by the time Hoover sent his memo to the White House, details of the Manhattan Project already were known. The top secret project taking place at Los Alamos, New Mexico, under the direction of physicist J. Robert Oppenheimer, was developing the first atomic bomb. The prototype, tested on July 14, 1945, some 230 miles south of Los Alamos, was a success, prompting the new president to authorize its use against the Japanese.

A year earlier, an army sergeant named David Greenglass had transferred to the Los Alamos project, where he worked as a machinist on elements of the bomb's interior. It was an easy job for Greenglass and a convenient connection for his sister, Ethel, a onetime member of the Communist Party.

For Ethel and her husband, Julius Rosenberg, however, playing at being a Communist was not enough. They were eager to do more for the Russian war effort and found the perfect opportunity through the Manhattan Project. Persuading Greenglass to feed them information from inside Los Alamos was easy. He himself had been a member of the Young Communist League as a teenager, a fact somehow overlooked in his security clearance.

It was simple for Greenglass to draw up plans of the triggering device, his own contribution from the machine shop, as well as list the names of the various scientists involved in the research and development of the warhead. Greenglass passed the information on to a courier he later learned was Harry Gold, who himself had been recruited by Soviet vice consul Anatoli A. Yakovlev.

Even as these amateurs were successfully stealing parts of America's most top secret plans, J. Edgar Hoover was reassuring the country that it was safe from the talons of Communist predators. "Foreign powers tried to steal not only the atomic bomb but other military secrets," he said in a speech delivered before the International Association of Chiefs of Police in Miami in 1945. "The counter-espionage program which we developed did more than encircle spies and render them harmless. It enabled us to learn of their weaknesses and aims."[8]

The names and faces of those involved in the Los Alamos theft would not become clear for another five years, and only after Britain's MI5, the security intelligence agency responsible for counterespionage in England, captured an atomic physicist named Klaus Fuchs. Fuchs, who had worked at Los Alamos, provided clues that led to Harry Gold, who provided information on David Greenglass, who provided the leads to Ethel and Julius Rosenberg.

In 1950, the FBI managed to gain considerable notoriety over the capture of Gold, Greenglass, and the Rosenbergs, which Hoover predictably lauded as an example of the efficiency of the Bureau. There was no mention that the alleged spies had operated untethered in the United States for well over five years and the memory of Alger Hiss was still fresh in people's minds.

Two years earlier, on August 3, 1948, *Time*'s senior editor Whittaker Chambers was called before the House

Un-American Activities Committee (HUAC) to repeat his charges against Alger Hiss. As he walked into HUAC's suite in the Old House Office Building, Chambers sported a wrinkled suit, stained tie, and furrowed brow, prompting one representative to remark that he had the look of a "walking potato sack" and the happiness of a "nauseated stomach."

His appearance notwithstanding, Chambers presented a straightforward portrayal of an adult life spent spying for the Russians. In the 10 years since he resigned from the Communist underground, Chambers had made every attempt to spread the truth about the organization, he said. Among the truths he wanted to reveal was that during the thirties, Hiss had worked with him on behalf of the Soviet Union.

> For a year, I lived in hiding, sleeping by day and watching through the night with a gun or revolver within easy reach. I had sound reason for supposing that the Communists might try to kill me. For a number of years, I had myself served in the underground, chiefly in Washington, D.C. I know it at its top level, a group of seven or so men. A member of this group was Alger Hiss.[9]

The charge was an old one and had been repeated often in front of various FBI and State Department officials. This was the first time, however, that Chambers took his accusation before Congress, and the difference was crucial. Hiss immediately demanded an opportunity to answer the charges, and on August 5, the HUAC accepted his request. In his response, Hiss was direct and firm in his absolute denial of every charge Chambers had placed before the committee.

> I am not and have never been a member of the Communist party. I do not and have not adhered to the tenets of the Communist party. I have never followed the Communist party line. To the best of my knowledge, I never heard of Whittaker Chambers until 1947, when two representatives of the Federal Bureau of Investigation asked me if I knew him. So far as I know, I have never laid eyes on him, and I should like to have the opportunity to do so.[10]

That same day, a somewhat embarrassed President Truman labeled the HUAC probe "a red herring" that the House had launched "to keep from doing what they ought to do . . . They are slandering a lot of people that don't deserve it," he said. Privately, Truman suggested that J. Edgar Hoover was secretly providing fuel to the fire in the belly of the HUAC.[11]

Hoover certainly was a resource to Richard M. Nixon, who took Truman's words as a challenge to prove the worth of the HUAC, beginning with the prosecution of Alger Hiss. What followed was an all-out assault to confirm Chambers's allegations, with Hoover eventually assigning 263 agents to the case.

Nixon, who had been appointed head of the subcommittee to determine the validity of Chambers's accusations, was at the time an unknown junior congressman from California with aspirations of greatness. Like Hoover, he saw that there was glory to be delivered in the successful fight against Communism, and proceeded to fight for that glory on the back of Alger Hiss.

Much has been written about the Hiss case that eventually found the onetime State Department official tried for perjury (the statute of limitations had expired on espionage charges), found guilty, and sentenced to five years in prison. Hoover was featured on the cover of *Time* surrounded by American flags, while *Newsweek* wrote, "The foot that kicked the planks the hardest and the eye that watched the resulting commotion most closely belonged to J. Edgar Hoover, chief of the Federal Bureau of Investigation."

> He was one of the first to recognize the Communist underground for what it was—a volunteer Russian espionage service and potential sabotage ring. He infiltrated the Communist Party, U.S.A. with FBI agents and informers and listened in on telephone conversations of Red suspects. Following the leads thus established, he learned something of the relationship between American agents and their Russian masters, and between these agents and their informers inside the United States Government.[12]

Not everyone shared *Newsweek*'s enthusiasm for the efficiency of Hoover's Bureau. For one, the president of the United States still found the routine trouncing of civil liberties to be against the freedom that was America, and approaching the Gestapo tactics that concerned him in 1945. Writing to his wife, Bess, in 1947, Truman explained: "I am sure glad the Secret Service is doing a

better job. I was worried about that situation. Edgar
Hoover would give his right eye to take over and all Congressmen and Senators are afraid of him. I'm not and he
knows it. If I can prevent [it], there'll be no NKVD [*Nar-
odnij Kommisariat Vnutrennih Del* (Soviet Secret Police)]
or Gestapo in this country. Edgar Hoover's organization
would make a good start toward a citizen spy system. Not
for me."[13]

Fighting Hoover proved no easy task for the belea-
guered president, who found his own popularity sinking
compared to the heroic image of America's chief crime
fighter: Hoover the great, the incorruptible, the preserver
of justice and the American way. With the headlines tout-
ing the start of the Cold War with Russia, no amount of
logic from the halls of the White House could convince an
alarmed public that Hoover's power should be reduced, his
ability to snoop in the most private places encumbered.

Hoover's cause was aided considerably when Julius
and Ethel Rosenberg were branded guilty long before the
actual verdicts were handed down. Walter Winchell, still
holding court in booth 50 at the Stork Club, gave daily
updates of the trial in his column, having received whispered news from Hoover as well as from a truculent
young attorney named Roy Cohn, who was serving on the
prosecution team.

The 21-year-old Cohn had been introduced into café
society by *New York Post* writer Leonard Lyons, who
found Cohn's acerbic wit and photographic memory helpful in filling his column with anecdotes full of detail and
sophistication. Where Lyons provided Cohn entrée,
Winchell delivered him fame as he repeatedly mentioned

the newly hired assistant U.S. attorney on his radio broadcast, coupling his name with such words as "bright," "charming," and "clever." Cohn admitted to being all that and more, including "biting," "ambitious," and "ruthless."

Hoover, too, was impressed by Cohn, particularly his ability to ferret out secret information on attractive socialites and their gentlemen escorts. In the world of gossip, Hoover's appetite was notoriously insatiable. It did not matter if the subject was named Muffy or Franklin; it mattered only that they had committed some act of lechery. And it was even better if sex was involved and the subplot was set in Washington, D.C.

During the Rosenberg trial, Cohn and Hoover interacted frequently, each maneuvering to gain the biggest career boost on the backs of the accused. From Hoover's perspective, Cohn was untried and thus not to be trusted—at least until the Bureau's director could uncover something, *anything*, in his background that would leave him vulnerable to Hoover's less-than-subtle brand of career blackmail. Hoover did not have long to wait.

Cohn had been hired as the confidential assistant to Irving Saypol, the new U.S. attorney in Manhattan who had previously been involved in the Alger Hiss case. Distantly related by marriage, Saypol and Cohn had dispositions well suited to each other—both were belligerent and rude to those they found useless in furthering their cause of the moment. For Cohn, the opportunity to assist in the prosecution of the Rosenbergs pushed him into the limelight, a move highly beneficial to his personal life. Not only did he gain entrance into the celebrity of the Stork Club, but he was able to attract the attention of the handsome, rich heir to a theater empire, G. David Schine, who in turn attracted the attention of J. Edgar Hoover.

After graduating from the prestigious Phillips Academy (Andover), Schine attended Harvard University, where, local legend suggests, he had a secretary attend his classes, take notes in shorthand, and present him with a typed transcript of the lecture at the end of the day. According to the *Harvard Crimson,* the prototype playboy was best known for the radiophone he had installed in his Cadillac and for flaunting his wealth. "He took great pains to impress his contemporaries. He once carried a valise, containing nothing but $1,100 in cash, through Harvard Yard—'just for fun,' he explained. On another occasion, he staggered his colleagues with the announcement that he was signing a check for $3,000, asking, 'Have you ever signed a check for that much?'"[14]

Apparently Cohn was so impressed by Schine's aplomb and looks, which one critic described as "in the style that one associates with male orchestra singers,"[15] that he made special arrangements to help the student when Saypol introduced the two to each other. Soon Schine was spouting Cohn's anticommunist jargon and even wrote a six-page pamphlet that condemned Communism in America. *The Definition of Communism* was distributed free to hotels owned by a division of Schine Circuit Theaters, including the Boca Raton Club in Florida and the Ambassador Hotel in Los Angeles. In it, Schine wrote that the Communist Party was guilty of "stealing words, such as freedom, security, and equality from the Bible, and other good covenants to confuse issues, and deceive the mind into ensnarement."

Hoover's interest in the pair had less to do with Schine's anticommunist leanings than with his close relationship to Cohn. In an effort to discover the exact nature of their friendship, Hoover placed Cohn under surveillance—a scrutiny that continued long after the espionage trial ended in April 1951 with Julius and Ethel Rosenberg sentenced to death. It was the beginning of a lifelong interest that Hoover took in Cohn, one that found them both locked in an interdependent struggle of deception and denial. For the moment, however, the FBI director was content with boosting Cohn's career, confident that his skills as an attorney were an ideal match for the needs of the junior senator from Wisconsin, Joseph McCarthy.

McCarthy, the onetime chicken farmer and high school dropout turned U.S. senator, was considered by many to be the most dangerous politician in America, not so much for what he knew but for whom he would accuse. Unethical to a fault, McCarthy built his political foundation based on a campaign of lies and distortions that left Robert La Follette Jr., the incumbent Wisconsin senator he defeated, in such a state of emotional distress that he later committed suicide.

Swept into office on a wave of patriotic furor based on an exaggerated war record, McCarthy spent his first several years as a senator in relative obscurity. By 1950, his political base was eroding as the public began to catch up with his lies and learned that the IRS was investigating him for a variety of tax offenses. Desperate to shore up his flagging popularity, McCarthy searched for a cause that might save his career in the Senate. The answer came by way of a dean at Georgetown University, Edmund A. Walsh, who suggested that McCarthy investigate the prevalence of Communists within the Truman administration.

Lightning had hit the rod of revelation. In an instant, McCarthy, crusader for good against evil, was born. The midwife was J. Edgar Hoover, who eagerly joined the senator's campaign by quietly supplying him with an endless stream of confidential files on hundreds of suspected Communists then living in the United States. Hoover's support was given freely, if secretly, allowing McCarthy to bathe in the reflected glory while Hoover accomplished his own goal—the clearing of Communists from America.

Though McCarthy previously had made occasional references to Communism in the United States, his legendary effort to purge Communists from the U.S. government began on February 9, 1950, when he spoke before a Republican women's club in Wheeling, West Virginia. Labeling Secretary of State Dean Acheson a "pompous diplomat in striped pants, with a phony British accent," McCarthy held up several sheets of paper and proclaimed, "I have in my hand, fifty-seven cases of individuals who appear to be either card-carrying members or certainly loyal to the Communist party, but who nevertheless are still helping to shape our foreign policy."

It was a shocking revelation at a time when America's paranoia about Russia and the Cold War was building to extraordinary levels. Reaction was swift and predictable. An outraged public demanded an investigation into the charges, and a clean sweep of the Truman administration to ensure that it was purified of its "pinko population." Painted as a president under the control of his own cabinet, Harry S. Truman had little choice but to agree when the Democrats called for a thorough investigation into the charges, totally unaware that his real enemy was neither McCarthy nor Communism, but J. Edgar Hoover.

While the country was seeing Red, Hoover found that he was finally able to relax, putting his feet up on a lounge chair at the Roney Plaza Hotel in Miami. He was on yet another working vacation, with Clyde Tolson in the adjoining suite, compliments of the hotel's owner, J. Myer Schine. J. Myer Schine, father of David Schine, Roy Cohn's best friend. Yes, life was good.

It was a happy time for the Bureau's director. Never had he felt so secure in his position or more needed by his country. He was sure this was the beginning of the end for Truman. *Any time I need the services of the FBI, I will ask for it through my attorney general.* Finally, Truman would regret those words.

As McCarthy macheted his way through Washington, armed with information supplied by the Bureau's director, Hoover toyed with the participants, dangling his support, friendship, and the Bureau's files just out of reach. It was more game than performance for Hoover, who looked at McCarthy as a bombastic diversion from whose chaos he could resurrect calm.

There was nothing calming, however, about a writer named Max Lowenthal, whose book, *Federal Bureau of Investigation,* was about to be published by William Sloane Associates. The first writer to actually tackle the FBI's complex infrastructure, Lowenthal was immediately discredited by Hoover for his folly in attempting to crack the walls of secrecy that surrounded the institution.

Part of Hoover's frustration lay in the fact that Lowenthal had managed to write the book without his knowledge. Hoover only learned of its pending publication through a listing in the trade magazine *Publishers Weekly.* He naturally placed blame in as many places and on as many individuals as possible, the hardest hit being Assistant Director Louis Nichols, head of the FBI's public relations operation. "If I had known this book was going to be published," Nichols was said to have commented in his own defense, "I would have thrown my body between the presses and stopped it."[16] More important, Hoover would have no doubt allowed it.

As it was, the Bureau's director attempted to strong-arm the publisher by persuading ACLU cofounder–Hoover personal attorney Morris Ernst to write a letter suggesting that the book was filled with errors. At that point, Hoover had yet to see the book, or even the endnotes. If he had, he would have seen that the bulk of Lowenthal's book was taken from congressional documents, read much like a legal brief, and contained little in the way of detail on the inner workings of the FBI. Nevertheless, Hoover was determined to stop its publication, and demanded that both author and publisher be questioned before the House Un-American Activities Committee.

With no small amount of angst, Hoover wrote to the president suggesting that Lowenthal might be a "Communist sympathizer." Hoover most likely did not know that Max Lowenthal was the primary motivator behind Truman when he was chosen to run as Roosevelt's vice president. Hoover also seemed unaware that Truman had helped Lowenthal edit portions of the manuscript and had already seen a copy of the finished book.

Never one to take Hoover's rantings seriously, Truman sent a copy of the letter to Lowenthal along with one of his own saying that he "got a kick out of [reading the book]."[17] Publicly, Truman denied having time to peruse the book, preferring to avoid a direct confrontation with the Bureau.

Congressman George Dondero of Michigan, already in Hoover's camp for his condemnation of abstract art as a "Communist conspiracy" because of its failure to "glorify" America, found his voice on the House floor as he accused Lowenthal of "serving the cause of Moscow" with his still unpublished book. Proclaiming that the FBI "stands four-square for the American way of life," Dondero stomped and preened his way through a 10-minute diatribe condemning Lowenthal, who he said was "not unknown at the White House." Further, the congressman struck the tenor of the times when he suggested that Lowenthal was guilty of crimes against the country, and that "when he is caught, the revelation will be a bigger shock than the expose of Benedict Arnold. It must be done. The Nation can take it. But it cannot win the war of survival with Russia if this man is allowed to continue his clever, diabolical scheme to undermine our national security."[18] It is a speech that found its origin with the FBI's Louis Nichols, who had Hoover's authorization for its use.

The Senate was not immune to Hoover's sledgehammer touch, courtesy of Bourke B. Hickenlooper from Iowa, who labeled Lowenthal's work an "utterly biased piece of propaganda," and Homer Ferguson from Michigan who said that "at the bottom, the book is evil, a monstrous piece of libel."[19] Had the pair known that the book consisted of excerpts from the *Congressional Record,* their opinions might have been different. As it was, the ruckus created by Hoover over the slightest hint of criticism only served to promote the book's arrival in 1950 and gave it what few sales it finally managed to achieve.

With the Lowenthal book resigned to history, and without the slightest ripple in Hoover's widespread public appeal, the Bureau's director placed his office at McCarthy's disposal in the senator's mission to eradicate Communists on native soil. If McCarthy and Hoover were using each another—and they were—there is no doubt that Hoover was pulling the strings of the various puppet players. It was Hoover who decided which names to supply to McCarthy for questioning. It was Hoover who provided the supporting documents. And it was Hoover who molded the senator's scathing attacks on Adlai Stevenson when the former governor of Illinois became the Democratic nominee for president in 1952.

Hoover's hatred of Truman was so resolute that no candidate the president endorsed had any hope of winning favor within the halls of the FBI. Hoover's dislike for Stevenson, however, surmounted mere loathing by association. He admitted privately to Clyde Tolson that he was intimidated by the Illinois governor's wit and intelligence, and for that reason would never allow himself to be caught in a one-on-one conversation with the Princeton graduate.

Stevenson took full advantage of his verbal skills in attacking the Republican presidential candidate General Dwight D. Eisenhower. His intellect coupled with his bald head earned Stevenson the label of "egghead," but it was his liberal politics that provided Joseph McCarthy the ammunition for his spirited attacks.

On October 27, 1952, McCarthy traveled to Chicago, where the city was awash in Halloween celebrations as goblins and witches ruled the night. Their fright factor had nothing on McCarthy as he unexpectedly announced during an unscheduled press conference that he was about to expose Adlai Stevenson "for the man he is." That announcement caught Eisenhower and his campaign team by surprise, and Eisenhower expressed concern that any scandalous revelations might have a backlash effect on his own candidacy. Undeterred, McCarthy bought airtime on some 50 television stations and more than 550 radio outlets, ballyhooed with the energy normally reserved for fire sales and lynchings in the South.

It was a Hoover-inspired moment, choreographed by Louis Nichols and documented by FBI files. Rumor suggested that McCarthy was going to call Stevenson a Communist and a homosexual. In front of 1,700 well-wishers, each of whom had paid $50 for dinner and a speech, McCarthy did not disappoint.

Holding up a fistful of papers, McCarthy accused Stevenson of having defended Alger Hiss, "the arch-traitor of our time." He claimed that Stevenson successfully introduced Communists into the coalition government of Italy, and that he covered up his membership in Americans for Democratic Action, which McCarthy labeled "left-wing." McCarthy dramatically held up a photograph of a barn in South Lee, Massachusetts, which he claimed held an elegant conference room that contained "over 200,000 astounding documents. They were the hidden files of the

Communist controlled Institute of Pacific Relations."[†20](Stevenson's only connection with the organization was an invitation he received to attend its annual conference in Mont Tremblant, Quebec, Canada.)

Though the Democrats would claim that McCarthy's accusations were riddled with errors, pointing specifically to 18 false statements, the damage to Stevenson's campaign was irreversible. True to his threats, McCarthy later made unfounded references to Stevenson's sexual inclination, bandying about such epithets as "pansies" and agreeing with the New York Daily News, which began referring to the Democratic candidate as "Adeline."

The defeat of Adlai Stevenson in November 1952 saw a Hoover-supported Dwight Eisenhower ascend to the White House. While all of America and much of the world was swept up in paranoia about the future of the Cold War, J. Edgar Hoover found unusual solace in the unrest. His popularity at a peak, the country at its neediest, Hoover celebrated Christmas in Washington with Clyde Tolson, receiving friends in his home and attending church for the first time in years. He posed for photographs outside the National Presbyterian Church on Connecticut Avenue with pastor Edward L. R. Elson, before retreating to Tolson's apartment for Christmas dinner and Jack Daniels Black Label.

Hoover's black housekeeper, Annie Fields, had packed several suitcases for his annual "working" vacation in

---

† The Institute of Pacific Relations was organized in Hawaii in the 1920s to inform businesspeople, educators, and politicians about social, economic, and historic developments in Asia and the Pacific. It had no direct association with Communism, although Alger Hiss was on its board of directors.

Florida, looking forward to *her* vacation which coincided annually with his trip. Not that she actually went anywhere or took any time off. Hoover would allow none of that. But with her employer a thousand miles away, the routine was altered enough to make the coming month seem like a true holiday.

This year, George Allen would be joining Tolson and Hoover on their vacation—Allen headed the Reconstruction Finance Corporation under Truman, and was a longtime friend of Eisenhower's dating back to his work with the Red Cross during World War II. He shared a love of racetracks with Hoover and Tolson, and the three planned to spend their days at Hialeah and Gulfstream Park.

The assembled staff at Schine's Roney Plaza Hotel tripped over themselves in excitement when the trio finally made their way through the turquoise lobby with overstuffed round banquets, a gaggle of bellmen handling suitcases and attaché cases filled with imagined secret files. The basket of fruit—a collect of papaya, apples, and pears—addressed to Mr. J. *Edward* Hoover, did not go unnoticed. "Edward" made quick note of the error, but did not relinquish the fruit or basket for replacement.

On the outdoor lanai, the winter heat had left a layer of moisture too fine to be called dew. Hoover maneuvered his 200-pound frame into a wrought iron lounge chair and felt the hot Miami sun. His gray sharkskin pants were pulled high over his thick waist, his stomach seemingly magnified by a fluorescent blue Hawaiian shirt that the director reserved for just such occasions. His Countess Mara ties had been hung precisely in line, next to his starched Van Heusen shirts and tailor-made worsted wool suits. Freshly polished shoes, eight pairs, all identical, stood sentry on the closet floor, as if nothing was wrong or out of place in Hoover's world.

Back in Washington, however, a kernel of ugly gossip had taken flight, winding its way through members of a dinner party. The host, a onetime CIA operative assigned to the Psychological Warfare Division, was anxious to share a piece of news with his male guests. A mutual friend had been approached by Hoover "several times," it was said. "When it was found that no progress could be made, [Hoover] had turned him in."[21]

The hush that followed the revelation quickly dissolved into a shotgun of whispers as each guest returned home and began to spread the rumor. Even as Hoover was reaching for the old-fashioned glass, filled with his favorite whiskey over ice, the fallout had started. The director was now the hunted, and someone eventually would pay the price.

TEN

A PANSY IS
ONLY A FLOWER

Joseph St. George Bryan III looked every bit like the Princeton University graduate he was. Tall and slender, with sharp, handsome features, he had a refined presence that reflected his ability to move in upper-class society. He was, he often reminded people, "a casual friend of the Windsors"—as in the duke and duchess of Windsor, the onetime king of England and his American divorcée wife. It was hardly surprising, for Joseph St. George Bryan came from one of Virginia's oldest and wealthiest families, which counted judges, scholars, and publishers among its moneyed ranks.

After graduating from Princeton, Bryan was employed as an editorial writer for his father's newspaper, the *Richmond News Ledger,* then worked for several magazines before serving in Naval Intelligence during World War II. In 1947, Bryan joined the CIA, where his work in the Psychological Warfare Division gave him access to the FBI's "Obscene" file, begun in 1925 to hold "all obscene matter such as booklets, leaflets, photographic prints, etc." in an effort to keep the material from being placed in the readily accessible files in the FBI's Central Records. Bryan's access was approved by Hoover personally, the director having met the agent when Bryan interviewed him for a profile in the *Saturday Evening Post,* where Bryan was once an editor.

That was, to be sure, the last J. Edgar Hoover had heard of Joseph Bryan III until he received a letter from Richard Hood, special agent in charge of the Bureau's Los Angeles office, with details of a dinner party Bryan hosted just before election night in 1952. In addition to revealing the contents of the "Obscene" file, Bryan is said to have labeled Hoover "the worst pansy in Washington" and a piranha who preyed on innocent males, including a mutual friend whom he refused to name at the time—though he did offer to "testify to it, and . . . name the person and prove it."[1]

When Hoover received the letter in April 1953, he raged in a note to Tolson: "I want this skunk Bryan to be made to put up or shut up. I want no effort to be spared to call his bluff & promptly."[2]

Nothing demanded a faster response from the FBI than an aspersion on the sexual orientation of the Bureau's director. Nothing. Since the early thirties, it had been a long-standing policy to answer any and all accusations with immediate investigations and demands for proof. Writing in his official blue ink on the bottom of his note to Tolson, Hoover scrawled: "I am puzzled why SAC Richard Hood waited from last Nov. till April to advise us of this."[3]

The following day, Assistant Director Louis Nichols memoed back to Clyde Tolson that he had interviewed a guest at the dinner, as to whether Bryan had said the derogatory comments. "He denied that Bryan had made such a statement. He said that he had left early that evening because [text censored], that such a statement could have been made after he left, but that he did not hear such a statement on the part of Bryan or anyone either on this occasion or any other. He said that it was contrary to the character of Bryan to speak of individuals in this manner; that he either accepts them or does not, but that Bryan is not inclined to speak maliciously of other individuals."[4]

Not inclined perhaps, but apparently willing, for with his casual comment at a dinner party Joseph Bryan III joined a growing list of Americans who found it fashionable to dress the Bureau's director in an overcoat of homosexuality. It was mere rumor, of course; the kind of idle speculation that has been exchanged over backyard fences and across clotheslines for centuries. The difference here was that those who dared to take Hoover's name and wash it in the mud were uncovered and exposed, like rock beetles bared to the sun.

There was the overweight hairdresser and her rich society matron from Georgetown who risked talking about Hoover between set and perm. The trucker who thought he was being clever by bringing up the subject over a casual burger at the Orange Diner in Tenafly, New Jersey. And the fox-trot instructor at the Thayer LeRoy Dance Studios on Connecticut Avenue, who told it to an employee of the National Labor Relations Board, who went to the Sportsmen's Club dance at the Coral Theater on Marlboro Pike and discussed it after a particularly exhilarating tango.

None of these men and women had proof of their allegations. Just talk. Gossip, really. But gossip that was accepted as truth and, as such, had a life of its own. Each received a personal visit from a pair of FBI special agents; each professed total innocence; each received a warning;

and all were placed under surveillance for the remainder of their lives.

Attorney Roy Cohn, himself a closeted homosexual, knew why there was never any proof. It was not because Hoover was so clever or even clandestine with his relationships. It was because Hoover was too scared of his own desires to even *have* relationships—male or female. "J. Edgar Hoover was the most frightened man I ever met," Cohn said in 1982 to publicist Peter Simone, with whom he had a relationship. "The most frightened—and the most frightening. He wouldn't do anything, certainly not in public, not in private either. Hoover was always afraid that somehow who he saw, where he went, what he said, it would impact that all-important image of his. He would never do anything that would compromise his position as head of the FBI—*ever.*

"There was supposed to be some scandalous pictures of Hoover and Tolson—there were no pictures. Believe me, I looked. There were no pictures because there was no sexual relationship. Whatever they did, they did separately, in different rooms, and even then, I'm sure Hoover was fully dressed."[5]

In the 1992 book *Official and Confidential: The Secret Life of J. Edgar Hoover,* author Anthony Summers quotes Susan Rosenstiel, former wife of Hoover's friend Louis Rosenstiel,* as she described attending an orgy at the

---

* Louis Rosenstiel was a 67-year-old multimillionaire who had made his fortune by distilling and importing liquor through his company, Schenley Industries. Rosenstiel met Hoover through Joseph Kennedy, patriarch of the Kennedy family, who created his wealth in the twenties as a bootlegger with Rosenstiel.

Plaza Hotel in 1958 in which Hoover was "wearing a fluffy black dress, very fluffy, with flounces, and lace stockings and high heels, and a black curly wig. He had makeup on, and false eyelashes. It was a very short skirt, and he was sitting there in the living room of the suite with his legs crossed. Roy [Cohn] introduced him to me as 'Mary . . .'"[6]

Cohn's 1982 comments obviously dispute those facts, which were later refuted as well by others, including author Peter Maas. Writing in *Esquire* magazine, Maas, who thought Hoover "a fatuous, personally corrupt, evil ass," knew better than to accept the cross-dressing story as fact.

> The trouble is that the sole source for this is Susan Rosenstiel. The trouble also is that she'd been trying to peddle this story for years. Among those she had approached was Robert Morgenthau, a former U.S. attorney in New York and current Manhattan D.A. On paper, she couldn't have made a better choice. Morgenthau had tried, unsuccessfully, to convict Cohn three times for various transgressions. He and Hoover were not on speaking terms. Morgenthau discovered that Rosenstiel—no paragon of civic virtue—had dumped Susan and an ugly divorce ensued. She hated Hoover, convinced he put FBI agents on her to help her husband's cause. "I didn't believe her then," Morgenthau told me, "and I don't now."[7]

Having spent years exposing Hoover's prejudices and shortcomings in his role as Bureau director, columnists

Jack Anderson and Les Whitten spearheaded an investigation into the autocrat's private life, turning the tables on a man whose later career was devoted to invasion of others' privacy. Anderson assigned a reporter to sort through Hoover's garbage looking for clues to a hidden lifestyle, while Whitten tailed Hoover and Tolson to lunch at the Mayflower Hotel, hoping to overhear stories told out of school. The garbage revealed nothing more than empty liquor bottles and the wrappings from gifts, while the lunch conversation was a disappointing extension of Hoover's office banter.

Years later Whitten interviewed William C. Sullivan, a career special agent who at one time was thought to be in line to take over Hoover's position at the Bureau. When questioned about Hoover's sexual orientation, Sullivan, who broke with Hoover in 1971 and was an outspoken critic, told Whitten he was almost certain that Hoover was not a practicing homosexual. He, like others, had heard the stories of early romances, but credited them to efforts by Hoover's friends and subordinates to deflect any rumors of his homosexuality.

Whitten also questioned one of Hoover's vacation hosts in the Florida Keys where Hoover and Tolson once shared a room. According to Whitten, "He had suspicions, but had absolutely nothing to back them up. Personally," Whitten added, "I feel that Hoover was too uptight, too fearful of scandal to venture anything sexually clandestine with either a man or a woman, assuming he even wanted to."[8]

Hoover's life was one of denial, of pulled window shades and dark screens that kept out the light of prying eyes, holding the world at bay and maintaining an image of perfection. No one saw the solitary nights he spent compulsively reading and rereading FBI files. No one knew of the toilet raised from the floor to keep bathroom germs at bay. No one uncovered the real truth: Hoover had no private life, no moments when he could stop being the director, the one in control. To maintain the illusion required constant monitoring, especially of scandal and any hint of salacious sex—the kind told in stories that people repeated, no matter how many times Hoover denied their existence.

"I helped spread the rumors," Truman Capote said in a 1983 interview. "I used to call them 'Johnny and Clyde.' Was it true? Who knows? It didn't matter, and I didn't care; it was a *fabulous* story. It got Hoover upset, that much I know. And it got me—well, about 200 pages in an FBI file."[9]

Joseph Bryan III knew a fabulous story when he heard it as well, but he made the mistake of repeating it once too often—the last time being in 1955, when he called Hoover a "pansy in pants." Hoover heard about it from William Jenner, the ultraconservative chairman of the Senate Internal Security Subcommittee (the Senate's answer to the House Un-American Activities Committee), and who was considered by Hoover to be a "friend on the Hill." Jenner had been told by an unnamed office visitor that Bryan had told *him* that Hoover was a homosexual. Three steps removed from the original source, Hoover prepared to do battle with the onetime CIA agent who, at the time, was a freelance writer living in the Virginia home of his great-great-great-grandfather amid wealth and convenience. For Hoover, there was now "enough evidence in this matter to tackle Joseph Bryan and make him put up or shut up."

Assistant Director Nichols asked for the assignment to interrogate Bryan, "I think we should try to get a signed statement from him," he wrote to Tolson, "and then in view of the contacts which I had with Bryan some years ago, I would like to personally go see him and have the pleasure of making him put up or shut up. If we can verify this, I think we should really try to make an issue because Bryan is a former CIA agent and knows better than to be permitted to get by with such."[10] It was, of course, now familiar territory for Nichols and his assistant, Cartha D. "Deke" DeLoach, who accompanied him to Bryan's house situated among the seasoned oaks and poplar trees of old Richmond.

The arrival of two FBI agents on the doorstep of the Bryan home became big news. That sort of event did not happen often in Richmond, and particularly not to one of the oldest and richest families in town. No one knew that better that Joseph Bryan, who was properly intimidated by the arrival of Nichols and DeLoach, as the fine bead of sweat on his upper lip confirmed.

"Mr. DeLoach and I called on Joseph Bryan at his home this morning," Nichols reported back to Tolson that afternoon. "It was pointed out to Bryan that approximately two years ago, we had received information from a reliable source attributing to him the statement that the Director was a homosexual. He very promptly stated that he could tell us the details; that this occurred at a dinner at his house at which [names censored] were present. They were discussing rumors and gossip in Washington and he made the statement that he wouldn't be surprised any day to hear that Admiral Halsey was beating his wife or that J. Edgar Hoover was a homosexual. He denied anything more was said."[11]

Nichols was skeptical of the last statement, since he knew a second accusation had been directed at Bryan in an unrelated incident:

> We then told him that just recently another presumably reliable source had made a similar statement attributing to him the same type of statement pertaining to the Director. He denied this categorically. He stated he never made any such statement; had no reason for making such a statement; that he admired the Director; that such a statement was not true; and that he does not spread scandal about others.
>
> At that point, I took from my pocket the [name censored] statement and read him the pertinent paragraph. Bryan shook his head and said how anybody could say that. He didn't react like the normal individual would react, demanding to know who said it.
>
> Accordingly, I told him that this statement was made by [name censored]. In addition, [name censored] had made a statement in the Senate Office Building in connection with a hearing which had been called to our attention. He . . . shook his head and asked how [name censored] could do that to him. He stated that only yesterday [name censored] had been to see him about a job. . . .[12]

Faced with irrefutable evidence from two unconnected sources, Bryan was openly nervous in the face of a potentially devastating lawsuit. In a gesture of sincerity, he extracted a sheet of watermarked, engraved stationery and composed a note to the director of the FBI.

Dear Mr. Hoover:

Lou Nichols has just told me that I am charged with a piece of slander against you. I can only give you my word that never did I make any such statement. I do not slander anyone. Specifically, I do not tell lies. I hope most sincerely that you will believe this.

Yours,
Joseph Bryan III[13]

Now totally rattled and shaking, the erudite Bryan had not helped his cause in the eyes of Nichols and DeLoach, who stepped up their intimidation, threatening to "take care of anyone who made such a statement." Exactly *how*, of course, was not revealed, but Bryan apparently got the message, for Nichols reported that when the pair left Bryan's home, "his eyes were watery"—and so they would stay, as Hoover spent the next 17 years building a file that grew to over 80 pages.[14]

By 1955, however, Hoover had had his fill of exaggerators and storytellers, the biggest of which was none other than his friend and fellow Communist-hater, Joseph Raymond McCarthy, who in his rush to ferret out Communists in America, had decided to forge a star for himself. When the 83rd Congress convened at the start of 1953, McCarthy had announced he would become chairman of the Senate's watchdog Committee on Government Operations, as well as head its Permanent Subcommittee on Investigations. And therein lay the problem for Hoover.

The Permanent Subcommittee had operated in the past to investigate charges of homosexuality and sexual perversion in government. McCarthy planned to enlarge its scope and use its private investigative team in an anti-communist effort. It was an investigative team independent of Hoover, and not within his control.

In a fascinating twist of irony, the hard-drinking, foul-mouthed McCarthy had been the subject of homosexual rumors himself, which were given a face when an army lieutenant named David Sayer, stationed in New York, had alleged that he had a sexual encounter with the junior senator from Wisconsin. According to a letter Sayer was said to have written to Connecticut senator William Benton, McCarthy picked up the young lieutenant at the Wardman Park Hotel in Washington, D.C., "gotten him drunk and had committed an act of sodomy on him"—the Wardman Park being the same hotel where Jess Smith and attorney general Harry Daugherty shared an apartment in the Twenties.

Benton, who had previously voiced a resolution to have McCarthy and his tactics investigated by the Senate, passed the letter on to a Senate investigator who in turn contacted J. Edgar Hoover to request "derogatory information" on McCarthy. It was a request that Hoover denied.

He did, however, alert McCarthy to the existence of the Sayer letter. The senator professed innocence and credited the accusation to columnist Drew Pearson, and his assistant Jack Anderson, then campaigning to expose

McCarthy's excesses. When the FBI subsequently interviewed Sayer, though he denied writing the letter as well as participating in sex with McCarthy, the lieutenant did reveal in the pressure of the moment that he, himself, was a homosexual, a disclosure that got him promptly discharged from the service.[15]

Several weeks later, *Las Vegas Sun* publisher Hank Greenspun wrote in his column Where I Stand that McCarthy had had consensual sex with a onetime Communist named Charles Davis. Further, Greenspun alleged that Ed Babcock, a McCarthy intern, had been arrested by the D.C. police and charged with "solicitation for a lewd and lascivious purpose." Moreover, Greenspun wrote that "McCarthy spent the night with William McMahon, formerly an official of the Milwaukee County Young Republicans, in a Wausau hotel room, at which time, McCarthy and McMahon engaged in illicit acts with each other"—this purportedly during the Wisconsin Republican Convention.[16]

McCarthy went on the attack immediately upon reading the newspaper column, threatening to sue, and being calmed only by Hoover's caution that any legal filing against Greenspun would amplify the charges that had been given little credence outside of Las Vegas. McCarthy acquiesced to Hoover's logic, as he aggressively organized the staff that would support his Permanent Subcommittee on Investigations.

When it was time to hire the committee's chief counsel, McCarthy followed Hoover's recommendation and selected attorney Roy Cohn over a disappointed 27-year-old Robert Kennedy who had lobbied for the job. Cohn, in turn, invited his friend G. David Schine to work as an unpaid "chief consultant." That was unexpected. So, too, was McCarthy's acceptance of the inexperienced playboy on his staff.

It was a close-knit world, Hoover-protected and Hoover-inspired, but hardly Hoover-controlled. As the Bureau director was about to learn right along with the rest of the country, McCarthy was out to imprint his name on America, carved in the carcass of roadkill if necessary.

In the early months of 1953, as McCarthy was launching his campaign against Communists, Eisenhower assumed the presidency and welcomed Hoover into his fold, including him in decision making at a level not experienced since the Roosevelt era. As with each arriving president, Hoover extended his offer of support and assistance. In Eisenhower's case, however, the proposition included some information. Eisenhower, Hoover advised, would be wise to reconsider the appointment of Arthur Vandenberg Jr. as the presidential secretary. The reason was made clear by information contained on a three-by-five card extended with his handshake.

Since the middle of 1951, Hoover had been aggressively organizing the "Sexual Deviates" index program within the FBI filing system.[†] The purpose was to maintain an index of known homosexuals "for furnishing information concerning allegations concerning present and past employees of any branch of the United States government." Included among them: Arthur Vandenberg Jr.[17]

---

† In 1977, when the "Sexual Deviates" indexes and files were destroyed by the FBI, the files numbered over 300,000 pages.

His father, Arthur Hendrick Vandenberg, was the senior senator from Michigan and the powerful chairman of the Foreign Relations Committee. Highly respected and charismatic, the elder Vandenberg died in office in 1951, prompting Junior to pick up the political mantle and utilize his father's contacts to help elect Eisenhower the following year. As a reward for his valuable assistance, the president-elect offered Vandenberg Junior the post of White House secretary, a highly coveted and responsible senior position.

The revelation from Hoover impressed the president, with the public knowledge of his homosexuality forcing Vandenberg to pull his name from consideration. Unfortunately for Eisenhower, he was deprived of the services of a man whose contacts and understanding of government and politics would have made him an invaluable aide.

Eisenhower rewarded Hoover's loyalty by involving him in the decision-making process of the White House as well as that of the attorney general's office. Eisenhower had appointed his campaign manager Herbert Brownell as the new attorney general, who in turn assigned his assistant William Rogers to interface with Hoover and the FBI. It would be a match that opened Hoover's vistas and awarded him unprecedented power.

Hoover had first met Rogers in 1947, when the young attorney was serving as counsel on the Senate War Investigation Committee. It was Rogers who advised Nixon during the hearings that lead to Hiss's conviction on perjury charges. Hoover never forgot what he considered to be brilliant legal work on Rogers's part, and welcomed him as a both a confidante and friend.

To Clyde Tolson's disbelief, Hoover occasionally asked Rogers to join the pair on their lunch outings at the Mayflower Hotel, and included Rogers and his wife Adele at dinner parties at Hoover's Rock Creek Park home. For a man who had not altered his personal associations in years, it was a highly unusual move for the otherwise predictable head of the FBI. Yet it was just the beginning of a number of changes that Hoover began to manifest in his life.

It was as if the election of Eisenhower and the president's subsequent effort to revalidate Hoover's role within the government had sparked his confidence level and freed him to expand his boundaries. Despite Hoover's excessively pompous demeanor and self-assured stature, he had grown increasingly insecure during the years of the Truman administration. His drinking had increased, and his ability to withstand criticism had fallen, leaving Hoover a rather isolated and anachronistic Washington veteran.

By late 1953, however, Hoover began to open up his private life, if not his sexual one. Ginger Rogers's mother, Lela, who had continued to see the Bureau director off and on for years, was suddenly persona non grata after she revealed that she found portions of the Communist manifesto to be valid. Muriel Viner, wife of FBI agent Leonard Viner, whose father, Harry, often paid the Hoover-Tolson tab at Harvey's Restaurant, remembered that Lela and Hoover were considered an "item" for years. "Everyone thought they would get married one day. I know I thought so. They used to frequent Harvey's together—not alone though. Clyde was always there and my father-in-law on occasion. Hoover was definitely a man's man."[18]

So too were Sid Richardson and Clint Murchison, two wildcatters from Texas who struck oil together in 1919 and remained friends for life. Richardson and Murchison met Hoover at the racetrack in Del Mar, during his late summer trip to the West Coast in 1949. For billionaires Richardson and Murchison, Hoover was a powerful friend in Washington who shared their conservative views on crime and Communism. For Hoover, the Richardson-Murchison coupling was a direct connection to wealth. In the early fifties, the oil barons included both Hoover and Tolson in their oil exploration investments, promising to pay dividends if their wells produced, and protect the pair from losses if the wells did not.

By 1953, Murchison had bought the Del Mar track as well as built a new luxury hotel—the Del Charro Hotel in nearby La Jolla, which included finely appointed bungalows with private verandas and commanding views of the Pacific. A two-bedroom bungalow was reserved for the use of Hoover and Tolson. The Bureau chief and his assistant lacked for nothing—except a bill, since Murchison happily picked up the tab for the pair's annual monthlong stay.

It was at the Del Charro that Hoover also first met Haroldson Lafayette Hunt, "H.L." to his friends and foes, another excessively rich oilman and a bigamist who had fourteen children. Like Murchison and Richardson, Hunt endorsed Joseph McCarthy and liberally funded his investigations that were based, of course, on Hoover provided material.

Hoover's basis for his friendship with all these men was generosity—theirs. Hoover openly exchanged his power

position in Washington for accommodations in the form
of entertainment, lodging, and investment advice—perks
Hoover thought little of accepting as an adjunct to his
salary, which had recently jumped to $20,000 per year, for
a wartime high of $16,000.

The men also provided Hoover with something far more
inestimable: introductions to members of organized crime.

In May 1950, Senator Estes Kefauver, as chairman of
the Senate Special Committee to Investigate Organized
Crime in Interstate Commerce, opened hearings to identify members of the Mafia operating within the borders of
the United States. It was, on the eve of those hearings,
that then secretary of state J. Howard McGrath quoted J.
Edgar Hoover in announcing that there was no such thing
as a "national crime syndicate." At the time of that statement, Hoover had met socially with Frank Costello,
Meyer Lansky, Sam Giancana, and Santos Trafficante, representing the heads of the New York, Las Vegas, Chicago,
and Miami Mafia families. The introductions had been
handled by Louis Rosenstiel, Clint Murchison, and Myer
Schine.[19]

Publicly, Hoover stated that while he was aware of
individual crime families operating within states, any illegal activities properly fell under the jurisdiction of the
various state police departments. Even as Kefauver televised the hearings, Hoover steadfastly maintained his
position.

Yet it was three years later, with a different president,
different attorney general, different senator, and different
hearings that Hoover found himself in a far more dangerous position. Senator Joseph McCarthy, with Roy Cohn

and G. David Schine at his side, was conducting a televised inquisition, using material generated by the FBI as his source. What had started as an investigative hearing on Communism had turned into a witch hunt that was shocking the nation and appalling the president. For Hoover, the real threat was where McCarthy questions would lead, organized crime being a small jump from political subversives.

Fortunately for Hoover, McCarthy's ego, which had grown even larger than that of the Bureau's director, exacerbated the problem yet provided the answer. When McCarthy deliberately enlarged his attack by accusing the U.S. Army of harboring Communists within its ranks, the president took it as a personal affront. Eisenhower was, after all, not only a general in the army but its commander in chief as well.

The president called upon Hoover to use his influence on McCarthy to redirect his attacks, something McCarthy had no intention of doing. Moreover, the army revealed that even as the senator's committee was looking into misconduct on the military's staff, they were applying pressure for favorable treatment of G. David Schine who was about to be drafted into the service of his country.

While Joseph McCarthy had little use for the overt antics of Schine, Cohn had taken a passionate liking to his friend, who luxuriated in the attention. He was flattered when Cohn attempted to have Schine commissioned as an officer, though disappointed when he failed. Cohn next appealed to Secretary of the Army Robert T. Stevens to allow Schine to return from basic training on weekends to work on the subcommittee hearings. Further, he requested that Schine be relieved of KP duties and be allowed to leave the post in the evenings for visits with Cohn.

The army, incredulous but accommodating, attempted to placate the insidious Cohn by giving Private Schine special consideration. After several months of continuous requests—Cohn would call army counsel John G. Adams three, four, sometime five times day—the army had had enough. Reports reached the president and Hoover that Schine was being granted special privileges, being driven to rifle-range exercises, and afforded special equipment.

> He had special mitten-shaped gloves, with one finger, the trigger finger, separated from the rest. He had special boots with straps and buckles on the side. He claimed the Army didn't have any that fitted him. He had a fur-lined hood which he wore. He had an air mattress and a heavy down sleeping bag—and he never had to sweat out a full-time bivouac period at that.[20]

The army ordered a special investigation into the treatment of Schine on January 29, 1954. It took nearly three months for the army to issue its report—a scathing attack on both McCarthy and Cohn—Cohn for his arrogant and belligerent behavior, and McCarthy for allowing his chief counsel to run rampant through established protocol and military regulations.

After reading the report, Republican senator Charles Porter from Michigan said, "Assuming the information is accurate, Mr. Cohn should be removed immediately."[21]

The editorial in the March 13, 1954, edition of the *New York Times,* read: "We should have preferred to see the present crackdown on Mr. McCarthy based on moral indignation over his whole philosophy—if one can call it that—instead of the specific outrages he has committed in recent weeks against the Army. But in any case, the senator and his friends have now been truly hoist with their own petard."[22]

Hoover, having seen the change in the public and presidential temperament concerning the McCarthy hearings, immediately began supplying the White House with regular briefings on the errors contained in McCarthy's statements. Cutting his losses, and covering his flank, Hoover rejected McCarthy's telephone calls, and became unavailable, disappearing into his fort of layered access through which no one could penetrate, not even the president.

McCarthy had made a fatal error, revealing his source of material when pressed for substantiation. Hoover immediately denied that McCarthy ever had any direct access to FBI files, which was, in fact, true, since Hoover supplied him with summaries of various files, prepared specifically to impact the senator's case.

When, on December 2, 1954, McCarthy was censured by his peers in the Senate by a vote of 67 to 22, his career was in ruins, his reputation shattered, yet his friendship with Hoover balanced behind a mysterious shroud of silence. In three years, McCarthy was dead, the victim of alcoholism.

As the McCarthy hearings ended, the mood in America was changing. For the first time, the world seemed at peace, and the country was flocking to suburbia with its homespun family life. The first color televisions were making their way into homes, though hits like *I Love Lucy* and *Father Knows Best* were still filmed in black and white. Doris Day was recording "Que Sera, Sera" and kids across the country were singing "The Legend of Davy Crockett." The Cold War was a fact of everyday life—something to worry about but not actually see—and Communists, despite all the fuss from McCarthy, were clearly not invading America.

Under the docile exterior of peace and harmony in the country, however, a festering discontent was beginning to surface as African Americans began to demand the inalienable rights granted them by the constitution and the Fourteenth Amendment. Rights of equality and equal protection under the law. Rights that had been routinely denied them when they were excluded from restaurants, hotels, nightclubs, and schools—the latter being examined in 1954 with the U.S. Supreme Court decision in *Brown v. Board of Education.* In that decision, the Court determined that "separate educational facilities are inherently unequal" and denied the legal basis for segregation in the 21 states that still allowed it.

By 1955, it was apparent to civil rights leaders in America that a door had been opened illuminating the potential of a bright future in which all men, and women, were indeed created equal. With the courts firmly on the side of equality, for the first time in his life, Hoover found himself obliged to enforce laws that he personally found in conflict with his own beliefs. He was, if nothing else, a gentleman of the Old South who believed that blacks were fine "in their place," which to Hoover meant as servants, handymen, laborers, and field-workers.

Those beliefs extended into an FBI that was, and had been, basically an all-white organization. The occasional Asian who became a special agent was subjected to frequent background checks far in excess of their white counterparts, while blacks were not considered FBI material at all under Hoover's standards of hiring.

The few blacks who had been hired by the Bureau worked exclusively for Hoover. James Crawford, his chauffeur, was expected to be on-call around the clock, and even worked weekends at the director's home on general maintenance and gardening—on FBI wages. Sam Noisette, the cheery receptionist in Hoover's outer-office, was the gatekeeper to the inner office, having joined the Bureau as a messenger in 1927. When Noisette moved into the receptionist spot, Worthington Smith took his place as Hoover's personal messenger. Hoover had a black driver at his exclusive disposal in Los Angeles and another in Miami. The black men of the FBI.

Officially, Hoover made an effort to dictate that no special agent should allow his or her own beliefs on civil rights to interfere with the performance of duty. "I am very much concerned over the fact that some of our personnel have apparently expressed themselves to the effect that the FBI does not favor Civil Rights investigations. I want it clearly understood that all Bureau personnel should be most careful not to indicate any views or expressions of opinion regarding any matters over which this Bureau has investigative jurisdiction."[23] It then became a matter of limiting the jurisdiction to exclude cases dealing with civil rights.

The issue came to the forefront on August 27, 1955, when a 14-year-old boy named Emmett Till was beaten and shot to death by two white men in Money, Mississippi, in the heart of the cotton-growing Delta, on a night that hung thick with humidity and fireflies. Till's crime was having talked to a 21-year-old white woman in Bryant's Grocery Store at the far end of Main Street as he purchased two cents worth of bubble gum. Till had come down to Money from Chicago to visit relatives and stay with Preacher Moses Wright. His body was found, bloated and decomposing, several days later in the Tallahatchie River, a cotton gin fan tied around his neck with barbed wire.

A horrified nation watched as the FBI did nothing, though Till had been kidnapped by two local men, taken from his bed at gunpoint. "We had no right to investigate because there was no violation of federal law," Hoover said, speaking about the case later on the Monitor Radio network. "Three days later, we received word that the body of the boy had been found in the Tallahatchie River. . . . The Department ruled that there was, on the facts, no violation of federal civil rights statutes, and, accordingly, the FBI was to conduct no investigation."[24]

It was no secret who committed the crime—Roy Bryant and J. W. Milam were identified as the killers. It had been Bryant's wife, Carolyn, who had sold Till the gum and later testified at the trial that he made "ugly remarks" to her. The local businesses raised $10,000 to pay for the defense of the murderers, who were found not guilty by a jury of 12 white men who had deliberated for only a hour. "We wouldn't have taken so long if we hadn't stopped to drink pop," they said.

The local newspaper reflected the town's irritation caused by the influx of national press and publicity. The headline in the *Jackson Clarion-Ledger* read: SUMNER FOLK ALREADY PLENTY BORED WITH ALL THIS RUCKUS. So too was the Bureau's director. J. Edgar Hoover was about to learn, however, how very wrong he was.

With reinforcement from an Eisenhower White House, Hoover was becoming lazy. For the first time in his life, he actually relaxed, and literally slept on the job. He was still arriving early with Tolson by his side, being dropped off a few blocks from the Department of Justice and walking into work—walking now his only form of exercise. The Mayflower was still the preferred spot for lunch, with Hoover and Tolson taking their normal one hour and fifteen minutes.

"He returned to the office at one-fifteen," according to "Deke" DeLoach, "but his door would be closed till three [while he napped]. Then he was in until quarter to five."[25]

No more late nights at the Stork Club. No more tuxedoed dinners with movie stars. This was a calmer Hoover who felt more secure with his position than at any other time of his life. The occasional sexual slur was to be expected, even anticipated, for life had become routine, predictable.

Yet even as Hoover became ever more set in his ways, the country began to change—evolving, moving, at a pace unlike anything in its history. Spurred on by the movement in the courts toward equal rights, African Americans were mobilizing. If Communism was no longer a threat, and homosexuality was more scandal than danger, the blacks of America were taking a stand that would have far-reaching implications across every facet of life in America.

Hoover had only a few months peace in the sanctity of post-McCarthy Washington when a black woman named Rosa Parks let it be known in Montgomery, Alabama, that she was not going to ride in the back of the bus any longer. She had not boarded the bus on December 1, 1955, to get arrested. She only wanted to return home after a long day of work as a seamstress. But this one-time secretary to the president of the NAACP was arrested when she refused to move, resulting in a boycott of the entire Montgomery bus system. It was to be the start of movement lead by Dr. Martin Luther King Jr., pastor of the Dexter Avenue Baptist Church in Montgomery, which would impact race relations from that day forward.

Hoover assessed the situation for the Eisenhower cabinet on March 9, 1956, with a report he titled "Racial Tension and Civil Rights." It was, of course, not personally written by Hoover—Louis Nichols took care of the text. It did, nevertheless, reflect the director's thoughts on the direction in which America was moving, and the new dangers it was facing.

The 24-page report moved to attack extremists on both sides of the issue, attempting to defuse a situation that was progressing toward violence. More than clarifying the status of civil rights in the country, however, it served to pinpoint Hoover's personal perception of the issue when he said that "delicate situations are aggravated by some overzealous but ill-advised leaders of the NAACP and by the Communist party."

By linking the Communist Party to the campaign for civil rights, Hoover piggybacked an issue he knew well to a concept that he was totally ill-prepared to discuss or accept. Hoover was, if nothing else, a product of his youth, and the strict moral code dictated by his mother. In that world, blacks remained separated from whites, joining only when economics forced them to coexist.

He lectured the cabinet that the law of master and slave in the South was "still the rule." He talked of intelligence, stating that "the claim is made that Southern Negroes are usually below the intellectual level of white children. The further claim is made that it would take a generation to bring the races to a parity." He added that southern whites were frightened to share bathrooms and gymnasiums for "colored parents are not as careful in looking after the health and cleanliness of their children." And as for the Court-mandated "mixed education," Hoover stated that it "stalks the specter of racial intermarriage."[26]

Privately, Hoover worried that blacks were gaining too much power; that their priorities were too confined to their own issues. For Hoover, equality of the races was of less interest than making certain that southern senators—the ones responsible for his annual appropriations—found him decidedly on the side of whites. To accomplish this sleight of hand without seeming to be bigoted, Hoover attempted to sidestep the issue of civil rights entirely, passing jurisdiction along to another federal bureau—any other federal bureau—willing to take on the hotbed of controversy.

It was, however, an election year—a year when civil rights would be very much in the campaign news. The president, who had suffered a near-fatal heart attack in

September 1955, had fully recovered and planned to run for a second term. The Democrats faced a harder choice, one that focused on Adlai Stevenson, but left the door ajar for a full spectrum of grassroots candidates.

Joseph Kennedy, Hoover's longtime friend, had his own concept of the presidential race—one that featured his son, John F. Kennedy, running for vice president with the director of the FBI leading the Democratic Party to victory as president of the United States.

Joseph Kennedy had met Hoover during his junior years in the Justice Department and, like Hoover, had grown in power with each successive administration. A major contributor to the Democratic Party, Kennedy was rewarded with the ambassadorship to England under Roosevelt. As a courtesy to his old friend, since the early fifties, Hoover had maintained a satellite team of four special agents in Hyannisport, Massachusetts, where the Kennedy family maintained a compound of homes, with the FBI at the ambassador's deposal. It was therefore more than just a courtesy that inspired the elder Kennedy to write Hoover about the upcoming presidential election.

Dear Edgar:

I think I have become too cynical in my old age, but the only two men I know in public life today for whose opinion I give one continental both happen to be named Hoover—one John Edgar and one Herbert— and I am proud to think that both of them hold me in some esteem.

I listened to Walter Winchell mention your name as a candidate for president. If that should come to pass, it would be the most wonderful thing for the United States, and whether you were on a Republican or Democratic ticket, I would guarantee you the largest contribution that you would ever get form [sic] anybody and the hardest work by either a Democrat or Republican. I think the United States deserves you. I only hope it gets you.

My best to you always,

Sincerely,
Joe

Hoover was not interested in becoming president of the United States. He didn't see the point. He already had more power, at least in his own country, which was, after all, all he cared about.

Winchell knew that when he broadcast the suggestion—just one of any number of ploys the journalist was using to keep Hoover's friendship. His column's readership had been slipping, his radio broadcast on the Mutual Broadcasting System was so opinionated as to be disregarded, and a new television show on NBC was struggling to find an audience. The struggle ended when Winchell's sponsor dropped the show after Winchell alluded on the radio to presidential candidate Adlai Stevenson's alleged homosexuality. "A vote for Adlai is a vote for Christine Jorgensen,"‡ Winchell had said. The tip had come from his friend J. Edgar Hoover.

---

‡   George Jorgensen was a 98-pound ex-GI who, in 1952, traveled to Denmark, and had a sex change operation, returning to the United States as Christine Jorgensen.

In November 1956, Dwight D. Eisenhower was reelected as president of the United States in a landslide victory over Adlai Stevenson, ensuring Hoover another four years of power and domination of American law enforcement. Yet, it would be four years that pushed him over the line of legality, a position from which there was no return, in an effort to maintain the inside track on a war he had no way to win.

ELEVEN

CIVIL RIGHTS, CIVIL WRONGS

C lyde Tolson allowed his knife to cut slowly through the prime rib, his plate overflowing with blood and fat that splattered on the tablecloth. He considered the question carefully before speaking, for to answer Hoover in haste was to risk instant mocking and the residual cruelty that always followed.

"There would be no room for error," Tolson, ever the skeptic, said when he finally spoke. "I'm not certain we could ensure that."

"If no one knows the entire operation, any screw-up is self-containing," the Bureau's director countered, then pursed his lips as he sniffed superiority. "Make certain of it."

Seagulls from the La Jolla beach circled overhead, their cries signaling the coming sunset in a nightly ritual familiar to all the guests at the Del Charro Hotel, who witnessed, but did not hear the conversation around the pool that evening. Against the backdrop of refined elegance, the talk of counterintelligence seemed academic like a textbook discussion of theory, not the groundwork for illicit activity. Yet that was in fact what Hoover was suggesting, without the slightest reservation of its legality.

As with most things that occupied the director's mind, the concept had its heart in Communism. It was, as

Hoover explained it, nothing more than what the Communists were doing already. The FBI only needed to play the game better: plant stories with cooperative columnists to ensure that the actions of the Communist Party leaders became publicly known. The more untrue the story, the more dramatic the impact. Forged letters, hotel bills, telephone records, and medical histories were gold mines of potential scandal. The disruption of everyday activities was the point. If the discovery led to arrests, so much the better. The planting of evidence was a skill every bit as difficult as the uncovering of evidence. Who better to do it than the skilled special agents of the FBI?

Labeled "COINTELPRO" for counterintelligence programs, the first operations targeted the Communist Party in late 1956 but quickly expanded to the New Left, the Ku Klux Klan, and the civil rights movement, where there was unlimited opportunity for infiltration. Informants had long been a valuable source to the FBI. With COINTELPRO, the effort was enlarged to include on-the-job harassment plus intimidation through IRS audits and police interrogations.

When Hoover first suggested the initial operation, placing it under the auspices of Alan Belmont, assistant director of the Domestic Intelligence Division, it seemed that caution controlled every aspect of the plan. But as the tactics became increasingly successful, they were expanded without regard to potential risk or legality, particularly in the area of black bag jobs and the use of eavesdropping devices. Hoover never failed to remind others that results were what mattered; curtailing crime was the goal. Even Assistant Director "Deke" DeLoach, a longtime admirer of the Bureau's director, said that "Hoover had sometimes found it necessary to work with less than full authority. The FBI adhered rigidly to most of the restrictions placed on it; but occasions arose when Hoover believed the end justified the means, that regulations should give way to expediency."

Publicly, it seemed that Hoover could do no wrong. His popularity was cresting, crowned in glory by the release of a new book, *The FBI Story* by Pulitzer Prize winner Don Whitehead. Not only did the book have the full cooperation of the Bureau, but it also was the brainchild of Louis Nichols, who personally proofed every page, making suggestions that would seal the FBI's place in the history of criminology to dramatic effect. Publicized as it was by the nation's FBI-favored journalists, the Whitehead book became a best seller overnight, boosted by the public appearances of Hoover, basking in the adulation like a lizard warming itself on a rock ledge.

As the latest brick in a life spent building a wall of propriety and honor, the book was cast in tones of glory that overlooked many of the Bureau's inefficiencies. Not the least of these was Hoover's continued denial of the existence of a national crime syndicate, and his refusal to address the growing number of gangland kidnappings and executions. A single event in a large stone house in a remote section of New York State would change all that, however, and leave the Bureau's director little choice but to play catch-up in the dirty game of organized crime.

The sodium light of a late autumn afternoon edged the pines like a pencil drawing against a sky too clear to be believed. It had rained the night before, and the damp, clean smell of wood shavings—the kind that are scattered on the bottom of a hamster's cage—mixed with the strong scent of aftershave. Men in suits and fedoras, Italians with names like Genovese, Profaci, Gambino, Maggadino, Bonanno, and Bernardo had gathered for a barbecue. Yet this was no ordinary party. This was a powwow of Mafia bosses, underbosses, capos, and soldiers.

That New York state trooper sergeant Edgar Croswell happened upon the meeting in Apalachin, a sleepy village in the Susquehanna River valley, was a combination of seasoned intuition and blind luck. Croswell had driven to the 58-room Parkway Motel in nearby Vestal to speak to the manager about the writer of a bounced check. While there, Croswell spotted Joseph Barbara Jr., the dark-haired son of reputed crime lord Joseph Sr., verifying multiple room reservations being held under his father's name.

For some time, Croswell had been watching the movements of the elder Barbara, a local resident and distributor for Canada Dry soda for the region. The curious trooper convinced his partner, Vincent Vasisko, and two U.S. Treasury agents to accompany him on a visit to the elegant 53-acre Barbara estate where he discovered the lunchtime party in progress, the barbecue pit at the rear of the home stocked with burgers, Enrico Caruso's "Recitar! . . . Vesti la giubba" blaring from the record player. The assembled Cadillacs, Lincolns, and Rolls-Royce suggested the wealth of those inside the house.

As the officers began to run license plates, there was a mass exodus from the property. Some of the partiers attempted to leave in their cars, others fled on foot, running into the woods. Sixty-three of the men were subsequently taken to the Vestal substation, where they were questioned and released. Of the group, 50 had police records with 35 convictions for a variety of crimes. All were of Italian descent, many related to one another.

As word of the Apalachin incident reached the headquarters of the FBI, J. Edgar Hoover had little choice but to admit the existence of La Cosa Nostra. Like most challenges at the FBI, he approached the task of tracking the organization through a system of indexes and files. Project Top Hoodlum was put into effect two weeks after the November 14 Mafia get-together, with Hoover instructing his field offices to prepare a list of the top 10 organized crime figures within their jurisdictions.

The entire concept was flawed of course. Certain areas of the country struggled to identify even a single Mafia member, while others had to whittle down their lists from several hundred to ten. Special agents in charge of FBI offices in New York, Philadelphia, Boston, Chicago, Las Vegas, and Miami were particularly hard-pressed to deliver the requested names, and instead sent lists of families. Though not effective, at least it was progress.

Robert Kennedy, then chief counsel for the McClellan Committee, the Senate committee investigating labor unions and organized crime, concluded that the "methods of our law enforcement agencies have not kept pace with the improved technique of today's criminals. We are still trying to fight the modern Al Capone with the weapons that we used twenty-five years ago. They simply are not effective."[1]

Hoover took the criticism personally, certain that Robert Kennedy was targeting him for his part in denying the attorney a role in the disastrous McCarthy hearings. The stage was set for a running battle between the two men that would hit its peak in another five years. For now, Kennedy watched as Hoover floundered. Hoover watched as Kennedy philandered. It was, by any unbiased account, an even match.

Though organized crime stole many of the headlines right along with massive amounts of cash, the mood of the country was decidedly racist. African Americans adopted "Black is Beautiful" as a mantra and attempted to convince a mostly bewildered public that their civil rights had been trampled upon. Northern whites were largely perplexed by the claim, since blacks and whites in the Northeast seemed to mix freely in churches, schools, and public places.

In the South, however, race was a lens through which all else was viewed. It determined a position in society that defied education, wealth, talent, and logic. Born in a place of bigotry and hate, it surfaced on the streets of Little Rock, Arkansas, as nine African American students attempted to enter the previously all-white Little Rock Central High School, only to be blocked by the National Guard and a wall of white racists who failed to understand the principle of equality and kindness to all. That the lawlessness was supported by the governor of the state spoke volumes to the need to educate and enlighten.

Martin Luther King Jr. later said, "Segregation . . . not only harms one physically but injures one spiritually. . . . It scars the soul. . . . It is a system which forever stares the segregated in the face, saying 'You are less than . . .' 'You are not equal to . . .'"

Hoover had no interest in seeing that southern schools were legally integrated as required by the courts. On the surface, he thought it a danger to the peace of the region, predicting, accurately as it happened, that violence was the natural by-product of enforced behavior. Privately, he considered the education that blacks were already receiving in segregated southern schools to be "totally adequate."[2]

As he had with previous localized hostilities, Hoover considered the Little Rock situation to be outside FBI jurisdiction. He did, however, order several dozen special agents into the area to help operate the local FBI office. The agents were housed in the Sam Peck Hotel,* directly across from the Federal Building, necessitating the removal of an equal number of national press reporters.

Though it was widely assumed that the FBI would be at Central High on the morning of September 23, 1957, no agents were present, having been told to stay at the Federal Building and not approach the school, which was over a mile away. It was only after a riot broke out at the school that Hoover authorized the agents to move in and begin questioning students. By then, the identities of those who had participated in the riot were nearly impossible to prove, since the white students closed ranks and refused to speak openly about the incident. Three months

---

* Built in 1913, the Sam Peck Hotel was named after its second owners, Sam and Henrietta Peck. Remodeled and restored in 1984, it was renamed the Legacy Hotel. During the Whitewater hearings, special windows were installed so that television announcers could broadcast from the hotel with a view of the federal courthouse across the street in the background.

later, the agents were pulled back to Washington, without ever gaining an indictment.

By that time, Hoover had been sidetracked by the news that reporters from the *New York Post* were preparing a multipart series on his life, the first to appear since the early thirties, when *Collier's* magazine printed an article titled "Hist! Who's That?" by Ray Tucker and the *New Yorker* published a three-part profile by Jack Alexander. There had been attempts to write books on the FBI itself, all either controlled or sabotaged by the Bureau. No one had ever dared write at length about Hoover, however. Or at least until *Post* publisher Dorothy Schiff announced her intention to do just that.

Almost immediately, doors were closed to the team of reporters seeking interviews. Congressmen and senators would voice opinions only off the record. And Schiff began to receive warnings that any article on Hoover would likely never see print. Any hope the publisher held that the First Amendment's freedom of the press would allow her free rein in pursuing the piece quickly evaporated a week after she met with a major *Post* advertiser for a casual lunch. Her luncheon date was Joseph L. Eckhouse, a chief executive with Gimbel Bros. department store, who had been approached by Hoover and Tolson in New York's Pavillon restaurant, when the pair joined him for coffee and dessert.

To Eckhouse's astonishment, Hoover revealed that the *Post* was preparing a "smear campaign" against the FBI, fingering Jimmy Wechsler, the *Post's* editor, as the crusader. When Eckhouse rallied to the *Post's* defense, Hoover claimed that Wechsler's wife, Nancy, had been fired from her job as chief counsel of President Truman's Civil Rights Committee "for being a Communist." The assertions were blatantly false. Nancy Wechsler was neither fired nor a Communist, and her husband was not the one behind the profile of J. Edgar Hoover. That honor fell squarely on Dorothy Schiff, who was only beginning to feel pressure from the Bureau's director.

Convinced that Schiff was determined to tarnish his image or, more precisely, that there was something derogatory in the series about his private life, Hoover authorized the assignment of several special agents to uncover the scope of the charges and disrupt the writing of the profile. In the months that followed, both Schiff and her reporters were followed, their telephone lines tapped, their sources intimidated, and their advertisers forewarned.

Dorothy Schiff was not an easily intimidated woman. Yet within weeks of Hoover's initial volley, she found herself both paranoid and suspicious. "Sitting on the sofa with my husband in our living room, I was overwhelmed by a strange feeling that I was talking for the record," Schiff wrote in 1959. "Nervously, I looked around under the furniture, but found nothing. This did not ease my tension. Often I had been told that 'bugs' could be very cleverly concealed. So I kept my voice low, behaving like Americans visiting Moscow hotels, and the refugees from Nazi Germany who had not yet been able to break the habit of searching the room and speaking in whispers when indoors."[3]

For an entire year, a sextet of *Post* reporters—William Dufty, David Gelman, Edward Kosner, Irving Lieberman, Carl J. Pelleck, and Joseph Barry—attempted to unravel the mystery of J. Edgar Hoover. As they did, Hoover wrote a letter to the journal *America* that said in part, "It has been quite obvious to us that a carefully organized campaign is under way to undermine confidence in the groups charged with the responsibility of protecting our nation's security."

Although the *Post* series was not mentioned by name, Hoover's friends in the media picked up the torch. Walter Winchell wrote about the maligning series. So too did Westbrook Pegler and George Sokolsky. John Marshall Butler, the Republican senator from Maryland, and Gordon Harry Scherer, the Republican congressman from Ohio, introduced the issue into the *Congressional Record*.

In the end, despite thousands of man-hours and a nearly unlimited budget, the reporters found nothing scandalous, or even remotely provocative. What they did uncover was the stuff of fan magazines. Hoover kept a clean desk, liked to watch wrestling on television, didn't read detective stories, valued efficiency, listened to music by Lawrence Welk, and hated to exercise. While hardly revelations, the facts were more than most people previously knew about America's top cop. If Hoover was prepared for salacious gossip, he found none in the 12-part series. The reporters declared that "prudence is one of his least advertised but most persistent virtues. There is little recklessness or daring in the Hoover saga."[4]

It was hardly surprising when the newspaper reported that Hoover brought his propensity for order into the Bureau. "In the main FBI office in Washington, for example, window shades must be raised or lowered to a perfectly uniform level, just as in Hoover's house," the reporters uncovered. They quoted a former maid who claimed that Hoover's red bedspread had to hang "precisely and evenly" on the sides of the bed.[5]

They made mention that bow ties weren't proper office attire. Neither were suspenders or short socks. Blue tones were encouraged in neckwear; gray tones in three-piece suits. Hardly shocking revelations considering the nature of FBI work.

The *Post* noted that Mervyn LeRoy had produced and directed the $3 million film version of *The FBI Story* starring James Stewart and Vera Miles. The film opened at Radio City Music Hall several weeks before the newspaper began running its exposé. Hoover had provided two special agents as technical advisers on the film at government expense, and five other agents appeared in acting roles.

"Dear Mervyn," Hoover wrote to LeRoy, the day after seeing the film at the FBI headquarters. "As I told you yesterday, words cannot express my complete delight at seeing *The FBI Story*. I felt certain the picture would be a great credit to the FBI, but what I saw and heard was beyond my greatest expectations. Your treatment of the development and growth of our bureau, interwoven with a warm family story, will have a great impact on the American public. It was done with great warmth, humility and dignity. . . . It can truly be said that you are one of us."[6]

While it was reported Hoover cried when he saw the film, it was not reported that he received $50,000 in unreported income for his services as a technical consultant.[7] Nor was it ever mentioned that Hoover received another $50,000 in royalties from his 1958 book *Masters of Deceit*, published by Clint Murchison's Henry Holt & Company. Clyde Tolson, Louis Nichols, freelance writer Bill Nichols (no relation), and the FBI Recreational Association each received $50,000 as well. Hoover's total royalties eventually totaled $71,000, all funneled through the FBI Recreational Association to avoid taxes.

There was confirmation that Hoover publicly dated Lela Rogers, and "enjoyed a friendship with Dorothy Lamour . . . model Anita Colby, and a correspondence with Shirley Temple." Even more fascinating was the total void of any suggestion of homosexuality on Hoover's part. According to Dorothy Schiff, none was ever found. In 1988, writer Anthony Summers, who would subsequently make the claim in his book *Official and Confidential,* nevertheless wrote to Schiff and revealed to her, "My own researchers so far have failed to substantiate the rumours that he was homosexual."[8]

In the area of civil liberties, the newspaper quoted ACLU founder Roger Baldwin, who said that over his 40-year history with Hoover, "If I were asked to produce evidence of transgression of citizens' rights by the FBI, I could cite only scattered cases."[9] Hardly a blanket condemnation of the Bureau that the *Post* had expected.

Regarding Communism and the FBI, civil libertarian Norman Thomas said that he was "concerned at the increasing tendency of J. Edgar Hoover to set himself up as an infallible interpreter of facts." Hoover, of course, knew more about Communism than any other law enforcement official—he would be happy to tell you in couched terms, free for the asking. Who better to interpret facts? Certainly the president thought Hoover was performing superbly, having awarded the director of the FBI the very first Gold Medal "for exceptionally meritorious civilian service" to the government.

For all its effort and intention, the *Post* was left to summarize its findings by admitting that "at the far end of over 40 years of history, [Hoover is] still recognizable in terms of the promising youth of long ago: still aloof, still solemn, still full of the ambitious energy that brought him quickly to the notice of his superiors when he was putting in overtime as a young mail clerk in the Justice Department."

Despite its total lack of controversy or revelation, Hoover's reaction to the piece was predictable, if only because the story was absent of laudatory phrases. When Harry Hoffmann, editor of the *Charleston Gazette,* wrote to Hoover requesting a comment to attach to the reprinting of the series in his West Virginia newspaper, he received this response: "As you no doubt can readily understand, I did not care to dignify the scurrilous unjustified attack upon the FBI by the *New York Post* at the time the original articles were running. My opinion remains the same."[10]

What the *Post*'s reporters failed to realize and subsequently uncover was that Hoover was *not* the same, was not "still recognizable." Having built the Bureau on his back and successfully developed filing systems, fingerprint records, ballistic testing, and all the other essential elements of the fully functioning FBI, Hoover had essentially completed his job. America was no longer entertaining a landscape where hoodlums freely roamed the countryside robbing banks and taking hostages for ransom. The Eisenhower era had provided peace. The country no longer had a fear of Nazis or Fascists. Communists were people who lived in Russia and China, and despite all that Hoover continued to say about the threat, it seemed a distant one at best, far removed from the Levittowns of American suburban life.

Had Hoover chosen to address the threat of organized crime, which was freely operating in the country under the guise of legitimate business, he might have been able to resurrect his importance to both the Bureau and America. Instead, he chose to pursue the issue of civil rights for African Americans. Hardly a crime, yet he tried to make it one by implicating the movement's leader, Dr. Martin Luther King Jr., suggesting that Communists had infiltrated the campaign to achieve equal rights for all citizens.

Hoover's interest in King developed gradually, his file originally a part of the records kept on the Southern Christian Leadership Conference (SCLC), which he and other black ministers launched in 1957. Hoover knew of King's visit to the Eisenhower White House with civil rights pioneers A. Philip Randolph and Roy Wilkins, having discussed the meeting with Attorney General William Rogers, who judged the meeting "pleasant, if cold."

King's rise to prominence occurred in 1961 as Hoover witnessed yet another change in the White House and King received national coverage for his involvement in the Freedom Rides. That John F. Kennedy had narrowly beaten out the Hoover-supported candidate, Richard M. Nixon, was enough of a surprise. With Kennedy in the White House and his brother Robert now attorney general and Hoover's boss, the nation's attitude turned toward youth. It was, as Hoover told Clint Murchison, a time when "experience gave way to inexperience and a pretty wife."

Robert Kennedy had long been a supporter of equal rights, and he took a special interest when King, then a rising leader in the civil rights movement, wrote an article in *Nation,* the bastion of left-wing journalism in America. In it, King called on the federal government in general and the FBI in particular to make employment available to all races.[11] Special agent M. A. Jones sent a copy of the article to "Deke" DeLoach with a memo recommending no action. "Although King is in error in his comments relating to the FBI," Jones wrote, "it is believed inadvisable to call his hand on this matter as he obviously would only welcome any controversy or resulting publicity that might ensue."[12]

There was no ongoing investigation into King at the time, but as the year progressed and King's fame and influence grew, Hoover became ever more interested in a man who he discovered in 1962 had "Communist ties." In a memo to Attorney General Kennedy, Hoover wrote that Stanley D. Levison, "a member of the Communist Party, USA . . . is allegedly a close advisor to the Reverend Martin Luther King, Jr."[13]

Levison was a white attorney and businessman who had taken an interest in King's civil rights efforts, counseling the minister on fund-raising projects and legal issues. He provided editorial help on King's first book, *Stride Toward Freedom.* The FBI had originally focused on Levison's dealings with the Communist Party in the early fifties when Levison had given the party advice on the handling of its finances in an effort to keep the group hidden from the federal government. That Levison eventually thought better of his totally legal activities and ultimately divorced himself from any association with the party never made it into the FBI's documentation or outlook.

Hoover's once-a-Communist–always-a-Communist mind-set was fueled by the increasing tension across America, brought on by the sharp political rhetoric of Soviet premier Nikita Khrushchev. The personification of the Iron Curtain and all things Communist, Khrushchev was playing a high stakes game of intimidation and subversion that rivaled Hoover's own—even though Khrushchev was playing it on an international stage, with nuclear weapons in his arsenal.

While Hoover's campaign against the influence of Communism was based on textbook knowledge and gut instinct, President Kennedy had seen Russia and the effects of Communism on domestic life from an up close and personal vantage point. At the age of 23, Kennedy went to Moscow on a diplomatic passport. It was an experience that would have a profound impact on the young future president.

"While working in the Paris Embassy in the summer of 1939," the *Harvard Crimson* reported, "[Kennedy] succeeded in touring Russia and will tell you that it wouldn't be a very nice place to live. He views Russian expansionist policies as a real threat to this country, supports the halting of Communist influence no matter what the cost. 'Russia is the main threat, the only power militarily strong enough to constitute a threat to peace.'"[14]

Yet even from a foundation of Communism bred in apprehension and caution, Kennedy made little attempt to restrict the party's growth. Hoover watched incredulously as the Bay of Pigs, a covert CIA operation in Cuba to over-throw dictator Fidel Castro, went disastrously wrong, only to be followed by a Kennedy-Khrushchev summit in Vienna in the spring of 1961 in which an unprepared Kennedy was bullied by the Communist leader.

For Hoover, it was a humbling experience, despite the fact that he was not directly involved. He had not been consulted on the Bay of Pigs, though former FBI agent Robert Maheu had run interference for the CIA with his organized-crime connections. He had not been privy to any of the discussions that Attorney General Kennedy had with Russian intelligence officer Georgi Bolshakov prior to the Vienna conference. And he knew nothing about Operation Mongoose, an ongoing CIA operation to invade Cuba and oust its leader. What he *did* know was that the Kennedys refused to listen to his repeated warnings about Communist infiltration across America, and now, it seemed, the brothers refused to take seriously Hoover's information that the Rev. Martin Luther King Jr. had deliberately allowed himself to be surrounded by Communists.

Not since Harry Truman was in office had Hoover been unable to reach the White House with a single call. Worse, his titular boss, the attorney general, seemed almost disinterested. Twice the Bureau's director had written letters condemning the administration's inactivity, and twice the letters were left unsent after Hoover rethought what the president's reaction might be.

It was not until August 1962 that Hoover was brought into the president's confidence, and only because Kennedy wanted surveillance on Georgi Bolshakov. Hoover had first heard the name the previous year when the attorney general introduced him to the man posing as an information officer in the Soviet Embassy. Feigning praise, Bolshakov compared Hoover to the head of the KGB, which was of course the *wrong* thing to say to the lifelong anti-communist.

The CIA already had Bolshakov under surveillance, even though he was acting as a go-between for the Soviet government and the president of the United States. Hoover's assignment was more salacious: determine what interested Bolshakov sexually, and coerce him into a relationship with an informant. The president knew Hoover was a specialist in this particular line of work. John Kennedy had, after all, first encountered the techniques of the FBI and its director while having a sexual relationship in Washington with Inga Arvad, a blonde beauty-contest winner from Denmark. It was the early forties, Kennedy was in the navy, and Arvad was the target of the surveillance. She had sat with Hitler at the 1936 Olympic Games and was therefore believed to have Nazi ties. Before he could shout "smorgasbord," Kennedy was shipped off to the South Pacific and out of Arvad's life, though he continued to correspond with her until the time of his marriage to Jacqueline Bouvier in 1953.

Hoover knew about Kennedy's subsequent relationships with Mob moll Judith Campbell Exner, actresses Marilyn Monroe and Angie Dickinson, former secretary Pamela Turnure, artist Barbara Kopsynska (who had changed her name to the far more easily pronounced Alicia Darr), and Ellen Rometsch, an Elizabeth Taylor look-alike who just happened to be an East German Communist. He also kept a record of a collection of prostitutes who were repeat visitors to the White House. Yes, Hoover knew how to keep tabs on clandestine affairs, and Kennedy needed a favor.

Learning as much about Bolshakov as possible was vital for the president, for it was Bolshakov who was providing information from the Soviets on the buildup of military installations in Cuba. While the CIA was insisting that missiles capable of delivering nuclear warheads to precise targets in the continental United States were in place in the small island country, Bolshakov was relaying the official Soviet explanation that all the armaments were solely for air defense.

Hoover had yet to uncover any valuable information on Bolshakov when he learned, along with the rest of America, exactly why the White House was so preoccupied with Cuba. At seven in the evening on October 22, 1962, President Kennedy delivered an address to the nation over radio and television. Seventeen minutes long, it struck fear in the hearts and minds of the world as he revealed that Russia had constructed a "series of offensive missile sites" whose sole purpose was "a nuclear strike capability against the Western Hemisphere." Kennedy said the United States would not allow the missiles to remain on Cuban soil. "We will not prematurely or unnecessarily risk the costs of worldwide nuclear war in which even the fruits of victory would be ashes in our mouth—but neither will we shrink from that risk at any time it must be faced."[15]

Hoover conveyed his support of Kennedy's stand, labeling Russian diplomats "liars of the worst sort." Yet even as the president was organizing a naval blockade of missile-laden Soviet ships heading toward Cuba, Hoover did not stray from his own determination to see that the missteps of Martin Luther King Jr. were kept in the headlines.

The FBI maintained wiretaps in Stanely Levison's home and office, as well as the offices of the SCLC in New York, where Levison had hired Jack O'Dell, a black man with a history of Communist Party ties. The association of O'Dell and King provided Hoover with the perfect opportunity to plant publicity releases through COINTELPRO.

Two days after the president's Cuban Missile Crisis speech, the Bureau sent press releases to the *Augusta Chronicle,* the *Birmingham News,* the *St. Louis Globe-Democrat,* the *New Orleans Times-Picayune,* and the *Long Island Star-Journal.* O'Dell's Communist Party ties were linked with the SCLC and King, and O'Dell was deliberately misidentified as the "acting executive director of the SCLC." Although King was quick to deny both the story and the position that O'Dell held within the organization, public association had been made between the Communist Party and King—an association supporters were hard-pressed to explain and unable to dismiss.[16]

On October 28, the president learned that Khrushchev had given in to pressure and agreed to remove Russian missiles from Cuban soil and return them to the Soviet Union. The nation, indeed the world, exhaled in unison as the threat of certain nuclear war came to an end. Hoover, however, found no relief in the moment, suggesting that this was no occasion to celebrate, no victory won. To him, the threat of Communism had merely gone underground, a subterranean stream that flowed invisibly throughout the country.

By November, as winter was pushing the last of autumn leaves off the stark maples in Manhattan, King had circled the country and returned to New York to deliver a sermon at the interdenominational Riverside Church. The gothic stone structure, with its dominant bell tower, was inspired by a thirteenth-century cathedral in Chartres, France. King's voice echoed through the nave, commanding in its power and beseeching the packed congregation to demonstrate tolerance and acceptance. After the service, a reporter from the *New York Times* questioned King about a statement made by historian Howard Zinn in a report for the Southern Regional Council, released four days earlier. In the report, Zinn wrote that there was a "fair amount of distrust among Albany (Ga.) Negroes for local members of the Federal Bureau of Investigation" who Zinn said "appear . . . as vaguely-disinterested observers of injustice, who diffidently write down complaints and do no more."[17]

King was familiar with the work and was in complete agreement with Zinn on the complacency of the FBI. "One of the great problems we face with the FBI in the South," King told the *Times* reporter, "is that the agents are white Southerners who have been influenced by the mores of the community. To maintain their status, they have to be friendly with the local police and people who are promoting segregation. Every time I saw FBI men in Albany, they were with the local police force."[18]

Alerted to the content of the *Times* article by a special agent in his Atlanta office whose local newspaper also carried the piece, Hoover became the defensive parent out to protect his only child. Angry, unforgiving, determined. To arm his cadre with the ammunition of facts, he ordered an immediate breakdown of special agents working in the Albany, Georgia, office, certain of the information he would receive in return. It was, after all, a fundamental practice of the Bureau to place agents outside familiar territory, away from the comforts and friendships of home, to allow them to operate impartially and without compromise. And so it was in Albany, Hoover discovered. In that office, four of the five agents were from the North. Hoover gloated, he pondered, then allowed himself the release of constrained anger, his tongue a ladle stirring the cauldron of intimidation.

The FBI director responded with an order to "educate" the civil rights leader, to eliminate any chance "that such misinformation should be reported again." Chuck Harding, a special agent in the Atlanta office, was instructed to call King and request an appointment to clarify the issue. Assistant Director "Deke" DeLoach telephoned King as well. The messages were left with King's secretary in Atlanta and noted in his message log on November 30: DeLoatch [sic] Wash DC cancelled and Chuck Harding FBI JA1-3900.[19]

Whether King actually received the messages is unknown. What is known is that he did not return the telephone calls, and for that slight he would be punished for the remainder of his life. For what was to some a passing disparagement, to J. Edgar Hoover the King comment in the *Times* was as direct a challenge as a glove smacked against the face.

Corporate executive George E. Allen, who joined Hoover and Tolson on their Christmas vacation in 1962, remembered that Hoover "seethed with anger" over King's failure to show respect to the FBI. "Edgar was set to a slow boil. On the surface, he seemed normal enough. Then suddenly, out of nowhere, his mind would remember the Dr. King issue, and then he would fume about it. He kept fuming the entire trip."[20]

Frustrated by the perceived disrespect, Hoover was also bothered by the reality that King was, for the most part, correct in his assessment of the situation in Albany. While four of the five men in the "Quail Hunting Capital of the World" were indeed from the North, the special agent in charge, Marion Cheeks, was from the South and a bigot, according to special agent Arthur L. Murtagh, who had also worked in Albany. "Marion was a nice guy, [but] he was a racist, and he had very strong feelings and he made them known to everybody around him."[21]

The following January, DeLoach wrote a memo to his supervisor, John Mohr, in which he labeled King a "vicious liar" who had no "desire to be given the truth." As DeLoach analyzed the situation, he determined that King "obviously used deceit, lies and treachery as propaganda to further his own causes," causes for which he still "takes instruction from Stanley Levison who is a hidden member of the Communist Party."

Mohr, who joined the Bureau in 1939, was third-in-command at the Seat of Government, having previously served as Tolson's assistant. There was little in Mohr's makeup that allowed any variance from official FBI protocol. His duty was to Hoover, and Hoover was being disrespected. At the time, there were nearly 6,000 special agents in the FBI and an additional 8,000 in support staff.

All were rallied against Martin Luther King Jr. with a concentrated effort not seen in the Bureau since the days of John Dillinger. To Hoover, King was the new enemy, and no effort was to be spared in bringing him to justice.

It was not that King was black or that Hoover was racist. It was that King, in Hoover's eyes, was dishonest and was leading his faithful followers into the arms of a Communist conspiracy. At first, Hoover's claims were considered exaggerated, at best. Certainly, Robert Kennedy felt as much, though he did take the precaution of warning King that "close aides" had been discovered to have Communist ties. After a year passed and King had done nothing to rid himself of the influence of either Levinson or O'Dell, even Robert Kennedy became alarmed.

In the early months of 1963, Hoover continued to monitor Levison and tap the phones at the SCLC in New York. Through that phone surveillance alone, Hoover was able to maintain a running dialogue of King-Levison conversations, including their favorable reaction to a speech the president delivered to the nation in June on civil rights. It was a moving endorsement of equal rights for all Americans that called for immediate legislation from Congress to end segregation in public accommodations and discrimination based on race in hiring.

When King and other civil rights leaders met with the president and attorney general at the end of that month, Hoover pushed for Robert Kennedy to speak formally with King about his Communist ties. Not only did the attorney general strongly suggest that King distance himself from Levison and O'Dell "for the good of the civil rights movement," but the president himself went for a stroll with King in the Rose Garden of the White House for a private conversation on the matter.

Despite repeated assurances from King that neither he nor anyone on his staff had any connection with the Communist Party, doubts lingered within the Kennedy administration due in no small part to Hoover's dogged determination. Hoover persisted, even in light of an internal FBI report, prepared by Assistant Director William C. Sullivan. Sullivan's 67-page report categorically denied that the Communist Party had any involvement in the civil rights movement, was "not the instigator" of the forthcoming March on Washington, and was "unable to control or direct" it.[22] Additionally, Sullivan stated that the Communist Party, now reduced in size to fewer than 5,000 members in the United States, was manageable through current resources.

Hoover was astounded by the report. Although it implied that the FBI had been successful in minimizing the impact of the Communist Party in America, it totally negated Hoover's continuing cry for increased surveillance of party members. Attempting to humiliate Sullivan into retreat, Hoover took his blue pen to the margins and wrote that the report reminded him "vividly of those I received when Castro took over Cuba. You contended then that Castro and his cohorts were not Communists and not influenced by Communists. Time alone proved you wrong."[23]

Only days later on August 28, King marched triumphantly onto Capitol Hill, leading a quarter of a million people to the foot of the Lincoln Memorial in what was to be the high point of his career and a pivotal moment in the

civil rights movement. When King declared, "I have a
dream," millions across America shared his vision. J. Edgar
Hoover was not one of them. Already aggravated at having
had to return early from his annual vacation in La Jolla, he
had spent several weeks venting his anger by attempting to
disrupt the efforts of the event's organizer, Bayard Rustin.

Rustin had three faces that Hoover habitually loathed:
a black who had stepped outside of a traditional role by
becoming a leader in the civil rights movement, a former
Communist who had joined the party as a youth, and a
homosexual who had been arrested for lewd conduct.
That Rustin would be investigated was a given. Hoover
even wondered aloud to Tolson if that "damned King had
picked him on purpose just to raise my blood pressure."[24]

Once he realized that stopping the march was impossible, Hoover concentrated on sabotaging its success by
having his agents telephone the celebrities who had
agreed to participate. Actor Charlton Heston, who led the
arts contingent at the march, received multiple calls, to no
effect. Heston said, "We will march because we recognize
the events of the summer of 1963 as among the most significant we have lived through; and we wish to be part of
these events and these times, when promises made a century ago will finally be kept." His reward was an FBI file,
some 200 pages deep. Also qualifying for files of their
own were Bob Dylan, Joan Baez, and the folk trio Peter,
Paul & Mary.

In the aftermath of the march's astounding success—
even King was impressed by the turnout and response—
Hoover sulked around the Seat of Government, venting
his frustration on Tolson and Helen Gandy. Assistant

Director Sullivan attempted to slip back into Hoover's graces via a memo to his superior Alan Belmont reassessing the role of Communism within the ranks of the King movement.

"The director is correct," Sullivan wrote. "We were completely wrong. . . . I believe in the light of King's powerful demagogic speech yesterday, he stands head and shoulders over all other Negro leaders put together when it comes to influencing great masses of Negroes. We must mark him now, if we have not done so before, as the most dangerous Negro of the future in this Nation from the standpoint of Communism, the Negro and national security." Apparently Sullivan was willing to break the law if it meant compromising King and pleasing Hoover, for he added that "it may be unrealistic to limit ourselves as we have been doing to legalistic proofs or definitely conclusive evidence that would stand up in testimony in court or Congressional Committees."[25]

On several occasions, Hoover had appealed to the attorney general to wiretap King's home as well as his Atlanta office, and each time the request was denied. After the March on Washington, however, the White House's opinion of King changed markedly. President Kennedy was both impressed and challenged by the power King possessed to inspire his followers to action; Robert Kennedy was worried that King had not completely divorced himself from Levison and O'Dell and continued to rely on them for advice and support. With those apprehensions in mind, the attorney general reexamined the request for a personal wiretap on the civil rights leader. He knew the risks were great should the tap be discovered; the controversy and scandal would likely cost him his job. Yet the potential for advance information was tempting— so tempting, in fact, that on October 10, 1963, Kennedy gave his permission for the taps "on a trial basis." The amount of information would determine if the taps would continue.

When Courtney Evans, the FBI's liaison to the attorney general, delivered the signed permission to J. Edgar Hoover, he anticipated that the director would be pleased—no, jubilant. What Evans received was official acknowledgment and polite gratitude. The work would be done, efficiently and surreptitiously. Jubilation would have to wait for King's downfall.

TWELVE

MOBSTERS
AND MURDERS

Norman Ollestad looked every bit like the surfer he was—or rather, used to be, before he joined the FBI. The fact was, he had once lived on Topanga Beach not far from the famed Malibu Colony, where movie stars, producers, and other Hollywood types pretended they didn't mind paying millions of dollars for a house that in any other part of town would have gone for a tenth of the price, been gutted for scrap wood, and been replaced by a mansion. Here, however, on the environmentally protected beachfront, there were laws against such wholesale remodeling. As a result, the area had kept its charm and look far longer than it had any right to expect in Los Angeles, a city that nipped and tucked itself into an artificial illusion of youth so complete that not even houses were allowed to age.

In the early sixties, however, Ollestad had given up the surf and the West Coast to travel east for what was to be a life of crime fighting as a special agent of the FBI. It was an age of infinite potential, led by the Camelot of President John F. Kennedy and built on the incorruptibility of the nation's top crime fighter, J. Edgar Hoover.

Ollestad, like all new agents, got to meet the director and shake his hand amid the awards and glory of the director's office in the Department of Justice. It was part of the rite of passage from agent-in-training to full-fledged special agent, a bar mitzvah of sorts, that was approached with trepidation, and, once accomplished, was held close to the heart like a badge of distinction.

The experience, however, was something of an epiphany for Ollestad—not so much because of his meeting with the director, though the formal handshake and introduction certainly was impressive and unforgettable. Hoover was, to be sure, a little older than anticipated. "Forty years on the job was a long time for any man," Ollestad later reasoned. "And the man *should* look old, that was only human. Why then had we been shown a photo that was more than twenty years old? The trophies were old, too, most of them dating from the twenties and thirties. Why none of a more modern vintage? Why none of the *Cosa Nostra*?" he questioned.[1] He would discover why in the coming years, but for now the *real* epiphany was far more immediate.

As Ollestad left the Justice Department building, snow had begun to fall, the flakes big as blueberries. He was joined on Pennsylvania Avenue by Sam Noisette, Hoover's receptionist and the office's token black, as they pushed into the bitter wind that always seemed to blow up from the river. Huddled against each other, Noisette was in a talkative mood; Ollestad the eager listener. The subject was respectability, and the need to conform.

"That's why we got all these agents' rules," Noisette said, shivering from the cold. Ollestad watched the white vapor that escaped his mouth as he spoke, only to freeze in the wind. "The boss likes everything to go like clockwork. The people do too. The people know what to expect from the FBI; they know we're on the job and that makes them feel safe. Those rules keep us looking respectable in the community, and that's the most important thing to the boss. We got to act *respectable!*"

Respectability meant everything to Hoover. Everything. There was no room for the slightest slip, suspicion of impropriety, or deviation from the norm. It was the reason he fought so hard against the gossip that swirled around his sex life. Especially the gossip about homosexuality. "The truth of the matter is that the boss don't understand *queers*, but he's scared to death of them. . . . The big thing is that queers are just like some colored folk—they been fightin' all their lives. Fightin' and hidin' so much that they've just given up and they ain't got nothing to lose anymore so they aren't scared of nothin'. The boss can't mold people like that. And that's the thing that scares him most."[2]

Noisette was only half right. Though Hoover was scared—more paranoid really—it was not that he feared the gossip about his sex life. He knew that his sex life was over, gone with the evenings spent in Manhattan nightclubs and penthouse suites surrounded by starlets. They were nothing more than dalliances anyway, harmless flirtations. Ultimately of no consequence, but totally without any deviation from respectability.

By the early fifties, however, Hoover's fantasies had replaced actual relationships, and had moved beyond longed-for normality expose a dark side fed by pornography. The black-market pictures of bondage and masochism; the magazines with names like *Eros East* and *SMNE*, brought to light by special agents in the course of

business and funneled to Hoover for placement in his
"Obscene" file. It was the perfect cover, actually. Should
anyone accidentally find the prints, the books, the slick
magazines with their dog-eared pages, they could always
be dismissed as being in his possession for safekeeping
and review.

By 1963, the "Obscene" file filled 18 filing cabinets,
accompanied by numerous containers of pornographic
films, which often made their way into Hoover's personal
collection at home. Though special agents watched some
of the films at the offices of the Justice Department as a
matter of business, Hoover made a practice of privately
screening films, alone in his home on his 16mm Koda-
scope projector, a gift from Eastman-Kodak back in 1936.

When the "Obscene" file was first created, Hoover
issued a memo to ensure that its contents stayed off limits to all Bureau employees with the exception of a select
few. Hoover instructed that when "obscene material
which may arouse the curiosity of employees" needed to
be filed in field offices, it should be locked in the "gun
vault or the SAC's safe. At no time should it be kept in a
place which is readily accessible to other employees, such
as the stock room or mail room." Moreover, Hoover gave
strict orders that "it not be shown to other personnel in
the office who have no need to observe it," thus eliminating "undue curiosity about such filth."[3]

Roy Cohn, who had continued to rise in fame among
organized-crime families after his association with Joe
McCarthy, resurfaced in Hoover's life in 1963 when his
home was burglarized and a collection of films, which
Cohn described in a 1980 interview as "kinky—even to

me," was stolen. He later learned from Hoover that the films were in Hoover's possession. "It was a warning to me never to get too far out of line since, unfortunately, I had made an investment in the company that produced the 'entertainment.' I thought I was making a joke when I told him to enjoy them. He didn't crack a smile when he told me that he already was."[4]

William Sullivan, who was promoted to assistant director of the Domestic Intelligence Division in 1961, admitted to writer Anthony Summers that he had rummaged through Hoover's desk and found "lurid literature of the most filthy kind . . . naked women and lurid magazines will all sorts of abnormal sexual activities."[5] Sullivan presumed it to be "pre-nap reading material."

Sullivan was a chief conduit of much of the material that made its way into the "Obscene" file in the early sixties. It was the by-product of prying into people's private lives which had been elevated to a science by the special agents. Placing a microphone under a mattress in a bedroom was certain to produce some interesting tapes, and no one gave the Bureau more material than the Reverend Martin Luther King Jr.

Hoover's determined assault on the Kennedy White House to authorize wiretaps of King's homes and offices had antagonized the attorney general to such an extent that Robert Kennedy had completely ceased direct communications with the director of the FBI. All messages were relayed through intermediaries, and rumors had been heard throughout the corridors of the Department of Justice that the president was looking forward to replacing the director on the occasion of his seventieth birthday, two years hence.

It was therefore not without a certain degree of relief that some 20 days after the King wiretaps were officially in place and functioning, Hoover received a telephone call from Gordon Shanklin, head of the Bureau's office in Dallas, alerting him that the president of the United States had been the victim of an assassin's bullets. Ironically, it was Hoover who relayed the news to the president's brother, Robert. The attorney general was at home in McLean, Virginia, hosting a luncheon when Hoover called with the devastating news: "The president's been shot." It was a cold, unemotional delivery of information that not only shocked a nation but forever changed its fabric. Hoover seemed to be announcing just another crime statistic: 1963, one president shot and killed. Kennedy later remembered that the Bureau's director was "not quite as excited as if he was reporting the fact that he found a Communist on the faculty of Howard University."[6]

The assassination of John F. Kennedy spelled political survival for Hoover as Lyndon B. Johnson, a longtime Hoover supporter and fellow gossip enthusiast, was sworn in to replace the fallen president. The name Lee Harvey Oswald would become an addition to history books around the world as the suspected assassin, though few would note that the FBI had detained Oswald for questioning the previous year when he reentered the country from his extended visit to Russia, yet failed to keep track of his whereabouts.

The day after the assassination, flags were lowered to half-staff at government offices around the country. Schools and businesses were closed as America held its collective breath in wonder about the future. Hoover had no such trepidation, however, nor, apparently, any sorrow. He spent the day in Baltimore at the Pimlico racetrack with Clyde Tolson at his side. During the running of the sixth race, Tolson felt a numbness in his right shoulder, flashes in his right eye, and a sudden need to sit down as the ground shifted in spite of his solid stance. In what was later diagnosed as a transient ischemic attack—a TIA, or ministroke—Tolson was made aware of his own mortality. Though the symptoms were gone as quickly as they came, the fear of death remained. Tolson began to worry incessantly about his health, much to the irritation of his boss, who openly mocked his apparent hypochondria. There was no denying that Tolson had long suffered from a duodenal ulcer, for which he had been hospitalized earlier in the year. Now a TIA only added to the strain of what should have been a triumphant period in his life.

With the ascension of Johnson to the White House, Hoover had renewed access to the president, with "Deke" DeLoach, his emissary. DeLoach had established a congenial, five-year relationship with Johnson, which started when the new president was the Senate majority leader.[7] The Johnson White House and Hoover's FBI operated as a united team, and Hoover's loyal support of the president never wavered for the entire length of his administration. At the moment that support translated into a speedy and efficient analysis of the Kennedy assassination, a report Hoover delivered to the new president on December 5, laying sole blame for the assassination on Lee Harvey Oswald.

It was in effect an effort to blindside any other interpretation of the facts. Unfortunately, as Hoover's investigative team, led by William Sullivan, examined the FBI's performance in the case, it found enormous inefficiencies in its agents. Oswald, it seemed, was well known to the Dallas office of the FBI. Agents already knew of his Communist affiliation, his visit to the Soviet Embassy in Mexico, his efforts to contact Cuban officials for a visit to Havana, and his hiring by the Texas Book Depository, from which the fatal shots were said to have been fired.

While Hoover had no knowledge of Oswald, Oswald was well aware of the FBI's interest in him. His Russian wife, Marina, had been interviewed by the FBI in her home, and Oswald later raged in defense of his privacy. He even threatened to blow up the Bureau's Dallas office in a note he wrote to special agent James Hosty, who was in charge of the Marina Oswald file. Despite all this information, Oswald was not placed on the FBI's Security Index, an omission that kept his every movement from being scrutinized.

Finding fault with the system, Hoover ordered censures placed in the files of 17 FBI employees for "shortcomings in connection with the investigation of Oswald prior to the assassination." According to Sullivan, who received a censure himself, "[Hoover's] theory was that if he was scored with having mishandled the investigation, he could say: 'The moment the assassination occurred, I looked into the matter and fixed the responsibility for what happened on individuals to whom I gave letters of censure, transferred, or both.'"[8]

Feeling the need to reinforce the FBI's report and answer to the public, President Johnson established the U.S. Commission to Report upon the Assassination of

President John F. Kennedy, commonly known as the Warren Commission, headed by Supreme Court Chief Justice Earl Warren. Although entire books have been written on the commission's report, which concurred with the FBI on Oswald's guilt, and many theories are still argued regarding the possibility of a conspiracy, there is no denial of the fact that the FBI's Dallas office was lax in its surveillance of Oswald prior to the assassination. Even Hoover privately admitted as much and was determined to keep that element of the investigation from ever being revealed. To that end, Hosty later testified in 1975 that he had destroyed Oswald's written threat on instructions from his superior, Gordon Shanklin.

In the months following the assassination, America attempted to regain its footing while openly acknowledging that nothing would ever be the same. With Camelot gone, so too was the innocence of a gentler world. Robbed of the glamour of the Kennedys in the White House, Americans were cast adrift and forced to take a hard look at a world that had decayed while the United States played. The Cold War was no longer academic but was now revealing itself in scenes of horror that unfolded in nightly newscasts, giving graphic relevance to the divide between democracy and Communism.

In Vietnam, the carnage of war in a country split by ideology began to insert itself into an American daily life turned harsh despite itself. Even as television commercials of Speedy Alka-Seltzer and Swanson TV dinners promised a bright future, reality grated a different message. One hundred miles east of Saigon, a South Vietnamese Buddhist monk calmly walked into a square, doused himself with gasoline, lit a match, and turned himself into a human pyre. His country's president, Ngo Dinh Diem, had been assassinated two weeks before the United States' own.

Americans desperately needed to be reassured that the world was indeed safe, that this violence had not set sail for its own shores. President Johnson, struggling to set a tone for domestic peace, turned to his one nonvariable: J. Edgar Hoover, bedrock of justice and propriety. Though slowed by age and circumstance, Hoover had not been detoured from his goal of a Communist-free America. By virtue of the parameters of his job, he was freed of any need to look at the grim reality of a combatant world, using the blinders of his position to focus on preserving the reputation of the Bureau, and with it his own.

His hatred for Martin Luther King had not softened in light of the changing mood of the country. If anything, Hoover saw in King the very embodiment of deceit—a leader who espoused equality and peace while crafting a personal life that mocked the very traditions he claimed to embrace. Fueling Hoover's vendetta against the civil rights leader, the Bureau's relentless surveillance of King had yielded a bounty of incriminating evidence. According to an FBI memo written by William Sullivan to his supervisor Alan Belmont, while the purpose of the surveillance was to "neutralize" King as a "Negro leader" and document his "dependence on Communists for guidance and direction," his personal activities were of equal interest.

"Although King is a minister," Sullivan wrote, "we have already developed information concerning weakness in his character which is of such a nature as to make him unfit to serve as a minister of the gospel." Sullivan suggested to Belmont that "at the proper time," when protection of the Bureau's own credibility could be assured, King should be exposed "as an immoral opportunist who is not a sincere person, but is exploiting the racial situation for personal gain."[9]

The FBI soon had what was a watershed opportunity when King checked into the Willard Hotel on January 5, 1964. Early that morning, special agent L.W. P. Cherndorf of the Washington office alerted Sullivan that a microphone had been placed in King's hotel suite—news that Sullivan passed along to Belmont, warning that "trespass is involved."[10] It was the first bugging of King's private sanctuary, and its placement would produce amazing, if illegally obtained, results.

Just as *Time* magazine was hitting the newsstands naming Martin Luther King its Man of the Year, FBI bugs were taping the married King, a few male associates from the SCLC, and two female workers from the Philadelphia Naval Yard drinking and engaging in sex. The tapes were transcribed, with excerpts played for Hoover in his office on Friday, January 10, 1964. According to Sullivan, upon hearing the tapes Hoover was said to have exclaimed, "This will destroy the burrhead."[11]

Eager to do just that, Hoover dispatched "Deke" DeLoach to the White House with an eight-page report on the surveillance, excited at finally having obtained recorded proof of King's extramarital affairs. DeLoach later said that King's dalliances "seemed incongruous in a leader who claimed his authority as a man of God. So extravagant was his promiscuity that some who knew about it questioned his sincerity in professing basic Christian beliefs and in using the black church as the home base of his movement."[12]

Johnson reacted with predictable interest, suggesting that the Bureau make the information available to the press "for the good of the country." Tricky business, of course—exposing King without also exposing the FBI's blatant violation of his civil liberties. It was, however, worth the risk, for as Hoover labeled him, King was a "'tomcat' with excessive degenerate urges" who needed to be exposed.[13]

Hoover further authorized the bugging of King's hotel rooms in New York, Milwaukee, and Honolulu. While none of those efforts produced any information of value, the Bureau's luck improved on February 22, 1964, when it planted microphones in King's rooms at the Hyatt House in Los Angeles. Special agents checked into an adjoining suite. During this two-day surveillance operation, the FBI taped the most damaging evidence against King—tapes so inflammatory they were later sealed by a judge and currently are unavailable even through the Freedom of Information Act. The contents of those tapes are said to include racially profane revilements as well as King's description of John F. Kennedy's sex life, with an off-color reference to the late president's widow. Again, copies of the tapes were made, highlights were played for Hoover, and the president was advised.

The close relationship that Johnson shared with Hoover was advantageous to both men, for each knew what to expect from the other. Their friendship dated back to 1945, when Johnson became Hoover's neighbor on Thirtieth Place NW. Hoover had watched the Johnson daughters mature and flourish, shared Sunday brunch on occasion with the family, and genuinely liked Johnson's down-home brand of politics that had its origins in the president's Texan heritage.

So it was hardly a surprise when Johnson took the occasion of Hoover's fortieth year as director of the Bureau to formally waive his mandated retirement at the age of 70, several months hence. On May 8, 1964, in the relaxed setting of the Rose Garden of the White House, members of the Senate and House came together to pay tribute to a friend. The gathering was a ceremonial gesture, to be sure. The president had already signed Executive Order No. 11154. Yet hearing Johnson's words was important to Hoover, for appearance was now everything to him.

> All during [my] last trip* . . . I kept thinking—what a great nation this is. And I kept thinking that the foundation of our greatness is the ability of our people to solve our problems by reasonable and compassionate means.
>
> There is another reason for America's greatness: the tireless devotion of those men and women who serve the public's welfare.
>
> J. Edgar Hoover is such a man. . . . He is a hero to millions of decent citizens, and an anathema to evil men. No other American, now or in our past, has served the cause of justice so faithfully and so well. . . .

---

* The president had just returned from a two-day tour of the poverty-stricken areas of Appalachia.

J. Edgar Hoover has served the government since 1917—he has served *nine* Presidents, and this Sunday, he celebrates his fortieth year as Director of the FBI. Under his guiding hand, the FBI has become the greatest investigation body in history.

I am proud and happy to join the rest of the nation in honoring this quiet, humble, and magnificent public servant.

Edgar, the law says that you must retire next January when you reach your seventieth birthday, and I know you wouldn't want to break the law.

But the nation cannot afford to lose you. Therefore, by virtue of and pursuant to the authority vested in the President, I have today signed an Executive Order exempting you from compulsory retirement for an indefinite period of time.

Again, Edgar, congratulations on behalf of a grateful nation.[14]

At the time of the ceremony, Johnson was becoming concerned that the civil rights movement might disrupt the upcoming Democratic National Convention, made all the more real with the expectation that the Mississippi Freedom Democratic Party would attempt to be seated on the convention floor. It was hardly surprising in light of the fact that the Democratic National Convention was overwhelmingly a white affair. African Americans were finding it nearly impossible even to register to vote in the South. The MFDP had been formed by black Mississippi Democrats in an effort to have a voice in their future.

Not only was Johnson in favor of encouraging African Americans to vote, he also was the favored candidate of the MFDP. The official Mississippi Democratic Party, in contrast, was so upset by Johnson's pro–civil rights stance that it actually favored the Republican candidate, Barry Goldwater. Nevertheless, with DeLoach running interference for the FBI in Atlantic City, New Jersey, as the Democrats met and crowned Johnson their candidate in the 1964 presidential election, the MFDP achieved only marginal television coverage, and were never allowed on the floor of the convention despite repeated attempts at compromise.

After Johnson's successful nomination, Hoover placed the entire facilities of the Bureau at his disposal to ensure his reelection and thus keep his job as head of the FBI. Hoover maintained a relatively low profile until November, though several incidents served to spotlight his stress level, one that was not to be calmed until Johnson was safely back in the White House.

In September, the Warren Commission issued its official report on the Kennedy assassination, placing responsibility solely in the hands of Oswald, while pointing an accusatory finger at the FBI. "An alert agency such as the FBI," the report claimed, should have seen Oswald as "a potential threat to the safety of the President." As with all criticism of the Bureau, Hoover took it personally, agreeing in part that the Bureau "will never live down this smear which could have been so easily avoided if there had been proper supervision and initiative."[15]

The arrest of Warren Jenkins was a further blow to Hoover, if only by association. Jenkins, a top adviser to the president, a friend of 25 years, and a key contact for the Bureau within the White House, was arrested on October 14, while having sex with a former soldier in the men's room of the YMCA. After being fingerprinted and identified, Jenkins was so close to a nervous breakdown that he was immediately admitted to George Washington University Hospital.

While much of Washington was abuzz about the arrest, Helen Gandy, on Hoover's instructions, sent flowers to Jenkins in the hospital with a get-well card from the Bureau's director. The gaffe was quickly picked up by the press and turned against Hoover, who knew Jenkins only as a well-respected member of the president's staff and a family man with a wife and six children. In their rush to embarrass Hoover, who for once was innocent of any wrongdoing, the press overlooked the actions of Johnson's friend and legal counsel Abe Fortas, who was told to empty Jenkins's safe of its contents before the police could seal it. Obstruction of justice at its best and an impeachable offense at its worst, Fortas nevertheless complied. He was appointed by Johnson to the Supreme Court the following year. Jenkins, released to his family's custody, returned to Texas and never set foot in the White House again.

By November, after Johnson's landslide win in the presidential election (the Republican candidate, Barry Goldwater, carried only the southern states of Georgia, South Carolina, Alabama, Mississippi, and Louisiana, as well as his home state of Arizona), Hoover returned to form, surprising his own staff when he agreed to be interviewed by the Women's National Press Club to "set the record straight." What was to be one of Hoover's last mass press conferences turned into a three-hour monologue infused with an undercurrent of hostility and frustration with the South in general and the Reverend Martin Luther King Jr. in particular. Even for the rather worldly women of the National Press Club, the words were unexpected as Hoover characterized the South as "filled with water moccasins, rattlesnakes and red-necked sheriffs, and they are all in the same category as far as I am concerned." On King, Hoover was no less guarded, reflecting the civil rights leader's claim that all special agents in the South were bigots, with Hoover branding King the "most notorious liar in the country."[16]

King immediately responded, sending a telegram expressing his outrage.

> I was appalled and surprised at your reported statement maligning my integrity. What motivated such an irresponsible accusation is a mystery to me. . . . I have sincerely questioned the effectiveness of the FBI in racial incidents, particularly where bombings and brutalities against Negroes are at issue, but I have never attributed this merely to the presence of Southerners in the FBI. This is a part of the broader question of federal involvement in the protection of Negroes in the South and the seeming inability to gain convictions in even the most heinous crimes perpetrated against civil rights workers.

King went on to say that he had "sought in vain for any record" of a request from the FBI to meet with him. He offered to discuss the issue of civil rights and the FBI's efforts to assist African Americans "at length in the near future."[17]

King interrupted his vacation on Bimini Island in the Bahamas—that slice of white sand that had inspired Ernest Hemingway to write *Islands in the Stream* nearly 30 years earlier. King had gone to Bimini to compose his acceptance speech for the Nobel Peace Prize. It was the honor of a lifetime, and one that irritated Hoover to the point where he angrily poked his finger in the air on hearing the news and scribbled on a copy of an article announcing the news: "King would well qualify for the 'top alley cat' prize."

Hoover's deliberate affront called for immediate retaliation from King. This was no time for forgiveness or even Christian charity. This was, in very real terms, a fight for reputation. "I cannot conceive of Mr. Hoover making a statement like this without being under extreme pressure. He has apparently faltered under the awesome burden, complexities and responsibilities of his office. Therefore, I cannot engage in a public debate with him. I have nothing but sympathy for the man who has served his country so well."[18]

To challenge Hoover's capacity to lead was to challenge his very purpose in life. Petulant, vindictive, with the red-angry look of a cartoon thermometer about to explode, Hoover ordered that copies of material on King's recorded transgressions be made available to government officials and privately to assorted media. That it was against the law to release information to anyone other than approved government officials was irrelevant. Hoover wanted vindication by the nation's press. The response, however, was silence; media outlets refused to attack the civil rights leader on personal issues. Gone were the days when a telephone call from Hoover was enough to ensure instant press coverage of leaked material.

Hoover reacted impulsively, frantically. He did not have the balancing influence of Tolson, who was recovering from surgery to repair an aortic abdominal aneurysm. Without formally authorizing its preparation, Hoover had Sullivan assemble an abridged tape for King, featuring the audio highlights of the Bureau's bugging of the civil rights leader. The letter Sullivan wrote to accompany the tape stands as uncontested witness to Hoover's fragile state of mind.

KING,

In view of your low grade . . . I will not dignify your name with either a Mr. or a Reverend or a Dr. And, your last name called to mind only the type of King such as King Henry the VIII. . . .

King, look into your heart. You know you are a complete fraud and a great liability to all of us Negroes. White people in this country have enough frauds of their own but I am sure they don't have one at this time that is anywhere near your equal. You are no clergyman and you know it. I repeat you are a colossal fraud and an evil, vicious one at that. You could not believe in God. . . . Clearly you don't believe in any personal moral principles.

King, like all frauds, your end is approaching. You could have been our greatest leader. You, even at an early age, have turned out to be not a leader, but a dissolute, abnormal moral imbecile. We will now have to depend on our older leaders like Wilkins,† a man of character and thank God we have others like him. But you are done. Your "honorary" degrees, your Nobel Prize (what a grim farce) and other awards will not save you. King, I repeat you are done.

No person can overcome facts, not even a fraud like yourself . . . I repeat—no person can argue successfully against facts. You are finished . . . And some of them to pretend to be ministers of the Gospel. Satan could not do more. What incredible evilness . . . King you are done.

The American public, the church organizations that have been helping—Protestant, Catholic and Jews will know you for what you are—an evil, abnormal beast. So will others who have backed you. You are done.

King, there is only one thing left for you to do. You know what it is. You have just 34 days in which to do (this exact number has been selected for a specific reason, it has definite practical significant [sic]). You are done. There is but one way out for you. You better take it before your filthy, abnormal fraudulent self is bared to the nation.[19]

The smear effort, now in full swing, was picked up by DeLoach, who presented a carefully prepared surveillance transcript on King to *Newsweek*'s local bureau chief, Ben Bradlee, who would go on to fame as executive editor of

---

† Civil rights leader Roy Wilkins, who, at the time, was 64 years old.

the *Washington Post*. Again, the response was apparent disinterest. Actually, Bradlee was *very* interested—not so much for what the transcript said about King, but in what its offering said about Hoover.

As talk swirled in Washington about Hoover's efforts to besmirch King's name and reputation, the Bureau itself became a hotbed of suspicion. Unwilling to believe Hoover's contention that the Communist Party was backing the civil rights effort, reporters began to look underneath the FBI's agenda for a deeper, more desperate schema. When word reached the Bureau that a concerted effort was under way to unravel the plot behind the King attacks, Hoover begrudgingly agreed that a face-to-face meeting with the civil rights leader might be beneficial. On December 1, 1964, Martin Luther King Jr. arrived at FBI headquarters 30 minutes late for a 3 P.M. appointment. He was accompanied by top aides Andrew Young, Ralph Abernathy, and Walter Fauntroy, and greeted by a gaggle of assembled press who had received advanced word of the meeting from the SCLC.

A restrained Hoover met with King that afternoon— restrained in the sense that he made no threats, direct or otherwise, and refrained from any mention of his knowledge of King's sexual activities. Abernathy, who spoke first, was conciliatory, alleging that the SCLC was gratified by the FBI's accomplishments on civil rights.

When King spoke, he suggested that while "many Negroes have complained that the FBI has been ineffective, I myself discount such criticism . . . and I want to assure you that I have been seriously misquoted in the matter of slurs against the FBI."[20]

Having had the floor for a little over five minutes, the King contingent paused just long enough for Hoover to reply. His response filled the remaining 50 minutes of the meeting, prompting King to remark during a subsequent wiretap: 'The old man talks too much."[21]

What Hoover talked about was the effort the FBI was making to help blacks in the South, including the ongoing investigation into the killing of three civil rights workers—Michael Schwerner, Andrew Goodman, and James Chaney—all from the North. The trio had traveled to Mississippi and vanished, leaving only the burned-out remains of their car. Their bodies were subsequently discovered by the FBI at an isolated farm, buried in an earthen dam. To Hoover, the efforts in Mississippi were proof of his sincerity in helping the civil rights movement.[‡] He was sincere in the sense that the FBI did investigate cases when it determined it had jurisdiction, though hardly as many as King and others would have liked.

After the meeting was concluded, King told the collected press it was "amicable." Hoover refused to comment, though later he made up a scenario for *Time* magazine that had him calling King a liar to his face. "He said he never criticized the FBI. I said, 'Mr. King—I never called him reverend—stop right there, you're lying.' He then pulled out a press release that he said he intended to give to the press. I said, 'Don't show it to me or read it to me.' I couldn't understand how he could have prepared a press release

---

‡   The case and subsequent trial formed the basis for the 1988 film *Mississippi Burning*, starring Gene Hackman and Willem Dafoe.

even before we met."[22] No mention was made of King's sexual habits or the audiotape sent to his office, which was later opened and played by his wife, Coretta.

Time magazine wrote, "J. Edgar Hoover has many old foes, has made a legion of new ones recently; undoubtedly there will be vastly increased pressures on the White House from now on to boot the old fellow out of his job." *Time* was being naive. President Lyndon Johnson had J. Edgar Hoover exactly were he needed him to be—about to turn 70, desperate to keep his job and power, and willing to do almost anything to accomplish that end. Just how far Hoover was willing to go, however, was discovered a few months later, when another wiretap in another state uncovered shocking plans for a murder about to be committed.

The players in this game of kill-the-hoodlum were small-time gangsters in Massachusetts, members of the New England crime family run by Raymond Salvatore Loreda Patriarca, who ran the National Cigarette Service and a vending machine company called Coin-o-Matic out of his Atwells Avenue office in the Italian neighborhood of Providence, Rhode Island, known as Federal Hill. Patriarca had risen to power in the area, having taken over the local Mafia family business from Frank "Butsey" Morelli after Morelli's death in the early fifties.

While Hoover was presumably ignorant of the New England crime syndicate, Providence locals knew that Patriarca ran a money-laundering and loan-sharking business from the "Office" on Atwells. It was to be the location of one of the more interesting microphone bugs planted by the FBI in 1962. Though authorized by Robert

Kennedy in a loosely based hear-no-evil, see-no-evil agreement with Hoover, the bug was highly illegal and anything heard would not be admissible in court.

Up until 1965, the bug served mainly to provide details of the extent of payoffs apparently rampant within the offices of the governors of both Rhode Island and Massachusetts, plus a few judges and what seemed like half the police officers in Boston on the payroll of the Italian vending machine king. Then, in the middle of an otherwise uneventful March day in 1965, Patriarca received a call that would change everything and sweep Hoover into a conspiracy that would become an addiction.

Joseph "the Animal" Barboza and Vincent James "Jimmy the Bear" Flemmi, two Boston thugs heavy on testosterone and meatball sandwiches, placed a call to *Patrone* Patriarca to get his blessing for an upcoming hit. The target was a onetime boxer and sometime hood named Edward "Teddy" Deegan.

According to the field memo Hoover received from the Boston office, "[Names censored] advised on 3/9/65 that [Vincent] Flemmi and Joseph Barboza contacted [Raymond] Patriarca, and they explained that they are having a problem with Teddy Deegan and desired to get the 'OK' to kill him. . . . Flemmi stated that Deegan is an arrogant, nasty sneak and should be killed. Patriarca instructed them to obtain more information relative to Deegan and then to contact [underboss] Jerry Angiulo at Boston who would furnish them a decision." While Angiulo's response has been lost in history, just three days later, on March 12, Deegan turned up facedown in an alley in Chelsea with six slugs in his chest.

Hoover had done nothing to stop the murder. More-over, the information on the Deegan "rub-out" did not end there. On March 15, James L. Handley, special agent in charge of the Boston office, notified Hoover that an inform-ant had revealed details of the crime, including its perpe-trators. "On 3/12/65, Edward 'Teddy' Deegan was found killed in an alleyway in Chelsea, Mass. in gangland fashion. Informants report that Ronald Casessa [correctly spelled Cassessa], Romeo Martin, Vincent James Flemmi and Joseph Barboza, prominent local hoodlums, were responsi-ble for the killing. They accomplished this by having Roy French, another Boston hoodlum, set Deegan up in a pro-posed 'breaking & entering' in Chelsea, Mass. French apparently walked in behind Deegan when they were gain-ing entrance to the building and fired the first shot hitting Deegan in the back of the head." "Casessa and Martin immediately thereafter shot Deegan from the front."[23]

To the nation's top cop, such news should logically have hit some sort of button, triggering a response to have local law enforcement apprehend the hit men. Yet logic was not occupying the Bureau director's mind in 1965 or the following year. He was in a scramble to prove he was still in top form, capable of protecting America against—he hated to admit it—organized crime. That a murder was committed under his watch was hardly a problem if a much bigger target, the entire Mafia organization, could be exterminated. The agents in Boston certainly under-stood. Particularly H. Paul Rico.

Rico had been a charter member of the Organized Crime Squad, an elite team of special agents established to place the FBI on the fast track for inside information on

La Cosa Nostra. With an affinity for gold rings, gold watches, gold cuff links, and Chesterfield overcoats, Rico had made a name for himself cultivating connections within the Mob as well as a certain gaudy sartorial splendor. At Hoover's prodding, Rico was pushing to "turn"— the FBI's word for forced coercion—Barboza into an FBI top echelon informant. "The Animal" was a prime target despite his public braggadocio of having killed 40 men. As long as Barboza supplied information, Hoover apparently did not care how many hits the killer scored, Teddy Deegan among them.

Having been told, however, who was actually responsible for Deegan's slaughter complicated the FBI's responsibility. Rico sent a memo to Hoover on March 19, 1965, stating that for Barboza to be a useful source, he had to remain embedded in the gang. Likewise Flemmi, who was likely to "turn" toward the FBI now that he needed protection from prosecution as well.

What Hoover and his Boston office needed were scapegoats to take the fall for the murder, allowing Barboza and Flemmi to remain free. According to Barboza, he targeted Joseph Salvati, Peter J. Limone, Louis Greco, and Henry Tameleo because they were all "pains in the ass"— Salvati because he had not paid back a $400 debt, Tameleo because he was an underboss for Patriarca, the others because they were local hoods. The names seemed to please Hoover and the agents of the FBI office in Boston, for they stood by silently as the men were arrested, tried, and falsely convicted of the killing, thanks to the testimony of the government's star witness: Joseph "the Animal" Barboza.

At the time, Barboza, the self-proclaimed tough guy, was running for his life—Patriarca having decided that the killer was too unpredictable and talkative to have a continuing future within the Family. The previous year, while jailed on a concealed-weapons charge, Barboza not only learned that Patriarca refused to post his $100,000 bail, but thanks to the still-operative bug, he also heard the Mafia don swear, "Barboza's a fuckin' bum. He's expendable." So too were Barboza's two friends, who attempted to raise the bail themselves.

Unfortunately for Arthur "Tash" Bratsos and Thomas "Joey" DePrisco Jr., they stopped at the Nite Lite Café, "Ralphie Chang" Lamattina's joint in Boston, and ended up getting shot to death. Their bodies were unloaded on the South side of town, but their $59,000 didn't make the trip, eventually finding its way into Patriarca's wallet. The FBI, keeping track of the scenario, used it to convince Barboza that he might be safer in *their* protection. The tradeoff was that he would have to testify in the Deegan case, plus provide information in several others. Only *then* was Barboza released from jail, having served five months for his part in the murder, and became the first person officially placed in the Federal Witness Protection Program. Barboza changed his name to Joseph Baron ("that way I get to keep my monogrammed handker-chiefs") and was sent to Santa Rosa, California, where he was enrolled in a cooking school, a favorite pastime—he was Italian, after all.

With Barboza out of town and Flemmi in jail for an unrelated attempted murder, Rico next moved to con-vince Flemmi's brother, Stevie—who preferred to be called by his nickname "the Rifleman"—that it was *his* turn to cooperate. Stevie Flemmi was only too happy to inform on those around him in exchange for protection and some extra money under the table. Business wasn't great at Flemmi's newly opened auto body shop, and he needed the cash. He told a similar story, of course, to Raymond Patriarca when he was invited for lunch at the family home in Providence. "The Rifleman" talked with the don and left the house that day with $5,000 in cash and a promise that Patriarca would send cars to Flemmi's shop in Boston.[24]

Hoover was pleased at Rico's progress in turning informants within the Mafia, and with the quick resolution of the Deegan trial as well. "The successful prosecution of these subjects," Hoover wrote, "was a direct result of your noteworthy development of pertinent witnesses. I want you to know that I am most appreciative of your fine services."[25]

During the period between the Deegan murder and the arrests of the accused killers, Hoover had been preoccupied—some say emotionally handicapped—and unable to focus with his characteristic precision. His alter ego and best friend, Clyde Tolson, had suffered a series of massive strokes—the first in 1966, which affected his right side. Tolson's walking, speech, and ability to write were impaired to the extent that he remained at Hoover's home recuperating under the watchful eye of Annie Fields.

For Tolson, it was as if life itself had stopped. Even the simplest task required arduous rehabilitation. Instead of persevering, Tolson seemed to succumb, preferring to linger in the haze of his limitations rather than conquer his physical and mental disabilities. Perhaps it was just that he knew what lay ahead. In 1967, he suffered another stroke; this one even more profound. His left side was affected, further decreasing his mobility and his ability to concentrate, and severely limiting his contribution at work. The once strapping 5' 11" Tolson, who was never more than two steps behind his famous boss, dropped to under 140 pounds, a scarecrow that had stayed too long in the field.

Sensing Tolson's lack of resolve, his failure to fight, Hoover tugged at his alter ego, waxed poetic about his indispensable contribution at work, and insisted he appear at the office even if only for a few hours, just for show. The director of the FBI had lost his rudder, for that was what Tolson had become—the mechanism that steered Hoover through a maze of memos and regulations, attacks and outcries, to allow him to remain the leader.

Tired now, and floundering, Hoover reached out for support and consolation from a surprising source. Not "Deke" DeLoach or William Sullivan, his two trusted lieutenants. Not his family, for they had not spoken to Hoover in years. Instead, he turned to a Hollywood actress whom he once described as "the most beautiful woman in the world." She, more than anyone, knew this man—his fears, his hopes, his passion, and the secret to his long-rumored sexuality, left untouched for nearly 40 years.

THIRTEEN

THE EMPEROR HAS NO CLOTHES

When J. Edgar Hoover first met Dorothy Lamour in 1935, she was not yet known as the sultry actress who exchanged wisecracks with the likes of Bob Hope and Bing Crosby on the road to somewhere or other. She had not yet become famous for her long brown hair and wide-set eyes, or for wearing her trademark sarong that showed off a body thin and fit with a delicate femininity. Truth be told, she had just turned 20, and, as such, had yet to develop much in the way of style or poise. But to J. Edgar Hoover, she was wonderful.

Walking into the Stork Club on the arm of singer-bandleader Rudy Vallée, Lamour pretended not to notice as the movie stars and famous writers in the room stole glances in her direction, their whispers buzzing like swarming mosquitoes. She wore a pale blue satin gown that draped across her hips, catching the lights from the ceiling and bathing her in a glow of mystery. Her mother was there that night as well, but no one noticed Carmen Louise Lambour.* This was to be her daughter's night.

---

* An accidental misspelling of Lambour to Lamour changed Dorothy's stage name.

Lamour had arrived the previous week from Chicago, where she had worked as a singer with the Herbie Kaye Band, then a sensation on WGN radio, broadcasting from the ballroom of the Blackhawk Hotel. It was Vallée who had convinced Stork Club owner Sherman Billingsley to give Lamour an audition, and pay her $125 a week for her considerable talent. Though just one of many attractive singers who seemed to propagate themselves in nightclubs along the Great White Way and various side streets, Lamour had an innocence that captivated Hoover.

"I brought her up to Walter Winchell's table and introduced her before the show," Vallée recalled in 1980. "The place was full of famous people. But Dottie made a particular fuss over J. Edgar Hoover. He stood up like a gentleman and shook her hand, and said he hoped she would join the table after the show. I don't think Winchell was too excited about it, but I know Hoover was."[1]

For the next several months, Hoover romanced the young singer with weekend dinners at the Stork Club, nervously chattering away about crime statistics and shootings of "Pretty Boy" Floyd and John Dillinger, and inviting her to Washington for a tour of the Bureau's forensic labs. If it wasn't exactly romantic, it was at least sincere, for the singer, who never got to know her real father, saw in Hoover a successful, driven, and respectful substitute.

On weekdays, with Hoover back in Washington, Lamour was wooed by Vallée, then the reigning king of crooners with a radio show on NBC and a popular New York nightclub, Villa Vallée, on Fiftieth Street. Special agents from the Bureau's New York office, dispatched to watch

Lamour, discovered the relationship and, on Hoover's instructions, interfered with the budding romance. "Phone messages would mysteriously disappear, taxis would drop her off at the wrong restaurant, and her mother, Carmen, was everywhere we went," Vallée said. "Mr. Hoover saw to it."[2]

It was to be bandleader Herbie Kaye who eventually captured the singer's heart, however. "When Herbie came into town to do some special industrial engagements at the New York Hotel, he called me right away," Lamour later wrote. "I knew how *I* felt about him, but it came as a total surprise when he said he loved me and wanted to marry me."[3] The pair eloped to Waukegan, Illinois, on May 10, 1935, though pledged to keep their wedding a secret to boost their growing careers. They had not counted on J. Edgar Hoover, of course, or the Chicago office of the FBI, which alerted columnist Ed Sullivan, who broke the news of the nuptials on May 15.

Privately, Hoover was devastated by the loss of Lamour to another man. Publicly, he moved directly into the arms of Ginger Rogers's mother, Lela, who had been patiently waiting to reacquaint herself with the well-known, respected bachelor. It was convenient to be seen with Lela, and Hoover admitted he enjoyed the spotlight that followed the pair for the next four years on Manhattan's tuxedoed nightclub circuit. Yet, his heart remained with Dorothy Lamour, whose star was rising quickly in Hollywood. When her marriage disintegrated under the pressures of show business, Hoover was the first to offer his shoulder in support. However, it took a president and a birthday party to reunite the unlikely pair.

The fifty-eighth birthday celebration of President Franklin D. Roosevelt brought both Dorothy Lamour and J. Edgar Hoover to the White House—she escorted by Tyrone Power, her most recent co-star, and he with Lela Rogers, who was excited about an anticipated marriage proposal. Yet neither Power nor the hopeful Rogers held on to their dates, who were discovered together the next morning in Lamour's suite at the Willard Hotel by Walter Winchell. While Winchell was blackmailed into secrecy by Hoover, he revealed the story to film producer Allan Carr, who had purchased Winchell's Manhattan apartment on Central Park.[4] The romance was later verified by author Charles Higham in 1971, interviewing the actress for an audio history of her life. When asked about her sexual relationship with Hoover, she commented simply, "I cannot deny it."

As Higham says, "A lady never tells."[5]

Though Lamour married William Ross Howard III in 1943, she maintained a close friendship with Hoover for the remainder of her life. The Bureau's director visited the Howard home in Beverly Hills once a year for an extended stay, and a portrait of the actress remained in Hoover's bedroom until the day he died. It was hardly surprising therefore that Hoover turned to Lamour for support after Tolson suffered two massive and debilitating strokes in the mid-sixties.

Lamour had long suspected Tolson's health was declining, though she was shocked at his appearance when Tolson joined Hoover at the debut of the singer's nightclub act in 1965—so shocked that she referred him to her own physician for a complete physical. Both Tolson and Hoover dismissed the associate director's weight loss to overwork. It was a legitimate excuse. Tolson was working harder than ever, thanks to Hoover's sale of his 1958 book, *Masters of Deceit*, to ABC for $75,000 as the basis for a new television series, *The F.B.I.*

The Quinn Martin production starred Efrem Zimbalist Jr. as fictional FBI inspector Lewis Erskine, whose office was said to be next to the director's own. To some, it was the ideal telling of the Bureau's story. To Hoover, it was the ultimate vindication. His Bureau, his life, was placed on the pedestal of fictional television and passed off as fact, to the extent that in the initial years of the show, authentic case file numbers were listed in the opening credits of the hour-long drama.

Hoover had handpicked Zimbalist for the actor's clean-cut, immaculate image, and saw to it that every script, every movement, was approved by someone within his department—at first Tolson, then DeLoach, who grudgingly assumed the task. They were, in a very real sense, crafting the Bureau's image for a new generation of American consumers, and the audience bought the illusion wholesale.

Zimbalist as well became convinced of the FBI's integrity and strength, based on his initial meeting with Hoover soon after he was cast. "I don't recall his ever pausing in his conversation once," Zimbalist remembered. "He just talked at breakneck speed on every subject imaginable and with such a command of thought and language that there wasn't room to get in the amenities of conversation. When it was over, I looked at my watch, and I'd been there two hours and four minutes. He was a great conversationalist, had a great sense of humor, and wide knowledge of every area of life, and he just chatted most charmingly and interestingly about every subject— he crossed decades and continents and everything else."[6]

The actor was subjected to a full FBI investigation into his past in Hoover and Tolson's attempt to prevent even the slightest hint of scandal from being injected into the program. Despite their caution, however, both men approached the series' debut with apprehension, particularly Hoover, whose voice opened the premiere episode on Sunday, September 19, 1965. Seated in Hoover's downstairs den, surrounded by mementos of a career nearing its end, the director and his assistant sat transfixed as the show unfolded. The sets, the cast, even the Ford automobiles used in the production were perfectly polished. Yet into this wholesomeness of good vs. evil slipped an incipient villain with a problem: the bad guy was no ordinary crook, no mere bank robber or kidnapper. To Hoover's horror, the villain had a fetish—the touch of human hair made him kill. Hoover demanded that in the future, the criminal element on the drama would be "dishonest, rather than psychologically imbalanced."[7]

The pressure was on Tolson to keep the program exciting yet pure, dramatic if uncontroversial. It was, of course, not his only assignment, and had grown in manhours to encompass a full quarter of his workweek. Adding to the pressure, Tolson was being pushed by Hoover to protect the Bureau against an ever-suspicious Senate—particularly Senator Edward V. Long, who, in 1966, had launched an investigation into the Bureau's use of electronic surveillance, including the use of microphone listening devices installed through black bag jobs.

Long, a Democrat from Missouri, claimed that federal agents had embarked on a "nationwide campaign of wiretapping, snooping and harassment of American citizens."[8] His opinion was based on several hundred reports of uncovered wiretaps and electronic surveillance, including multiple installations authorized by the FBI. To Long, America was "a naked society, where every citizen is a denizen in a goldfish bowl."[9] No one felt the invasion more than Dr. Martin Luther King Jr., who remained at the top of Hoover's list of "low-life filth."

Hoover had found a willing underling in William Sullivan, whose ascent into the executive ranks in the Seat of Government was all but assured by his success in invading the sanctity of the civil rights leader. At least, that is, until Senator Long began to investigate Sullivan's late-night break-ins and illegal bugging. At that point, Hoover immediately distanced himself from any culpability.

In March 1965, Attorney General Nicholas Katzenbach had informed Hoover that authorized wiretaps would be reviewed every six months, and that microphone surveillance would be subject to the same strict authorization procedures. For Hoover, the notice was tantamount to a challenge; the taint of disapproval hanging in the wind.

The revelation of King's sexual habits had failed to impeach the integrity of the civil rights leader. With many SCLC wiretaps and bugs already in place, and information on King flowing into Bureau headquarters in sporadic fashion, Hoover needed immediate proof that the Communists were actively involved in the operation of the SCLC. As usual, Hoover looked to Tolson to achieve the results. Hoover's second-in-command, whose mandate had always been to perform as well as protect, felt himself faltering, consumed by the very work that was draining him physically. His was a piquant world where past sins could no longer be ignored or handled with a wink, yet whose excitement urged him to continue to play among the political minefields.

For Tolson, it was William Sullivan, not J. Edgar Hoover, who was the source of most concern. Sullivan, out to trump his predecessors in the Domestic Intelligence Division, pushed to plant more bugs, further invading the privacy of King in an effort to locate the single piece of damning evidence to prove his collusion with the Communist Party.

On January 22, 1966, Tolson received a memo from Sullivan through "Deke" DeLoach, routinely advising him of the latest microphone surveillance of the civil rights leader: a bug installed at the Americana Hotel in New York. In his enthusiasm for information, Sullivan had failed to secure Hoover's authorization. Now, he felt Tolson's anger. "Remove this surveillance at once," Tolson wrote in pencil across the memo. "No one here approved this. I have told Sullivan again not to institute a mike surveillance without the director's approval.[10] Reluctantly, Sullivan obeyed, even as the pressure within the Bureau mounted. Seven weeks later, Tolson was stricken by a massive ischemic stroke. Just as with the ministrokes that had preceded it, Tolson became dizzy and disoriented at work. The most recent stroke had come when he joined Hoover to open the new Bureau office in Jackson, Mississippi, on July 10, 1964. And as he did with the ministrokes, Tolson ignored the warning signs, thinking they would pass. They always passed; yet, not this time.

Hoover received the news with typical efficiency, removing Tolson from his office and rushing him to the hospital—not in an ambulance, but rather his in own limousine. All the better to minimize confusion—and publicity. As always, the FBI had to remain impenetrable, its leaders impervious to calamity. Yet, as the weeks and months that followed would show, Hoover and Tolson were both vulnerable and increasingly pushed to protect a fast-dissolving illusion.

On the surface, Hoover continued to play hardball politics and go through the motions of control via intimidation. One casualty was Attorney General Katzenbach. Determined to openly admit the extent of the government's wiretapping and electronic surveillance, Katzenbach fought against Hoover and lost. He could not compete with what he labeled "the historical accident of J. Edgar Hoover."[11] It was Katzenbach's naiveté as much as his revelations about Bureau surveillance that sealed his fate. To think that an attorney general actually controlled the behavior of the Bureau's director was serious folly. Katzenbach's resignation had nothing to do with justice, and everything to do with secrets. His replacement, Ramsey Clark, was not about to make the same mistake.

Clark had worked as Katzenbach's deputy and had been in charge of the Office of Criminal Justice. His mandate was to fight crime, but not by any standard Hoover deemed reasonable. For Clark, the root of crime was poverty, not the permissive society that Hoover railed against—a society that allowed its young people to grow their hair to shoulder length, launch demonstrations against duly elected officials, and adopt a mantra of "Make Love, Not War."

It was a time of urban civil war, where rioters in the inner city competed with men burning draft cards and women burning bras. Hoover watched in amazement as America seemed to be disintegrating around him—at least the America he knew, the democracy he loved and fought to protect. He continued to report daily to work, preaching his message of Communist infiltration and disrespect for the law, only to be labeled anachronistic in a world where free speech took precedence over covert surveillance.

"At all levels of our society, a pervasive contempt for law and order" was consuming America, Hoover told former FBI agents in a speech in 1967. "The soaring crime rate, widespread, open defiance of constituted authority, threaten, if unchecked, to plunge our Nation into the abyss of violence and anarchy."[12]

Although much of America still saw Hoover as a bastion of integrity and its stalwart defense against anarchism, his own proclamations had become so parochial as to be comical in light of the times. While the flower children of Haight-Ashbury were claiming the headlines along with photos of annihilation in Vietnam, Hoover's suited perfection and grandiose pontifications were being relegated to the sidelines. The louder he proclaimed America's detour into crime, the louder Clark countered that the crimes of riot were ignited by anger over poverty. Though Hoover labeled Clark "a spineless jellyfish," during the remainder of the Johnson administration he largely ignored the ruminations of his titular boss and conducted business as usual. That, however, was the problem for many who began to see Hoover as outdated, a prepackaged product allowed to remain on the shelf too long.

"Hoover lives in the past . . . surrounded by aged or incompetent men who have spent their careers looking backward and telling [him] what he wants to hear," an anonymous writer declared in a letter to Clark. Apparently making a veiled reference to Tolson's former roommate Guy Hottel, the writer further stated that one SAC was allowed to remain in place despite his alleged wife-beating because he "has openly stated that Hoover and Tolson, whom he knows intimately, and some of their friends, are homosexuals."[13] The letter was written on stationary from the Bureau's Los Angeles office.

Without the calming effect of Tolson, Hoover flailed wildly in an effort to strike down his opponents and cast the largest shadow. Antiwar protests against the U.S. presence in Vietnam were characterized as the product of "Communists who are taking advantage of disaffected young Americans." Civil rights activists were seen as puppets of Martin Luther King whom Hoover continued to include among "vociferous firebrands who are very militant in nature and who at times incite great numbers to activity."[14]

In the South, churches were being burned as the Ku Klux Klan continued its victimization. In the North, 50,000 marchers descended on Washington to protest the Vietnam War. In the West, students were painting flowers on their faces and experimenting with hallucinogenic drugs, preferring the magical fantasy of LSD to the reality of a country that seemed to be collapsing around them. It was no longer the America that Hoover remembered or even recognized. More important, it was not an America he could control.

Though his schedule was perceived as the same—9-to-5 days at the office, dinners spent with Clyde Tolson—almost nothing in Hoover's world remained the same. There was, of course, his home in the suburbs, with his two dogs and longtime housekeeper. Yet, even there, the appearance of normalcy was only that—an illusion designed to preserve what little remained of Hoover's world.

Tolson was damaged beyond repair, his physical shell pushed and prodded by the power of Hoover's expectations but accomplishing little. Now visually impaired and partially paralyzed, Tolson limped into the office, commanded into the chair behind his desk by an emperor who refused to accept defeat. James Crawford, Hoover's driver, was no longer able to chauffeur the man who had pulled him from the ranks of truck drivers and into the FBI. Afflicted with a recently diagnosed brain tumor, Crawford suffered more watching Hoover flounder in his absence than he did from the surgery to remove the cancerous growth.

Each day brought news of more protests, increased disruptions in the order of things. Blacks against whites, poor against rich, students against war. If any sense was to be made of the paradigm shift in American culture, Hoover did not grasp it. Nor did he care to try. It was lunacy. There could be no other explanation.

In Memphis, the lunacy presented itself in the form of a garbage strike. Black sanitation workers demanded the right to be represented by their union, which was calling for a 40-cents-an-hour raise. That Memphis was in the heart of the Old South, with its firmly entrenched segregationist policies, helped lather legitimacy on the city's policy of refusing to recognize a trade union of black workers.

By April 1968, the strike was nearing the end of its second month, with no movement toward settlement. Memphis mayor Henry Loeb had resisted demonstrations and marches, riots and litigation to resolve the issue. It was therefore hardly unexpected that Dr. Martin Luther King should fly into Memphis to attempt to terminate the strike, preaching tolerance and peace along the way. On April 3, while addressing the striking sanitation workers assembled in the Masonic Temple, King declared that he had "been to the mountaintop." His speech was so eloquent it inspired not only those present but a nation that would hear it repeated in tribute.

The following day, an anticipated thunderstorm failed to materialize, and King thought it a wonderful sign for the march that was planned in support of the workers. Just before 6 P.M., the civil rights leader stepped onto the balcony outside his room at the Lorraine Motel. The scene was bathed in red-orange light as the sun began to set across the Mississippi River. Even as King laughed and joked with visitors in the motel's courtyard below, an unseen man was stepping into a bathtub in a rundown rooming house some 70 yards away, propping the barrel of a brand-new rifle against the weathered sill of an open window.

The single shot that severed King's spine and killed him instantly echoed round the world. When Hoover learned of the assassination a half hour after it occurred, he reacted with practiced speed and efficiency. Publicly, he ordered the Bureau to cooperate with the Memphis police in its investigation. Privately, he rejoiced in the death by going to Baltimore's Pimlico racetrack just as he had done after the assassination of John F. Kennedy. Two months later Hoover repeated the performance, this time upon learning of the assassination of Robert Kennedy, who had been celebrating his victory in the California Democratic presidential primary. Again, since no federal law had been broken, the investigation was the responsibility of local police. And again, the horse races beckoned, all the better to draw a curtain over an unrecognizable America that had failed to live up to the standards of its chief law enforcement officer.

Attorney General Ramsey Clark pressed a reluctant Hoover into doing more than merely "cooperating." Clark expected the FBI to lead the investigation to track down King's killer. (Kennedy's assassin, a Palestinian Arab named Sirhan Sirhan, had been captured at the scene of the shooting.) At the time of Kennedy's murder in the kitchen of the Ambassador Hotel in Los Angeles, more than 2,000 special agents were actively investigating the King assassination, the largest single manhunt in the nation's history. In a remarkable coincidence, King's alleged killer was arrested in London on the eve of Kennedy's burial.

The twist of fate provided Hoover with one final opportunity to prove his contempt for both Kennedy and King. The Bureau's director ordered a press release detailing the capture of James Earl Ray, a small-time crook who had fled to England after the King shooting. The rifle allegedly used in the shooting, covered with Ray's fingerprints, was discovered minutes after the assassination, wrapped in a bedspread along with an unopened can of Schlitz beer, and tossed in front of Canipe's Amusement Company, a used-record store on Main Street.

It was midway through the Kennedy funeral that "Deke" DeLoach alerted Attorney General Clark that Ray had been captured in London. The official word was that while the Bureau had attempted to keep the arrest quiet until after the burial, England's Scotland Yard had announced that Ray was in custody. As Kennedy's casket was being carried down the steps of St. Patrick's Cathedral, the echo of the "Battle Hymn of the Republic" still caught in the nave of the great church, the atmosphere changed from funeral to carnival as news reporters tripped over one another in their rush to report the Ray arrest.

When Clark learned that Hoover had orchestrated the news release, he called DeLoach into his office and summarily criticized the agent. According to Clark, "The thing I couldn't take was that I'd been lied to. You can't function that way."[15]

DeLoach recalled the encounter differently. He claimed Clark was upset not by the timing of the release but rather by its content. "Why weren't the attorney general and the Justice Department mentioned more often?" DeLoach remembered Clark asking. "We should have gotten more credit."[16] Regardless, the confrontation was to be DeLoach's undoing. Clark immediately replaced him as the liaison to the attorney general.

The capture of Ray and his eventual conviction did little to end the rebellion taking place across America. If anything, the hopelessness that gripped many blacks and caused the civil rights unrest to continue to boil just beneath the surface of everyday life was aggravated by King's death, as the movement struggled to regain its footing under a new leader.

The havoc in the streets found its way to Chicago where the Democratic National Convention convened to select a candidate for president. Hoover, on vacation in La Jolla, watched in disbelief as protesters with long hair and love beads openly fought with local police in riot gear and gas masks, the scene playing out on national television. More than 200 protesters and police were injured in the melee, which left Hoover so depressed that he refused to leave his hotel room even for the Del Mar races, seeing only Clyde Tolson plus Dorothy Lamour, who had flown in for a visit on a break from her starring role in the national tour of *Hello, Dolly!*

Winning the Democratic nomination, Vice President Hubert Humphrey instantly became the target of the street violence and protests against the current administration and its policy on the Vietnam War. Richard Nixon, a longtime Hoover friend and admirer, turned quietly to the Bureau's director for help in securing inside information that would benefit his Republican presidential campaign. The FBI's files were opened to Nixon in a manner unprecedented for a political candidate. To Hoover, Nixon represented America's best hope to regain its stability in a climate of violent social upheaval. Certainly Hoover was incapable of controlling the situation, perplexed at the rampage of protest and disrespect for American ideals. The values of Seward Square were distant memories, forgotten by a new generation anxious to make its mark.

Hoover's open-door policy toward Nixon had as much to do with keeping his job as it did with calming America's turmoil. Now obviously aging and increasingly resistant to change, he needed the balm of an old friend in a high place almost as much as Nixon needed the information Hoover could supply.

The aggressive posture of a country rebelling played out in the presidential election of 1968 through violent graphics and antiwar slogans. Campaigning on a platform of law and order, Nixon crept into power by the slimmest of majorities—hardly a popular mandate by any means. Yet, to fulfill his promise of restoring peace across the land of the free, he positioned the welcome mat to the Bureau's director in a grand gesture that was more pomp than circumstance. In a pre-inaugural meeting with Hoover at Manhattan's Hotel Pierre, Nixon lauded Hoover's status, his accomplishments, his indispensability to the administration. According to incoming White House counsel John Ehrlichman, who was present at the meeting, Nixon said, "Edgar, you are one of the few people who is to have direct access to me at all times. I've talked to [Attorney General-Elect John] Mitchell and he understands."[17]

It was the type of fawning that appealed to Hoover, the kind of grand sweep bestowed by medieval kings on victorious knights. Unfortunately, Hoover was no longer battle ready, not to the point needed by the incoming Republican administration.

"The director of the Federal Bureau of Investigation was 74 years old when I first met him," Ehrlichman remembered of that moment at the Pierre. "His appearance surprised me. His big head rested on beefy, rounded shoulders, apparently without benefit of neck. He was florid and fat-faced, ears flat against his head, eyes protruding. He looked unwell to me."[18]

Hoover in fact *was* in poor health, hiding high blood pressure and heart palpitations under layers of bombast. Bravado substituted for energy, for more often than not, Hoover was weary, pushing himself just to complete the day ahead. Beginning in 1969, Hoover began to receive early morning visits from nurse Valerie Stewart, who administered an injection of a prescribed elixir alleged to have been a combination of vitamins spiked with amphetamines—a combination Hoover referred to as his "therapy." It became his lifeline at the Seat of Government, and the only way to maneuver through a complete day. The 9-12 shift, with its maniacal activity, followed by lunch and a two-hour nap. No variations; no surprises.

The illusion of normalcy disappeared with the sun, however, for as night fell and Hoover retired to his home, he reentered the time warp of trophies and long-forgotten accolades yellowing on faded walls amid the scent of dried flowers and Asian antiques. The ritual dinner with Clyde Tolson was no longer a daily repast peppered with talk of crime-busting exploits and the newest technology. With Tolson's illness, the meal became an exercise in determination as the crippled lieutenant was pushed to find muscles that failed to function. For Hoover, the evening ended predictably in a valley of depression—the polar opposite of the amphetamine high. Often jags of tears poured forth in the solitude of a bedroom blackened against nothing. The prying eyes of reporters no longer thought it newsworthy to search through Hoover's garbage, or watch from across the street for signs that a visitor was in residence.

Late-night calls to Dorothy Lamour were occasional diversions that played like holidays, for even the ritual vacations to Miami and La Jolla were held hostage to medical equipment, doctors' exams, and extra blankets to protect against chills. The mighty G-men, who once held their own against gangster legends, now were susceptible to chronic coughs and irritable bowels.

Yet, if the human condition was weakening Hoover's ability to control the FBI, human nature was helping it appear that the Bureau was an invaluable resource for the president. No sooner had the new administration taken control of the White House than confidential information began to leak into the media, particularly the *New York Times*. Initially, these leaks were cause for little more than embarrassment. When Nixon's highly confidential war plans for Vietnam found their way into the news, the president launched a counterattack to identify the source of the hemorrhage.

Henry Kissinger, the German-born head of Nixon's National Security Council, moved immediately to trace the leaks, which apparently came from within his own organization. In what was to be a massive internal effort, the president authorized Hoover to "take the necessary steps—including wiretapping."[19] Hoover immediately issued instructions to install 17 separate wiretaps—13 within the White House and the Departments of State and Defense, and the remainder on reporters including the *New York Times*' William Beecher, whose article revealed details of Cambodia's authorization for bombing raids on Vietnam.

Though Attorney General John Mitchell officially approved the wiretaps, Hoover never fully accepted his legal authority to maintain them. Now growing increasingly nervous over any activity that could be judged politically incorrect or, worse, totally illegal, Hoover segregated the Kissinger wiretaps and kept details of their existence in a file completely separate from others involving FBI electronic surveillance. Despite the wiretaps, however, privileged information continued to spring from unidentified sources within the Nixon administration, driving the president to ever more desperate measures.

In a marked about-face from his years of black bag jobs and aggressive surveillance, Hoover flatly refused Nixon's request to expand wiretap coverage of news reporters. This single gesture spawned the formation of a team of covert investigators under White House direction, led by former New York police officer John J. Caulfield. Hoover wanted nothing to do with what he labeled as Caulfield's "scurrilous activities," and he attempted to minimize the investigator's effectiveness at uncovering information. According to John Ehrlichman, Caulfield was "able to secure far better data for the president . . . than we could get from Hoover."[20]

Nixon was not yet ready to dispense with the Bureau's director, despite his reluctance to serve unquestioningly. Needing the faith of the conservative base that held Hoover in high esteem, the president continued to praise the FBI and its leader for their contribution to the administration. It was little more than posturing, to be sure, since Nixon was finding the FBI's inefficiency shocking in its depth—dealing "excessively in rumor, gossip and conjecture."[21] That did not, however, make it any less necessary, as Nixon proved when he accepted Hoover's invitation to have dinner at his home on the edge of Rock Creek Park. Mitchell and Ehrlichman accompanied the president to Hoover's home, which Ehrlichman later characterized as "seedy," with walls covered by "brown or faded" photographs and mementos. The meal consisted of steak flown in by Clint Murchison, chili from Chasen's Restaurant in Beverly Hills, and fresh fruit from Florida.

"After dinner we were led down the narrowest of basement stairs to the recreation room for an after-dinner drink," Ehrlichman recalled. "Near the door was a small bar. All the walls over and near this counter were decorated with girlie pinups of the old *Esquire* vintage. Even the lampshade of a small lamp on the bar had a naked woman pasted on it. The effect of this display was to engender disbelief—it seemed totally contrived. That impression was reinforced when Hoover deliberately called attention to his naughty gallery, as if it were something he wanted us to know about J. Edgar Hoover."[22]

The evening reinforced Nixon's image of Hoover as a man living in the past, lost in a world of accolades and medals, combating an enemy settled in a mind filled with statistics that proved his worth. The irony of the situation was hardly lost on the nation's chief executive. Hoover had kept his hold on the Bureau by virtue of the secrets he clutched tightly to his chest—the most cherished of all being the illusion of his own power.

Where it had once been the unknown contents of secret files that motivated politicians to maintain the throne on which Hoover sat, now it was the public's perception of the director as protector of the country that preserved his power. Like the bald eagle, Hoover had become an endangered species, a symbol of might more legend than reality.

Although he rarely appeared in public these days, Hoover was still polished and poised, immaculately turned out in custom-made suits and manicured nails. His thinning hair was pomaded with Yardley brilliantine, casting the lingering fragrance of English lavender as he minced through the halls of the Justice Building. In contrast, Tolson, dragging his right leg and trailing several yards behind, struggled to keep up with his famous boss, who seemed to walk even faster in his assistant's company. Unable to keep his former schedule of tasks, Tolson nevertheless made a daily effort to come to work. It was a symbolic effort now that Tolson was doing little more than reviewing scripts for the television series, *The F.B.I.*, which Hoover continued to refer to as "my series."

"I understand that in the last television (TV) script which Mr. Tolson had to review," Hoover memoed DeLoach in late 1969, "there were three killings, and he returned it in order to have it rewritten so as to eliminate these acts of violence. I want to make it emphatically clear that I do not want any extreme acts of violence portrayed on our TV program. I have stated this previously, but apparently it is not being given the attention that it should. There is a nationwide feeling that TV presents entirely too much violence and various groups and organizations have publicly stated the same and testimony has been given before Congressional committees to that effect. I do not intend that the FBI's TV program be in that category and you must, therefore, give more attention to the review of these scripts before they are sent to Mr. Tolson for final approval."[23]

As popular as the Hollywood version of Hoover's FBI was across America, the series had little in common with the reality gripping the country. There was no mention of the campus unrest, sit-ins, and walkouts, nor the political wiretapping orchestrated by the president. Equally absent was any effort to depict the continuing civil rights movement, which had grown more violent with the creation of the Black Panthers.

The activist, antiestablishment group was as militant as it was controversial, a combination that placed it on Hoover's "most hated" list from its inception. Hoover took particular umbrage toward Eldridge Cleaver, the group's minister of information. Cleaver's 1966 book, *Soul on Ice,* written in prison, provided a philosophical foundation for the organization—an organization that Hoover told Congress was funded by East Coast celebrities such as pianist Peter Duchin and conductor Leonard Bernstein. The Bureau's director was often a target for Cleaver, whose name Hoover repeatedly mispronounced *Cleavenger.*

In tapping COINTELPRO to "expose, disrupt, misdirect, discredit or otherwise neutralize the activities of black nationalist hate-type organizations and groupings, their leadership, spokesmen, membership and supporters,"[24] Hoover routinely used the U.S. mail to send forged letters and publicity releases aimed at embarrassing the militants and their agenda. It mattered little that innocents were hurt if blame could be cast on the Black Panthers.

Jean Seberg, the complex actress who rose to fame playing the title role in Otto Preminger's 1957 film *Saint Joan*, and who starred in the 1960 masterpiece *Breathless*, was swept onto Hoover's crosshairs with her alleged financial support of the Black Panthers in Paris. As pay back for this indiscretion, Hoover set about ruining her life. With his permission, a plot was hatched in the Bureau's Los Angeles office. On April 27, 1970, SAC Richard W. Held sent a memo to Hoover in which he requested authorization to "publicize the pregnancy of Jean Seberg, well-known movie actress," whom Held suggested had been impregnated by Raymond Hewitt, a Black Panther leader. Held wanted to advise "Hollywood Gossip-Columnists in the Los Angeles area of the situation. It is felt that the possible publication of Seberg's plight could cause her embarrassment and serve to cheapen her image with the general public."[25] To accomplish this goal, he proposed drafting a letter from "a fictitious person" reading as follows:

> I was just thinking about you and remembered I still owe you a favor. So —— I was in Paris last week and ran into Jean Seberg, who was heavy with baby. I thought she and Romaine[†] had gotten together again, but she confided the child belonged to a Raymond Hewit [sic] of the Black Panthers, one of its officers. The dear girl is getting around!

---

† Seberg's estranged husband, the novelist Romain Gary.

Anyway, I thought you might get a scoop on the others. Be good and I'll see you soon.

Love, Sol

"Usual precautions would be taken by the Los Angeles Division to preclude identification of the Bureau as the source of the letter if approval is granted," Held continued.[26] It was a heinous plan with only one purpose: the destruction of a career, a small price to pay in Hoover's mind if the Black Panthers were humiliated in the process.

"To protect the sensitive source of information from possible compromise and to insure the success of your plan," Hoover decided, "Bureau feels it would be better to wait approximately two additional months until Seberg's pregnancy would be obvious to everyone."[27]

Newly pregnant, the actress, who was alternately described as pert and pious, confused and convincing, elfish and elusive, had no idea she was about to become Hoover's latest COINTELPRO target. By methods still unclear, Joyce Haber, a gossip reporter from the *Los Angeles Times,* became aware of the FBI-generated rumor and ran a thinly veiled item in her May 19, 1970, column. Labeling the actress "Miss A," Haber wrote that the "beautiful and blonde" woman was the "current 'A' topic of chatter among the 'ins' of international show business circles." Stating that the actress arrived in Hollywood "with the tantalizing flavor of a basket of fresh-picked berries," Haber ended her column with a revelation:

And now, according to all these really 'in' international sources, Topic A is the baby Miss A is expecting, and its father. Papa's said to be a rather prominent Black Panther.[28]

In the months that followed, silence became Seberg's most cherished ally as the industry trade paper the *Hollywood Reporter*, picked up the Hoover campaign with the gossip "Hear a Black Panther's the pappy of a certain film queen's expected baby."[29]

Reeling from the whispers and emotionally unable to cope with the pressure created by the vortex swirling ever faster around her, Seberg attempted suicide in early August, taking a near-fatal dose of sedatives. She was 31 years old. That the pills failed to end her life became a millstone Seberg carried for the remainder of her life. Worn and damaged, the delicate actress struggled to find reason in the tragedy her life had become. Hollywood looked upon her with pity, believing each word Hoover leaked to an insatiable public. It took only a subsequent article in *Newsweek*—confirming that Seberg was remarrying her second husband, Romain Gary, "even though the baby Jean expects in October is by another man—a black activist she met in California"—to push her beyond her physical and mental limits.[30] The actress once described as "fragile, like a dandelion pod" went into premature labor on August 20. Her only child died two days after birth. At the funeral, Seberg ordered the infant placed on view in a Plexiglas coffin that revealed a white baby girl, a silent statement that refuted Hoover's claims.

Regrettably, Seberg never recovered. She attempted suicide in an annual ritual on the anniversary of her daughter's birth. In 1979 she finally succeeded, dying of a barbiturate overdose in the backseat of her car.

Never publicly admitting the FBI's involvement in the Seberg tragedy, Hoover instead went on record warning Americans that the Black Panther Party was "the most dangerous and violence-prone of all extremist groups."[31] The Bureau was particularly upset that "despite its record of hate, violence, and subversion, the Black Panther Party continues to receive substantial monetary contributions from prominent donors. With these funds, its representatives have been able to travel widely and make frequent public appearances at colleges, universities, and even secondary schools."[32]

As he had for the previous 40 years, Hoover presented his annual report on the activities of the Bureau, relying heavily on statistics to illustrate the effectiveness of his investigative organization. There were references to the Communist Party, of course, still high on Hoover's list of subversives, as well as mention of Students for a Democratic Society, identified as the "principal force guiding the country's violence-prone young militants." Yet, even as he sat sequestered in his fifth-floor suite of offices, overweight, short of breath, and dependent on drugs to stimulate his energy level, Hoover was a ghost of his former self.

The leader of the FBI still commanded respect from his special agents, now numbering 7,000 strong. But he had lost touch with the people seeking change—students, young politicians, and scholars who were behind a mass movement fueled by discontent. He labeled them enemies rather than prophets of the future, and in doing so was added to their list of hypocrites.

No longer comfortably shielded from criticism by the perception of his power, Hoover became an open target for ridicule by conservatives and liberals alike. Ramsey Clark, the former attorney general, was particularly harsh in his book *Crime in America,* saying Hoover ran the FBI with a "self-centered concern with his own reputation" while concentrating on Communists and ignoring organized crime. The Nixon administration leaped to Hoover's defense, suggesting that his years of service were proof of his success, but it seemed a hollow defense in light of a country seemingly intent on devouring itself.

The man noted for his stubborn dedication to justice and fierce pride in his country, reacted to Clark's criticism by dissolving into tears. Helen Gandy happened upon the uncharacteristic breakdown when she entered Hoover's office to announce an unexpected visit from attorney Roy Cohn one afternoon in December 1970. Though she credited overwork for the rare display of emotion, Gandy openly worried about the toll his job was taking on her 75-year-old boss.[33] His entire career, indeed the FBI itself, was being held hostage to age. What once worked in Hoover's favor now was an indicator of out-of-date philosophies and incapacitation. With each successive attack, Hoover attempted to crank up his activity level a notch as if mere movement was enough to suggest capability. Gandy knew the effect it was having on Hoover's health. She herself was 74 and had wanted to retire for years.

Clyde Tolson had reached the mandatory retirement age of 70 in May 1970, and given his precarious health, few expected him to remain in his post. Yet, Hoover was determined to keep his team in place, and so, as he had for the past 45 years, Tolson followed Hoover's lead. On Tolson's retirement day, at Hoover's request, Attorney General John Mitchell rehired the associate director as an annuitant, a sort of halfway house of employment status. Tolson continued to receive his full salary with complete benefits, though a large share of his pay came from his government pension, the FBI picking up the difference.

With Tolson now barely functioning and Hoover drawing on reserve merely to keep up appearances, the bulk of the actual daily responsibilities was handled by "Deke" DeLoach, who, at 49, was the baby among the barnacled. It was not a situation DeLoach relished, and with the re-upping of Tolson, Hoover's third-in-command decided to end his career at the FBI, resigning as deputy associate director to join PepsiCo as vice president of corporate affairs.

The move was as unexpected as it was painful. Hoover immediately branded his capable administrator a Judas and tapped William Sullivan, whom DeLoach disliked, to fill the position. It was to be what Hoover later labeled "the biggest mistake of my life." Not that the tough, buzz-cut Sullivan was inefficient. If anything, he was a younger, more aggressive version of Hoover himself—and a man determined to take Hoover's place at the top of the FBI hierarchy.

At the moment, however, Hoover's concern was not a palace coup but Jack Nelson, Atlanta bureau chief for the *Los Angeles Times,* whose fascination with the Bureau's director had evolved from his eager support during his cub years into his current resolve in exposing improprieties. Nelson, a gritty journalist with a Pulitzer Prize to his credit, began to ask questions and print answers that were making Hoover extremely uncomfortable. He probed into the royalty arrangements on Hoover's books, the director's liberal use of special agents to build the front portico and back wall at his home, the cost of his custom-made bulletproof limousine, and the annual vacations to Florida and California at taxpayers' expense.

Nixon as well was pressing for answers to the increase in student protests and demonstrations even as Sullivan was pushing for expanded wiretaps and black bag jobs to counter them. It was the stuff of paranoia—rumors that Big Brother was invading the privacy of the nation's elite and the nation's subversives. Suddenly, there was no safe haven from criticism as the merry-go-round of innuendo and suspicion splattered blame and accusation with equal effort.

Suffocating under the doubt being cast on his ability to control the country's largest investigative force, Hoover retreated inward, closeting himself behind the Department of Justice in offices that were becoming if not a prison, then at least a holding cell. Protecting his authority, his secrets, and his honor became Hoover's defense, against a population all too willing to forget his history, his accomplishments, his past.

The fragile house of cards that was Hoover's world came tumbling down around him on March 8, 1971. The air was particularly cool that Monday night, cutting sharp through Media, Pennsylvania, with scalpel precision. Snow flurries had been predicted but none arrived. Instead, that evening a group calling itself the Citizens'

Commission to Investigate the FBI arrived at the Bureau's offices in that Philadelphia suburb to steal confidential files—files Hoover could ill afford to be made public. It was two weeks before samples of the stolen files began to appear, first in the offices of Senator George McGovern, the Democrat from South Dakota, and then on the desk of Congressman Parren Mitchell of Maryland, the first African American elected to the House from that state.

This invasion of privacy was little more than the Bureau had been doing to others, yet to Hoover it was tantamount to treason. He characteristically accepted no blame and called for a widespread investigation into the culprits who successfully breached the Bureau's shell of impenetrability. Even as America was learning of the FBI's most clandestine operations, including the existence of COINTELPRO, the Bureau was circling its wagons in an effort to control the damage.

Like a robot on overload, Hoover began to shut down operations systematically as the chaperones of justice sniffed at his heels. Ripping out wiretaps, removing surveillance teams, releasing informants in a wholesale effort to mask rough edges and exposed vulnerabilities, Hoover closed doors and watched his back as never before.

The president, now unable to count on the FBI to perform his private investigations, organized his own team of detectives, nicknamed "White House plumbers" for their ability to stop leaks. Yet the leaks continued, revealing that the FBI tapped the phones of members of Congress and the Senate. Hale Boggs, the House majority leader led the attack on Capitol Hill. "When the FBI taps the telephones of Members of his body and of Members of the

Senate, when the FBI stations agents on college campuses to infiltrate college organizations, when the FBI adopts the tactics of the Soviet Union and Hitler's Gestapo, then it is time—it is way past time, Mr. Speaker—that the present Director no longer be the Director . . . I ask again that Mr. Mitchell, the Attorney General of the United States, have enough courage to demand the resignation of Mr. Hoover."[34]

House Minority Leader Gerald Ford argued in response that while the FBI had made "some mistakes," he felt the "Nation has been fortunate to have had the FBI and Hoover as its Head," adding, "They are humans, as we are."[35]

Hoover rushed to his own defense, stating that he was unaware of any wiretap of a politician on Capitol Hill. Attorney General Mitchell, speaking to Hoover by phone from Key Biscayne, Florida, advised him to "let the storm blow over and it will pass."[36] But Hoover was far too nervous, pressured by guilt and the knowledge that he had often approached both senators and congressmen with incriminating evidence about their personal lives—information he swore would remain secret. Yet, in light of the break-in in Media, Pennsylvania, who among them could be sure?

"I will be willing to step aside," Hoover told Mitchell, "if at any time I may be a burden or handicap to the re-election."[37] A grand gesture on Hoover's part, it was dismissed by Mitchell, who called Hoover, "a good American."

Others were not so kind. Reporters besieged him during his customary lunch at the Mayflower Hotel, pushing past the maître d' and interrupting Hoover's meal. Exposed and outflanked, the director declared Boggs "a very sick man" and fled the restaurant, taking refuge in his office. The pack of journalists followed, the townspeople holding torches high at the base of Frankenstein's castle.

Reporter Jack Nelson called for a congressional investigation, a move that Deputy Attorney General Richard Kleindienst seconded, much to Hoover's fury. Senator Edward Kennedy called for Hoover's resignation, as did Senators Edmund Muskie and George McGovern. *Newsweek* turned Hoover into its cover story with the banner, HOOVER'S FBI: TIME FOR A CHANGE?[38] Citing an anonymous congressional leader, the magazine reported there were "hopes and hints" that Hoover's end was near. "Hoover's replacement as the head of the FBI is no longer unthinkable," the congressional leader said. "In fact, there would be a sigh of relief that could lift the Capitol dome quite a few inches."[39]

Hoover was not, however, without his supporters, who rallied around the aging director by establishing Friends of the FBI, a nonprofit organization whose honorary chairman was none other than actor Efrem Zimbalist Jr., the star of television's *The F.B.I.* Calling the clamor for Hoover's resignation "a vicious smear campaign," Zimbalist declared that such a move threatened to "undermine the whole structure of law and order in the United States."[40]

To many, that was occurring already as lawlessness continued to invade towns across America, and every dawn seemed to bring new revelations and leaks. Such was the case on June 13, 1971, when the *New York Times* published the first of several reports of a confidential study prepared by Secretary of Defense Robert McNamara called the *History of the U.S. Decision-Making Process on Vietnam Policy*. The press shortened the ungainly title to the Pentagon Papers, and its revelations changed history.

The Nixon White House immediately demanded an FBI investigation into the source of the leaked material. Daniel Ellsberg, a former Defense Department analyst, was quickly charged, leaving the FBI to mop up any accomplices along the way. Unfortunately for Hoover, that included a man named Louis Marx, Ellsberg's father-in-law and America's leading toy manufacturer.[‡]

Marx and Hoover had a casual relationship. Marx contributed a truckload of toys annually to Hoover, who gave them away as Christmas gifts to friends. As the investigation into the Pentagon Papers intensified, an ultimately innocent Marx was placed on the list of people to be screened. Chick Brennan, special agent in charge of the Ellsberg investigation, notified the director via memo of his intention.

Hoover did not authorize Brennan's plan, marking the memo "No H." Brennan, however, mistakenly read the scribble as "H OK," and, believing he had Hoover's approval, proceeded to conduct the interview. Upon learning of the error, Hoover immediately moved to demote Brennan and transfer him out of the Seat of Government. It was typical punishment at Hoover's hands, nothing more than he had done on dozens of other occasions. To William Sullivan, who had groomed Brennan personally as head of the Domestic Intelligence Division,

---

[‡] Known as the Henry Ford of toys, Marx sold Louis Marx & Co. to Quaker Oats in 1972 for $52 million.

the punishment was far in excess of the crime. After complaining bitterly to the director, Hoover's third-in-command took his case directly to the attorney general, who passed it along to the White House. Ultimately, Brennan's job was spared, but not without a terse censure from Hoover, who now began to see Sullivan as the enemy.

Sullivan looked on his partial victory as an indication of support from the White House. After 30 years with the Bureau, Sullivan had failed to learn the first rule of conduct: Never disagree with the director. In this case, Sullivan not only had a problem with Hoover's conduct, but he openly discussed it with the attorney general. Sullivan had disagreed with Hoover before, most recently when the director authorized the expansion of the FBI's foreign attaché offices. Rather than being rubber-stamped through the Bureau's Tolson-led executive committee, the issue was a bone of contention, prompting Sullivan to write Hoover a memo deriding not only the idea but other members of the executive committee as well.

Of his colleagues on the committee, Sullivan wrote, "It was somewhat more than mildly distressing and saddening to me to observe the lack of objectivity, originality, and independent thinking in their remarks. While I am certain it was not the intention of these important Bureau officials, who occupy unique roles, to create the impression in the reader's mind that they said what they did because they thought this was what the Director wanted them to say, nevertheless it seems to me that this is the impression conveyed."[41]

Within days of receiving the memo, Hoover had assembled his troops for battle against one of their own.

Even as Sullivan was maneuvering within the Justice Department, seeking counsel from Robert Mardian, head of internal security, Hoover swiftly promoted Mark Felt to deputy associate director, which made him Sullivan's boss.

Suddenly finding himself slipping a notch in the executive ranks, Sullivan lobbied for position by demonstrating his loyalty to the Nixon White House. In a risky winner-take-all move, he conducted his own black bag job, transferring classified files on the Bureau's wiretapping operations from his office to chief of staff H. R. Haldeman's private safe. There was no turning back, no possibility of retreat. The Bureau's fourth-in-command had made his bid for a throne large enough for only one man.

At 76, Hoover was old in the way that curmudgeons are old—more ornery than just tired. He was a fussy, cantankerous perfectionist who ate upstarts like Sullivan for amusement. While he did not know that his assistant director had illegally transferred documents from the Seat of Government, he knew all he had to know. Sullivan would retire, but on Hoover's timetable, not his own. His insubordination was enough to demand that.

On Tuesday, August 31, the skies in Washington, D.C., were cast in blue so pure as to appear synthetic. But William Sullivan never noticed. At 2 P.M., he was escorted into Hoover's inner office for what was to be a protracted appointment. For the next two and a half hours, Hoover delivered a monologue outlining the special agent's faults. The reedy timbre of Hoover's voice rapped staccato-quick, pausing only occasionally when breath required.

It was late in the game to offer a defense. Instead, Sullivan merely listened to the onslaught of insults and put-downs, studying Hoover as he did. The director's perfectly pressed suit pulled at the buttons, his body unabashedly plump, the fat on his neck layered over his crisp white collar like icing melting in the sun.

Sullivan knew this was how it would end. The director had won yet again. Somehow Sullivan had misjudged his own strengths, or perhaps Hoover's. Either way, within days the Bureau's director wrote a memo commanding Sullivan to take a two-week vacation. As if out of spite, Sullivan wrote back that one week was all the vacation he actually needed. "Take two. H." came the reply. Sullivan did, only to return after a fortnight to find the locks on his office door changed, and a nameplate that read "Alex Rosen" in place of his own.

The disposal of Sullivan seemed to give Hoover renewed energy. But then, the transfusion of personnel always had that effect. He was reborn with each new memo, instructing, controlling, maneuvering the troops to do his bidding. It was, of course, an illusion, and he knew it. There was no denying his age or the constant harping of naysayers who nipped at his heels with the sole intent of making him stumble.

But Hoover did not waver. There was no hint that he was even listening to any talk of retirement. None. "I have never considered stepping down from my position in the FBI as long as I can be of service to my country and have the health, vigor and enthusiasm to perform my responsibilities in the manner my superiors and the public have a right to expect," he said just before his seventy-seventh birthday.[42]

On the day itself, January 1, 1972, Hoover was flying aboard Air Force One. The flight, a birthday present from the president, was returning him from his annual trip to Miami to a new year in Washington, D.C. The illusion was one of business as usual, but Hoover knew that wasn't so. He had even begun going through his most secret files, destroying those he could ill afford to reveal.

Perhaps he had heard that G. Gordon Liddy, former special agent–turned–special assistant to Richard Nixon, and only months away from the Watergate break-in, had been told to come up with ways to remove Hoover quietly from his post. Ease him into retirement, glorify him if necessary, but remove him at the president's request. Nixon had lost faith in his longtime friend, and Hoover was now more liability than asset. "Comment: Hoover is in his 55th year with the Department of Justice. Even his secretary dates from the First World War. There is no dishonor, express [sic] or implied, in asking a man in such circumstances to give up the burden of office." Liddy wrote in his autobiography.[43] The question, of course, was how to make it happen, and there, no one seemed to have a clue. Hoover, certainly, was in no rush to leave.

Suddenly losing the motivation to destroy his secret files, Hoover instead returned them to the safety of Helen Gandy's omnipresent gaze. He resumed his two-hour lunches at the Mayflower with a nearly blind and lame Tolson in tow. Now more a prop than an ally, Tolson listened dutifully to Hoover's nonstop monologues, rehashing his beliefs and annoyances, always saving a special moment for reporter Jack Anderson, still considered the "lowest form of human being to walk the earth."

Increasing his dose of vitamin-amphetamine elixir, Hoover became more agitated, jerking his arms and rubbing his hands in a cacophony of rigid movements. His temper raged unpredictably, followed by periods of depression that seemed to manifest themselves in extended silence. Even at 77, however, his memos never changed. Hoover remained as virile in print as he was in his youth, spewing with unrelenting power.

"Today, upon my return to Washington," he wrote to Tolson on April 26, 1972, "there were, ready for me to sign, letters to the President of TWA, the Federal Aviation Administration, and the Airline Pilots Association relative to the outrageous action of a Captain of a TWA plane at Chicago in compelling two of our Agents to leave the plane unless they surrendered their guns."

> I had to rewrite the letter to TWA because of the rather 'mouselike' contents of the same. I want any correspondence with TWA to be curt and to the point. The original letter drafted for my signature did not emphasize the angry and incensed actions of the Captain of the TWA plane at Chicago. In fact, it made no mention of the same. I had to change the salutation in that it was addressed to "Dear ...." and closed with "Sincerely yours." I want all correspondence going to TWA to be addressed either "Sir" or "Dear Sir" and closed "Very truly yours."
>
> I had to add to the letter a concluding sentence in which I demanded that TWA instruct their pilots to comply with the regulations of the Federal Aviation

Administration, which was approached rather 'lamb-like' in the original letter.

> We have been treated most shabbily by TWA . . . and I see no reason why we should not be aggressively pertinent when we are communicating with that organization.[44]

Brandishing his usual pen, he signed the memo "J.E.H." in dark blue ink, unaware that it would be his last.

In the days that followed, Hoover was near frantic with excess energy, welcoming guests into his office, posing for souvenir photos, and insisting on meeting agents' family members who were taking tours of the FBI headquarters. It was, one visitor remembered, as if he knew should he stop, even for a moment, he would die.

On the evening of Tuesday, May 2, Hoover, concerned about his old friend's health, had an early dinner at Tolson's house: Omaha steak, baked potatoes, baby peas, vanilla ice cream for dessert. At 8 P.M., complaining of indigestion, Hoover returned to his home, poured himself a short drink, played with his dogs, and retired for the night, much as he had done for years.

Six hours later, only the steady ticking of a mantel clock bore witness as Hoover lay dying on the floor. Unconscious in the master bedroom, he pulled at air in a futile struggle against the inevitable. Stubborn, obdurate, unwilling to accept his own mortality. But then, J. Edgar Hoover had always fought against the odds. This night, however, would be different. This night, he would lose.

THE LEGACY,
THE LEGEND

The days that followed J. Edgar Hoover's death were clearly unusual—not only at the FBI and the White House but surely for most of America. A major icon of stability had fallen, leaving a void that many found strangely frightening, the way one feels when lost in an unfamiliar neighborhood at night. There was a sense of imminent danger that no amount of reassurance from the country's leaders could assuage.

Even as newspaper editors, politicians, and police chiefs around the country rushed to laud the man whom the president praised for his "granite-like honesty and integrity," the air hung heavy with trepidation. The watchdog was dead, and now the kennel was unguarded. America had every right to be concerned, paranoid even. And it was—the White House included.

As Nixon glorified the man who above all others was the profile of law and order, the president commanded that Hoover's home be scoured for any trace of scandal: files, photographs, letters, telegrams—anything that might reveal what was happening inside the Executive Mansion, or the FBI for that matter. Any proof that the granitelike honesty of the director had been compromised by the need to keep his job or, worse, to cover his own indiscretions or those of the president.

Within hours, Nixon was reassured that nothing had been found inside the colonial home at 4936 Thirtieth Place NW. The president was satisfied, perhaps too easily, that in the end the old bulldog had left nothing to chance. Helen Gandy had her instructions and was busy shredding any documents of an incriminating nature. Methodical and unfazed, Gandy was, after all, the keeper of truth. It was therefore with all innocence that she was able to look up from her desk on May 3 and report to newly appointed acting director L. Patrick Gray III that the files through which she was anxiously sorting were merely the "personal papers" of her late boss.

In reality, her last official act for the Federal Bureau of Investigation was to protect its image by protecting that of J. Edgar Hoover. Gone was any proof of black bag jobs and hired killers. Gone were the requests for illegal activities and the meticulously itemized reports of their successful completion. Gone were the details of book royalties, stock options, free vacations, and political blackmail. Gone forever, as box after box of documents and files were shredded and burned, reduced to silence in piles of ash.

There was no hint that six weeks later, a break-in at the Democratic National Committee headquarters in the Watergate office complex would lead to the demise of the Nixon administration. No hint to suggest that in April 1973, acting director Gray himself would be forced to resign under a cloud of accusations after it was revealed that he had destroyed files of White House plumber E. Howard Hunt. And no hint to forewarn that in 1975 the House of Representatives would convene an official inquiry into the destruction of Hoover's files, and the Senate investigate the FBI's surreptitious acts, leading to the conclusion that the deceased director was responsible for authorizing activities that "threatened our constitutional system."

It evoked the dismantling of a great cathedral, one believed to be built of the purest stone, only to be revealed as illusion, like the false front of a movie set. Slowly, so slowly, bits and pieces of Hoover's empire were exposed through the most unlikely of sources: the very files that Hoover used to maintain his fiefdom. The files surfaced in unexpected places, to be sure, such as the garage of Louis Nichols. Assistant to the director until 1957, Nichols had kept personal copies of files Hoover thought long destroyed. Clyde Tolson, the trusted confidant and dearest friend who moved into Hoover's home on the very day of his death also kept files far longer than the FBI mandated six months.

Perhaps no one, however, circumvented Hoover's attempts at invulnerability more than Helen Gandy. For 53 years the bespectacled matron had meticulously filed and refiled the most damaging of memos, moving documents among cabinets labeled "Official and Confidential," "Obscene," "Personal and Confidential" and "Secret"—never revealing a word from the written pages. Yet not even the well-meaning, obedient executive assistant was infallible.

Through an act of fate, nothing more, a memo dated July 19, 1966, and labeled "Do Not File" found its way into the central filing system. Written by William Sullivan to "Deke" DeLoach, it detailed the procedures for black bag jobs, and was a response to DeLoach's request "concerning what authority we have for 'black bag' jobs and for the background of our policy and procedures in such matters." Sullivan wrote:

> We do not obtain authorization for 'black bag' jobs from outside the Bureau. Such a technique involves trespass and is clearly illegal; therefore, it would be impossible to obtain any legal sanction for it. Despite this, 'black bag' jobs have been used because they represent an invaluable technique in combating subversive activities of a clandestine nature aimed directly at undermining and destroying our nation.[1]

Helen Gandy received a copy of the memo, as she did all memos that passed through Hoover's office. Under her name, she wrote the initials "P.F." for placement in Hoover's personal files hidden from the scrutiny of prying eyes, and destined to be destroyed by Gandy after his death. The memo, however, never made it to the safety of Hoover's private filing cabinet. Instead, it was uncovered in the FBI's central filing system by investigators from the Senate and House.

Interrogated about the memo by Congresswoman Bella Abzug during the December 1975 House inquiry into the destruction of Hoover's files, Gandy was defiant.

> *Ms. Abzug.* My question is this: Was everything in the personal file destroyed?
> *Miss Gandy.* Everything in the personal file, as I reviewed them before I destroyed them, was destroyed

with the exception of a folder on the dogs. I kept the file on the dogs' pedigree for Mr. Tolson's information.

Ms. Abzug. Did you look at every single personal file?

Miss Gandy. Every single page and every single personal file.

Ms. Abzug. I am going to read you a list of names and subjects, and in each case I would like you to comment, tell me if there was anything in the personal files on any of these people or subjects. Mail openings?

Miss Gandy. No.

Ms. Abzug. Informants?

Miss Gandy. No.

Ms. Abzug. Wiretappings?

Miss Gandy. No.

Ms. Abzug. Black bag jobs?

Miss Gandy. No, indeed.

Ms. Abzug. What about the black bag job memorandum which indicates that it was a personal file?

Miss Gandy. It looks like a mistake on my part; that is, to put the P.F. on it when it should be O.C.

Ms. Abzug. Where did you actually put it? Where did you put it when you filed it?

Miss Gandy. I have no idea at this date. The date of that memorandum is what?

Ms. Abzug. The date of the memorandum is July 19, 1966.

Miss Gandy. How in the world could I remember that?

Ms. Abzug. That would be difficult.

Miss Gandy. At 78 years old, that would be difficult.

The congressional investigations and their subsequent revelations shattered what was left of the public's faith in government and the ethics of its institutions. Coupled with the Watergate scandal, the fall of the Federal Bureau of Investigation from its pillar of integrity and incorruptibility forever changed America and its perception of liberty. In 1966, a Gallup poll found 84 percent of Americans rating the FBI's work as "highly favorable." By 1975, the Bureau's approval quotient had fallen to 52 percent.[2] It was doomed to drop even further.

In 1976, a federal investigation discovered that Hoover had been liberally dipping into the $85,000 treasury of the FBI Recreational Association, as well as a $10 million fund set up to payroll informants, using the money to bankroll expensive dinners for himself and selected cronies at the Carriage House restaurant in Georgetown. One special agent told *Time* magazine, "It started with cocktails and crab meat, then there were oysters, followed by steak and wine and French pastries and brandy."[3] According to investigators, Hoover also used the FBI's exhibit section (a division whose primary responsibility was constructing models for demonstrations in court cases) to build the portico on the front of his home, plus add a back porch and statuary—work totaling nearly $100,000.

As a result of the Freedom of Information Act, news organizations gained access to the FBI's "Official and Confidential" files, forever destroying Hoover's illusion of propriety. The most direct assault on his reputation came via ABC News which marked the tenth anniversary of the director's death with a scathing exposé. Among the revelations: Hoover's falsification of evidence and official reports that misled Congress and the Warren Commission, as well as the orchestration of a massive campaign, which ABC correspondent Marshall Frady said was "conducted through illegal surveillance, burglaries, harassment, political sabotage and directed—the best authorities say— against many thousands of innocent citizens."[4]

Suddenly, the rush to crucify Hoover slid like mercury on a marble floor. The man who once could do no wrong now was seemingly guilty of everything short of sacrilege. Unfortunately, while much of the criticism was based on newly discovered truths, it failed to place the wrongdoings in the perspective of history—for indeed, that is how Hoover, who was born when the Civil War was a recent memory and died on the day Hanoi forces captured Quang Tri, must be judged.

The rigid love of country and belief in democracy that Hoover had learned in Seward Square at the turn of the century remained with him for his entire life, pushing him to mold the Bureau in his image and allow it to transgress in order to uphold his vision. In the end, it was Hoover's unshakable confidence in America's ideals that the country found so admirable. To many, he stood as a beacon of old-fashioned patriotism, a man unafraid to wave the American flag when flags were being burned around the world.

Perhaps it was a pedestal no mere mortal could occupy, though that concept never occurred to J. Edgar Hoover. He saw his role in American history no less vividly than did Washington or Jefferson, Lincoln or Roosevelt: to keep the United States free from crime, free from the tyranny of Communism, and free from subversion in the name of liberty—no matter the price.

Unfortunately, more than 30 years after his death, the costs of Hoover's excesses are still being played out across the landscape of America, and are now a part of history. His wholesale violation of privacy cannot be explained away by outlining a noble cause. Neither can we dismiss his cultivation of murderers and thugs to topple the organized crime families of which they were members. Though it is easier to understand the politics that encouraged him to deftly blackmail presidents, it is no less a transgression for a man appointed with investigating such crimes.

Yet for those who would demand that his name be removed from the architecturally monstrous FBI building in Washington, or who would label the man an American Beria,* it is wise to remember the turmoil he inherited when he first rose to power in the Bureau. Hoover battled the rampant corruption and wholesale favoritism with the same fervor he later applied to removing gangsters from America's cities and slowing the onslaught of Communists, who he rightly feared were looking to gain a foothold in the United States. Nor should it be forgotten that in between, Hoover created the nation's first crime laboratories and consolidated its fingerprint files.

That he was allowed to prosper without public scrutiny says less about Hoover than it does of the political climate in which he gained extraordinary power, and of the politicians and journalists who permitted him to flourish. Few investigative reporters of the day dared risk their own reputations by questioning his. Those who did—Jack Anderson, Les Whitten, Jack Nelson—paid a

---

* Lavrentii Beria was head of the Soviet Secret Police under Joseph Stalin.

high price as Hoover declared battle and silenced sources while planting scurrilous rumors in their stead.

Moreover, all eight presidents under whom the late director served knew of his illegal activities. If they did not in fact order these operations, they at the very least allowed them, encouraging an atmosphere that posed the most serious threat to American civil liberties since the Revolutionary War.

It was Supreme Court Justice Robert H. Jackson who said: "I cannot say that our country could have no central police without becoming totalitarian, but I can say with great conviction that it cannot become totalitarian without a centralized national police." Jackson's comment, made shortly before his death from a fatal heart attack in 1954, was not lost on Hoover, who made certain that few journalists missed the rumor that Jackson died while having sex in the home of one of his secretaries.

Hoover was a prisoner of his own design, living with secrets so dark and sinister they made him writhe in sleeplessness attempting to justify their existence. Of the lot, the worst by far was the conviction of four innocent men for murder. Congressman Tom Davis, chairman of the Committee on Government Reform, charged with investigating the FBI's role in protecting the known killers of small-time gangster Edward "Teddy" Deegan, labeled the episode "one of the greatest failures in the history of federal law enforcement" in his report titled *Everything Secret Degenerates: The FBI's Use of Murderers as Informants*.

In what can be seen only as an act of karma, H. Paul Rico, the FBI agent in charge of the Bureau informants who had carried out the Mafia hit, was arrested for murder and conspiracy in October 2003. Pointing the finger at his guilt was none other than Stevie "the Rifleman" Flemmi, brother of Vincent "Jimmy the Bear" Flemmi, one of the informants in the Deegan killing.

Ultimately, the real victims of the Bureau's downfall were the men and women of the FBI, who struggled to survive the dishonor that had become Hoover's legacy. These same special agents were the least surprised by the implosion of confidence, of course, for they had long been aware of Hoover's policy even if the public had not.

What is most incredible is that in the face of accusations and distrust, these survivors of the Bureau's disgrace remain loyal to their fallen chief. After all, it was Hoover who had given them their status by virtue of his dogged determination to uphold values that for the most part no longer existed in America. It was Hoover who convinced them that they were working toward something important: the protection of American ideals.

These men and women were not just FBI agents, they were, by Hoover's own designation, *special* agents, and each and every one of them—then as now—is unique in law enforcement. A college graduate with a degree in law or accounting mostly, and always neatly attired and remarkably fit. As special agents of the FBI, they were told they were diplomats, not police officers, representatives of the U.S. government investigating federal crimes.

They have little time for families and friends, having been trained to think of themselves on duty 24 hours a day. As James Stewart said in *The FBI Story*, he "belonged to the Bureau"; at home, he was merely on loan to his family. Even after retirement, agents bond with former colleagues in the Society of Former Special Agents of the Federal Bureau of Investigation. "Once a G-man, always a G-man" seems too easy a reason, but they'll tell you it's true.

And then, when pressed, they will share their pride in an organization that despite its history, or perhaps because of it, remains linked to the man who nursed it through infancy and into adulthood—a battered one it's true, but still the finest crime-fighting organization in the world. J. Edgar Hoover would have had it no other way.

WILL - John Edgar Hoover

I. John Edgar Hoover, a resident citizen of Washington, District of Columbia, being of sound and disposing mind, do hereby declare this to be my last will and testament, specifically revoking any and all wills heretofore made by me.

The following bequests I desire to be carried out:

(1) The perpetual care of the burial plots of my father, my mother, my sister Marguerite and myself in the Congressional Cemetery in Washington, D. C.

(2) To Helen W. Gandy, absolutely, the sum of five thousand dollars.

(3) To James E. Crawford, two thousand dollars to be paid over a period of three years.

(4) To John Edgar Ruch, my platinum watch with white gold wrist band, and two pairs of cuff links.

(5) To John Edgar Nichols, my small star sapphire ring, and two pairs of cuff links.

(6) To James E. Crawford and W. Samuel Noisette, equal distribution of all personal wearing apparel.

(7) To Annie Fields, three thousand dollars to be paid over a period of one year.

I would like Clyde Tolson to keep, or arrange for a good home, or homes for my two dogs.

I give, devise and bequeath all the rest, residue and remainder of my estate, both real and personal, unto Clyde A. Tolson, his heirs, executors, administrators and assignees forever.

In the event Clyde A. Tolson's death should occur prior to or simultaneously with mine, then the residue of my estate, both real and personal, after the above stated bequests are satisfied, is given, devised and bequeathed to the Boys' Clubs of America, Inc., and the Damon Runyon Memorial Fund for Cancer Research, Inc., equally.

I hereby nominate and appoint Clyde A. Tolson as Executor of this my last will and testament and direct that he serve with no bond.

In witness whereof, I subscribe my name and set my seal this 19th day of July, 1971.

John Edgar Hoover

The foregoing instrument was on the 19th day of July, 1971, signed and sealed and declared by the testator as his last will and testament in the presence of each of us, who, at the same time and in his presence, and in the presence of each other, hereunto subscribe our names as witnesses.

Erma D. Metcalf

Edna M. Holl : WITNESSES

408

n re Estate of
   JOHN EDGAR HOOVER
     also known as
     J. EDGAR HOOVER,
          Deceased

Administration No. 957-72

Address of Petitioner:

   4936 - 30th Place, N.W.
   Washington, D.C. 20008

PETITION TO PROBATE WILL
AND FOR LETTERS TESTAMENTARY

The petition of Clyde A. Tolson respectfully represents:

1. The petitioner Clyde A. Tolson is a citizen of the
nited States and a resident of the District of Columbia, of adult
ge, and not under any legal disability. The petitioner makes
his application as the executor nominated in the will of the
bove-named decedent.

2. John Edgar Hoover, also known as J. Edgar Hoover,
ate an adult citizen of the United States domiciled in the District
f Columbia, died on or about May 2, 1972, leaving a paper writing
ated July 19, 1971 in the nature of a will and testament. Said
aper writing is now on file in the Office of Register of Wills for
he District of Columbia. No other paper writing in the nature of
, testamentary disposition of said decedent's estate has been found,
lthough diligent search therefor has been made. The petitioner
elieves that such paper writing is in fact decedent's last will
nd testament.

3. The decedent was survived by the following persons
ho are the only heirs-at-law and next-of-kin of decedent, who
re all of adult age and sui juris, and whose respective names,
ddresses, places of residence and relationships are as follows:

Fred G. Robinette, nephew
(son of decedent's deceased sister)
5401 Whitfield-Chapel Road
Lanham, Maryland 20801

Mrs. Dorothy Robinette, niece
(daughter of decedent's deceased sister)
P.O. Box 911
Delano, California 93215

Mrs. Marjorie A. Stromme, niece
(daughter of decedent's deceased sister)
2040 Federal Avenue
Costa Mesa, California 92626

Mrs. Anna Hoover Kienast, niece
(daughter of decedent's deceased brother)
12004 Lisborough Road
Mitchellville, Maryland 20716

Mrs. Margaret Hoover Fennell, niece
(daughter of decedent's deceased brother)
12313 Shelter Lane
Bowie, Maryland 20715

Dickerson N. Hoover, Jr., nephew
(son of decedent's deceased brother)
The Rocks
Route 2, Box 107
Charlestown, West Virginia 25414

Decedent was not survived by a wife, child or descendants or by any parent or by a brother or sister or descendants thereof except as stated above.

4. The decedent at the time of his death owned the following described real estate in the District of Columbia:

> 4936 - 30th Place, N.W., known for purposes
> of taxation as lot 806 in square 2274, assessed
> for real estate tax purposes at $40,437, un-
> encumbered.

Decedent at the time of his death did not own or possess any other real estate or interest therein in the District of Columbia or elsewhere, except as indicated in paragraph 5 hereof.

5. The decedent owned at the time of his death approximately forty oil, gas and mineral leases (or parts thereof) for

interests in Texas and Louisiana, some of which may be considered
as real estate interests, the estimated value of which insofar as
petitioner can determine at this time is approximately $125,000.

6. The decedent at the time of his death was possessed
of personal property of a total estimated value of $326,500, con-
sisting of the following:

Stocks and bonds	$122,000.
Cash in banks and loan associations	84,000.
Insurance payable to estate	45,000.
Contributions to Civil Service retirement	45,000.
Unpaid salary and annual leave	18,000.
Household effects	7,500.
Jewelry	5,000.
	$326,500.

7. The decedent, so far as petitioner has been able to
ascertain, after diligent search and inquiry, left no debts except
(a) funeral expenses in the approximate amount of $5,000, which
have not been paid and (b) miscellaneous current expenses in the
approximate amount of $1,000, which have not been paid.

WHEREFORE, the petitioner prays:

1. That notice by citation or by publication or both
as may be necessary, shall issue to the above-named heirs-at-law
and next-of-kin.

2. That said paper writing dated July 19, 1971, be
admitted to probate and record as the last will and testament
of John Edgar Hoover as a will of both real and personal property.

3. That letters testamentary issue to the petitioner
as the executor named in the will.

4. And for such other and further relief as the nature of the case may require and to this Court may seem proper.

Clyde A. Tolson
Petitioner

HOGAN & HARTSON

By *George E. Monk*
George E. Monk

and

Robert J. Elliott
Robert J. Elliott

815 Connecticut Avenue, N.W.
Washington, D.C.   20006
298-5500

ATTORNEYS FOR PETITIONER

District of Columbia   ss:

    I, the undersigned,   Clyde A. Tolson   , do solemnly swear that I have read the foregoing and annexed petition by me subscribed and know the contents thereof; that I verily believe the facts as stated in said petition to be true.

Clyde A. Tolson

    Subscribed and sworn to before me this _____ day of .
_____, 1972.

Elizabeth S. Hill
Notary Public
My commission expires:
_____ MAY 23, 1973

412

ACKNOWLEDGMENTS

The celebration that follows the completion of a book is a rite of passage. What began as a fragment of a concept is born whole in paper and ink, bound in fabric and wrapped in a glossy cover that presents its face to the world. What is not as obvious, however, is the collaborative effort that every book is. Certainly this is true for *Puppetmaster: The Secret Life of J. Edgar Hoover,* a book that found its form and content through the generous contribution of time and fact from a wide variety of Hoover scholars, colleagues, relatives, friends and special agents of the Federal Bureau of Investigation.

Unknown but to a select few, this book had its genesis in the curiosity of writer Truman Capote, who, early in 1980, passed along his notes on interviews he had conducted while planning an exposé of J. Edgar Hoover and his tenure at the FBI. Occupied as he was at the time attempting to write his final novel, *Answered Prayers,* Truman thought that I might pick up the investigative trail and complete what he had started. Publisher Michael Viner agreed that the Hoover saga had never been completely explored, and authorized the book you now hold.

Puppetmaster combines Truman's early interviews with material recently uncovered through a labyrinthine route that led to the discovery of long-forgotten memos, notes, and papers—over 100,000 documents in all. Some of these papers are now part of the permanent collection maintained by the J. Edgar Hoover Foundation and housed at the Temple of the Supreme Council 33°, Scottish Rite of Freemasonry, in Washington, D.C. Grand Steward Arnold L. Flottman Jr. was extremely generous with both time and information regarding the Hoover exhibit and its material. Veteran journalist Les Whitten helped to separate illusion from reality, no small task where Hoover's life is concerned. My appreciation, Les, for your valuable input.

Thanks as well to the librarians and staff of the Provincetown Public Library, Provincetown, Massachusetts: director Debra DeJonker-Berry plus Karen Mac-Donald, Renee Gibbs-Brady, Laine Quinn, Arno Masters, Mary Smith, Andrew Aull, Martha Hyams, Jean Jarrett, Diana Maher, Nancy Sirvent, and Linton Watts. My gratitude always to Jane Wimer and her staff at the Port Orange branch of the Volusia County (Florida) Library—Pia Andersen, Kim Dolce, Liz Huffman, Beth Masterson, Charlotte Nettles, Mary Ann Sumner and Agnes Rivera. At the University of Delaware, Shelly McCoy and her staff in the Microforms unit of the Morris Library—Georgia Basso, Nadine Burroughs and Richard Campbell. Plus the staff and researchers at the Library of Congress, Manuscript Division, Washington, D.C.; Dwight D. Eisenhower Library, Abilene, Kansas; Harry S. Truman Presidential Museum and Library, Independence, Missouri; John F. Kennedy Library and Museum, Boston, Massachusetts; Franklin D. Roosevelt Presidential Library, Hyde Park, New York; Lyndon Baines Johnson Library and Museum, Austin, Texas; Richard Nixon Library and Birthplace, Yorba Linda, California; Herbert Hoover Presidential Library-Museum, West Branch, Iowa; and the Martin Luther King Jr. Memorial Library, Washington, D.C.

For New Millennium Press, Mary Aarons assembled a wonderful squad whose only purpose was to make me excel: copy editor Dianne Woo, typesetting/designer Carolyn Wendt, indexer Pam Rider, proofreader Carol Buckley, audio engineer Dave Maiden, jacket designer Steve Edelman, photo researcher Jill Cairns-Gallimore, article researcher Cathy Dawson, with data entry by Margaret Luke.

Carole White donated her condo in Beverly Hills as a base for my research in California; Patrick Gibbs in Washington, D.C., and Joyce Outlaw in Orlando did likewise; while my sister, Joan Henn, voiced not a complaint as I turned her home in Newark, Delaware, into a safe house for documents best kept hidden. As always, my thanks.

For Robert Maheu, Marilyn Richards, Tony Melluzzo, Evan Harlow, Annette Warner, Valerie Reynolds, Anne Jordan, Shelley Herman, Ronald Saleh, Daniel Eastman, David Hall, Betty and Phoebe, Deb and Jill, Laurie and Lu, Courtney and Jen, Patti and Harry, Traci and Michael, plus Melissa and Richard—special friends all.

To the very special Robert Deaton and Julie McCarron, my thanks for your encouragement and comments on the first read.

And Charlie Leporacci—who knows the reason why.

Finally, to my mother Anne, whose kindness and strength are an inspiration to all who know her well. There are no words to express my gratitude for your contribution to this book and my world.

— RICHARD HACK
PROVINCETOWN, MASSACHUSETTS

NOTES

PROLOGUE

1 Gentry, *J. Edgar Hoover: The Man and the Secrets*, p. 73.
2 Ibid., p. 28.
3 Nixon, *RN: The Memoirs of Richard Nixon*, p. 599.
4 *New York Times*, May 3, 1973, p. 53.
5 Nixon, *RN*, p. 599.
6 *New York Times*, May 3, 1972, p. 53.
7 *Washington Post*, May 3, 1972, p. A13.
8 Mohr to Kleindienst, memo, May 2, 1972, Bureau File 67-561-379.
9 Nixon Papers.
10 DeLoach, *Hoover's FBI*, p. 415.
11 Author's interview of confidential source.
12 *Inquiry into the Destruction of Former FBI Director J. Edgar Hoover's Files and FBI Recordkeeping: Hearings before a Subcommittee on Government Operations, House of Representatives*, 94th Congress, 1st session, 1975, p. 88.
13 Powers, *Secrecy and Power*, p. 482.
14 Robertson, *New York Times*, May 4, 1972, p. 18.
15 Ibid.
16 Smith, *New York Times*, May 4, 1972, p. 1.

CHAPTER ONE

1 Annie Hoover to Dalphinia Price, unmailed letter, April 12, 1895, J. Edgar Hoover Foundation Collection, Washington, D.C.
2 Ibid.
3 Ibid.
4 De Toledano, *J. Edgar Hoover: The Man in His Time*, p. 37.
5 Hoover, *U.S. News & World Report*, August 7, 1972, p. 80.
6 Ibid.
7 Interview with Truman Capote, November 1983.
8 Ibid.
9 Dickerson Hoover to Hoover, letter, April 14, 1904, Foundation.
10 Ibid.
11 Elson, *The J. Edgar Hoover You Ought to Know*; interview with Truman Capote.
12 Annie Hoover to Hoover, letter, September 9, 1912, Foundation.
13 Hoover, *Weekly Review*, undated, Foundation.
14 Hoover, *Diary*, June 10, 1906, Foundation.
15 De Toledano, *J. Edgar Hoover*, p. 37.
16 Annie Hoover to Hoover, undated letter, Foundation.
17 Interview with Margaret Hoover Fennell, August 1984.
18 Announcements, *Washington Post*, June 24, 1908, p. 6.
19 Hoover, *Diary*, July 30, 1909, Foundation.
20 Hoover, *Weekly Review*, undated, Foundation.
21 Hoover, *Diary*, September 11, 1910, Foundation.
22 Memorabilia collection, Foundation.
23 Interview with Margaret Hoover Fennell, August 1984.
24 Ibid.
25 Ibid.
26 Ibid.

27   Powers, *Secrecy and Power,* p. 31; Ammentorp, *The Generals of World War II,* www.generals.dk/usa.htm, April 2003.
28   De Toledano, *J. Edgar Hoover,* p. 39.
29   Memorabilia collection, Foundation.
30   *Centennial History of Central High,* p. 42.
31   De Toledano, *J. Edgar Hoover,* p. 40.
32   Ibid., p. 41.

CHAPTER TWO

1   O'Brian to Gregory, memo, December 14, 1917, Department of Justice file 190470, Thomas Gregory Papers, Box 2735, RG 60, National Archives.
2   Demaris, *The Director,* p. 51.
3   Goldman, *Conscription,* Department of War and Military Intelligence Division, Emma Goldman Papers, RG 165, National Archives.
4   O'Brian, CBS-TV interview, May 2, 1972.
5   United States, *Statutes at Large,* Washington, D.C., 1918, Vol. XL, pp. 553 ff.
6   Author's interview of confidential source.
7   Hoover, Report on Anarchist bombing, Foundation.
8   Hoover to Creighton, memo, August 23, 1919.
9   Palmer to Hoover, memo, August 29, 1919.
10   Vaile, *Congressional Record,* January 5, 1920.
11   Hoover to Division of Military Intelligence, memo, December 19, 1919.
12   Hoover to Caminetti, memo, December 19, 1919.
13   *New York Tribune,* December 22, 1919, Hoover collection, RG 65, National Archives.
14   Palmer to Hoover, memo, December 22, 1919.
15   Hoover to Palmer, memo, December 22, 1919.
16   Gentry, *J. Edgar Hoover,* p. 91.
17   Nash, *Citizen Hoover,* p. 21.
18   *New York Times,* January 27, 1920, p. 1.
19   Whitehead, *The FBI Story,* p. 50.
20   Transcript, House Rules Committee, June 1–2, 1920, 1–209.
21   Palmer, "The Case Against the Reds," Forum, 1920, p. 173.
22   *Hearings and Final Report before the Select Committee to Study Governmental Operations with Respect to Intelligence Activities of the United States Senate, 94th Congress, 1st session, 1975–76.*
23   Photograph collection, Foundation.

CHAPTER THREE

1   Author's interview of Truman Capote, November 1983.
2   Receipt, Hecht Company, Foundation.
3   Harding, speech, Boston, Massachusetts, May 1920.
4   Daugherty to Smith, undated memo, National Archives.
5   Author's interview of Truman Capote, November 1983.
6   Means, *The Strange Death of President Harding,* p. 82.
7   Hoover, *Persons in Hiding,* p. 255.
8   Anthony, *Florence Harding,* p. 295; undated article in *True* magazine.
9   Whitehead, *The FBI Story,* p. 61.
10   Ku Klux Klan advertisement, 1922.

11   Wade, *The Fiery Cross: The Ku Klux Klan in America*, p. 165; Calvin
     Coolidge Papers, case file 28, Manuscript Division, Library of Congress.
12   Hoover to Burns, memo, December 28, 1922, Bureau file 44-0-122.
13   Whitehead, *The FBI Story*, p. 62.
14   Wade, *The Fiery Cross*, p. 154; *Literary Digest*, September 24, 1921, p. 34.
15   Whitehead, *The FBI Story*, p. 62.
16   Hoover, *The Memoirs of Herbert Hoover*. Vol. 2, *The Cabinet and the Presi-
     dency, 1920–1933*, p. 49.
17   Anthony, *Florence Harding*, p. 407.
18   Ibid., p. 406; *Daily News*, December 21, 1923.
19   Cook, *The FBI Nobody Knows*, p. 131.
20   Author's interview of confidential source.
21   Hoover, *The Memoirs of Herbert Hoover*, p. 49.
22   Ibid., p. 51.
23   Werner and Starr, *Teapot Dome*, p. 57.
24   Whitehead, *The FBI Story*, p. 65.
25   Ibid., p. 67.

CHAPTER FOUR

1   Mason, *Harlan Fiske Stone: Pillar of the Law*, p. 159.
2   Whitehead, *The FBI Story*, p. 66.
3   Mason, *Harlan Fiske Stone*, p. 151; Stone to Hoover memo, May 13, 1924,
     National Archives.
4   Gentry, *J. Edgar Hoover*, p. 128.
5   Whitehead, *The FBI Story*, p. 69.
6   Baldwin to Stone, letter, August 6, 1924, Bureau file 67-561-8.
7   Stone to Hoover, memo, August 7, 1924, Bureau file 67-561-9.
8   Author's interview of Truman Capote, November 1983.
9   Author's interview of Fred Astaire, November 1981.
10   Small, *Washington Evening Star*, December 29, 1924.
11   Small, *Literary Digest*, January 24, 1925. p. 45.
12   Ibid.
13   Author's interview of Margaret Hoover Fennell.
14   Demaris, *The Director*, p. 7.
15   De Toledano, *J. Edgar Hoover*, p. 94.
16   Author's interview of Truman Capote.
17   Egan to Hoover, memo, February 23, 1928, Bureau file 67-952-18.
18   Ibid.
19   C. D. White to Hoover, memo, February 7, 1928, Bureau file 67-9524-15.
20   Author's interview of Margaret Hoover Fennell.

CHAPTER FIVE

1   Interview of Betty Gow by Truman Capote.
2   Ransom note, collection of the New Jersey State Police Museum, West
     Trenton, New Jersey.
3   Berg, *Lindbergh*, p. 245.
4   Hoover to President Hoover, memo, March 2, 1932, Foundation.
5   *New York Times*, March 5, 1932, p. 2.
6   Author's interview of confidential source.
7   Waller, *Kidnap*, p. 31.

8   Ibid.
9   Ibid., p. 32.
10   Turrou, *Where My Shadow Falls: Two Decades of Crime Detection*, p. 109.
11   Hoover, *Persons in Hiding*, p. 277.
12   *New York Times*, March 1, 1933, p. 1; Gentry, *J. Edgar Hoover*, p. 153.
13   Author's interview of Truman Capote.
14   *New York Times*, March 3, 1933, p. 1.
15   *New York Times*, August 1, 1933, p. 2.
16   Unger, *The Union Station Massacre: The Original Sin of J. Edgar Hoover's FBI*, p. 56.
17   Ibid.
18   Bureau files, 62-28915.
19   Hoover to Vetterli, memo, June 17, 1933, Bureau file, unindexed.
20   Unger, *The Union Station Massacre*, p. 79.
21   Whitehead, *The FBI Story*, p. 101.
22   Ibid., p. 227.
23   Tucker, *Collier's*, August 19, 1933, p. 15.
24   Ibid.
25   Author's interview of Margaret Hoover Fennell.
26   Hoover to Purvis, letter, April 3, 1934, Melvin Purvis Collection in the Department of Special Collections, Boston University.
27   *Time*, May 7, 1934, p. 18.
28   Toland, *The Dillinger Days*, p. 286.
29   Summers, *Official and Confidential: The Secret Life of J. Edgar Hoover*, p. 72.
30   Unger, *The Union Station Massacre*, p. 206.
31   Ibid., p. 208.
32   Ibid., p. 210.

CHAPTER SIX

1   Author's interview of Margaret Hoover Fennell.
2   Suydam, Department of Justice release, April 3, 1935.
3   Tolson Efficiency Rating Sheet, September 30, 1928, FBI Boston Office.
4   Hoover to Tolson, memo, October 20, 1934, Bureau file 67-9524-178.
5   Hoover to Tolson, memo, February 15, 1935, Bureau file 67-9524-187.
6   Hoover to Tolson, memo, November 8, 1934, Bureau file 67-9524-238.
7   Hoover to Tolson, memo, February 22, 1935, Bureau file 67-9524-185.
8   Hoover to Tolson, memo, March 25, 1935, Bureau file 67-691-135.
9   Hoover to Tolson, memo, July 23, 1935, Bureau file 67-22035-05.
10   Hoover testimony, Senate Appropriations Subcommittee, April 11, 1936.
11   Martin Grams Jr., *The G-men Take to the Airwaves*, Audio Classics Archive, www.audio-classics.com/mgarticle008.html, p. 2.
12   Hoover to Special Agents in Charge, Field Offices, memo, April 12, 1936, Bureau files.
13   Author's interview of Eddie Mount.
14   *New York Times*, May 2, 1936, p. 1.
15   *New York Times*, May 3, 1936, p. 1.
16   Hoover, *Persons in Hiding*, p. 70.
17   Karpis, *The Alvin Karpis Story*, p. 222.
18   Ibid.
19   Hoover to Tolson, memo, May 6, 1936, Bureau file 67-9524-232.

20 Author's interview of Eddie Mount.
21 *New York Times,* May 8, 1936, p. 8.
22 *New York Times,* May 9, 1938, p. 34.
23 *New York Times,* May 13, 1936, p. 22.
24 FBI brochure, circa 1936, National Archives.
25 Hoover to Tolson, memo, November 12, 1935, Bureau file 67-9524-215.
26 Author's interview with Ginger Rogers, 20th Century-Fox Studios.
27 Ibid.
28 *New York Times,* December 15, 1936, p. 1.
29 *New York Times,* December 16, 1936, p. 1.
30 Hoover to Tolson, memo, January 18, 1937, Bureau file 67-9524-245.

CHAPTER SEVEN
1   De Toledano, *J. Edgar Hoover,* p. 152.
2   *Hearings and Final Report of the Select Committee to Study Governmental Operations with Respect to Intelligence Activities of the United States Senate,* 94th Congress, 1st session, 1975–76, Book III, p. 396.
3   Gentry, *J. Edgar Hoover,* p. 207.
4   Ibid.
5   Burrus to Hoover, memo, February 12, 1936, Bureau file 66-801-185.
6   Summers, *Official and Confidential,* p. 85.
7   Ibid.
8   Durante, Kofoed, *Night Clubs,* p. 114.
9   Transcript of Winchell broadcast, December 20, 1936, Bureau file 62-31615-54X.
10 Whitehead, *The FBI Story,* p. 163.
11 Hoover to Cummings, memo, September 16, 1937, Bureau file 67-561-147.
12 Hoover to Tolson, memo, February 14, 1938, Bureau file 67-9324-263.
13 Tolson to Hoover, memo, July 1, 1938, Bureau file 67-9324-266.
14 Winchell, *Winchell Exclusive,* p. 147.
15 *New York Times,* August 25, 1939, p. 1.
16 Whitehead, *The FBI Story,* p. 171.
17 *Congressional Record,* January 5, 1940.
18 *Congressional Record,* February 27, 1940; Gentry, *J. Edgar Hoover,* p. 213; Whitehead, *The FBI Story,* p. 177.
19 Supplementary Detailed Staff Reports on Intelligence Activities and the Rights of Americans, Book III, *Final Report,* United States Senate.
20 Whitehead, *The FBI Story,* p. 175.
21 *Time,* March 11, 1940, p. 18.
22 Ibid.
23 De Toledano, *J. Edgar Hoover,* p. 148.
24 *Time,* March 11, 1940, p. 18.
25 Whitehead, *The FBI Story,* p. 177.
26 Roosevelt to Hoover, letter, June 14, 1940; Gentry, *J. Edgar Hoover,* p. 226.
27 Hoover to Roosevelt, letter, June 16, 1940; ibid.
28 Author's interview of Truman Capote.
29 *New York Times,* February 7, 1940, p. 12.

CHAPTER EIGHT
1   Hoover to Watson, memo, December 7, 1941, File 10-B, FBI report 1028; Powers, *Secrecy and Power,* p. 240.

2   Author's interview of Eddie Mount.
3   Popov, *Spy/Counterspy,* p. 168.
4   Ibid.
5   Ibid., p. 203.
6   Hoover, "The Enemy's Masterpiece of Deception," *Reader's Digest,* April 1946, p. 22.
7   Hoover to Early, memo, December 12, 1941, Stephen Early Papers, FBI, Franklin Delano Roosevelt Presidential Library; Powers, *Secrecy and Power,* p. 241.
8   Powers, *Secrecy and Power,* p. 243.
9   Author's interview of confidential source.
10 Powers, *Secrecy and Power,* p. 244.
11 Whitehead, *The FBI Story,* p. 187.
12 Ibid., p. 189.
13 Hoover to Roosevelt, memo, January 29, 1941, Franklin Delano Roosevelt Presidential Library.
14 Whitehead, *The FBI Story,* pp. 201–202.
15 Ibid.
16 Lardner, *Washington Post,* January 13, 2002, p. W12.
17 Hoover to Watson, memo, June 16, 1942, Roosevelt Presidential Library; Hoover to McIntyre, memo, June 22, 1942, Roosevelt Presidential Library; Hoover to McIntyre, memo, June 27, 1942, Roosevelt Presidential Library; Gentry, *J. Edgar Hoover,* pp. 290–291.
18 Wood, *New York Times,* July 5, 1942, p. E6.
19 Kantor, *Atlanta Journal and Constitution,* July 4, 1980, p. 1-A.
20 Roosevelt, Proclamation No. 2561, July 2, 1942.
21 Dasch, *Eight Spies Against America,* p. 92.
22 Ladd to Hoover, memo, February 4, 1942, Bureau files.
23 Burton to Ladd, "Do Not File" memo, December 31, 1943; Theoharis, *From the Secret Files of J. Edgar Hoover,* pp. 56–58.
24 Streitmatter, *Empty Without You: The Intimate Letters of Eleanor Roosevelt and Lorena Hickok,* p. 17.
25 Author's interview with Truman Capote.

CHAPTER NINE

1   Truman, personal memo, May 12, 1945, Truman Presidential Museum and Library, Box 333.
2   Hoover note, Bureau file.
3   Sullivan, Brown, *The Bureau: My Thirty Years in Hoover's FBI,* p. 38.
4   Donovan, *Conflict and Crisis,* p. 293.
5   Demaris, *The Director,* p. 106.
6   Tanenhaus, *Whittaker Chambers,* p. 163.
7   Powers, *Secrecy and Power,* p. 282.
8   Turner, *Hoover's FBI: The Men and the Myth,* p. 272.
9   Whelan, *New York Times,* December 12, 1948, p. 1.
10 Ibid.
11 McCullough, *Truman,* p. 652.
12 *Newsweek,* January 30, 1950, p. 16.
13 Ferrell, *Dear Bess: The Letters from Harry to Bess Truman, 1910–1959,* p. 550.
14 Von Hoffman, *Citizen Cohn,* p. 146.
15 Ibid.

16   Gentry, *J. Edgar Hoover,* p. 386.
17   Truman to Lowenthal, letter, July 25, 1950, Bureau files.
18   Dondero, *Congressional Record,* September 1, 1950.
19   Hickenlooper, *Congressional Record,* November 27, 1950.
20   Reeves, *The Life and Times of Joe McCarthy,* p. 445.
21   Hood to Hoover, memo, April 10, 1953, Bureau files, Library of Congress Manuscript Division.

CHAPTER TEN

1   Hood to Hoover, memo, April 10, 1953, Bureau files, Library of Congress Manuscript Division.
2   Hoover to Tolson, memo, April 13, 1953, Bureau files, Library of Congress Manuscript Division.
3   Ibid.
4   Nichols to Tolson, memo, April 14, 1953, Bureau files, Library of Congress Manuscript Division.
5   Author's interview with Peter Simone.
6   Summers, *Official and Confidential,* p. 254.
7   Maas, *Esquire,* May 1993, p. 58.
8   Author's interview of Les Whitten.
9   Author's interview with Truman Capote.
10   Nichols to Tolson, memo, June 1, 1955, Bureau files, Library of Congress Manuscript Division.
11   Nichols to Tolson, memo, June 3, 1955, Bureau files, Library of Congress Manuscript Division.
12   Ibid.
13   Ibid.
14   Ibid.
15   Theoharis, Cox, *The Boss,* p. 290.
16   Ibid., p. 291.
17   Theoharis, *J. Edgar Hoover, Sex, and Crime,* p. 109.
18   Author's interview of Muriel Viner.
19   Author's interview of Truman Capote.
20   Reeves, *The Life and Times of Joe McCarthy,* p. 537.
21   Ibid., p. 575.
22   Ibid., p. 575; *New York Times,* March 13, 1954, p. 14.
23   Hoover, memo, October 29, 1952, Bureau file 66-6200-44-n/a.
24   Rafferty, "Federal Protection of Civil Rights Against Acts of Violence," Unpublished Princeton University Thesis, 1976, p. 36-37; Powers, *Secrecy and Power,* p. 328.
25   Theoharis, Cox, *The Boss,* p. 304.
26   Ungar, *FBI: An Uncensored Look Behind the Walls,* p. 408; Powers, *Secrecy and Power,* p. 330.

CHAPTER ELEVEN

1   Kennedy, *The Enemy Within,* p. 263.
2   Hoover to Tolson, Memo, Bureau files, not indexed.
3   Schiff, *New York Post,* October 6, 1959, p. 33.
4   Dufty et al., *New York Post,* October 7, 1959, p. 3.
5   Dufty et al., *New York Post,* October 8, 1959, p. 58.

6 Hoover to LeRoy, letter, September 12, 1959, Bureau file, unindexed.
7 Author's interview with Truman Capote.
8 Summers to Schiff, letter, February 2, 1988, New York Public Library, Manuscripts and Archives Division, Dorothy Schiff Papers
9 Dufty et al., *New York Post,* October 14, 1959, p. 62.
10 Hoover to Hoffmann, letter, January 27, 1960, New York Public Library, Manuscripts and Archives Division, Dorothy Schiff Papers.
11 King, "Equality Now," *Nation,* February 4, 1961, p. 91.
12 Jones to DeLoach, memo, February 7, 1961, Bureau file 100-106670-12.
13 Hoover to R. Kennedy, memo, January 8, 1962, Bureau file 100-392452-131.
14 "At a Liberal," *Harvard Crimson,* October 19, 1946, p. 1.
15 Kennedy, radio and television report to the American people on the Soviet arms buildup in Cuba, October 22, 1962, John F. Kennedy Library and Museum.
16 Garrow, *The FBI and Martin Luther King, Jr.,* p. 53.
17 Zinn, *Albany: A Study in National Responsibility,* p. 31.
18 "Dr. King Says F.B.I. in Albany, Ga., Favors Segregationists," *New York Times,* November 19, 1962, p. 21.
19 King message book, Boston University, Contemporary Archive Collection.
20 Truman Capote interview of George E. Allen, 1969.
21 Garrow, *The FBI and Martin Luther King, Jr.,* p. 56.
22 Baumgardner to Sullivan, "March on Washington, August 28, 1963, Possible Subversive Influence," August 22, 1963, Bureau file 100-3-116-230; Baumgardner to Sullivan, "Communist Party, USA, Negro Question, August 23, 1963, Bureau file, 100-3-116-253X.
23 Ibid.
24 Truman Capote interview of George E. Allen, 1969.
25 Sullivan to Belmont, "Communist Party, USA, Negro Question; IS-C," August 30, 1963, Bureau file 100-3-116-253X.

CHAPTER TWELVE

1 Ollestad, *Inside the F.B.I.,* p. 165.
2 Ibid.
3 Hoover to Special Agents in Charge, Letter Number 512, March 24, 1925, Bureau file 66-04-X92.
4 Author's interview of Roy Cohn and publicist Peter Simone.
5 DeLoach, *Hoover's FBI,* p. 73.
6 Powers, *Secrecy and Power,* p. 383.
7 DeLoach, *Hoover's FBI,* p. 372.
8 Sullivan, Brown, *The Bureau,* p. 52.
9 Sullivan to Belmont, memo, December 24, 1963, Bureau file 100-3-115-684; House Committee on Assassinations, *Hearings—King,* v. 6, p. 156.
10 Sullivan to Belmont, memo, January 6, 1964, Bureau file 100-3-116-714; House Committee on Assassinations, *Hearings—King,* v. 6, p. 192.
11 Garrow, *The FBI and Martin Luther King, Jr.,* p. 106.
12 DeLoach, *Hoover's FBI,* p. 202.
13 Sullivan to Belmont, memo, January 27, 1964, Bureau files 100-3-116-792.
14 Johnson, Executive Order No. 11154, May 8, 1964, Federal Register, May 12, 1964, p. 29, FR 6233.
15 Powers, *Secrecy and Power,* p. 389.

16 Franklin, *New York Times*, November 19, 1964, p. 1.
17 King to Hoover, telegram, November 19, 1964, Bureau file 100-106670-584; Senate Committee to Study Governmental Operations with Respect to Intelligence Activities, *Final Report*, Book III, p. 157.
18 Garrow, *The FBI and Martin Luther King, Jr.*, p. 123.
19 Gentry, J. *Edgar Hoover*, p. 572; Garrow, *The FBI and Martin Luther King, Jr.*, pp. 125–26.
20 DeLoach, *Hoover's FBI*, p. 208.
21 Sullivan, Brown, *The Bureau*, p. 140.
22 Senate Committee to Study Governmental Operations with Respect to Intelligence Activities, *Final Report*, Book III, pp. 166–67.
23 Handley to Hoover, memo, March 19, 1964, Bureau file, unindexed.
24 Lehr, O'Neill, *Black Mass*, p. 10.
25 Hoover to Handley, memo, August 5, 1968, Bureau file, unindexed.

CHAPTER THIRTEEN
1 Author's interview of Rudy Vallée.
2 Ibid.
3 Lamour, McInnes, *My Side of the Road*, p. 38.
4 Author's interview of Allan Carr.
5 Author's interview of Charles Higham.
6 Demaris, *The Director*, p. 76.
7 Hoover to Martin, letter, September 20, 1965, Bureau files, unindexed.
8 Neary, *Life*, May 20, 1966, p. 38.
9 Ibid.
10 Sullivan to DeLoach, memo, January 21, 1966, Bureau file 100-106670-2192.
11 Senate Committee to Study Governmental Operations with Respect to Intelligence Activities, *Final Report*, vol. 6, p. 219; Gentry, J. *Edgar Hoover*, p. 584.
12 Hoover, speech , September 28, 1967, Bureau files.
13 Gentry, J. *Edgar Hoover*, p. 600.
14 Senate Committee to Study Governmental Operations with Respect to Intelligence Activities, *Final Report*, Book III, p. 492.
15 Gentry, J. *Edgar Hoover*, p. 607.
16 DeLoach, *Hoover's FBI*, p. 251.
17 Ehrlichman, *Witness to Power*, p. 156.
18 Ibid.
19 Nixon, *RN*, p. 388.
20 Ehrlichman, *Witness to Power*, p. 159.
21 Ibid., p. 158.
22 Ibid.
23 Hoover to Tolson, DeLoach, Bishop, memo, October 23, 1969, Tolson files, part 8.
24 Hoover to Tolson, memo, August 25, 1967, Tolson files, part 6.
25 Held to Hoover, memo, April 27, 1970, Bureau file 100-448006-1766.
26 Ibid.
27 Hoover to Held, memo, May 6, 1970, Bureau file 100-448006-1766.
28 Haber, *Los Angeles Times*, May 19, 1970, p. 42.
29 Richards, *Played Out: The Jean Seberg Story*, p. 241.

30 Ibid., p. 248.
31 *NewYork Times*, July 14, 1970, p. 21.
32 *U.S. News & World Report*, July 27, 1970, p. 24.
33 Author's interview of Roy Cohn.
34 *Congressional Record*, House of Representatives, April 5, 1971.
35 Ibid.
36 Hoover to Tolson, memo, April 5, 1971, Tolson files, part 8.
37 Ibid.
38 *Newsweek*, May 10, 1971, p. 23.
39 *Newsweek*, April 12, 1971, p. 39.
40 *Nation*, July 5, 1971, p. 6.
41 Sullivan to Hoover, memo, June 6, 1971, Bureau files, unindexed.
42 *New York Times*, December 26, 1971, p. 44.
43 Liddy, *Will*, p. 180.
44 Hoover to Tolson, memo, April 28, 1972, Tolson files, part 10.

EPILOGUE
1 Sullivan to DeLoach, memo, July 19, 1966, Bureau files, unindexed.
2 Theoharis et al., *The FBI: A Comprehensive Reference Guide*, p. 187.
3 *Time*, August 2, 1976, p. 17.
4 Reuben, *Nation*, June 19, 1962, p. 739.

BIBLIOGRAPHY

A Note from the Publishers
In order to keep the page count down, and to make the book more affordable and accessible to our readers, we have decided to make the extensive list of periodicals consulted by the author as he researched the book available on our website, *www.newmillenniumpress.com.*

BOOKS

Adams, Samuel Hopkins. *The Incredible Era: The Life and Times of Warren G. Harding.* Boston: Houghton Mifflin, 1939.

Allen, Frederick Lewis. *Only Yesterday.* New York: Blue Ribbon Books, 1941.

Ambrose, Stephen E. *Eisenhower: Soldier, General of the Army, President-Elect, 1890–1952.* New York: Simon & Schuster, 1983.

Anthony, Carl Sferazza. *Florence Harding.* New York: Morrow/Avon, 1998.

Bagby, Wesley M. *The Road to Normalcy: The Presidential Campaign and Election of 1920.* Baltimore: Johns Hopkins Press, 1962.

Baker, Elmer LeRoy. *Gunman's Territory.* San Antonio, TX: Naylor, 1969.

Ball, George. *The Past Has Another Pattern.* New York: Norton, 1982.

Berg, A. Scott. *Lindbergh.* New York: Penguin, 1998.

Berle, Beatrice, and Travis Jacobs, eds. *Navigating the Rapids, 1918–1971.* New York: Harcourt Brace Jovanovich, 1973.

Beschloss, Michael. *The Crisis Years: Kennedy and Khrushchev, 1960–1963.* New York: HarperCollins, 1991.

Biddle, Francis. *In Brief Authority.* Garden City, NY: Doubleday, 1962.

Blackstock, Nelson. *COINTELPRO.* New York: Pathfinder, 1988.

Blair, Joan, and Clay Blair. *The Search for JFK.* New York: Putnam, 1974.

Blumenthal, Ralph. *Stork Club.* New York: Little, Brown, 2000.

Bonanno, Joseph, and Sergio Lalli. *A Man of Honor.* New York: Simon & Schuster, 1983.

Boughton, James. *Bouton-Boughton Family.* Albany, NY: Joel Minnsell's Sons, 1890.

Bradlee, Benjamin. *Conversations with Kennedy.* New York: Pocket Books, 1976.

Brendon, Piers. *Ike.* New York: Harper & Row, 1986.

Breuer, William B. *J. Edgar Hoover and His G-Men.* Westport, CT: Praeger, 1995.

Britton, Nan. *The President's Daughter.* New York: Elizabeth Ann Guild, 1927.

Brogan, Hugh, and Charles Mosley. *Burke's Peerage & Baronetage: American Presidential Families.* Toronto: Maxwell Macmillan, 1993.

Brough, James. *Princess Alice.* Boston: Little, Brown, 1975.

Brown, Dorothy M. *Setting a Course: American Women in the 1920's.* Boston: Twayne, 1987.

Bruccoli, Matthew. *Selected Letters of John O'Hara.* New York: Random House, 1978.

Butler, Nicholas Murray. *Across the Busy Years.* New York: Scribner's, 1939.

Campbell, Rodney. *The Luciano Project.* New York: McGraw-Hill, 1977.

Capote, Truman. *Answered Prayers: The Unfinished Novel.* New York: Random House, 1987.

Caro, Robert. *Means of Ascent: The Years of Lyndon Johnson.* New York: Knopf, 1990.

———. *The Path to Power: The Years of Lyndon Johnson.* New York: Knopf, 1982.

Charns, Alexander. *Cloak and Gavel.* Chicago: University of Illinois Press, 1992.

Clapper, Olive. *One Lucky Woman.* Garden City, N.Y.: Doubleday, 1961.

Clark, Ramsey. *Crime in America.* New York: Simon & Schuster, 1970.

Cochran, Louis. *FBI Man.* New York: Duell, Sloan & Pearce, 1966.

Collins, Frederick. *The FBI in Peace and War.* New York: Putnam, 1943.

———. *The FBI in Peace and War.* New York: Simon & Schuster, 1970.

Collins, Herbert. *Presidents on Wheels.* New York: Bonanza, 1971.

Colman, Edna M. *White House Gossip: From Andrew Jackson to Calvin Coolidge.* Garden City, NY: Doubleday, 1927.

Comfort, Mildred. *J. Edgar Hoover, Modern Knight Errant.* Minneapolis: T.S. Denison, 1959.

Conners, Bernard. *Don't Embarrass the Bureau*. Indianapolis: Bobbs-Merrill, 1972.

Cook, Blanche Wiesen. *Eleanor Roosevelt*. Vol. 1, *1884–1933*. New York: Viking, 1992.

Cook, Fred. *The FBI Nobody Knows*. New York: Macmillan, 1964.

Corrill, Dale. *The Conciliator*. Philadelphia: Dorrance, 1969.

Cox, James M. *Journey Through My Years*. New York: Simon and Schuster, 1946.

Cressey, Donald. *Theft of a Nation*. New York: Harper & Row, 1969.

Crockett, Fred E. *Special Fleet: The History of Presidential Yachts*. Camden, Maine: Down East Books, 1983.

Cuneo, S.A. *From Printer to President*. Philadelphia: Dorrance, 1922.

Daniels, Jonathan. *The Man from Independence*. New York: Lippincott, 1950.

Dasch, George John. *Eight Spies Against America*. New York: R.M. McBride, 1959.

Daugherty, Harry M. *The Inside Story of the Harding Tragedy*. New York: Churchill, 1932.

Davis, John. *The Kennedys: Dynasty and Disaster*. New York: SPI Books, 1992.

———. *Mafia Kingfish*. New York: McGraw-Hill, 1989.

DeLoach, Cartha D. "Deke". *Hoover's FBI*. Washington, DC: Regnery, 1995.

Demaris, Ovid. *The Director*. New York: Harper's Magazine Press, 1975.

———. *The Last Mafioso*. New York: Times Books, 1981.

Denenberg, Barry. *The True Story of J. Edgar Hoover and the F.B.I.* New York: Scholastic, 1993.

De Toledano, Ralph. *J. Edgar Hoover: The Man in His Time*. New York: Manor, 1974.

Donner, Frank. *The Age of Surveillance*. New York: Vintage, 1981.

Donovan, Robert J. *Conflict and Crisis*. New York: Norton, 1977.

———. *Tumultuous Years*. Toronto: McLeod, 1982.

Dorman, Michael. *Payoff*. New York: David McKay, 1972.

Dorwart, Jeffrey. *Conflict of Duty*. Annapolis, MD: Naval Institute Press, 1983.

Downes, Randolph C. *The Rise of Warren G. Harding, 1865–1920*. Columbus: Ohio State University, Press, 1970.

Ehrlichman, John. *Witness to Power*. New York: Pocket Books, 1982.

Eisenberg, Dennis, Uri Dan, and Eli Lanau. *Meyer Lansky: Mogul of the Mob*. New York: Paddington Press, 1979.

Eisenhower, Julie. *Pat Nixon: The Untold Story*. New York: Zebra, 1986.

Elson, Edward L. R. *The J. Edgar Hoover You Ought to Know*. Westwood, NJ: F. H. Revell Co., 1954.

Exner, Judith, and Ovid Demaris. *My Story*. New York: Grove Press, 1977.

Felsenthal, Carol. *Alice Roosevelt Longworth*. New York: Putnam, 1988.

Felt, Mark. *The FBI Pyramid*. New York: Putnam, 1979.

Ferrell, Robert H. *The Strange Deaths of President Harding*. Columbia: University of Missouri Press, 1996.

Ferrell, Robert H., ed. *Dear Bess: Letters from Harry to Bess Truman, 1910–1959*. New York: Norton, 1983.

———, ed. *Off the Record: The Private Papers of Harry S Truman*. New York: Harper & Row, 1980.

Fisher, Jim. *The Ghosts of Hopewell*. Carbondale: Southern Illinois University Press, 1999.

Fox, Stephen. *Blood and Power: Organized Crime in the Twentieth-Century America*. New York: Morrow, 1989.

Freidel, Frank. *Franklin D. Roosevelt*. Boston: Little, Brown, 1990.

Fried, Albert. *The Rise and Fall of the Jewish Gangster in America*. New York: Holt, Rinehart and Winston, 1980.

Fuess, Claude M. *Calvin Coolidge*. Boston: Little, Brown, 1940.

Garrow, David. *Bearing the Cross*. New York: William Morrow, 1986.

———. *The FBI and Martin Luther King, Jr.* New York: Norton, 1981.

Gellman, Irwin. *Good Neighbor Diplomacy*. Baltimore: Johns Hopkins University Press, 1979.

Gentry, Curt. *J. Edgar Hoover: The Man and the Secrets*. New York: Norton, 1991.

Giancana, Sam, and Chuck Giancana. *Double Cross*. New York: Warner Books, 1992.

Goodwin, Doris Kearns. *The Fitzgeralds and the Kennedys.* New York: St. Martin's, 1987.

Goodwin, Richard. *Remembering America.* Boston: Little Brown, 1988.

Gosch, Martin, and Richard Hammer. *The Last Testament of Lucky Luciano.* Boston: Little, Brown, 1974.

Greene, Laurence. *The Era of Wonderful Nonsense.* Indianapolis: Bobbs-Merrill, 1939.

Guthman, Edwin, and Jeffrey Shulman, eds. *Robert Kennedy: In His Own Words.* New York: Bantam, 1988.

Haldeman, H.R. *The Ends of Power.* New York: Times Books, 1978.

———. *The Haldeman Diaries: Inside the Nixon White House.* New York: Putnam, 1994.

Haley, Evetts. *A Texan Looks at Lyndon.* Canyon, TX: Palo Duro Press, 1964.

Hersh, Seymour. *The Price of Power.* New York: Summit, 1983.

Hicks, John D. *Republican Ascendancy.* New York: Harper, 1960.

Hoover, Herbert. *Memoirs of Herbert Hoover.* Vol. 2, *The Cabinet and the Presidency, 1920–1933.* New York: Macmillan, 1952.

Hoover, Irwin A. *Forty-two Years in the White House.* Boston: Houghton Mifflin, 1943.

Hoover, J. Edgar. *J. Edgar Hoover on Communism.* New York: Random House, 1969.

———. *J. Edgar Hoover Speaks.* Washington, DC: Capitol Hill Press, 1971.

———. *Masters of Deceit.* New York: Henry Holt, 1958.

———. *Persons in Hiding.* Boston: Little Brown, 1938.

———. *A Study of Communism.* New York: Holt, Rinehart and Winston, 1962.

Huie, William Bradford. *Did the FBI Kill Martin Luther King?* Nashville: Thomas Nelson, 1977.

Hull, Cordell. *Memoirs of Cordell Hull.* Vol. 2. New York: Macmillan, 1948.

Ickes, Harold. *The Secret Diary of Harold L. Ickes: The First Thousand Days, 1933–1936.* 4 vols. New York: Simon & Schuster, 1953.

Jaffray, Elizabeth. *Secrets of the White House.* New York: Cosmopolitan Book Corporation, 1927.

Johnson, Lady Bird. *A White House Diary.* London: Weidenfeld & Nicolson, 1970.

Johnson, Lyndon. *The Vantage Point.* New York: Holt, Rinehart and Winston, 1971.

Kahl, Mary. *Ballot Box 13.* Jefferson, NC: McFarland, 1983.

Karpis, Alvin, with Bill Trent. *The Alvin Karpis Story.* New York: Coward, McCann and Geoghegan, 1971.

Kearns, Doris. *Lyndon Johnson and the American Dream.* New York: Harper & Row, 1976.

Keller, William. *The Liberals and J. Edgar Hoover.* Princeton, NJ: Princeton University Press, 1989.

Kelley, Clarence, and James Davis. *Kelley: The Story of an FBI Director.* Kansas City: Andrews, McMeel & Parker, 1987.

Kennedy, Robert. *The Enemy Within.* New York: Harper & Row, 1960.

Kiel, R. Andrew. *J. Edgar Hoover: The Father of the Cold War.* Lanham, MD: University Press of America, 2000.

Kirchner, L.R. *Triple Cross Fire! J. Edgar Hoover & the Kansas City Union Station Massacre.* Kansas City: Janlar Books, 1993.

Kissinger, Henry. *White House Years.* Boston: Little, Brown, 1979.

———. *Years of Upheaval.* Boston: Little, Brown, 1982.

Kobler, John. *Ardent Spirits: The Rise and Fall of Prohibition.* New York: G.P. Putnam's Sons, 1973.

Lacey, Robert. *Little Man.* Boston: Little, Brown, 1991.

Lamour, Dorothy, and Dick McInnes. *My Side of the Road.* Englewood Cliffs, NJ: Prentice-Hall, 1980.

Lamphere, Robert, and Tom Shachtman. *The FBI-KGB War.* New York: Random House, 1986.

Lash, Joseph. *Eleanor and Franklin.* New York: Norton, 1971.

———. *Love, Eleanor.* New York: Doubleday, 1982.

Lasky, Victor. *It Didn't Start with Watergate.* New York: Dell, 1977.

———. *JFK: The Man and the Myth.* New York: Macmillan, 1963.

Lehr, Dick, and Gerard O'Neill. *Black Mass*. New York: HarperCollins, 2001.

Liddy, G. Gordon. *Will*. New York: St. Martin's, 1980.

Lincoln, Evelyn. *Kennedy and Johnson*. New York: Holt, Rinehart and Winston, 1968.

———. *My Twelve Years with John F. Kennedy*. New York: David McKay, 1965.

Littell, Norman. *My Roosevelt Years*. Seattle: University of Washington Press, 1987.

Lovegrove, Richard, and Tom Orwig. *The FBI*. New York: Brompton, 1989.

Lowenthal, Max. *The Federal Bureau of Investigation*. New York: Sloane, 1950.

Lynum, Curtis. *The FBI and I*. Bryn Mawr, PA: Dorrance, 1987.

Maas, Peter. *The Valachi Papers*. New York: Bantam, 1969.

Martin, John Bartlow. *Adlai Stevenson and the World*. Garden City, NY: Doubleday, 1977.

Mason, Alpheus. *Harlan Fiske Stone: Pillar of the Law*. New York: Viking, 1956.

McClure, Ruth, ed. *Eleanor Roosevelt: An Eager Spirit, Letters of Dorothy Dow, 1933–45*. New York: Norton, 1984.

McCoy, Donald R. *Calvin Coolidge*. Lawrence: University Press of Kansas, 1988.

McCullough, David. *Truman*. New York: Simon & Schuster, 1992.

McKeever, Porter. *Adlai Stevenson: His Life and Legacy*. New York: William Morrow & Co., 1989.

Means, Gaston B., and May Dixon. *The Strange Death of President Harding*. New York: Guild, 1930.

Messick, Hank. *John Edgar Hoover*. New York: David McKay, 1972.

———. *Lansky*. New York: Berkley Medallion, 1971.

Milan, Michael. *The Squad*. New York: Berkley, 1989.

Miller, Merle. *Ike the Soldier*. New York: Putnam, 1987.

———. *Lyndon*. New York: Putnam, 1980.

———. *Plain Speaking*. New York: Berkley, 1973.

Millspaugh, Arthur. *Crime Control by the National Government*. Washington, DC: Brookings Institute, 1937.

Moley, Raymond. *After Seven Years*. New York: Harper, 1939.

Morgan, Ted. *FDR*. New York: Simon & Schuster, 1985.

Morris, Edmund. *The Rise of Theodore Roosevelt*. New York: Ballantine Books, 1979.

Morris, Roger. Haig: *The General's Progress*. New York: Playboy Press, 1982.

———. *Richard Milhous Nixon: The Rise of an American Politician*. New York: Henry Holt, 1990.

Munves, James. *The FBI and the CIA*. New York: Harcourt Brace Jovanovich, 1975.

Nash, George H. *The Life of Herbert Hoover*. New York: Norton, 1988.

Nash, Jay Robert. *Citizen Hoover*. Chicago: Nelson Hall, 1972.

Nelson, Jack, and Ronald Ostrow. *The FBI and the Berrigans*. New York: Coward, McCann, 1972.

Nixon, Richard. *Memoirs of Richard Nixon. RN: The Memoirs of Richard Nixon*. New York: Grosset & Dunlap, 1978.

———. *Six Crises*. Garden City, NY: Doubleday, 1962.

North, Mark. *Act of Treason: The Role of J. Edgar Hoover in the Assassination of President Kennedy*. New York: Carroll & Graf, 1991.

Ollestad, Norman. *Inside the FBI*. New York: Lyle Stuart, 1967.

O'Reilly, Kenneth. *Racial Matters*. New York: Macmillan Free Press, 1989.

Parmet, Herbert. *Richard Nixon and His America*. Boston: Little, Brown, 1990.

Payne, Cril. *Deep Cover*. New York: Newsweek Books, 1979.

Perret, Geoffrey. *Eisenhower*. New York: Random House, 1999.

Phillips, John W. *Sign of the Cross*. Louisville: Westminster John Knox Press, 2000.

Popov, Dusko. *Spy/Counterspy*. New York: Grosset & Dunlap, 1974.

Powers, Richard Gid. *Secrecy and Power*. New York: Free Press, 1987.

Purvis, Melvin. *American Agent*. Garden City, NY: Doubleday, Doran, & Co., 1936.

Ranelagh, John. *The Agency*. Berkeley: University of California Press, 1972.

Ray, James Earl. *Who Killed Martin Luther King?* Washington, DC: National Press Books, 1992.

Reeves, Thomas C. *The Life and Times of Joe McCarthy.* New York: Stein and Day, 1973.

———. *A Question of Character: A Life of John F. Kennedy.* New York: Free Press, 1991.

Reid, Ed. *The Grim Reapers: The Anatomy of Organized Crime in America.* New York: Bantam, 1970.

Reid, Ed, and Ovid Demaris. *The Green Felt Jungle.* New York: Trident Press, 1963.

Richards, David. *Played Out: The Jean Seberg Story.* New York: Random House, 1981.

Robins, Natalie. *Alien Ink.* New York: William Morrow, 1992.

Roemer, William. *Man Against the Mob.* New York: Donald Fine, 1969.

Rosenfeld, Susan. *The History of the J. Edgar Hoover Building.* Washington, DC: FBI Office of Congressional Affairs, 1987.

Salinger, Pierre. *With Kennedy.* Garden City, NY: Doubleday, 1966.

Schlesinger, Arthur M., Jr. *Robert Kennedy and His Times.* Boston: Houghton Mifflin, 1978.

Schott, Joseph. *No Left Turns.* New York: Praeger, 1975.

Sherwood, Robert. *Roosevelt and Hopkins.* New York: Bantam, 1950.

Smith, R. Harris. *OSS: The Secret History of America's First Central Intelligence Agency.* Berkeley: University of California Press, 1972.

Stevenson, William. *Intrepid's Last Case.* New York: Ballantine, 1984.

Streitmatter, Rodger. *Empty Without You: The Intimate Letters of Eleanor Roosevelt and Lorena Hickok.* New York: Free Press, 1998.

Sullivan, William C, with Bill Brown. *The Bureau: My Thirty Years in Hoover's FBI.* New York: Norton, 1979.

Summers, Anthony. *Official and Confidential: The Secret Life of J. Edgar Hoover.* New York: Putnam, 1993.

Tanenhaus, Sam. *Whittaker Chambers.* New York: Random House, 1997.

Terrace, Vincent. *Radio's Golden Years.* San Diego: A. S. Barnes & Co., 1981.

Theoharis, Athan. *From the Secret Files of J. Edgar Hoover.* Chicago: Ivan R. Dee, 1991.

———. *J. Edgar Hoover, Sex, and Crime.* Chicago: Ivan R. Dee, 1995.

———. *Spying on Americans.* Philadelphia: Temple University Press, 1978.

Theoharis, Athan, and John Stuart Cox. *The Boss.* Philadelphia: Temple University Press, 1988.

Theoharis, Athan, with Tony G. Poveda, Susan Rosenfeld and Richard Gid Powers. *The FBI: A Comprehensive Reference Guide.* New York: Checkmark Books, 2000.

Toland, John. *The Dillinger Days.* New York: Random House, 1997.

Trani, Eugene, and David Wilson. *The Presidency of Warren G. Harding.* Lawrence: University Press of Kansas, 1977.

Troy, Thomas. *Donovan and the CIA.* Frederick, MD: University Publications of America, 1981.

Tully, Andrew. *Inside the FBI.* New York: Dell, 1987.

———. *Treasury Agent.* New York: Simon & Schuster, 1958.

Turkus, Burton, and Sid Feder. *Murder, Inc.* New York: Farrar, Straus & Young, 1951.

Turner, William. *Hoover's FBI: The Men and the Myth.* Los Angeles: Sherbourne Press, 1970.

Turrou, Leon. *Where My Shadow Falls: Two Decades of Crime Detection.* Garden City, NY: Doubleday, 1949.

Ungar, Sanford J. *FBI: An Uncensored Look Behind the Walls.* Boston: Atlantic-Little, Brown, 1975.

Unger, Robert. *The Union Station Massacre: The Original Sin of J. Edgar Hoover's FBI.* Kansas City: Andrews McMeel, 1997.

Vallée, Eleanor, with Jill Amadio. *My Vagabond Lover.* Dallas: Taylor Publishing, 1996.

Villano, Anthony, and Gerald Astor. *Brick Agent.* New York: New York Times Books, 1977.

Von Hoffman, Nicholas. *Citizen Cohn.* Garden City, NY: Doubleday, 1988.

Wade, Wyn Craig. *The Fiery Cross: The Ku Klux Klan in America.* New York: Simon & Schuster, 1987.

Waller, George. *Kidnap.* New York: Dial Press, 1961.

Watters, Pat, and Stephen Gillers, eds. *Investigating the FBI.* Garden City, NY: Doubleday, 1973.

Welch, Neil, and David Marston. *Inside Hoover's FBI.* Garden City, NY: Doubleday, 1984.

Werner, M.R., and J. Starr. *Teapot Dome.* New York: Viking Penguin, 1959.

Whitehead, Don. *The FBI Story.* New York: Random House, 1956.

Williams, David. *Without Understanding: The FBI and Political Surveillance 1908–1941.* Ann Arbor, MI: University Microfilms International, 1981.

Wills, Garry. *Nixon Agonistes.* New York: New American Library, 1971.

Winter-Berger, Robert N. *The Washington Pay-Off.* Secaucus, NJ: Lyle Stuart, 1972.

Wise, David. *The American Police State.* New York: Random House, 1976.

Wofford, Harris. *Of Kennedys and Kings.* New York: Farrar, Straus & Giroux, 1980.

Wolf, George, and Joseph DiMona. *Frank Costello: Prime Minister of the Underworld.* New York: William Morrow, 1974.

Wright, Peter. *Spycatcher.* New York: Viking, 1987.

Wright, Richard. *Whose FBI?* LaSalle, IL: Open Court, 1974.

Zinn, Howard. *Albany: A Study in National Responsibility.* Atlanta: Southern Regional Council, 1962.

GOVERNMENT DOCUMENTS

United States. *Statutes at Large.* Washington, DC, 1918. Vol. XL.

U.S. Congress. House. *Hearings before the Subcommittee on Civil and Constitutional Rights of the Committee on the Judiciary, on FBI Oversight.* Serial No. 2, Part III, 1976.

———. *Hearings before the Subcommittee of the Committee on Appropriations, Testimonies of J. Edgar Hoover, 1926–1972.*

———. *Inquiry into the Destruction of Former FBI Director J. Edgar Hoover's Files and FBI Recordkeeping: Hearings before the Government Information and Individual Rights Subcommittee of the Committee on Government Operations,* 94th Congress, 1st session, 1975.

———. *Report of the Select Committee on Assassinations of the U.S. House of Representatives.* U.S. Government Printing Office, 1979.

U.S. Congress. *Memorial Tributes to J. Edgar Hoover in the Congress of the United States and Various Articles and Editorials Relating to His Life and Work.* Washington, DC: U.S. Government Printing Office, 1974.

U.S. Congress. Senate. *Hearings before the Select Committee to Study Governmental Operations with Respect to Intelligence Activities of the United States Senate.* 94th Congress, 1st Session, vols. 2 and 6.

———. *Investigation of the Assassination of President John F. Kennedy: Performance of the Intelligence Agencies, Book V, Final Report of the Select Committee to Study Governmental Operations, with Respect to Intelligence Activities.* Senate Report No. 94-7559. 94th Congress, 2nd Session. 1976.

INDEX

Note: The initials JEH stand for
J. Edgar Hoover (John Edgar Hoover)
throughout this index.
Note: Photographs in the special section
are identified as on pages 1ph–8ph.

A

Abercrombie, John (acting labor secretary,
  1920), 68, 71
Abernathy, Ralph, 347
Abraham Lincoln Brigade, 205, 208
Abzug, Rep. Bella, 400–401
Acheson, Dean (secretary of state), 250n,
  260
ACLU (American Civil Liberties Union),
  108, 262, 310
Acton, Lord John Emerich Edward
  Dalberg, iii
Adulthood, early (JEH). *See also*
  Childhood (JEH); JEH
  acceptance, George Washington
  University, 48. *See also* George
  Washington University
  and Bureau corruption (Harding
    administration), 82
  career advancement, 52–53, 54, 58–59,
    62, 64. *See also* Justice Department
  employment, Library of Congress, 48, 53
  JEH as family income source, 58–59
  and Harding "Love Nest," 79
  joining Bureau of Investigation (1921),
    77–78
  passing bar, 49
  and patriotism, 49
  and Radical Division leadership, 62. *See*
    Radical Division (c. 1919–1920s)
  and Selective Service, 53
  as special agent (first time), 52
  25th family birthday party, 66, 68
  work habits, 52, 53
AEB (Alien Enemy Bureau), 51–56
African Americans
  in FBI (1955), 290
  JEH views on, 83, 195, 289, 294, 305
Alien Enemy Bureau (AEB), 51–56
Allen, George (JEH friend), 267, 320, 321
Allen, Robert S. (columnist), 163
The Alvin Karpis Story (1971), 177
Ambassador Hotel, Los Angeles, 258
American Civil Liberties Union (ACLU),
  108, 262, 310
American Protective League (APL), WWI,
  53
American Youth Congress (AYC), 234–235
Anderson, Jack (columnist), 274,
  279–280, 394–395, 404–405
Angiulo, Jerry, 350
Answered Prayers (Truman Capote), 243–244

Anticommunism (JEH), 186. *See also*
  Atomic secret spying; McCarthy,
  Sen. Joseph Raymond
  Anarchist deportations, 65–66
  atomic spy suspects, 250n, 250–251
  and Baughman (Thomas), 66–67
  and Bureau of Investigation post, 77–78
  and civil rights movement, 294, 312, 313
  Communism knowledge of JEH, 310–311
  Communist Party informants, 67, 251
  and Congressional red-baiting, 263–264
  conspiracy belief, 73, 318, 322
  false charges of JEH, 307
  and FURW raids, 65
  Hiss (Alger). *See* Hiss, Alger
  infiltration, 249, 300
  JEH mind-set on Communism, 314
  and Kennedy, John, 315
  and Kennedy, Robert, 315
  and King, Martin Luther, Jr./SCLC, 318,
    322, 363–365
  and McCarthy (Sen. Joseph), 260, 261
  and 1960s, 366–367
  open-ended surveillance, FBI, 187
  recognized by *Time, Newsweek,* 255
  and Rogers (Lela), 283
  scope, 187
  surveillance authority, 186n
  unwritten monitoring, 187–188
  WWII end rededication to, 248–249
Antifascism (JEH), 197. *See also* German
  American Bund
  open-ended surveillance, FBI, 187
  scope, 187
  surveillance authority, 186n
  unwritten monitoring, 187–188
Apalachin Mafia meeting, 302–303
APL (American Protective League), WWI,
  53
Appel, Charles (special agent), 121, 136
Appleby, Paul (Budget Bureau), 250n
Arlington Hotel, 141
Army investigation on David Schine,
  287–288
Army-McCarthy televised hearings, 285,
  286, 288
Arnaz, Desi, 233
Arthur, Art (screenwriter), 194
Arvad, Inga (JFK girlfriend), 316
Astair, Fred and Adele, 111–112
Atomic secret spying, 250n, 250–252,
  256–257, 259
AYC (American Youth Congress), 234–235

B

Babcock, Ed (McCarthy intern), 280
"Baby Face" Nelson. *See* Nelson, Lester
  "Baby Face"

431

trusted by FDR, 208
and U-boat vs. New York, 228–233
and undercover informants, 67
vacations, 188–193, 199, 206, 218, 261, 267, 320, 386
vanity, 19
view of Prohibition-era gangsters, 126
views of other nationalities, 213
and vigilantism, 85
vs. subversives, 52, 57, 66, 403. See also Anticommunism (JEH); FBI: and subversive activity
wealth, connections to, 284–285
Welles (Sumner) sex scandals, 225–226, 243–244
and whiskey, 171, 266, 268
White Slave Traffic Act prosecution (1922), 87–88
and white supremacy, 85
and Willebrant (Mrs. Mabel Walker), assist. attorney general, 1920s–1930s, 101–102
will of, 408
and Winchell (Walter) friendship, 202. See also Winchell, Walter (columnist)
wiretapping qualms, 376
and wiretaps, 209, 215, 351. 363. See also Wiretapping
without Tolson restraint, 367
Women's National Press Club appearance, 342–343
World War II. See also Pearl Harbor; World War II
Jenkins, Warren (LBJ aide/JEH friend), 341–342
Jenner, Sen. William (Internal Security Subcommittee chair), 275
Jentzer, Emma (female Bureau agent), 106n
Johnson, Hugh S. (FDR top administrator), defending JEH, 206–207
Johnson, President Lyndon B., 8ph
and DeLoach (Cartha D. "Deke"), 333
and FBI, 333
and JEH, 332, 333, 338–340, 341
and King, Martin Luther, Jr. promiscuity report, 338
U.S. Commission to Report upon the Assassination of President John F. Kennedy, 334–335, 341
Warren Commission, 335
Jones, Gus T., (Kansas City Massacre SAC), 144
Jones, Lawrence Biff, 44
Jones, M. A. (special agent), 313
Jorgensen, George/Christine (sex-change), 296, 296n
Joseph Gawler's Sons Inc. (JEH funeral arrangements), 8, 13, 15, 19, 25

Junior G-Man Club, Melvin Purvis Junior G-Man badge, 165
Justice Department. See also Suydam, Henry (Justice Department publicist)
and APL "auxiliary," 53
bribes/payoffs, Prohibition, 80
career advancement, 52–53, 54, 58–59, 62
co-worker associations, 57
Department of Justice building, 168n
Goldman/Berkman deportations, 62–66
Harding admin. intimidation during Senate probe, 93, 95
JEH, post-WWI, 56–57
and JEH named acting Bureau chief (1924), 105
Lindbergh kidnapping. See Lindbergh kidnapping
Radical Division creation, 60. See also Radical Division
Sedition Act of 1918, 57
War Emergency Division (WWI), 51

K
Kansas City Massacre
autopsies, 145
Bailey (Harvey), suspect, 143
Brady (Robert "Big Bob"), suspect, 143, 157
Caffrey (Raymond J.), special agent, killed, 140, 141, 142, 145–146
event, 142–143
files of, 142
and firearms for agents, 141
Floyd (Charles "Pretty Boy"), suspect, 143–144, 149, 150, 156, 157
Galatas (Richard "Tallman"), 141
Grooms (Bill), killed, 140, 142
Gross, Stephen J., Jr. (aka Verne Miller), 146–147. See also Miller (Verne) in this section
Hermanson (Frank), killed, 140, 142, 143, 145–146, 158
and JEH, 140–141, 143, 149
Jones (Gus T.), SAC, 144
Lackey (Joe), victim , 142, 146, 149, 158
Miller (Verne), suspect, aka Stephen J. Gross Jr., 143, 146–147, 149–150, 157
Nash (Frank), escapee, killed, 140, 141, 142, 145–147
Reed (Otto), killed, 140, 142, 146
Richetti (Adam), suspect, 146, 149, 156, 157–158
and shotgun bullet/firing, 145–146
Silvers/Silverman (Al), suspect's friend, 146, 150
slapstick suspect getaway, 147
Smith (Frank), witness, 142, 143, 149, 157

RICHARD HACK has been an investigative writer for over 20 years. Among his works are biographies of media moguls Ted Turner and Rupert Murdoch, billionaire businessman Ron Perelman, and pop star Michael Jackson. In 2001, he wrote the critically acclaimed national best seller, *Hughes: The Private Diaries, Letters and Memos,* whose film rights were sold to Castle Rock Entertainment. He currently is at work on *Michael Eisner's Tragic Kingdom.* Richard divides his time between homes on the shores of Cape Cod, Massachusetts, and Maui, Hawaii.